Eco Illusions

Eco Illusions: Unmasking Greenwashing in the Shared Economy

EDITED BY

PAWAN KUMAR
Lovely Professional University, India

SUMESH S. DADWAL
London South Bank University, UK

POOJA KHANNA
Lovely Professional University, India

RAJESH VERMA
Lovely Professional University, India

AND

GORDON BOWEN
Anglia Ruskin University, UK

emerald PUBLISHING

United Kingdom – North America – Japan – India – Malaysia – China

Emerald Publishing Limited
Emerald Publishing, Floor 5, Northspring, 21-23 Wellington Street, Leeds LS1 4DL

First edition 2026

British Library Cataloguing in Publication Data
A catalogue record for this book is available from the British Library

ISBN: 978-1-83662-783-8 (Print)
ISBN: 978-1-83662-782-1 (Online)
ISBN: 978-1-83662-784-5 (Epub)

INVESTOR IN PEOPLE

Contents

About the Editors

Pawan Kumar is working as a Professor in the Department of Marketing at Mittal School of Business, Lovely Professional University, Punjab, India. He has 18 years of experience in business academic research. His areas of interest in research include entrepreneurship, marketing, e-commerce, consumer behaviour, marketing research, etc. He is an avid researcher. He is active in Ph.D. research supervision and has good number of publications in Q1 and Q2 journals to his credit in various research papers published Scopus indexed journals namely: *The TQM Journal* from Emerald, *Visions: Journal of Business Perspectives* from Sage, *International Journal of Business and Globalization*, *International Journal of Business Information Systems* from Inderscience and other national/international journals of repute. He also served as editor of Edited Book of IGI Global Publishers.

Sumesh S. Dadwal has 23 years of experience in research, teaching, e-Learning, quality management and examination assessment in a wide range of business subjects. Currently, Sumesh is working as a Sr. Lecturer of Strategy and Course Director at LSBU Business School. Before joining LSBU, he worked as a Sr. Lecturer, Dissertation Lead, and Programme Leader with Northumbria Universities London campus and also as an associate with London Graduate School and Regent College London (Bucks New University and the University of Bolton, UK). Dr Dawdal has also worked as an Associate Lecturer with Birkbeck College (UoL), University of West London, Plymouth University (GSM, London), Uni of Roehampton UK, and also worked as a Sr. Lecturer and Programme Leader (MBA) at Glyndwr University London. Sumesh has hands-on experience in managing departments and in supporting the implementation of effective quality management systems. Previously, Dr Dawdal has also worked with QAA, UK. He has designed, developed and supported for validation and review of various programmes. He has published in journals and books.

Pooja Khanna is working as an Associate Professor in the Department of Marketing at Mittal School of Business, Lovely Professional University, Punjab, India. She has 20 years of experience in industry and academia. Her research interests encompass marketing, with a particular emphasis on consumer behaviour, sustainability and business practices and market research. She has publications in peer-reviewed journals and has presented her work at numerous national and international conferences. She has also chaired sessions in national and international conferences. She has written various research papers and book chapters published in SCOPUS indexed books and journals namely *Indian Journal of Marketing* indexed in Elsevier's Scopus, *International Journal of Intelligent Systems and Applications in Engineering, Demystifying the Dark Side of AI in Business* – IGI Global Publishers, *Digital Transformation for Business Sustainability and Growth in Emerging Markets* – Emerald. In addition, Pooja also has hands on industry experience in operations management and Six Sigma.

Dr. Rajesh Verma is a Sr. Dean and Professor of Strategy at Mittal School of Business, LPU, Punjab. His research and teaching interests entails areas like business models, market orientation and political marketing. He is the recipient of Junior Research Fellowship from University Grant Commission of India and other research grants from bodies like UK-India Education and Research Initiative (UKIERI); European Commission; and Department of Science & Technology (DST), Government of India. He is a Wiley Certified Design Thinking Practitioner and has conducted several training programmes on design thinking, selling skills, changing business models, brand building and customer orientation, etc. for corporates like India Oil, Radington, etc. He is avid researcher and excellent publication in highly reputed journals.

Gordon Bowen is an internationally experienced Non-Executive Director, consultant and academic specialising in strategy, marketing and corporate governance. Currently an Associate Professor in Management at Anglia Ruskin University, he also supervises doctoral research at the University of Wales Trinity Saint David and the University of Warwick. His academic contributions include published work on governance, performance management and competitive social media strategies, alongside reviewing for the European Academy of Management (EURAM). With over 40 years of professional experience, Gordon spent 17 years at Nortel Networks, where he led strategy and business development across EMEA, driving growth initiatives in public switching and broadband wireless networks. He has since advised SMEs worldwide, embedding governance frameworks, supporting growth strategies and guiding market entry initiatives.

About the Contributors

Shyam Sunder Agrawal is a Professor and Researcher in Environmental Policy and Management. His expertise includes green growth strategies and regulatory frameworks for corporate responsibility.

M Ruben Anto is an Early-Career Researcher focusing on consumer awareness and trust-building strategies.

Laiba Anwar researches climate finance, green investments and the risks of greenwashing in global markets.

G N P V Babu's interests lie in sustainability communication and consumer engagement.

Sanjay Bahl is a Management Academic focusing on brand communication and sustainability strategies.

Rohit Bansal is a Researcher in management studies focusing on green branding, consumer behaviour and transparency in Indian markets.

Deepak Bisht is a scholar of sustainable marketing and ethical consumerism.

Anvita Chitrapu specialises in empirical research on consumer attitudes and brand communication strategies.

Dalwinder Kaur Dhillon specialises in consumer behaviour, industry analysis and green communication strategies.

Rohit Duggal's expertise includes data analysis, bibliometrics and emerging areas of research in greenwashing.

Mohd Farhan is an Academic Researcher specialising in sustainable development, green growth and environmental policy. His work focuses on linking economic models with environmental responsibility to achieve the Sustainable Development Goals (SDGs). He has authored several research papers and actively contributes to global debates on green economy transformation.

Sumayya Fatima's research examines consumer trust, online marketing strategies and green consumer behaviour.

Krishan Gopal is an Interdisciplinary Researcher focusing on corporate ethics, governance and sustainability. He has contributed extensively to literature on organizational behaviour, transparency and responsible corporate communication.

Jyoti Grover's research centres on social identity theory, sustainability and consumer psychology.

Shabnam Gulati researches ethical fashion, sustainability narratives and influencer culture.

Kritika Gupta is a Researcher in consumer behaviour, specialising in demographic influences on perceptions of sustainability and ethical consumption.

Jana Al Hajj focuses on consumer engagement, digital literacy and the intersection of sustainability and communication.

Essa Yessuf Hussen is a Sustainability Practitioner with expertise in environmental governance and policy analysis. His research interests include the green economy, renewable energy and sustainable business practices in developing countries.

Labaran Isiaku studies digital communication strategies and their role in exposing unsustainable practices. His research examines how communities use media to challenge corporations.

Shamily Jaggi is a Marketing Expert specialising in fast fashion, rebranding and consumer perception.

Sonal Jain is a Researcher in legal and regulatory frameworks of the sharing economy, with a focus on sustainability policies.

Narinder Kaur's work focuses on corporate storytelling, sustainability narratives and consumer trust in the digital age.

P B Narendra Kiran's work examines corporate branding and consumer perception in the digital economy.

Ruchika Kulshrestha is an academic with a focus on sustainable development, responsible business practices and global economic transformation. She has presented her work at several international conferences.

Arun Kumar specialises in digital media, green communication and influencer marketing.

Arvind Kumar's expertise lies in sustainable fashion, consumer behaviour and eco-branding.

Jyoti Malik focuses on consumer behaviour, ethical consumption and cruelty-free product research.

Abubakar Sadiq Muhammad is a Sustainability Researcher with expertise in social media, green branding and corporate accountability.

Abdillahi Mohamoud Sheikh Muse is a Researcher and Policy Analyst, Mr. Muse specialises in the role of technology and media in shaping corporate behaviour. His work focuses on digital advocacy and sustainability.

Soumya Nedunuri is an Early-Career Academic focusing on digital media studies and sustainability narratives.

Dheeraj Nim specialises in digital marketing, corporate strategy and the ethical challenges of green communication.

Fazla Rabby works on sustainability research, particularly the role of developing economies in greenwashing narratives.

Suma N. Reddy is an Academic Leader in artificial intelligence applications for sustainability. Her work focuses on machine learning, green business models and the detection of corporate greenwashing.

Mahnoor Sahrash is a Researcher in marketing and sustainability. Her work combines empirical approaches with consumer psychology to understand the impact of greenwashing.

Ankitha Sharma researches the ethical role of influencers in shaping consumer sustainability perceptions.

Animesh Kumar Sharma researches bibliometric approaches to sustainability, with an emphasis on greenwashing literature.

Rahul Sharma studies sustainability practices in industries transitioning toward circular models. He specialises in bibliometric analysis, academic publishing and sustainability research trends.

Avtar Singh's research interests include circular economy models, outdoor industry practices and green consumerism.

Pritpal Singh works in the fields of business management and environmental economics. His research explores the intersection of economic growth, corporate responsibility and environmental sustainability.

Ram Singh researches Indian corporate practices and greenwashing, with a focus on regulatory challenges and sustainable growth.

Rupesh Roshan Singh focuses on international finance, development economics and sustainability governance.

Vinay Pal Singh's work explores greenwashing detection, consumer activism and corporate responsibility in the Indian context.

Arpit Tiwari specialises in corporate governance and ethics. Dr. Tiwari's research emphasises transparency in sustainability reporting and the prevention of greenwashing practices.

Pinnika Syam Yadav is a scholar of social media marketing and influencer engagement in the sustainability context.

Seda Yıldırım is an international scholar specialising in sustainability communication, marketing and consumer studies. She brings cross-cultural perspectives to the study of corporate transparency and ethics.

Foreword

In an era when the urgency of climate change and environmental degradation can no longer be ignored, the rhetoric of sustainability has become a dominant feature of business strategy and consumer culture. From eco-friendly branding to promises of carbon neutrality, companies across sectors are eager to demonstrate their commitment to building a greener world. Yet, beneath this growing wave of 'green talk' lies a critical problem: not all that is presented as sustainable truly is.

This is where the notion of eco illusions becomes both powerful and necessary. Eco illusions describe the subtle, and often deliberate, ways in which organisations create a façade of environmental responsibility – through vague claims, selective disclosures or misleading ecolabels. While the appearance of sustainability may comfort consumers and appease stakeholders, it too often conceals superficial practices that do little to address the structural challenges of environmental or social responsibility.

The shared economy, once celebrated as a transformative model for resource efficiency and social inclusion, is a telling example. Platforms that emphasise sharing, recycling and community empowerment frequently market themselves as inherently green. Yet, as this book shows, these models can harbour their own contradictions. When environmental promises serve more as branding strategies than as genuine commitments, the result is a widening gap between perception and reality.

Eco illusions: Unmasking Greenwashing in the Shared Economy is an important and timely intervention. By shining light on the tactics of greenwashing and the risks of misplaced trust in sustainability claims, it challenges us to look more critically at the narratives we accept and the systems we support. The book does not merely expose deception – it encourages accountability. It reminds us that awareness is the first step towards change and that meaningful sustainability requires transparency, integrity and verifiable action.

For scholars, policymakers and everyday consumers alike, this work offers an invaluable guide to navigating the complex terrain of environmental responsibility in the 21st century. Its insights compel us to ask difficult questions and demand higher standards from those who claim to act in the name of sustainability.

The journey to a truly sustainable economy will not be easy, but it is only through unmasking illusions that we can clear the path towards authentic, lasting change. This book makes that journey a little clearer, a little sharper and, most importantly, a little more honest.

Preface

In recent years, the global conversation on sustainability has gained tremendous momentum. Businesses, governments and individuals increasingly emphasise their commitment to environmental stewardship and social responsibility. Yet, beneath this promising surface lies a more complex and troubling reality – one where the language of sustainability is often used more as a marketing tool than a genuine call to action. This phenomenon, known as eco illusions, is at the heart of this book.

Eco illusions describe the deceptive practices through which companies and organisations present themselves as environmentally friendly or socially responsible while masking the superficiality – or even absence – of their true commitment. From vague claims of being 'green' to misleading ecolabels, these practices distort consumer choices, undermine trust and ultimately slow down progress towards authentic sustainability.

The shared economy, celebrated for its collaborative and resource-efficient models, is not immune to such challenges. In fact, it has become one of the most prominent spaces where eco illusions thrive. Businesses that claim to 'reduce waste', 'cut emissions' or 'empower communities' often provide only partial truths, exaggerating their contributions to sustainability. This book explores those realities, seeking to highlight instances where well-intentioned narratives about environmental and social responsibility mask practices that are far less impactful than they appear.

The goal of eco illusions: Unmasking Greenwashing in the Shared Economy is not merely to critique but to cultivate awareness. By exposing the tactics of greenwashing and examining how misleading ecolabels or ambiguous sustainability claims operate, this book aims to empower readers – be they consumers, researchers, policymakers or business leaders – to identify eco illusions and respond more critically to them. Only by separating illusion from reality can society ensure that sustainability becomes more than a slogan and instead transforms into a lived practice with genuine impact.

This book is thus an invitation: an invitation to question, to discern and to demand accountability. In doing so, we take a vital step towards unmasking the deceptive layers of greenwashing and moving closer to an economy that does not just promise sustainability but truly embodies it.

Chapter 1

The Association Between Greenwashing, Green Economy and Green Growth in Achieving the Sustainable Development Goals for Global Transformation

Mohd Farhan[a], *Essa Yessuf Hussen*[b], *Rajesh Verma*[c], *Krishan Gopal*[c], *Pooja Khanna*[c], *Pritpal Singh*[c] *and Ruchika Kulshrestha*[d]

[a]Mittal School of Business, Lovely Professional University, India
[b]Wolkite University, Ethiopia
[c]Lovely Professional University, India
[d]GLA University, India

Abstract

This article aims to explore the relationship between green growth and green economy in the accomplishment of the sustainable development goals (SDGs) to transform the world. This study is important because a green economy concept is crucial at the global level. In the face of worsening resource constraints and climate crisis, the concept of a green economy is necessary to achieve SDGs. This study also determined that how greenwashing is a hindrance to green growth and achieving sustainable development since it diverts attention and resources from real environmental solutions to mere propositions. It erodes consumer confidence, discourages investment in truly green innovations and creates unfair competition with truly sustainable businesses. A secondary source of information was used to understand the relationship, and the results of the investigation demonstrate that a strong correlation between green growth and a green economy is an essential concept to achieve SDGs. This study is beneficial for policymakers

Eco Illusions, 1–12

Published under exclusive licence by Emerald Publishing Limited
doi:10.1108/978-1-83662-782-120261001

to prepare policies in favour of green growth and green economy to achieve SDGs and transform the world towards sustainability.

Keywords: Greenwashing; green growth; green economy; SDGs; ecology; environment; sustainable development

Introduction

Currently, the global community has the problem of a growing population and continuous pressure on limited resources. The persistent growth of the worldwide population drains and pollutes the limited resources of the planet (Ogisi & Begho, 2023). Hence, the development of sustainable production and consumption systems and optimization of the use of resources becomes a necessity. Such systems should focus on the sustainable management of wastes, energy, water, transport and agriculture (Waseem et al., 2024). The OECD (2025) expects that air pollution might cause more deaths than any other global risk factor by the year 2050. The exposure to ozone pollution due to terrestrial urban pollution is expected to cause the highest rapid scale of mortality rates by the year 2050, among OECD nations. More than 10% global biodiversity loss is predicted, with the highest impact falling on the continents of Asia, Europe and Southern Africa. A little less than 40% of the world's population today lives in conditions of water scarcity, and water-related disasters account for 70% of all deaths caused by natural disasters. It is expected that forested areas will diminish by 13% within the succeeding decades. As it stands, approximately two-thirds of the biodiversity of lakes and rivers around the world has been lost, and further loss is expected by 2050. These situations are going to put at risk water availability for irrigation. The OECD (2015) foresees a global water demand rise by 55%, a 140% rise in energy generation and a 130% rise in domestic use, within the next decade. To ensure that water is used sustainably, the World Bank is putting in place initiatives aimed at improving integrated management and enhancing climate resilience (Arabameri et al., 2021).

According to a recent report from an energy agency, a linear projection of the present pace of activities indicates that emissions of CO_2 from the energy sources within the boundaries of the United States would amount to 6.9 billion metric tons by 2030 (IEA, 2022). On a global scale, it is anticipated that energy-related CO_2 emissions will increase to 42.3 billion metric tons in 2030 (IEA, 2022). In order to protect the environment, it is important to utilize all necessary measures aimed at combating environmental pollution. Along with it, greenwashing, by disguising environmental damage, serves to slow the pace of climate goal achievement and misalign resources, as well as make public accountability weaker, and thereby sap the systemic change needed for sustainability. With a distinction between clean and dirty, greenwashing distorts market signals, complicates policy enforcements and entrenches inequities by hiding the differentially heavy environmental burdens borne by vulnerable communities. Thus, it is necessary to put the issue of greenwashing on the agenda so as to create a harmonious balance between economic growth and environmental and social equity objectives central to sustainable development.

These challenges, that of air and water protection, are very well resolved in a transition to a green economy which aims at lowering carbon emissions and pollution, improving the efficiency of resource use and conserving trees and species diversity. Dealing with greenwashing is important in the entire process of sustainable development because it links economic growth with environmental preservation and social equity.

Objective of the Study

- To assess the contribution of green growth and economy for the accomplishment of the sustainable development goals (SDGs).

Conceptual Framework

Greenwashing

Greenwashing implies the allegations made to the customers by company or an organization that misled them into believing that their products, services or operations are more environmentally friendly than really they are often realized by deceptive marketing or vague and superficial claims, gestures which do not have a meaningful environmental impact. Very much often, it is like using things that say 'eco-friendly' or 'sustainable', but in the end, there is no proof to back such initiatives; creating fake eco-labels, emphasizing comparatively non-significant green initiatives and so on, ignoring major harmful effects environmentally or making claims that have no relevance at all, such as being 'CFC-free', even if these chemicals are banned already. They will corrode trust consumerism and suppress genuine eco-businesses and divert resources from real impactful sustainability efforts. Thus, it is the real harm of progress to environment goals: detecting green-wash by looking at measurable data, checking for certifications, judging an organization's overall practices and being doubtful of 'green-washing'.

Green Economy

For the first time, the term 'Green Economy' was used in 1989 in the report entitled Blueprint for a Green Economy, prepared in the United Kingdom by a panel of environmental economists (Barbier & Markandya, 2013). In 2011, the UNEP described the green economy as 'one that results in improved human well-being and social equity, while significantly reducing environmental risks and ecological scarcities. It is low carbon, resource efficient, and socially inclusive' (UNEP, 2018). The creation and maintenance of the earth's natural resources, as well as the reduction of ecological deficits and environmental dangers, are the hallmarks of the green economy. In order to 'green' traditional resource-based and polluting sectors of the economy and garner support for such sectors, UNEP launched the Green Economy Initiative (Allen & Clouth, 2021). According to Hamdouch and Depret (2021; UNEP, 2018), these initiatives are concentrated on clean technologies, energy-efficient buildings, low-emission transportation, renewable energy, waste management improvement, sustainable agriculture, sustainable fishery and forest management.

As noted by the International Chamber of Commerce (2021), social development, to which the growth of the green economy also contributes, is 'the interaction of economic development and environmental protection cohesive with one another in a circular flow'.

The idea of the 'green economy' seeks to greatly reduce ecological deficits and environmental dangers while promoting social welfare, economic transformation and justice. The main ways to accomplish this kind of change are by making 'green' investments, generating 'green' jobs and expanding markets for novel goods, which promote global trade and the circular economy (Kasztelan, 2021). Good health and well-being (SDG 3), peace, justice, strong institutions (SDG 16), climate action (SDG 14) and responsible consumption and production (SDG 12) are the four fundamental facets of the green economy. The green economy concept also fits with the ideas of the circular economy which is a business model with a primary focus on recycling and other forms of reuse of products and materials over extended periods. The development of usable materials and energy to factors or resources that can be used or consumed within the ecological means is necessary to achieve sustainability (United Nations, 2022).

Green Growth

According to the OECD (2015), 'Green growth means fostering economic growth and development while ensuring that natural assets continue to provide the resources and environmental services on which our well-being relies'. According to the Arabameri et al. (2021), green growth is 'growth that is efficient in its use of natural resources, minimizes pollution and environmental impacts, and resilient in that it accounts for natural hazards'.

Green growth strategies ought to promote eco-friendly business and consumer behaviour, enhance the most efficient use of labour, capital and technology for greener operations and stimulate the creation of eco-innovations (OECD, 2015; Siwal et al., 2023). Social welfare, the environment and the development of new jobs should all be considered in the green growth strategy (OECD, 2025). It is necessary to encourage businesses and consumers to adopt greener practices, improve the utilization of resources towards greener practices (labour, capital and technology) and motivate the generation of eco-innovations in growth strategies developed at the national level (OECD, 2015; Siwal et al., 2023). The approach of green growth, however, does not neglect the social aspects such as environmental protection or the creation of new jobs (OECD, 2025). Green growth is concerned with motivating people and institutions to devote their efforts to environmentally sound behaviours, promoting the spatial equilibrium of factors such as capital, labour and technologies and, finally, providing the necessary conditions and means for the growth of environmentally friendly technologies (OECD, 2015).

Acosta et al., in 2019, affirm that Green Growth Index encompasses a composite measure in which each nation's attempts at achieving specific sustainability objectives are assessed within four components of green growth: social inclusion (SDG 1, SDG 3, SDG 5, SDG 6, SDG 7, SDG 8, SDG 9, SDG 10, SDG 11, SDG 17), environmental preservation (SDG 3, SDG 9, SDG 11, SDG 12, SDG 13, SDG 14, SDG 15), environmentally friendly business activity (SDG 9, 12) and the efficient use of resources and/or sustainable sourcing of raw materials (SDG 2, SDG 6, SDG 7, SDG 8, SDG 12, SDG 15). This index is the first to connect the concepts of sustainable and green growth.

Sustainable Development

Sustainable development is defined as 'development that meets the needs of the present without compromising the ability of future generations to meet their own needs' by the World Commission on Environment and Development (WCED, 1987). This notion garnered substantial attention after the Rio de Janeiro Earth Summit (1992), which approved a model blueprint for pursuing sustainable development, 'Agenda 21'. Many nations have embraced the idea of sustainable development, which has had a big impact on how important environmental objectives are prioritized (Satbyul et al., 2021; UNESCAP, 2020). According to Van Stappen (2008),

> Development that meets the basic needs of all human beings while conserving, protecting, and restoring the health and integrity of the Earth's ecosystem, without compromising the ability of future generations to meet their own needs and without exceeding the long-term capacity of the earth's ecosystem.

A Green Economy and Anti-Greenwashing Initiative Taken by the Countries

Green economy initiatives were taken by different countries as announced in Dubai, promoting extensive national activities to build a green economy in the United Arab Emirates under the slogan 'A Green Economy for Sustainable Development' (Terdiman, 2022). For example, Masdar City touted as the main green city globally, invests in sustainable energy sources, nuclear energy production and organic farming (Luo et al., 2021). According to the Brookings Institution, around 2.7 million Americans work in green jobs, and the United States Conference of Mayors estimates that this number will triple by 2040 (Matthew, 2021). Following America in rank, China leads in the total installed capacity of wind farms in the world with 91,000 MW produced. Wind energy provided Denmark with 30% of its electric energy in 2000 with plans to increase by 50% in the year 2020. While Germany manages to convert 8% of electricity renewals through wind farms, Lithuania, Spain, Portugal and Ireland each produce approximately 20%. Terrace farming is ecological since it encourages the use of minimal pesticides as well as the efficient production of food that does not deplete a lot of resources. Green roofs improve cities by minimizing energy loss, purifying air and creating places for leisure (Perivoliotis et al., 2023). Usage of electric vehicles results in decreased consumption of fossil fuels as well as emissions (Hooftman, 2021). Paper recycling has a significant positive impact on the environment, with the Environmental Protection Agency (EPA) indicating that recycling a metric ton of paper saves energy and reduces greenhouse gas emissions (Long & Schubert, 2021). Solar cell production has doubled in the past decade, with Europe generating 30% of the world's photovoltaic power, followed by the United States and Japan (Wawer et al., 2021). Wave energy production can generate grid energy offshore, although its use remains limited (Siwal et al., 2021). The green economy positively impacts employment in developing countries; for instance, solar energy technology in Turkey creates direct jobs and benefits the economy (Cetin & Erican, 2021). Africa's Green Jobs report indicates a long-term potential of around 462,567 jobs in green sectors (IDC, 2021). In the United States, clean energy policies have significantly boosted employment, creating around 660,000 jobs (Barrett et al., 2002). In Canada, renewable energy sector growth has led to substantial job increases (Rutovitz & Atherton, 2009). Approximately 150,000 direct jobs have been generated from wind energy production in the European Union (EU) (UNEP, 2018). Many nations established anti-greenwashing programmes for dissuading deceptive environmental claims and encouraging authentic sustainability. Green Claims Directive is a EU initiative, which mandates companies to substantiate their environmental claims with actual clear proof, while EU Ecolabel identifies and certifies products that meet strict quality and environmental standards. In the United States, for instance, the Federal Trade Commission's Green Guides specifies how claimants should be able to support their claims, such as eco-friendly. Following the same trend, California enacted laws that would expand transparency on environmental practices. Under Australian Consumer Law, the Australian Competition and Consumer Commission protects consumers through the enforcement of laws against misleading green claims; while in Canada, the Competition Bureau sees to it that companies do not mislead regarding environmental advertising. The United Kingdom came up with the Green Claims Code, which basically sets out guidelines for organizations on how to make accurate statements concerning environmental attributes and started investigating misleading green marketing on issues related to recycling of plastics. Eco Mark Programme certifies products in Japan as environmentally friendly. It has Fair Trade Commission that deals with violations of false advertising. All these programmes which have international standards like the Global Reporting Initiative (GRI) or ISO 14021 aim at protecting consumers, ensuring transparency and nurturing trust in green markets from being misled through deceptive greenwashing practices.

A Relationship Between Green Growth, Green Economics and Sustainable Development Goals

Green growth is considered to be the first step to achieving the goal of sustainable development. Green growth is an important element of the green economy on the path to sustainable development. The picture below illustrates the proposed relations between sustainable development, green growth and the green economy. Both concepts are aimed at identifying productive paths through which the excesses of economic engagement can be realized with the ongoing climate change and reduction of resources, predominantly through energy and resource-efficient technologies. The primary aim of the Green Growth Plan is to sustain economic expansion while acknowledging the significance of natural resources in the transition to a sustainable economy. The primary measure to achieve this goal is to ensure proper measurement of pollution and resource utilization (Endl & Sedlacko, 2021). The focus of Green Growth is to accelerate innovations and investments, providing new economic opportunities to achieve sustainable development. Green growth directs the economy towards consumption patterns and technologies that create economic growth and jobs while reducing the harmful impact on the environment (Khan et al., 2025).

To achieve sustainable development, the first stage is green growth (Dogaru, 2020). It can provide effective utilization of scarce resources and reduce energy consumption. Green growth can enhance the sustainability of green manufacturing to minimize its environmental impact, by helping to reduce pollution and waste (Khaloie et al., 2020). The green economy can happen once green growth is achieved (Scott, 2023). The green economy, by definition, includes any activity that relies on natural resources. Activities such as transport, energy, organic farming and production of renewable energy sources are resource-saving oriented to a high degree. A green economy may limit the negative influence on the environment, reduce the consumption of natural resources and energy and offer a secure environment for workers and consumers (Rusinko, 2022). According to UNEP, a green economy increases employment (UNEP, 2018). It shows the influence of the green economy on the labour force. Green energy policy and the establishment of a green economy are interlinked (UNEP, 2018).

In the United States, green energy policies will raise employment by creating an estimated 660,000 jobs (Barrett et al., 2002). It has also been noted that the growth of the renewable energy sector in Canada has increased job opportunities significantly. Within the realm of wind power generation in the European territory, some reports estimate that approximately 150,000 direct jobs have been created (UNEP, 2018). Green growth is a method that runs on low-carbon sources and is integrated into the green economy on the pathway to sustainable development. Fig. 1.1 outlines the model of relationships among sustainable development, green economy and green growth. A new, low-emission paradigm of sustainable development for fast-developing Asian nations has evolved, and it is called 'green growth' (UNESCAP, 2020). It provides a means of reaching sustainable development (OECD, 2015; UNEP, 2018; Arabameri et al., 2021).

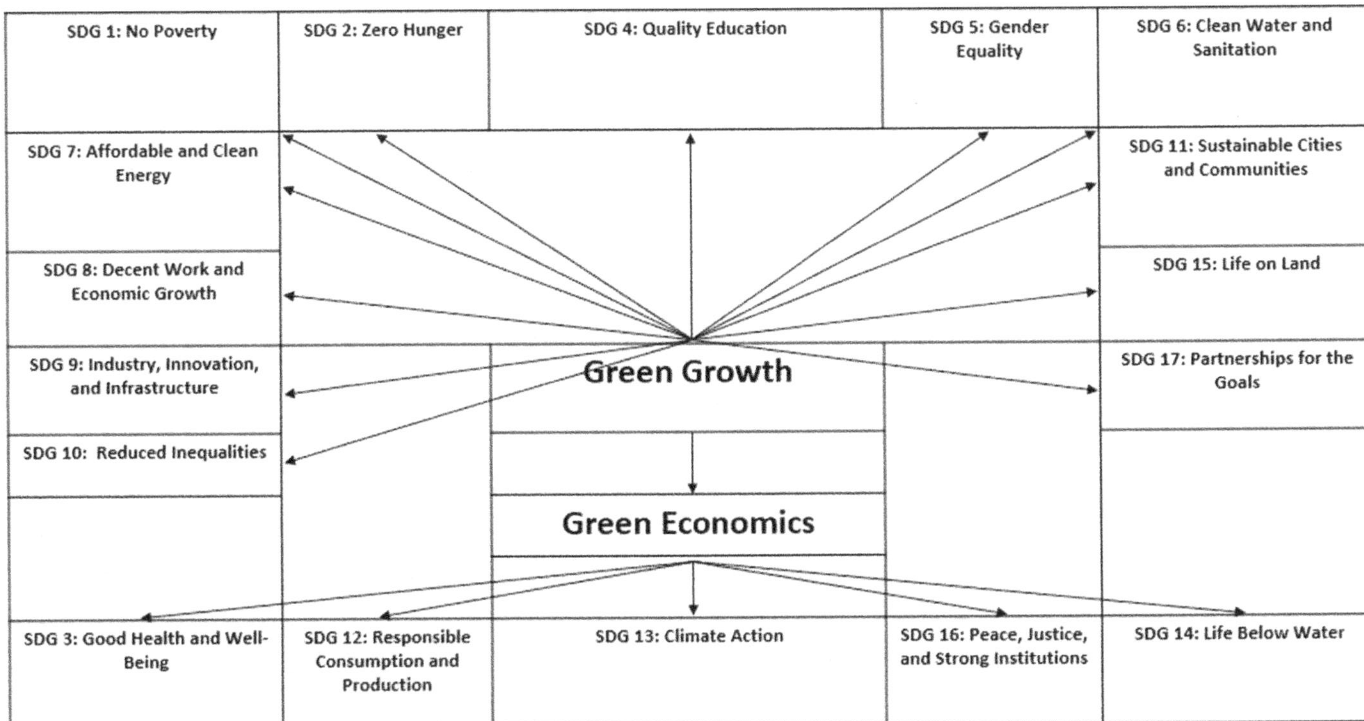

Fig. 1.1. Green Growth, Green Economy and Sustainable Development Goals. *Sources:* Pawlowski et al. (2020), UNEP (2018), OECD (2015), Jacobs (2022), and Fallah Shayan et al. (2022).

The 'green economy' is the creation of a framework for policymakers, economists, business and society in general, enabling them to find another way to sustainable development (Galik & Chelbi, 2021). The green economy has substantial potential to stimulate global growth (UNEP, 2018). The 'greening' of the economy can lead to achieving sustainable development (Eliezer & Bermann, 2022).

Conclusions and Future Directions of Work

Green activities are important in promoting a green economy, which is a fundamental step to achieving sustainable development. Green growth is a novel concept which implies economic development but in an 'ecological mode' where carbon emissions decrease and negative consequences on the environment are kept to a minimum, while, consequently, more jobs are created and more wealth is generated. Cinvestav (2021) explained that green growth can increase resource productivity, stimulate new markets in clean technologies and increase innovative activities while enhancing resource management. This vision of a sustainable economy often embraces the employability of science and technology not just for making a profit but for the conservation of the environment and social well-being (UNEP, 2018). A green economy will be built through economic growth framed within the wise management of available resources. This not only decreases environmental degradation but also goes towards enhancing the economic capacity and productivity of the output. According to the World Bank research (2023), countries that have implemented sustainable resource management and the acquisition of green technologies are likely to be better placed in the global economy. Measures supporting economic growth are hence required in addition to measures addressing climate change, and these measures are interconnected with green growth policy measures. The evidence suggests that regions that tend to embrace green growth manifest higher levels of creativity and economic performance. Renewable sources of energy also aid in employment creation while helping in combating climate change through the reduction of greenhouse gas emissions which addresses several SDGs. This connectivity is particularly important in addressing the SDGs as they seek to alleviate the interrelated economic, social and environmental problems sustainably. Greenwashing diverts the green growth and sustainable development initiatives by redirecting attention and resources towards false or misleading environmental solutions. It undermines consumer trust, neither invests in authentic green innovations nor offers real competition to genuinely sustainable companies. Therefore, it ultimately limits the availability of resources for additional investments in innovative, value-driven product lines, as companies focus excessively on profit-oriented marketing claims. Ultimately, it gives rise to a darkened environment that would hamper the progress towards the climate goal by cresting level misallocation points, diluting accountability to the constituents and halting changes in the entire system. Besides, it distorts the market premises, complicates the manner in which policies enforcement occurs and continues to widen the gap by concealing the unfair benefits accrued from unequal environmental impacts suffered by less privileged communities. The very essence of greenwashing needs to go by negating the link between economic growth and environmentally and socially equitable objectives, which, in turn, can achieve an end in itself for the development of sustainability. Above all, measures associated with green growth are very important in creating a green economy to achieve SDGs.

References

Acosta, L. A., Maharjan, P., Peyriere, H., Galotto, L., Mamiit, R. J., Ho, C., Flores, B. H., & Anastasia, O. (2019). *Green growth index: Concept, methods and applications* GGGI Technical Report No. 5, Green Growth Performance Measurement (GGPM) Program. Global Green Growth Institute.

Allen, C., & Clouth, S. (2021). *Green economy, green growth and low-carbon development: A practical guide*. UN Division for Sustainable Development.

Arabameri, A., Pal, S. C., Rezaie, F., Chakrabortty, R., Chowdhuri, I., Blaschke, T., & Ngo, P. T. T. (2021). Comparison of multi-criteria and artificial intelligence models for land-subsidence susceptibility zonation. *Journal of Environmental Management*, *284*, 112067. https://doi.org/10.1016/j.jenvman.2021.112067

Barbier, E. B., & Markandya, A. (2013). *A new blueprint for a green economy* (1st ed.). Routledge. https://doi.org/10.4324/9780203097298

Barrett, J. P., Hoerner, J. A., Bernow, S., & Dougherty, B. (2002). Clean energy and jobs: A comprehensive approach to climate change and energy policy. *Economic Policy Institute & Center for a Sustainable Economy*.

Cetin, M., & Erican, N. (2021). The economic impact of solar energy in Turkey. *Renewable Energy & Sustainability Reviews*, *143*, 110878. https://doi.org/10.1016/j.rser.2021.110878

Cinvestav. (2021). *Impact of greenwashing on consumer behavior: A Mexican case study*. Cinvestav Press.

Dogaru, L. (2020). Green economy and green growth—Opportunities for sustainable development. *Proceedings*, *63*(1), 70. https://doi.org/10.3390/proceedings2020063070

Eliezer, B., & Bermann, A. (2022). Greening the economy: Toward sustainable development. *Journal of Sustainable Development*, *15*.

Endl, A., & Sedlacko, M. (2021). Green growth strategies: Impacts on economic development. *Environmental Science & Policy*, *124*, 103–110. https://doi.org/10.1016/j.envsci.2021.07.011

Fallah Shayan, N., Mohabbati-Kalejahi, N., Alavi, S., & Zahed, M. A. (2022). Sustainable development goals (SDGs) as a framework for corporate social responsibility (CSR). *Sustainability*, *14*(3), 1222. https://doi.org/10.3390/su14031222

Galik, C. S., & Chelbi, L. (2021). Revisiting institutional stability: A systematic review and distillation of dominant modes. *Environmental Policy and Governance*, *31*(5), 463–473. https://doi.org/10.1002/eet.1941

Hamdouch, M., & Depret, M. (2021). Policy integration strategy and the development of the "green economy": Foundations and implementation patterns. *Journal of Environmental Policy Research*, *14*(2), 99–120.

Hooftman, N. (2021). Electric vehicles and their impact on urban air quality. *Transportation Research Part D, 90*, 102710. https://doi.org/10.1016/j.trd.2021.102710

International Chamber of Commerce. (2021). *ICC principles for sustainable trade (Wave 2)*. ICC.

International Data Corporation. (2021). *Africa's green jobs: A report on employment potential.* IDC. https://www.idc.com

International Energy Agency (IEA). (2022). *World energy outlook 2022*. IEA. https://www.iea.org/reports/world-energy-outlook-2022

Jacobs, R. (2022). Green economy frameworks: A comparative analysis. *Journal of Business Management and Research, 9*(1), 62–78.

Kasztelan, A. (2021). On the road to a green economy: How do European Union countries do their homework? *Energies, 14*(18), 5941. https://doi.org/10.3390/en14185941

Khaloie, H., Anvari-Moghaddam, A., & Hatziargyriou, N. (2020). Risk-constrained self-scheduling of a hybrid power plant considering interval uncertainty. *Journal of Cleaner Production, 282*, 125344. https://doi.org/10.1016/j.jclepro.2020.125344

Khan, R. Z., Razak, L. A., & Premaratne, G. (2025). Green growth and sustainability: A systematic literature review on theories, measures and future directions. *Cleaner and Responsible Consumption, 17*, 100274. https://doi.org/10.1016/j.clrc.2025.100274

Long, M., & Schubert, P. (2021). The impact of recycling on energy savings. *Environmental Protection Agency*. https://www.epa.gov/recycling

Luo, H., Zhao, S., & Yao, R. (2021). Determinants of housing prices in Dalian City, China. *Journal of Urban Planning and Development, 147*(3), 05021011. https://doi.org/10.1061/(ASCE)UP.1943-5444.0000698

Matthew, P. (2021). *Green jobs in America: Trends and projections.* Brookings Institution. https://www.brookings.edu/research/green-jobs-in-america-trends-and-projections/

OECD. (2015). *Towards green growth? Tracking progress.* OECD Publishing. https://doi.org/10.1787/9789264234437-en

OECD. (2025). *Environmental performance of agriculture in OECD countries: Key trends and insights.* OECD Publishing. https://doi.org/10.1787/2679ba38-en

Ogisi, O. D., & Begho, T. (2023). Adoption of climate-smart agricultural practices in sub-Saharan Africa: A review of progress, barriers, gender differences and recommendations. *Farming Systems, 1*(2), 100019. https://doi.org/10.1016/j.farsys.2023.100019

Pawlowski, J., Apothéloz-Perret-Gentil, L., & Altermatt, F. (2020). Environmental DNA: What's behind the term? *Molecular Ecology, 29*(22), 4258–4264. https://doi.org/10.1111/mec.15643

Perivoliotis, D., Arvanitis, I., Tzavali, A., Papakostas, V., Kappou, S., Andreakos, G., Paravantis, J. A., Souliotis, M., & Mihalakakou, G. (2023). Sustainable urban environment through green roofs: A literature review with case studies. *Sustainability, 15*(22), 15976. https://doi.org/10.3390/su152215976

Rusinko, C. (2022). Green economy: A comprehensive review of the current landscape. *Business Strategy and the Environment, 31*(1), 56–67. https://doi.org/10.1002/bse.2841

Rutovitz, J., & Atherton, A. (2009). *Energy sector jobs to 2030: A global analysis.* Institute for Sustainable Futures, University of Technology.

Satbyul, L., Kim, S., & Park, J. (2021). Advancing SDG 7: Policies for affordable and clean energy in emerging Asian economies. *Energy Policy and Sustainable Development*, *8*(4), 311–325.

Scott, G. (2023). The path from green growth to green economy: Lessons learned. *Sustainability*, *15*(2), 1090. https://doi.org/10.3390/su15021090

Siwal, S. S., Zhang, Q., Devi, N., Saini, A. K., Saini, V., Pareek, B., & Thakur, V. K. (2021). Recovery processes of sustainable energy using different biomass and wastes. *Renewable and Sustainable Energy Reviews*, *150*, 111483. https://doi.org/10.1016/j.rser.2021.111483

Siwal, S. S., Zhang, Q., Devi, N., Saini, A. K., Saini, V., Pareek, B., & Thakur, V. K. (2023). Efficient removal of heavy metals by Mg/Fe bimetallic oxide-modified biochar. *Journal of Cleaner Production*, *403*, 136821. https://doi.org/10.1016/j.jclepro.2023.136821

Terdiman, M. (2022). Green and smart cities in the developing world. In T. Angert (Ed.), *The Palgrave encyclopedia of urban and regional futures* (pp. 1–9). Palgrave Macmillan.

United Nations Economic and Social Commission for Asia and the Pacific (UNESCAP). (2020). *Asia and the Pacific SDG progress report 2020*. UNESCAP.

UNEP. (2018). *Towards a green economy: Pathways to sustainable development and poverty eradication*. United Nations Environment Programme. https://www.unep.org/greeneconomy

United Nations. (2022). *The sustainable development goals report 2022*. https://unstats.un.org/sdgs/report/2022/

Van Stappen, P. (2008). Redefining sustainable development: From theory to action. *International Journal of Sustainable Future*, *1*(1), 5–19.

Waseem, M., Ibrahim, S., & Khan, A. (2024). Leading green, innovating clean: Transformational leadership and eco-innovation through employee behavior. *Journal of Business Management and Research*, *9*(1), 62–78.

Wawer, A., Nowak, P., & Zieliński, Ł. (2021). Solar energy adoption in Central Europe: Challenges and opportunities. *Renewable Energy Insights*, *5*(2), 48–60.

World Bank. (2023). *Recipe for a livable planet: Reorienting the global agrifood system for SDGs*. World Bank Group.

World Commission on Environment and Development. (1987). *Our common future*. Oxford University Press.

Chapter 2

Intersecting Paradigms: Reducing Greenwashing, Ensuring Sustainable Claims and Achieving Corporate Transparency

Arpit Tiwari[a], *Shyam Sunder Agrawal*[a], *Pawan Kumar*[a] *and Seda Yıldırım*[b]

[a]Lovely Professional University, India
[b]Tekirdag Namik Kemal University, Turkey

Abstract

In the increasing competition in today's dynamic scenario, the industry has seen many instances of deceptive promises by organizations where the organizations have overstated their eco-friendly capacities. This chapter attempts to unleash such greenwashing practices and assess the combination of advanced technologies, like big data, blockchain and artificial intelligence, to identify and reduce the greenwashing in the industry. This chapter also addresses the issues related to corporate transparency. In an effort to dive deeper into the field of study, this chapter reviews a number of research papers by following a systematic literature review (SLR) methodology grounded in the Theory, Context, Characteristics, Methodology (TCCM) framework. The study utilized the 'Resource-based View' for establishing the relationship desired and proposed in the conceptual model. It combines existing literature, synthesizes it systematically to provide a comprehensive understanding of the greenwashing practices and integration of cutting-edge technologies for unmasking it and ensuring corporate transparency. This chapter identifies research gaps and bridges them by recommending a conceptual model that suggests how the above technologies can be integrated into a comprehensive strategy for detecting greenwashing and verifying the sustainable claims for improved customer trust. The findings also identify the substantial challenges in widespread implementation of these

Eco Illusions, 13–44

doi:10.1108/978-1-83662-782-120261002

technological advancements and encourage the organizations to adopt real green practices and improve their brand image effectively. The valuable insights gained through this study assist the academicians, researchers, policymakers and industry professionals to enhance their competencies and credibility by adopting sustainable practices and ensuring corporate transparency to a great extent.

Keywords: Greenwashing practices; technological advancement; systematic literature review (SLR); resource-based view; sustainable claims; corporate transparency; customer trust

Introduction

Background in Global Context

With the increased demand for green products in the customer market, several organizations have shifted their focus to green advertising (TerraChoice, 2009). At the same time, such increased demand for green products has also increased the difficulties for various brands to deal with the high competition and also tempted the organizations to get involved in greenwashing practices. The concept of greenwashing has become prevalent in the industry, particularly as customers and stakeholders have increased demand for businesses and sustainability (Furlow, 2010). Many organizations are making superficial claims strategically, rather than actually engaging in the environment-friendly practices (Polonsky et al., 1998). The term 'Greenwashing' was first coined by a renowned environmentalist Jay, Westerveld in 1986, who identified during his study that many organizations are communicating a strong environment-friendly image among their customers but without incorporating significant green-responsible behaviour into their action plan (Pimonenko et al., 2020). Besides being an evolving concept from the literature perspective, greenwashing has gained much popularity in the industry, considering its potential to deal with competition by making sustainability claims. Hence, greenwashing becomes ever more challenging, particularly in those industries where true sustainability efforts are manifold, costly or difficult to implement.

However, the customers today are more empowered and curious about the authenticity of the products' claims and demands for transparency (Alyahia et al., 2024). The rising awareness of greenwashing practices has led researchers to the study of various technological tools that might help the industry to minimize this problem. Technologies such as artificial intelligence (AI), big data analytics and blockchain are seen as main game-changers in increasing transparency and ensuring that corporate sustainability claims can be verified (Nygaard & Silkoset, 2023; Moodaley & Telukdarie, 2023). For instance, blockchain offers a fast method and transparency by validating the authenticity of tracking sustainability claims (Nygaard & Silkoset, 2023), while AI has the capability of data-driven decision making, which makes it feasible to identify the misleading advertisements or marketing content that may deceive customers

(Moodaley & Telukdarie, 2023). Even with the several appealing promises of these technologies, the challenges related to integration and effectiveness across various industries and regulatory environments are also huge and highlight the enormous scope of research in the field of study.

Research Gap

Notwithstanding the fact that significant research studies have been conducted on the concept of greenwashing. The key focus of all such studies was especially on exploring the concept in terms of its ethical implications and trust of customers (Lyon & Maxwell, 2011), very few studies have focused on the role of these emerging technologies in fighting this issue. The available literature relevant to this field of study primarily focuses on behavioural as well as psychological impacts of greenwashing on customers (Peattie & Crane, 2005), but still, there is a lack of exploration into how the integration of various advanced technologies, such as AI and blockchain, can specifically resolve the greenwashing challenge. To advocate the above-mentioned standpoint regarding the research gap, Table 2.1 outlines the key areas where current research is lacking and how this study seeks to address those gaps (see Table 2.1).

The identified research gaps in the above table stem from the limitations in existing studies, which predominantly focus on the conceptual and ethical dimensions of greenwashing without sufficiently discussing the technological integration required for real-time verification of sustainability claims and reduction of the greenwashing activities in the industry. Current literature, such as that by Delmas and Burbano (2011), emphasizes the drivers and characteristics of greenwashing, yet it does not explore how emerging technologies like blockchain, AI and big data can combat this issue effectively (Lyon & Montgomery, 2015).

Integrative models that make use of these technologies are desperately needed in order to ensure corporate transparency and improve accountability in business sustainability practices. Blockchain technology is also known for its ability to offer tamper-proof along with traceable records, according to Chaudhuri et al. (2023) and Navaratne (2024). However, the above research studies also fall short of proposing practical frameworks for their application across different industries. The lack of such frameworks creates a gap in understanding how blockchain can be scaled for a broader sense and resolve industry-specific challenges.

In the same way, AI-driven tools for identifying greenwashing are still in their initial stage, with limited research exploring their dual potential: not only to reveal misleading claims but also to unwittingly enable greenwashing through experienced data manipulation (Frank, 2021). Moodaley and Telukdarie (2023) focus on this ethical dilemma and the need for comprehensive research to ensure AI technology is employed responsibly in claiming for sustainability. Furthermore, the table also shows that big data analytics demonstrated a significant role in assessing environmental performance, but due to limited studies combining big data with blockchain and AI to create real-time solutions for cross-industry, that presents another important gap (Li et al., 2024). These integrations could enable more vigorous and reliable verification systems, yet the lack of a practical, conceptual framework leaves this potential uncovered.

Regulatory implications further synthesize these challenges. The importance of greenwashing regulations is properly documented (Lyon & Montgomery, 2015; Zhang, 2022), but its alignment with technological advancements remains insufficient. The slow adoption of frameworks that incorporate blockchain and AI into regulatory compliance mechanisms hinders the use of these tools for claim verification. Ultimately, the role of customer's trust in adopting technological verification systems remains untapped. Liu et al. (2023) and Delmas and Burbano (2011) underscore the importance of transparency in building credibility, yet there is little empirical evidence on how customers perceive blockchain and AI-enabled verification systems. Bridging these gaps is important to understand how these technologies can affect customer behaviour and drive widespread adoption.

Table 2.1 highlights their respective limitations and provides justifications for addressing them. While the available literature identifies blockchain's capacity to enhance transparency, the lack of research into its scalability across industries justifies further exploration. Similarly, AI's role in both detecting and potentially exacerbating greenwashing emphasizes the requirement for ethical guidelines and frameworks to govern its use. By focusing on the integration of these technologies with regulatory and customer perspectives, future research can develop holistic solutions to counter greenwashing effectively. Intending to bridge these research gaps, the chapter aligns the gaps with some of the research questions as listed below:

(1) How can the emerging technologies like AI, big data, and blockchain be employed to detect and combat greenwashing in corporate sustainability practices?
(2) Examine the challenges associated with integrating these technologies into existing corporate structures, and how can they be overcome?
(3) How can these technological interventions help improve corporate accountability and customer trust in sustainability claims?

While exploring the solution to the above-mentioned research questions, the chapter is structured by demonstrating the background and research gap in the above section, followed by the review of literature (RoL) in the next section, which shows the in-depth assessment of the available research papers relevant to the field of study. The RoL also covers the proposal of a conceptual model, which is followed by research methodology that represents the systematic literature review (SLR) method applied for reviewing the number of literature pieces. After the RoL section, the chapter led to the key finding areas based on the conceptual model designed for reducing the greenwashing issues and ensuring the corporate transparency. Furthermore, in the subsequent section, the book

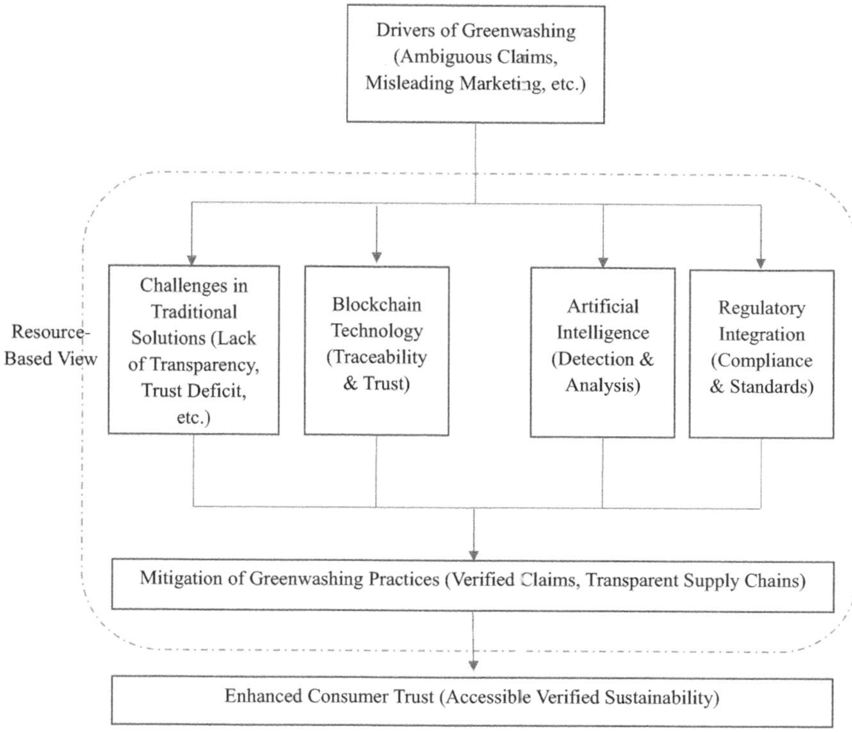

Fig. 2.1. Conceptual Mode.l *Source:* Prepared by author.

chapter covers the discussion on findings and their implications from diverse perspectives, which is finally followed by the conclusion of the chapter.

Review of Literature

It provides an in-depth investigation of greenwashing practices and the importance of emerging technologies to mitigate their impact. Following the Theory, Context, Characteristics, Methodology (TCCM) framework, the review examines the theoretical underpinnings, industry-specific contexts, attributes of greenwashing practices and methodological innovations. Each sub-part talks about a narrative, integrating insights from available literature to create a reliable understanding of the issue and its technological solutions.

Greenwashing: The Evolution of a Corporate Dilemma

The idea of greenwashing emerged from Corporate Social Responsibility practices or traditions, whose purpose is to fix corporate actions with environmental as well as societal well-being. In the beginning, it was found as a tool for

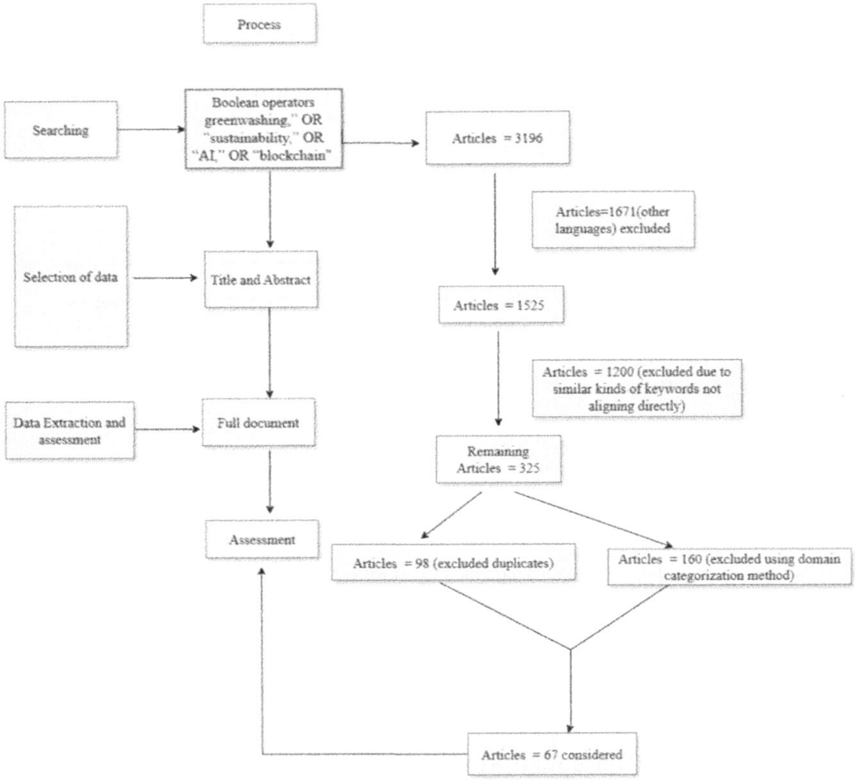

Fig. 2.2. Articles Extraction Through SLR Process. *Source:* Self prepared by authors.

encouraging transparency and accountability; corporate social responsibility unwittingly became a well-known platform for misleading practices or traditions as companies sought to optimize sustainability claims for competitive advantages (Marquis & Toffel, 2012). Greenwashing talks about the strategic distortion of environmental practices to improve social image without substantial action. Eventually, greenwashing has developed into a complicated marketing plan, with corporations making evasive statements, biased reporting, and unverified certifications to mislead stakeholders (Delmas & Burbano, 2011).

The fashion industry highlights companies that are prone to greenwashing, often claiming to use sustainable resources while masking exploitative actions in their supply chains (Fletcher, 2014). In the same way, in the energy sector, corporations highlight various token contributions to renewable energy while relying heavily on fossil fuels (Lyon & Maxwell, 2011). Such practices reduce

Table 2.1. Relevance of Existing Research Gap

Research Focus	**Key Literature (2010–2024)**	**Identified Gap**	**Justification for Bridging the Gap**
Greenwashing and Sustainability	Delmas, M. A., & Burbano, V. C. (2011). The drivers of greenwashing. *California Management Review.* Lyon, T. P., & Montgomery, A. W. (2015). The means and end of greenwashing. *Organization & Environment.* Beppato, C. (2024). *Greenwashing and sustainability: People's perception, awareness, and behaviour* (Master's thesis, Universidade NOVA de Lisboa (Portugal)). Bolton, M., & Chan, T. *Governing sustainability transitions in a world of AI-powered greenwashing.*	The challenge lies in verifying sustainability claims, as previous research often focuses on identifying greenwashing without identifying the technological tools needed to verify claims in real time (Lyon & Montgomery, 2015). Limited studies have fully explored blockchain, Artificial Intelligence, and big data's potential in real-time verification.	There is a need for models that use emerging technologies to verify sustainability claims clearly or transparently and effectively. Research should explore the integration of blockchain, Artificial Intelligence, and big data to increase accountability in sustainable practices for corporations and prevent greenwashing.
Blockchain Technology in Sustainability	Chaudhuri et al. (2023). Improving social sustainability and reducing supply chain risks through blockchain implementation: Role of outcome and behavioural mechanisms. *Annals of operations research*, 1–33.	Despite of numerous research papers available in the field of Blockchain technology, the area of Blockchain's capability to deal with the greenwashing concern is still	Integration of blockchain technology has immense capacity to play a critical role in offering transparency and traceability while making sustainability claims. However, current research

(Continued)

Table 2.1. *(Continued)*

Research Focus	Key Literature (2010–2024)	Identified Gap	Justification for Bridging the Gap
	Navaratne, N. (2024). The Promise of blockchain as a driver for sustainability in value chains: A critical theory analysis.	unexplored. The integration of blockchain technology into marketing practices can help organizations obtain authenticity of green promises with utmost transparency. There is limited research available on its application in the verification of sustainability claims, particularly across diverse industries	lacks a comprehensive framework showing how blockchain technology can authenticate the green promises made by different brands across industries. The chapter also identifies the gap of research for addressing the practical challenges of integrating blockchain for sustainability substantiation.
Artificial Intelligence and Greenwashing	Frank, B. (2021). Artificial intelligence-enabled environmental sustainability of products: Marketing benefits and their variation by consumer, location, and product types. *Journal of Cleaner Production, 285*, 125242. Moodaley, W., and Telukdarie, A. (2023). Greenwashing,	AI-driven tools for detecting greenwashing are still in the early stages, and there is insufficient research on how AI can be misused further. Available literature does not explore the dual role of Artificial Intelligence in detecting and potentially encouraging greenwashing (Frank, 2021).	The research highlights the potential of AI in detecting greenwashing concerns by analyzing the sustainability claims made by different organizations against real-world data. However, research should also emphasize the dark side of AI and ChatGPT in marketing (Tiwari

Table 2.1. *(Continued)*

Research Focus	Key Literature (2010–2024)	Identified Gap	Justification for Bridging the Gap
	sustainability reporting, and artificial intelligence: A systematic literature review. *Sustainability*, *15*(2), 1481.		et al., 2024). The available studies highlight the misuse of AI technologies by various organizations while manipulating the customer perceptions and advocate for the use of AI-enabled tools ethically and responsibly in reporting the sustainability.
Big Data and Greenwashing Detection	Jianjun, S. U. N., Nannan, Z. U., & Haorui, W. (2024). Effects of big data technologies on enterprises' greenwashing: Based on the perspective of greenwashing behaviours. *Collected Essays on Finance and Economics*, *40*(10), 92. Li, Q., He, Z., & Li, H. (2024). Uncovering corporate greenwashing: A predictive model	Big data plays a significant role in sensing the greenwashing practices, which is yet underexplored. The chapter identifies the gulf of insufficiency in the research based on blending big data with AI and blockchain to offer a more effective and real-time solution for detecting and reducing greenwashing activities across industries.	The chapter highlights a holistic approach of using the technologies like AI, blockchain and big data analytics in attempting to explore the significance in assessing the sustainability claims. However, the current research lacks in terms of availability of conceptual framework that defines the impact

(Continued)

Table 2.1. *(Continued)*

Research Focus	Key Literature (2010–2024)	Identified Gap	Justification for Bridging the Gap
	based on Chinese heavy-pollution industries. *Sustainability Accounting, Management and Policy Journal.*		of integration of these technologies in a practical, industry-specific manner to eliminate the greenwashing activities successfully.
Regulatory Context of Greenwashing	Zhang, D. (2022). Environmental regulation and firm product quality improvement: How does the greenwashing response? *International Review of Financial Analysis, 80*, 102058. Lyon, T. P., & Montgomery, A. W. (2015). The regulatory oversight of greenwashing. *Journal of Business Ethics.*	Regulatory bodies are slow to incorporate emerging technologies in their frameworks. While greenwashing regulations are evolving, they often lag behind technological advancements that could improve claim verification.	There's a need to align regulatory frameworks with new technologies such as AI, blockchain and big data. Research should focus on developing an updated regulatory model that ensures these technologies are effectively used to validate sustainability claims and prevent greenwashing.
Customer Perception and Trust	Chen, Y. S., & Chang, C. H. (2013). Greenwash and green trust: The mediation effects of green consumer confusion and green perceived risk. *Journal of business ethics, 114*, 489–500.	Little research has been done on how customers perceive technological verification of sustainability claims. The effectiveness of blockchain and AI	Understanding customer trust in technological verification systems is crucial for their adoption. Research should investigate how customers respond to blockchain and

Table 2.1. *(Continued)*

Research Focus	Key Literature (2010–2024)	Identified Gap	Justification for Bridging the Gap
	Szabo, S., & Webster, J. (2021). Perceived greenwashing: The effects of green marketing on environmental and product perceptions. *Journal of business ethics*, *171*, 719–739. Delmas, M. A., & Burbano, V. C. (2011). Customer response to corporate sustainability. *California Management Review*.	in building customer trust is still a largely unexplored area in the context of greenwashing (Delmas & Burbano, 2011).	AI-driven sustainability verification and whether such transparency leads to more trust and credibility in corporate sustainability efforts.

Source: Prepared by author.

customer trust and transform the competitive landscape by concentrating on superficial compliance over true environmental activity.

Governments & non-governmental organizations (NGOs) have made efforts to handle greenwashing through standards and regulations. Efforts such as the European Union's Corporate Sustainability Reporting Directive objective to foster or elevate transparency by mandating full disclosure of environmental practices. However, enforcement continues to be inconsistent, and corporations persist in taking advantage of regulatory loopholes (Zhang, 2022). This tendency of practising greenwashing brings the focus to the high-time requirement for adopting innovative tools and applications for detecting and eliminating greenwashing activities and rebuilding the credibility of sustainability claims in the business.

Table 2.2. Table for Technology-Based Functions to Address Greenwashing Issue

Component	Function	Example	Citations
Blockchain	Provides traceability and immutable records of sustainability claims.	Tracking sustainable sourcing of raw materials in the fashion or food industries.	Saberi et al. (2019), Navaratne (2024)
AI	Detects patterns of greenwashing and validates claims against real-world data.	Analysing corporate reports to detect ambiguous or misleading language in sustainability claims.	Moodaley and Telukdarie (2023), Frank (2021)
Big Data Analytics	Aggregates real-time data for comprehensive sustainability performance insights.	Monitoring environmental metrics across supply chains for discrepancies between claims and actions.	Chaudhuri et al. (2023), Li et al. (2024)
Regulatory Integration	Ensures compliance by aligning technologies with legal standards.	Policies mandating blockchain-based supply chain reporting and AI-powered claim verification.	Zhang (2022), Lyon and Montgomery (2015)
Customer Trust	Builds confidence in verified claims, driving informed decision-making.	Public dashboards showing blockchain-verified sustainability data for customer products.	Chen and Chang (2013), Delmas and Burbano (2011)

Source: Prepared by author.

Emerging Issues With Cutting-Edge Technologies

The rise of green awareness among the customers and the emergence of several technological advancements have opened up new doors of opportunities to identify the presence of misleading promises by enhancing sincerity and corporate accountability in sustainable practices. Blockchain, AI and big data analytics have emerged as major technological tools, offering specialized or varied yet complementary functionalities. However, such a shift towards new

Table 2.3. Key Theories Explaining Technological Integration, Greenwashing, and Corporate Transparency

Theory	Description	References
Legitimacy Theory	Legitimacy theory defines three different types of legitimacies including cognitive, pragmatic, and moral, where the pragmatic affect the disclosure regarding environmental problems and fosters a strategy aimed at gaining and improving legitimacy or at reconstituting a compromised legitimacy.	Baldini et al. (2018), Camilleri (2018), Lokuwaduge and Heenetigala (2017), Melloni et al. (2017), Reber et al. (2022)
Agency Theory	Greenwashing is a corporate governance issue. Conflict arises when managers and owners make misleading disclosures in their own interest.	Arayssi et al. (2016, 2020), Arif et al. (2022), Bătae et al. (2021), Bravo and Reguera-Alvarado (2018), Camilleri (2015), Clementino and Perkins (2021)
Stakeholders Theory	To manage their relational capital, stakeholders are involved in the companies' activities.	Capelle-Blancard and Petit (2019), Clementino and Perkins (2021), Coleman (2011)
Signalling theory	Signalling theory aims to improve accountability.	Coleman (2011), Giannarakis (2014), Melloni et al. (2017), Rezaee and Tuo (2017), Wang et al. (2020)
Disclosure Theory	Disclosure activities mainly rely on companies' resources; businesses take a competitive advantage of greenwashing.	Beretta et al. (2019), Fatemi et al. (2018), Grewal et al. (2019), Kim and Lyon (2015), Lu and Wang (2021), Melloni et al. (2017)
Resource Based View (RBV)	Resource-based View (RBV) advocates that the emerging technologies like Blockchain, Big Data, and AI are strategic assets that provide a competitive advantage. By leveraging these technologies,	Coates and McDermott (2002), Irwin et al. (1998), Barney (1991)

(Continued)

Table 2.3. *(Continued)*

Theory	Description	References
	organizations can enhance sustainability practices, improve transparency, and continuously adapt, thereby boosting performance, mitigating greenwashing, and strengthening relationships with eco-conscious customer	

Source: Prepared by author.

technology is not without its integration complexities, including technical, economic and regulatory barriers, which highlight the requirement for in-depth research. This chapter discusses these technological integration issues in detail as below;

- *Blockchain:* Blockchain technology is especially considered as an ideal technological advancement for authenticating sustainability claims due to its ability to trace the history in a decentralized manner and detect unauthorized access (Nygaard & Silkoset, 2023). By creating an unalterable and highly traceable ledger, blockchain technology allows the parties involved to trace the information source of products and materials, confirming that sustainability declarations are always reinforced by the evidence that can be validated (Saberi et al., 2019). One such evidence is the effective blockchain's implementation by Walmart in its supply chain processes to monitor food safety and sustainability performance metrics (Spicer & Hyatt, 2017; Vanleer et al., 2016). Despite its numerous potential advantages, heavy cost of implementation, along with the interconnection obstacles and inconsistent standards, continues to restrict the adoption of this technology (Navaratne, 2024).
- *Artificial Intelligence (AI):* The ability of AI to process extensive datasets and identify trends and positions makes it an essential tool in detecting greenwashing. Natural Language Processing (NLP) algorithms are capable of examining sustainability reports, advertisements, and marketing content for irregularities, although machine learning models can identify patterns of fraudulent and unethical behaviour (Moodaley & Telukdarie, 2023). However, the misuse of AI is an increasingly pressing issue. Organizations could employ AI to create more effective greenwashing tactics that highlight the ethical dilemmas connected to its usage (Frank, 2021).
- *Big Data Analytics:* It facilitates real-time tracking of environmental metrics throughout global supply chains, making it feasible. By combining data from

Table 2.4. Exemplary Articles Included in the Review as per Citation

Name of the Journal	Number of Documents	Area of Focus	References	Citations
Journal of Management	1	Business Management	Barney (1991)	107,928
International Journal of Information Management	1	Information Management, Blockchain	Kshetri (2018)	4,504
International Journal of Production Research	1	Supply Chain, Blockchain	Saberi et al. (2019)	3,693
MIS Quarterly	1	Information Systems, Business Management	Wade and Hulland (2004)	2,647
Qualitative Market Research: An International Journal	1	Marketing, Green Marketing	Peattie and Crane (2005)	1,606
Journal of Business Research	1	Business Research, AI, Blockchain	Zhao et al. (2021)	1,401
Journal of Economics & Management Strategy	1	Economics, Greenwashing	Lyon and Maxwell (2011)	1,153
International Journal of Process Management and Benchmarking	1	Benchmarking, Sustainability	Vanleer et al. (2016)	1,025
Business Strategy and the Environment	1	Environmental Business, Greenwashing	Nygaard and Silkoset (2023)	980
International Journal of Marketing Studies	1	Marketing, Customer Attitude	Chen and Chang (2013)	945
Organization & Environment	1	Environmental Business	Lyon and Montgomery (2015)	786
Journal of Manufacturing	1	Technology Management,	Samadhiya et al. (2023)	652

(Continued)

Table 2.4. *(Continued)*

Name of the Journal	Number of Documents	Area of Focus	References	Citations
Technology Management		Circular Economy		
Business Strategy and the Environment	1	Business, Sustainability	Grewal et al. (2019)	550
Sustainability	1	Sustainability, Greenwashing, Reporting	Alyahia et al. (2024)	480
California Management Review	1	Business Management, Greenwashing	Delmas and Burbano (2011)	412
The Journal of Applied Business and Economics	1	Business, Greenwashing	Furlow (2010)	401
Journal of Business Economics and Management	1	Business Economics, Greenwashing	Yang et al. (2020)	271
Journal of Engineering and Technology Management	1	Technology, Management	Irwin et al. (1998)	254
Journal of Operations Management	1	Business Management, Operations	Coates and McDermott (2002)	253
Water Science and Technology	1	Technology for Sustainability	Ho (2005)	209
Journal of Business Ethics	1	Ethics, Business	Polonsky et al. (1998)	180
Society and Business Review	1	Business, Corporate Social Responsibility	Rezaee and Tuo (2017)	180

Source: Author's Own Elaboration.

various sources, it offers a complete 360-degree view of corporate environmental performance, empowering stakeholders to recognize contradictions between claims and practices (Li et al., 2024). However, inadequate integration of big data with blockchain and AI technologies weakens the effectiveness of a comprehensive greenwashing detection framework.

While these technologies can revolutionize sustainability certification, their effectiveness depends on addressing implementation challenges. Regulatory frameworks must be reformed to accommodate these tools, and research should concentrate on developing cohesive models that leverage their benefits.

Intersecting Paradigm: Bridging Greenwashing and Technology

The industry is seeing an increased dependence on the greenwashing activities; the intersection of the emerging technologies discussed in the above section with the greenwashing practices has created a new paradigm concentrated on accountability and transparency. Technological advancements like AI, Blockchain and big data are not the isolated solutions; their real potential appears when they are incorporated into the processes together as part of an integrated system.

However, there are significant research gaps in the literature concerning the real-time utilization of these technologies. While the majority of the research studies explored are on the basis of applications of these technologies, very few studies are focused on their collaborative potential for addressing difficulties in the different industries (Li et al., 2024). Furthermore, the most significant hindrance in the pathway to the widespread adoption of these technological advancements is the limited customer awareness, low technical literacy and regulatory non-compliance. To bridge these important gaps, stakeholders – including policymakers, industrialists and the researchers, must work together to develop detailed frameworks that endorse the seamless implementation of these technologies. This chapter attempts to fill in the above research gap by offering a conceptual model that represents effective utilization of technologies for identifying and eliminating the greenwashing practices prevalent in the industry by validating the organization's sustainability claim and improving the real green image of various brands.

Preparing Conceptual Model

The chapter proposes a conceptual model highlighting the significant relationship between greenwashing practices and utilization of advanced technologies such as Blockchain, AI and big data analytics. The model was prepared by following the TCCM framework, which evaluates the literature based on four aspects including the theory used, the characteristics or constructs explored, the context examined and the method used (Bhardwaj & Kalro, 2024). As a part of the TCCM framework, the chapter examined six different theories, including legitimacy theory, stakeholder theory, signalling theory, disclosure theory and resource-based view, for explaining the relationship proposed in this conceptual model. It is observed from the literature that Legitimacy Theory explains the three categories of legitimacy, including pragmatic, cognitive, and moral legitimacy, where it emphasizes about the social, environmental and governance disclosures (Baldini et al., 2018; Reber et al., 2022). While the agency theory focused only on the corporate governance concern in the business practices (Arayssi et al., 2016; 2020; Clementino & Perkins, 2021). The third theory examined for the review structuring purpose is the stakeholder theory, which highlights managing the relational capital for the organizations, that encourage the stakeholders involved in the business activities to perform ethical behaviour (Capelle-Blancard & Petit, 2019). While the signalling theory mainly focuses on the accountability of the managers for green practices (Agarwal et al., 2020; Melloni et al., 2017; Wang et al., 2020). The chapter further evaluates the disclosure theory that explains the importance of a company's resources for making sustainable claims (Beretta et al., 2019; Melloni et al., 2017), however, the last theory considered for evaluation is the resource-based view (RBV) (Coates & McDermott, 2002). The RBV demonstrates the effective and collaborative utilizations of the cutting-edge technologies as the company's resources to create the competitive advantage (Irwin et al., 1998). The RBV lens also explains how the acquisition of these cutting-edge technological advancements can improve the organizational performance (Barney, 1991), which makes this theory the most suitable among the others for preparing the conceptual model for this chapter.

The model proposed intends to define the interrelationship between the implementation of advanced technologies to detect, mitigate, and prevent greenwashing activities performed by various brands in the context of their marketing plan. The model also considers the broader regulatory and contextual issues in the process of adoption of these technologies. This model follows a systems-thinking approach, establishing links between the drivers of greenwashing, technological solutions, their integration and the resulting outcomes that depict the characteristics that lead the organizations to achieve the desired outcomes.

Drivers of Greenwashing

The first stage of the model covers the identification of the key drivers that strengthen the greenwashing activities, such as misleading claims, selective reporting, false certifications, and deceptive marketing practices (Delmas & Burbano, 2011). Such unethical strategies succeed in surroundings characterized by intricate supply chains, weak regulations and a lack of transparency. This means that in such a weak regulatory and operational setting, the traditional solutions, including audits and manual verifications, can be ill-equipped to manage the wide scale and intricacy of greenwashing. With an intention to improve such contextual weakness, Delmas & Burbano (2011) also emphasized the requirement of a collaborative approach by managers, researchers, NGOs and policymakers to deal with the greenwashing issue. Such a coalition between the organizations and government entities will help improve the environmental impacts of the business practices and reduce the greenwashing activities (Yang et al., 2020).

Challenges in Traditional Solutions

The traditional approaches used for addressing greenwashing concerns are often insufficient for organizations, as they do not offer traceability, real-time monitoring and consistent industry standards (Bhagat, 2024). These significant characteristics of limitations only serve to broaden the trust shortfall between companies and customers, making the favourable scenario for adopting the innovative tools that can provide clearer transparency and stronger accountability (Zhang, 2022).

Integration of Cutting-Edge Technologies

The industry is consistently growing with the increased utilization of various emerging technologies. Such integration of the frontline and advanced technologies, including AI, blockchain and big data analytics, with the business practices can play a substantial role in attracting increased possibilities for enabling sustainability across various industries (Ho, 2005). Such increased technological adoption by the industry has been widely explained by various researchers using the RBV (Coates & McDermott, 2002; Wade & Hulland, 2004). These technologies collectively improve transparency, efficiency, and accountability in supply chains, thereby supporting sustainable practices (Moorthy et al., 2022). The following sections elaborate on their roles and interrelationships.

Blockchain Technology: Blockchain technology has the capability of validating the immutability and transparency due to its highly traceable and encrypted framework (Samadhiya et al., 2023). It ensures that the sustainability claims are verifiable through an immutable ledger, which is crucial for tracing material life cycles (Moorthy et al., 2022).

Artificial Intelligence (AI): AI algorithms work based on data-driven decision-making and can help organizations detect patterns revealing greenwashing activities and improve the credibility of sustainability claims (Chatterjee et al., 2022). Based on the AI-driven data analysis, the organizations can automate the authentication of blockchain data, safeguarding compliance and precision in sustainability reporting (Rane et al., 2025).

Big Data Analytics: Big data aggregates environmental metrics, providing real-time monitoring of corporate sustainability efforts (Trivedi et al., 2024). Such comprehensive insights extracted by big data analytics can be used by organizations in collaboration with blockchain and AI for improving the conformity of the sustainability evaluation mechanism (Chatterjee et al., 2022). Hence, the integration of the aforesaid technologies can enhance the verification potential of the organizations.

Regulatory Integration

The conceptual model proposed in the chapter also examines the regulatory context for effective implementation of these evolving technologies in an integrative approach. The model highlights how the regulatory framework of the business surroundings can be helpful in normalizing the usage of these technologies. It emphasizes the high requirement of a government policy implementation that mandates the organizations for adopting blockchain-based tracking (Nygaard & Silkoset, 2023), AI-enabled data-driven verification (Moodaley & Telukdarie, 2023), and big data analysis in reporting the sustainability promises. Regulatory integration ensures that greenwashing detection systems are aligned with legal standards and enforced uniformly across industries (Zhang, 2022).

Mitigation of Greenwashing Practices

As identified from the review of the literature, the root cause of any organization involved in greenwashing practices is the ill-equipped assessments of the sustainability claims (Marquis & Toffel, 2012), weak regulatory framework (Zhang, 2022) and wilful attempt to make fake promises (Delmas & Burbano, 2011). The conceptual model suggested in the chapter highlights the collective implementation of evolving technologies by industry professionals, NGOs and Government entities to address the roots of greenwashing activities. Such effective implementation of the integrative technologies provides substantiated claims, improves corporate transparency in terms of supply chain, marketing and other processes and eliminates the chances of misleading practices. Technological advancement empowers the businesses and relevant stakeholders to ensure accountability at every stage of marketing, distribution and the remaining value chain for mitigating greenwashing practices effectively.

Enhanced Customer Trust

The systematic approach to implement technological combinations and integrate the same with the business practices can enable the organizations potential to grow fast without involving greenwashing. The conceptual model suggested in the chapter also emphasize that such an intersection plays a pivotal role for re-establishing and enhancing the customer trust in corporate sustainability promises. The verified claims are made accessible through transparent systems that empower the customers with technology-empowered credibility to make informed purchasing decisions (Liu et al., 2023). The credibility and trust gained with this intersection not only offers capabilities for the businesses by improving the brand image but also encourages the industry for comprehensive adoption of the verified sustainable practices (Chen & Chang, 2013; Marquis & Toffel, 2012). The relationship explained above is further demonstrated below in the Fig. 2.1.

The model suggested in this chapter operates as a cohesive ecosystem by using a holistic approach for the application of three advanced technologies interactively, where the blockchain technology offers grounds for tracing and recording the claims of sustainability due to its tamper-proof frameworks (Chaudhuri et al., 2023; Navaratne, 2024). AI-powered data analysis enables organizations to validate the records of green promises and identify irregularities, whereas big data analytics enhances value by increasing the relevance of the promises made by organizations against broader environmental metrics. These technologies can also be further enhanced by regulatory frameworks, which establish consistent standards for their implementation. The technologies work in a collaborative approach to deal with the key drivers of greenwashing activities and offer a strong solution that is scalable, transparent and aligned with customer expectations from the firms.

The intersection of greenwashing activities and emerging technological advancements fosters accountability among industry players and builds trust and credibility among customers. By defining this relationship, the model not only eliminates the greenwashing issue in the industry but also provides a reason for the companies to implement authentic green practices, ultimately enhancing the contributory efforts for long-term environmental and societal benefits. Table 2.2 covers some the relevant examples from the literature, highlighting how the cutting-edge technologies can reinforce the sustainable growth of industry by effectively dealing with greenwashing issues. The table offers some of the examples of technology-based functions extracted from the literature that can be utilized to address the greenwashing.

Research Methodology

A SLR methodology based on the TCCM framework is used in this chapter for reviewing the relevant literature. According to Fink (2019), a literature review is crucial for various reasons, as it helps refine the research questions and gives a comprehensive or better understanding of a topic, and it also highlights methodological approaches that offer various insights into the conceptual framework. It also helps in identifying contradictory issues, formulating hypotheses (Torchia et al., 2015), and guiding the research design process. Researchers, academicians, and practitioners also refer to review papers, and they get a systematic and updated knowledge of the literature in the particular field (Tiwari & Kendurkar, 2019). This chapter is based on reviewing various research papers or articles using the systematic literature method. The following are the steps for conducting the (Systematic Literature Method) SLR:

(1) *Search Strategy:* Relevant research was identified using databases such as Scopus, Web of Science, and Google Scholar (Chadegani et al., 2013; Mongeon & Paul-Hus, 2016; Vieira & Gomes, 2009). Boolean operators were used for Scopus and Web of Science to define the search string, which involved systematically testing various keywords like 'greenwashing', OR

'sustainability', OR 'AI', OR 'blockchain', OR 'big data', AND 'technological integration', AND 'technology advancement', etc. The top-cited articles were considered by Google Scholar. Various keywords that were integrated with appropriate Booleans were used for searching the title, abstract, and keywords of the publications.

(2) *Inclusion Criteria:* Studies published between 2010 and 2024 were selected, focusing on topics related to corporate sustainability, greenwashing detection, and the role of emerging technologies. We applied a filter to the search result of 3,196 articles initially; after observing, we found that 1,671 articles were out due to other languages. The remaining 1,525 articles were found based on keywords, abstracts, and titles after those similar kinds of keywords were found, like 'AI in Green practices', and 'Corporate transparency' in all aspects, but they are irrelevant because they didn't directly align with the primary focus of the study. These papers on AI in green practices are related to the application of AI in green practices and not focused on addressing core issues related to the misleading green claims. Additionally, the term 'corporate transparency' is a broad concept; however, we have to align it with respect to greenwashing specifically. So, we have excluded 1,200 articles. We further filtered out and used the domain categorization method using specific categories of keywords from 325 articles. With this, we found 165 articles for further analysis, with 80 publications sourced from Scopus, 70 from Google Scholar, and 15 from the WoS database. To filter out irrelevant search results, 98 papers were duplicates. Eventually, 67 primary studies were included. We have excluded 98 articles, research papers, and conference papers due to duplicates and other domains like science and humanities.

(3) *Data Extraction:* Each research article or paper was reviewed in depth, and pertinent results for examining the research questions were extracted and stored. Key themes were extracted and categorized according to the TCCM framework (Sharma et al., 2020). This process involved identifying the theoretical foundations, contextual factors, characteristics of greenwashing practices, and the methodologies used to detect them (Olaleye et al., 2023).

(4) *Analysis:* The TCCM framework is employed to address the research questions. This framework talks about theories, contexts, characteristics, and methodologies (Mahajan et al., 2024). The literature was critically analyzed to identify research gaps in the current research and opportunities for the integration of emerging technologies. The process of literature inclusion and exclusion for analysis is depicted in Fig. 2.2.

Theory

Table 2.3 refers to various theories identified and analyzed to comprehend the relationship in the conceptual model. It compares different theories cited in several pieces of literature, but found the Resource-based View (RBV) as the most prominent and relevant one to analyze the technological integration and enhance the sustainable practices (see Table 2.3).

Context

This section of the chapter investigates the contexts where the literature review exercise on greenwashing was carried out, and the review observed that while a reasonable quantity of studies focused on emerging economies, most of the research is focused on developed economies (Bhagat, 2024). The studies focus on corporate transparency and consumer trust, drivers of greenwashing like Ambiguous Claims, and Misleading Marketing (Chen & Chang, 2013). It is worth noticing that a substantial portion of the literature did not specifically indicate the above aspects. Apart from this, regulatory integration has an impact on sustainable claims. Robust regulations can help mitigate greenwashing by promoting accountability and holding corporations responsible for their environmental claims (Arif et al., 2022), and fostering more authentic sustainability practices.

Characteristics

We have observed characteristics in existing literature, focusing on factors that have been aligned with understanding the subject. Many studies have examined the role of greenwashing disclosure and its related variables, highlighting drivers like Blockchain, AI, and regulatory harmonization that affect the challenges and effectiveness associated with improving transparency and sustainable practices (Nygaard & Silkoset, 2023). Further, regarding technological advancements, the literature review also determines various issues or challenges faced by standard solutions in focusing on greenwashing issues. One main issue is the lack of clarity or transparency in sustainability claims, which often diminishes the integrity of sustainability practices. In addition, researchers have pointed out the displacement of greenwashing practices – where corporations or firms shift from one fallacious strategy to another in an attempt to avoid detection. Lastly, another key issue or challenge revealed in the literature is the need to enhance the trust of customers. As today's customers become more knowledgeable, informed and discerning, ensuring the authenticity of sustainability claims becomes crucial. Discussing these challenges, it is crucial to confirm that corporations can promote a sustainable and trustworthy relationship with their customers (Harrison et al., 2020).

Methodology

We extracted 165 research papers or articles from the Scopus, Web of Science and Google Scholar databases, out of which 98 research articles or papers were eliminated through the process which has been explained in detail in the search strategy. After this scrutiny stage, the title and abstract were read thoroughly, resulting in 67 articles. Table 2.4 reports some of the exemplary articles included in the review structuring process based on their number of citations (see Table 2.4).

Synthesis

A conceptual model was proposed to integrate the findings into a coherent framework for combating greenwashing using advanced technologies. The systematic review structuring is a method in which various research papers selected for analysis are mapped and profiled as per different criteria, like: relevancy limitations. We have considered top-cited papers for conducting the review exercise so that an understanding of the research pattern can be developed and quality of work can be ensured (Arvidsson & Dumay, 2022; Tiwari & Kendurkar, 2019). The chapter considers the mapping of the literature, considering the specificity with respect to greenwashing and corporate transparency in the field of study. The SLR method ensures the objectivity of the research approach.

Key Findings

The review revealed several key findings:

- *Technological Solutions:* Cutting-edge technologies, like big data analytics, blockchain and AI, have shown significant potential in focusing on the challenge of greenwashing by promoting the transparency and credibility of sustainability claims. For example, blockchain offers a decentralized and unquestionable record that ensures clarity, transparency and monitoring of sustainability claims (Tapscott & Tapscott, 2016), allowing customers and other stakeholders to verify the origins and environmental impacts of products. On the other hand, AI can be used to analyze promotional and advertising materials, detecting potentially fallacious claims through NLP and (He & Wang, 2025) machine learning algorithms. Lastly, big data analytics can give insights related to the environmental performance of entire supply chains by aggregating and analyzing vast amounts of data, enabling companies to assess their sustainability practices more accurately and identify areas for improvement (Wang et al., 2020).
- *Challenges to Implementation:* Despite the promising potential of these technologies, several challenges remain that hinder their widespread adoption. One of the most significant barriers is the regulatory environment, which often lags behind technological developments. Many countries and industries lack clear standards for sustainability verification, making it difficult to establish consistent frameworks for integrating blockchain, AI, and big data analytics into corporate sustainability practices (Gurría, 2019). Additionally, the high cost of implementing these technologies, especially for smaller companies, can be a significant deterrent. Blockchain infrastructure, AI systems and data

analytics platforms often require substantial investment in both technology and expertise, posing a barrier to entry for firms that may not have the resources to implement these solutions (Zhao et al., 2021). Finally, the lack of industry-wide standards for sustainability verification makes it difficult to ensure that these technologies are being used effectively and consistently across sectors, further complicating efforts to combat greenwashing.

- *Customer Trust:* Research has shown that customers are more likely to trust companies that provide transparent, verifiable information (Nielsen, 2015), but there is also the potential for scepticism, particularly when customers do not fully understand how these technologies work or how to interpret the data they provide. Therefore, studies should explore both the constructive and harmful implications of these technologies on customer trust, examining how they are perceived by different customer groups and the role of education and awareness in overcoming potential doubts (Harrison et al., 2020). Educating customers about how blockchain and AI can be used to verify sustainability claims is critical to ensuring that these tools effectively contribute to building trust in corporate sustainability efforts.
- *Regulatory Alignment:* As technologies like blockchain and AI become increasingly sophisticated, it is crucial that policymakers update existing regulations to ensure that these tools are used to prevent greenwashing and promote authentic sustainability practices (Gurría, 2019). Policymakers must develop guidelines that encourage the adoption of these technologies while also addressing issues related to data privacy, security, and ethical considerations in AI applications (Binns, 2018).

Discussion and Implications of the Study

The study has important implications across various sectors:

- *Academic Implications:* This chapter contributes to the consistently evolving body of literature on the intersection of technology and sustainability, offering a conceptual model that integrates technological solutions to address greenwashing. Greenwashing, or the deceptive practice of overstating environmental benefits, has become a significant challenge in the realm of corporate sustainability (Lyon & Montgomery, 2015). Recent studies highlight how cutting-edge digital technologies, such as blockchain and AI, can help address this issue by providing transparent, verifiable data and improving accountability in sustainability claims (Wang et al., 2020).
- *Social Implications:* By providing greater transparency, these technologies can foster more informed customer choices, contributing to a broader social movement towards sustainability. AI-driven data analytics can help customers track the sustainability performance of brands in real time, encouraging them to support businesses that align with their values and further strengthening demand for ethical practices in the marketplace. In a customer-driven

economy, where more individuals are prioritizing sustainability in their purchasing decisions (Nielsen, 2015).

- *Research Implications:* Future research should explore the practical challenges and limitations of implementing technologies like blockchain and AI in real-world scenarios and assess their effectiveness across different industries. While the theoretical potential of these technologies to combat greenwashing is promising, empirical studies are needed to investigate how they can be operationalized in diverse sectors, from agriculture to fashion, and whether they achieve the intended outcomes in terms of increased transparency and reduced deception (Kshetri, 2018).
- *Industry Implications:* Companies must adopt transparent practices and integrate emerging technologies to stay competitive and maintain customer trust. As customers become increasingly aware of corporate sustainability efforts, companies are under growing pressure to substantiate their claims (Cone Communications, 2017).
- *Policy Implications:* Policymakers have a critical role to play in promoting the adoption of technologies like blockchain and AI in sustainability reporting. Policymakers could incentivize companies to adopt technologies that enhance transparency, such as through tax breaks or certification programmes that recognize the use of verified sustainability practices (Gurría, 2019). Furthermore, regulation can ensure that sustainability claims are subject to rigorous scrutiny, with legal consequences for businesses that misrepresent their environmental impacts.

Conclusion

The study delves into the drivers of greenwashing practices, including ambiguous claims, misleading marketing strategies and lack of transparency, which undermine sustainability efforts. It highlights the pivotal role of advanced technologies, particularly blockchain and AI, in combating these issues (Binns, 2018). Blockchain ensures traceability and trust through transparent supply chains, allowing stakeholders to access verifiable sustainability claims. AI complements these efforts by detecting and analyzing greenwashing behaviours, integrating regulatory standards and ensuring compliance with sustainability frameworks (He & Wang, 2025). Findings, structured using the TCCM framework and a SLR, provide a comprehensive view of technological solutions, challenges to implementation, customer trust dynamics and regulatory alignment. Technological interventions have demonstrated significant potential in mitigating greenwashing practices. Verified claims supported by transparent operations not only enhance consumer confidence but also improve brand reputation. However, implementation challenges remain, including high integration costs, interoperability issues, and resistance to technological adoption across industries.

The study emphasizes the critical requirement for regulatory alignment to explore and utilize the utmost potential of these technologies. Clear compliance standards and globally accepted frameworks can streamline the adoption process, fostering accountability and ethical practices (Capelle-Blancard & Petit, 2019). Moreover, customer trust plays a vital role, as accessible verified sustainability claims empower consumers to make informed choices and demand higher accountability from organizations. Key findings reveal that while technological solutions like blockchain and AI are transformative, they require robust support from regulatory bodies and industry stakeholders to overcome adoption barriers (Coleman, 2011). Stronger regulatory compliance collectively contributes to mitigating greenwashing and fostering enhanced customer trust. This approach not only aligns the industry with the increasing consumer demand for ethical practices but also supports long-term sustainability goals, positioning businesses as leaders in responsible and transparent operations. However, the customers, too, play a crucial role in demanding transparency and holding companies responsible. With growing awareness and access to information, empowered customers can drive the demand for authenticity and ethical business practices, pushing brands to substantiate their sustainability claims (Harrison et al., 2020).

Ultimately, achieving true sustainability requires a collective effort from corporations, regulators, and customers. By aligning business strategies with rigorous sustainability criteria (Agrawal & Mukti, 2025), fostering open communication and ensuring continuous improvement, businesses can reduce the occurrence of greenwashing, restore public trust and contribute to a more sustainable and equitable future. The intersection of responsible corporate practices, transparent reporting, and customer advocacy holds the key to transforming corporate sustainability (Lyon & Maxwell, 2011). This chapter emphasizes the need for further research on force for positive change. While emerging technologies offer promising solutions, their integration into business practices faces the challenge of how these technologies can be effectively implemented to combat greenwashing and ensure that companies' sustainability claims are credible (Moodaley & Telukdarie, 2023).

References

Agarwal, S., Lenka, U., Singh, K., Agrawal, V., & Agrawal, A. M. (2020). A qualitative approach towards crucial factors for sustainable development of women social entrepreneurship: Indian cases. *Journal of Cleaner Production*, *274*, 123135.

Agrawal, S. S., & Mukti, S. (2025). *Chapter 12: Role of sustainable finance in contributing to the growth of Indian economy*. Emerald Publishing Limited.

Alyahia, M., Azazz, A. M., Fayyad, S., Elshaer, I. A., & Mohammad, A. A. (2024). Greenwashing behavior in hotels industry: The role of green transparency and green authenticity. *Sustainability*, *16*(3), 1050.

Arayssi, M., Dah, M., & Jizi, M. (2016). Women on boards, sustainability reporting and firm performance. *Sustainability Accounting, Management and Policy Journal*, *7*(3), 376–401. https://doi.org/10.1108/SAMPJ-07-2015-0055

Arayssi, M., Jizi, M., & Tabaja, H. H. (2020). The impact of board composition on the level of ESG disclosures in GCC countries. *Sustainability Accounting, Management and Policy Journal*, *11*(1), 137–161. https://doi.org/10.1108/SAMPJ-05-2018-0136

Arif, M., Gan, C., & Nadeem, M. (2022). Regulating non-financial reporting: Evidence from European firms' environmental, social and governance disclosures and earnings risk. *Meditari Accountancy Research*, *30*(3), 495–523. https://doi.org/10.1108/MEDAR-11-2020-1086

Arvidsson, S., & Dumay, J. (2022). Corporate ESG reporting quantity, quality and performance: Where to now for environmental policy and practice? *Business Strategy and the Environment*, *31*(3), 1091–1110. https://doi.org/10.1002/bse.2937

Baldini, M., Maso, L. D., Liberatore, G., Mazzi, F., & Terzani, S. (2018). Role of country- and firm-level determinants in environmental, social, and governance disclosure. *Journal of Business*. https://doi.org/10.1007/s10551-016-3139-1

Barney, J. (1991). Firm resources and sustained competitive advantage. *Journal of Management*. https://doi.org/10.1177/014920639101700108

Beppato, C. (2024). *Greenwashing and sustainability: People's perception, awareness, and behavior*. (Master's thesis). Universidade NOVA de Lisboa.

Beretta, V., Demartini, C., & Trucco, S. (2019). Does environmental, social and governance performance influence intellectual capital disclosure tone in integrated reporting? *Journal of Intellectual Capital*, *20*(1), 100–124. https://doi.org/10.1108/JIC-02-2018-0049

Bhagat, C. (2024). Greenwashing vs. Genuine efforts: The role of transparent communication in building corporate credibility. *Multidisciplinary Journal of Law for Future Security*, *1*(2), 51–62.

Bhardwaj, P., & Kalro, A. D. (2024). Consumer well-being—A systematic literature review and research agenda using TCCM framework. *International Journal of Consumer Studies*, *48*(1), e12991.

Binns, A. (2018). *AI and data ethics: A critical guide for the 21st century*. Springer.

Bolton, M., & Chan, T. *Governing sustainability transitions in a world of AI-powered greenwashing*.

Bravo, F., & Reguera-Alvarado, N. (2018). Sustainable development disclosure: Environmental, social, and governance reporting and gender diversity in the audit committee. *Business Strategy and the Environment*. https://doi.org/10.1002/bse.2258

Bătae, O. M., Dragomir, V. D., & Feleagă, L. (2021). The relationship between environmental, social, and financial performance in the banking sector: A European study. *Journal of Cleaner Production*, *290*, 125791. https://doi.org/10.1016/j.jclepro.2021.125791

Camilleri, M. A. (2015). Environmental, social and governance disclosures in Europe. *Sustainability Accounting, Management and Policy Journal*, *6*(2), 224–242. https://doi.org/10.1108/SAMPJ-10-2014-0065

Camilleri, M. A. (2018). Theoretical insights on integrated reporting. *Corporate Communications: An International Journal*, *23*(4), 567–581. https://doi.org/10.1108/CCIJ-01-2018-0016

Capelle-Blancard, G., & Petit, A. (2019). Every little helps? ESG news and stock market reaction. *Journal of Business Ethics*, *157*(2), 543–565. https://doi.org/10.1007/s10551-017-3667-3

Chadegani, A. A., Salehi, H., Yunus, M., & Farhadi, H. (2013). A comparison between two main academic literature collections: Web of science and Scopus databases. *Asian Social Science*. https://papers.ssrn.com/sol3/papers.cfm?abstract_id=2257540

Chatterjee, S., Sreen, N., Rana, J., Dhir, A., & Sadarangani, P. H. (2022). Impact of ethical certifications and product involvement on consumers decision to purchase ethical products at price premiums in an emerging market context. *International Review on Public and Nonprofit Marketing*, *19*(4), 737–762.

Chaudhuri, A., Bhatia, M. S., Kayikci, Y., Fernandes, K. J., & Fosso-Wamba, S. (2023). Improving social sustainability and reducing supply chain risks through blockchain implementation: Role of outcome and behavioural mechanisms. *Annals of Operations Research*, 1–33.

Chen, Y.-S., & Chang, C.-H. (2013). Greenwash and green marketing: A study of their influence on customer attitude. *International Journal of Marketing Studies*, *5* (5), 79–89.

Clementino, E., & Perkins, R. (2021). How do companies respond to environmental, social and governance (ESG) ratings? Evidence from Italy. *Journal of Business Ethics*, *171*(2), 379–397.

Coates, T. T., & McDermott, C. M. (2002). An exploratory analysis of new competencies: A resource based view perspective. *Journal of Operations Management*, *20*(5), 435–450.

Coleman, L. (2011). Losses from failure of stakeholder sensitive processes: Financial consequences for large US companies from breakdowns in product, environmental, and accounting standards. *Journal of Business Ethics*, *98*(2), 247–258. https://doi.org/10.1007/s10551-010-0544-8

Cone, C. (2017). *Cone communications CSR study: The next era of responsibility*. Cone Communications Website.

Delmas, M. A., & Burbano, V. C. (2011). The drivers of greenwashing. *California Management Review*, *54*(1), 64–87. https://doi.org/10.1525/cmr.2011.54.1.64

Fatemi, A., Glaum, M., & Kaiser, S. (2018). ESG performance and firm value: The moderating role of disclosure. *Global Finance Journal*, *38*, 45–64. https://doi.org/10.1016/j.gfj.2017.03.001

Fink, A. (2019). *Conducting research literature reviews: From the internet to paper*. Sage publications.

Fletcher, K. (2014). *Sustainable fashion and textiles: Design journeys*. Earthscan.

Frank, B. (2021). Artificial intelligence-enabled environmental sustainability of products: Marketing benefits and their variation by consumer, location, and product types. *Journal of Cleaner Production*, *285*, 125242.

Furlow, N. E. (2010). Greenwashing in the new millennium. *The Journal of Applied Business and Economics*, *10*(6), 22.

Giannarakis, G. (2014). Corporate governance and financial characteristic effects on the extent of corporate social responsibility disclosure. *Social Responsibility Journal*, *10*(4), 569–590. https://doi.org/10.1108/SRJ-02-2013-0008

Grewal, J., Riedl, E. J., & Serafeim, G. (2019). Market reaction to mandatory nonfinancial disclosure. *Management Science*, *65*(7), 3061–3084. https://doi.org/10.1287/mnsc.2018.3099

Gurría, A. (2019). *Harnessing the potential of AI for sustainable development*. OECD. https://www.oecd.org/

Harrison, J., Reid, S., & Tisdell, C. (2020). Customer trust and corporate sustainability: The role of transparency and technology. *Journal of Customer Research*, *47*(5), 745–762. https://doi.org/10.1093/jcr/ucz056

He, L. Y., & Wang, L. (2025). Can artificial intelligence curb greenwashing? Firm-level evidence based on large language model. *Energy Economics*, 108954. https://doi.org/10.1016/j.eneco.2025.108954

Ho, G. (2005). Technology for sustainability: The role of onsite, small and community scale technology. *Water Science and Technology*, *51*(10), 15–20. https://doi.org/10.1007/s10551-020-04441-4

Irwin, J. G., Hoffman, J. J., & Lamont, B. T. (1998). The effect of the acquisition of technological innovations on organizational performance: A resource-based view. *Journal of Engineering and Technology Management*, *15*(1), 25–54.

Jianjun, S. U. N., Nannan, Z. U., & Haorui, W. (2024). Effects of big data technologies on enterprises' greenwashing: Based on the perspective of greenwashing behaviors. *Collected Essays on Finance and Economics*, *40*(10), 92.

Kim, E.-H., & Lyon, T. P. (2015). Greenwash vs. Brownwash: Exaggeration and undue modesty in corporate sustainability disclosure. *Organization Science*, *26*(3), 705–723. https://doi.org/10.1287/orsc.2014.0949

Kshetri, N. (2018). Blockchain's roles in meeting key supply chain management objectives. *International Journal of Information Management*, *39*, 80–89. https://doi.org/10.1016/j.ijinfomgt.2017.12.001

Li, Q., He, Z., & Li, H. (2024). Uncovering corporate greenwashing: A predictive model based on Chinese heavy-pollution industries. *Sustainability Accounting, Management and Policy Journal*. https://doi.org/10.1108/SAMPJ-11-2023-0813

Liu, Y., Heinberg, M., Huang, X., & Eisingerich, A. B. (2023). Building a competitive advantage based on transparency: When and why does transparency matter for corporate social responsibility? *Business Horizons*, *66*(4), 517–527.

Lokuwaduge, C. S. D. S., & Heenetigala, K. (2017). Integrating environmental, social and governance (ESG) disclosure for a sustainable development: An Australian study. *Business Strategy and the Environment*, *26*(4), 438–450.

Lu, J., & Wang, J. (2021). Corporate governance, law, culture, environmental performance and CSR disclosure: A global perspective. *Journal of International Financial Markets, Institutions and Money*, *70*, 101264. https://doi.org/10.1016/j.intfin.2020.101264

Lyon, T. P., & Maxwell, J. W. (2011). Greenwash: Corporate environmental disclosure under threat of audit. *Journal of Economics and Management Strategy*, *20*(1), 1–25.

Lyon, T. P., & Montgomery, A. W. (2015). The means and end of greenwashing. *Organization & Environment*, *28*(2), 223–249. https://doi.org/10.1177/1086026615575332

Mahajan, Y., Bindra, S., Mann, S., & Hiremath, R. (2024). A systematic review of green creativity to develop future research agenda: A bibliographic and TCCM analysis. *Global Knowledge, Memory and Communication*. https://doi.org/10.1108/GKMC-10-2023-0373

Marquis, C., & Toffel, M. W. (2012). *When do firms greenwash?: Corporate visibility, civil society scrutiny, and environmental disclosure* (pp. 11–115). Harvard Business School.

Melloni, G., Caglio, A., & Perego, P. (2017). Saying more with less? Disclosure conciseness, completeness and balance in integrated reports. *Journal of Accounting and Public Policy*, *36*(3), 220–238. https://doi.org/10.1016/j.jaccpubpol.2017.03.001

Mongeon, P., & Paul-Hus, A. (2016). The journal coverage of Web of science and Scopus: A comparative analysis. *Scientometrics*, *106*(1), 213–228. https://doi.org/10.1007/s11192-015-1765-5

Moodaley, W., & Telukdarie, A. (2023). Greenwashing, sustainability reporting, and artificial intelligence: A systematic literature review. *Sustainability*, *15*(2), 1481.

Moorthy, S., Balakrishanan, S., Nithish, K., & Rohith, C. M. R. (2022). Blockchain and artificial intelligence feasibility, implementation and sustainability in supply chain. In *2022 8th international conference on advanced computing and communication systems (ICACCS)* (Vol. 1, pp. 2112–2116). IEEE. https://doi.org/10.1109/ICACCS54159.2022.9785273

Navaratne, N. (2024). *The promise of blockchain as a driver for sustainability in value chains: A critical theory analysis.*

Nielsen. (2015). *The sustainability imperative: New insights on customer expectations.* Nielsen Global Corporate Sustainability Report. https://www.nielsen.com/

Nygaard, A., & Silkoset, R. (2023). Sustainable development and greenwashing: How blockchain technology information can empower green customers. *Business Strategy and the Environment*, *32*(6), 3801–3813.

Olaleye, S. A., Mogaji, E., Agbo, F. J., Ukpabi, D., & Gyamerah Adusei, A. (2023). The composition of data economy: A bibliometric approach and TCCM framework of conceptual, intellectual and social structure. *Information Discovery and Delivery*, *51*(2), 223–240. https://doi.org/10.1108/IDD-02-2022-0014

Peattie, K., & Crane, A. (2005). Green marketing: Legend, myth, farce or prophecy? *Qualitative Market Research: An International Journal*, *8*(4), 357–370.

Pimonenko, T., Bilan, Y., Horák, J., Starchenko, L., & Gajda, W. (2020). Green brand of companies and greenwashing under sustainable development goals. *Sustainability*, *12*(4), 1679.

Polonsky, M. J., Bailey, J., Baker, H., Basche, C., Jepson, C., & Neath, L. (1998). Communicating environmental information: Are marketing claims on packaging misleading? *Journal of Business Ethics*, *17*(3), 281–294.

Rane, J., Chaudhari, R. A., & Rane, N. L. (2025). Resilience and sustainability in supply chains through circular economy: Environmental impact, climate change mitigation, and waste management. In *Enhancing sustainable supply chain resilience through artificial intelligence and machine learning: Industry 4.0 and Industry 5.0 in Manufacturing* (p. 111). Deep Science Publishing. https://doi.org/10.70593/978-93-7185-621-8

Reber, B., Gold, A., & Gold, S. (2022). ESG disclosure and idiosyncratic risk in initial public offerings. *Journal of Business Ethics*, *179*(3), 867–886.

Rezaee, Z., & Tuo, L. (2017). Voluntary disclosure of non-financial information and its association with sustainability performance. *Advances in Accounting*, *39*, 47–59. https://doi.org/10.1016/j.adiac.2017.08.001

Saberi, S., Kouhizadeh, M., Sarkis, J., & Shen, L. (2019). Blockchain technology and its relationships to sustainable supply chain management. *International Journal of Production Research*, *57*(7), 2117–2135.

Samadhiya, A., Agrawal, R., Kumar, A., & Garza-Reyes, J. A. (2023). Blockchain technology and circular economy in the environment of total productive maintenance: A natural resource-based view perspective. *Journal of Manufacturing Technology Management*, *34*(2), 293–314.

Sharma, D., Taggar, R., Bindra, S., & Dhir, S. (2020). A systematic review of responsiveness to develop future research agenda: A TCCM and bibliometric analysis. *Benchmarking: An International Journal*, *27*(9), 2649–2677. https://doi.org/10.1108/BIJ-12-2019-0539

Spicer, A., & Hyatt, D. (2017). Walmart's emergent low-cost sustainable product strategy. *California Management Review*, *59*(2), 116–141.

Szabo, S., & Webster, J. (2021). Perceived greenwashing: The effects of green marketing on environmental and product perceptions. *Journal of Business Ethics*, *171*, 719–739.

Tapscott, D., & Tapscott, A. (2016). *Blockchain revolution: How the technology behind bitcoin and other cryptocurrencies is changing the world*. Penguin.

TerraChoice, E. (2009). *The seven sins of greenwashing*. https://www.scribd.com/document/14475597/The-Seven-Sins-of-Greenwashing

Tiwari, A., & Kendurkar, P. (2019). A synchronized implementation of green supply chain management (GSCM) & green innovation for long-term business sustainability. *Journal of Current Science*, *20*(06), 1–17.

Tiwari, A., Kumar, P., & Jasrai, L. (2024). ChatGPT in Marketing 5.0: Gold is real or just a gold plating. In *Market grooming: The dark side of AI marketing* (pp. 79–95). Emerald Publishing Limited. https://doi.org/10.1108/978-1-83549-001-320241004

Torchia, M., Calabrò, A., & Morner, M. (2015). Public–private partnerships in the health care sector: A systematic review of the literature. *Public Management Review*, *17*(2), 236–261. https://doi.org/10.1080/14719037.2013.792380

Trivedi, S., Negi, S., & Tiwari, S. (2024). Business sustainability in aviation industry in post-COVID era through information technology and triple bottom line perspective. *International Journal of Sustainable Aviation*, *10*(1), 43–59.

Vanleer, M., Jain, R., & Squires, A. F. (2016). A systems approach to creating a sustainability performance benchmarking and reporting framework. *International Journal of Process Management and Benchmarking*, *6*(2), 190–215.

Vieira, E. S., & Gomes, J. A. N. F. (2009). A comparison of Scopus and Web of Science for a typical university. *Scientometrics*, *81*(2), 587–600. https://doi.org/10.1007/s11192-009-2178-0

Wade, M., & Hulland, J. (2004). The resource-based view and information systems research: Review, extension, and suggestions for future research. *MIS Quarterly*, 107–142.

Wang, S., Wang, H., Wang, J., & Yang, F. (2020). Does environmental information disclosure contribute to improve firm financial performance? An examination of the underlying mechanism. *Science of the Total Environment*, *714*, 136855. https://doi.org/10.1016/j.scitotenv.2020.136855

Yang, Z., Nguyen, T. T. H., Nguyen, H. N., Nguyen, T. T. N., & Cao, T. T. (2020). Greenwashing behaviours: Causes, taxonomy and consequences based on a systematic literature review. *Journal of Business Economics and Management*, *21*(5), 1486–1507.

Zhang, D. (2022). Environmental regulation and firm product quality improvement: How does the greenwashing response? *International Review of Financial Analysis*, *80*, 102058.

Zhao, H., Zhou, Y., & Zhou, J. (2021). Blockchain and AI in business: A survey of applications and research challenges. *Journal of Business Research*, *131*, 1–13. https://doi.org/10.1016/j.jbusres.2020.11.056

Chapter 3

Leveraging Artificial Intelligence to Detect Greenwashing in Shared Economy Business Models

Suma N. Reddy[a] *and Pooja Khanna*[b]

[a]St Ann's College for Women, India
[b]Lovely Professional University, India

Abstract

The rise of the shared economy has transformed traditional business models by promoting sustainability through resource optimization. However, the prevalence of greenwashing—misleading environmental claims aimed at enhancing brand image without substantial ecological benefits—has raised concerns about the credibility of sustainability efforts. This study explores how artificial intelligence (AI) can be leveraged to detect greenwashing within shared economy business models. By focusing on key factors such as AI-driven detection accuracy (ADA), transparency in sustainability reporting (TSR), and environmental, social, and governance (ESG) compliance levels (ECL), the study assesses their impact on consumer trust (CT). A regression analysis based on data from 253 respondents in Hyderabad reveals that ADA and TSR significantly enhance CT, while ECL shows a positive but weaker effect. According to the research, AI can help reduce greenwashing by enhancing the veracity and accuracy of sustainability claims, which in turn boosts CT. The study lays the groundwork for further research in this field by shedding light on how AI may promote ethical business practices and improve accountability in the shared economy sector.

Keywords: Greenwashing; artificial intelligence; consumer trust; shared economy; sustainability

Eco Illusions, 45–65

doi:10.1108/978-1-83662-782-120261003

Introduction

The global surge in shared economy business models, which emphasize collaborative consumption and resource sharing, has catalyzed new conversations around sustainability and corporate responsibility. These models, encompassing sectors such as ride-sharing, home-sharing, and peer-to-peer services, are often marketed as inherently green and socially beneficial. However, an increasing body of research highlights the potential for greenwashing—where businesses exaggerate or fabricate their environmental and social contributions to gain a competitive advantage or public favor. In this context, artificial intelligence (AI) presents a promising avenue for detecting and mitigating such deceptive practices.

Greenwashing undermines genuine sustainability efforts, erodes public trust, and distorts market dynamics. Leveraging AI technologies to detect greenwashing can provide more objective, data-driven evaluations of corporate claims. Recent studies emphasize AI's transformative role in enhancing accountability and transparency within corporate frameworks, including environmental, social, and governance (ESG) reporting. For instance, Chen and Zhang (2024) examine how AI applications can enhance ESG performance, suggesting that the digital transformation of enterprises plays a pivotal role in promoting sustainable development. Similarly, de Villiers et al. (2024) highlight AI's potential in revolutionizing sustainability reporting through automated text generation and analysis, offering a conceptual framework for future research in this area.

Despite the widespread adoption of ESG frameworks, their effectiveness remains inconsistent across industries and regions. Agnese et al. (2024) reassess the impact of ESG practices on firm profitability, revealing a complex relationship that often depends on contextual factors such as industry dynamics and regulatory environments. Banerjee and David (2024) further explore the significance of ESG in investment decision-making within the Indian context, noting a growing investor preference for sustainability-aligned firms. However, they caution against overreliance on ESG scores, which can be manipulated through selective disclosure or superficial initiatives.

AI's ability to process vast amounts of data in real time provides unique opportunities for monitoring shared economy business models. This capability is particularly relevant in sectors prone to greenwashing due to their fragmented and decentralized nature. Luan et al. (2024) demonstrate how industrial robots and other AI technologies contribute to corporate environmental governance, providing empirical evidence from Chinese firms. Their findings underscore the potential of AI to enhance operational efficiency and environmental stewardship simultaneously.

AI applications extend beyond operational efficiencies to strategic decision-making. Khan and Gupta (2024) discuss how AI can boost the efficacy of green accounting, emphasizing its role in improving firm performance through enhanced accounting quality. Their study suggests that AI not only streamlines sustainability reporting but also strengthens internal controls, thereby reducing the risk of greenwashing.

Traditional corporate processes are being reshaped by digital transformation, which is providing new tools and approaches to improve accountability and transparency. The effects of digital knowledge integration on sustainable accounting, reporting, and assurance are examined by de Silva et al. (2024). Their study emphasizes how crucial digital integration and literacy are to producing solid and trustworthy sustainability reporting. Similar to this, Abu Afifa et al. (2024) use Vietnam as a case study to investigate how AI might digitize accounting procedures. Their results show notable gains in financial reporting efficiency and accuracy, which can be helpful in spotting irregularities or anomalies that point to greenwashing.

While the adoption of AI in combating greenwashing offers numerous benefits, it also raises ethical and regulatory concerns. The use of AI in sensitive areas such as ESG reporting and sustainability assessment necessitates careful consideration of data privacy, algorithmic bias, and regulatory compliance. Capaldi (2023) critiques the Corporate Social Responsibility (CSR) movement for its inherent flaws, emphasizing the need for a more principled approach to CSR and ESG practices. His work underscores the importance of aligning AI-driven initiatives with broader ethical and regulatory frameworks to ensure their legitimacy and effectiveness.

The integration of AI into shared economy business models has profound implications for both research and practice. As highlighted by Ferreira and Murphy (2023), the rapid advancements in AI, blockchain, and other digital technologies are redefining the boundaries of entrepreneurship and innovation. This evolving landscape presents new challenges and opportunities for researchers, policymakers, and practitioners alike. The need for interdisciplinary research is particularly evident in the context of greenwashing detection. Carter (2024) advocates for a holistic approach to sustainability, emphasizing the importance of transformative policies and mindsets. His work aligns with the broader call for systemic change in how businesses approach sustainability, moving beyond rhetoric to actionable and measurable outcomes.

Baker et al. (2024) explore the implications of fintech innovations for sustainability, offering insights into how financial technologies can support green initiatives. Their research highlights the potential for AI-driven tools to enhance financial stability and resilience, particularly in sectors such as banking and finance.

The rapid growth of shared economy models has sparked widespread interest in how businesses can harness collaborative consumption and resource sharing for greater sustainability. These business models, which include services like ride-sharing, home-sharing, and peer-to-peer platforms, are often framed as inherently eco-friendly and socially responsible alternatives to traditional consumption patterns. However, the increasing prominence of such models has also given rise to concerns about the authenticity of sustainability claims, with greenwashing becoming a significant issue. Greenwashing occurs when businesses exaggerate or fabricate their environmental or social contributions to attract customers or investors, without implementing substantial changes in their operations. This misrepresentation not only misleads consumers but also undermines genuine efforts to address sustainability challenges.

One promising solution to combat greenwashing is the use of AI, which has the ability to scrutinize corporate claims with unprecedented speed and accuracy. AI technologies, particularly those designed for natural language processing and data analytics, can sift through vast amounts of unstructured data to detect inconsistencies in sustainability reporting. This ability to cross-reference and validate information in real time makes AI an essential tool for ensuring transparency in CSR and ESG reporting. AI-driven systems can identify patterns of deception, enabling consumers and stakeholders to make more informed decisions about the companies they engage with. The potential for AI to enhance accountability in corporate practices is further explored in recent studies, which suggest that AI can act as a watchdog, minimizing the opportunity for businesses to manipulate ESG metrics or make false claims about their environmental impact.

The growing adoption of AI in ESG reporting is transforming how companies approach sustainability. For example, AI can automate the analysis of corporate reports, detecting discrepancies or areas where companies may be overstating their environmental or social contributions. This type of automated evaluation allows for more objective assessments of a company's sustainability efforts. Researchers have shown that AI can also contribute to the digital transformation of firms, improving their sustainability performance by optimizing operations and providing more reliable data for decision-making. Through the integration of AI technologies, companies can not only streamline their reporting processes but also gain deeper insights into their environmental footprint and social impact, enabling them to take more informed and effective actions toward sustainability.

The relationship between ESG practices and firm profitability remains complex and variable, with multiple studies illustrating that ESG performance does not always correlate with financial success. Factors such as the industry in question, market dynamics, and the regulatory environment can all influence how effectively ESG initiatives are implemented and whether they result in tangible business outcomes. In emerging markets like India, where sustainability and ESG frameworks are still developing, there is a growing interest in how AI can support ESG integration and improve corporate governance. AI can help streamline decision-making processes related to ESG investments, providing tools that allow investors to better assess the sustainability of companies and predict future performance based on their environmental and social practices.

While AI can significantly enhance the effectiveness of sustainability initiatives, it should not be viewed as a panacea. It is essential that AI-driven solutions be implemented alongside broader efforts to promote systemic change in corporate behavior. Scholars like Carter (2024) have emphasized the need for a holistic approach to sustainability, which involves transformative policies that encourage businesses to move beyond superficial greenwashing tactics and toward more meaningful, measurable outcomes. AI can support these efforts, but it must be part of a larger framework that encourages long-term, sustainable practices across industries.

The integration of AI into shared economy models presents both opportunities and challenges for businesses and policymakers. As the technology continues to evolve, AI's role in enhancing corporate transparency and accountability will become increasingly important. At the same time, businesses must be vigilant in ensuring that their sustainability claims are genuinely reflective of their actions and not simply a marketing tool designed to appeal to eco-conscious consumers. In this rapidly changing landscape, interdisciplinary research will play a critical role in shaping the future of AI, sustainability, and corporate responsibility, ensuring that these technologies are leveraged in ways that promote genuine progress toward a more sustainable future.

Literature Review

The shared economy, characterized by peer-to-peer resource sharing, has emerged as a transformative business model, promoting sustainability by maximizing resource utilization. However, its sustainability claims are increasingly scrutinized due to the prevalence of greenwashing—misleading environmental claims aimed at enhancing brand image without substantial ecological benefits. This literature review explores how AI can be leveraged to detect greenwashing within shared economy models, drawing insights from recent research on sustainability, CSR, ESG practices, and AI applications.

Greenwashing undermines the credibility of sustainability initiatives, leading to consumer skepticism and reduced trust. Qayyum et al. (2023) highlight the adverse impact of greenwashing on green brand equity, emphasizing that consumers often struggle to distinguish between genuine and misleading sustainability claims. Silva et al. (2020) explore nuances of green skepticism across different economies, illustrating how varying levels of consumer awareness and regulatory oversight influence perceptions of corporate sustainability.

Panigyraki and Polyportis (2024) delve into the psychological effects of consumer suspicion, noting that skepticism toward corporate green claims can erode brand loyalty and increase scrutiny of corporate practices. Their findings underscore the importance of transparent and verifiable sustainability communications to mitigate the negative effects of greenwashing.

ESG frameworks have become a cornerstone for assessing corporate sustainability performance. Agnese et al. (2024) analyze the impact of ESG practices on firm profitability, demonstrating that effective ESG integration can enhance financial performance and stakeholder trust. However, Sætra (2024) critiques the politicization of ESG practices, warning that superficial compliance with ESG metrics may mask underlying sustainability challenges, contributing to greenwashing.

Greenwashing poses a significant threat to the credibility of corporate sustainability efforts, leading to consumer skepticism and potentially reducing the effectiveness of sustainability campaigns. As Qayyum et al. (2023) highlight, greenwashing can diminish green brand equity by creating confusion among consumers, making it difficult for them to discern between legitimate and deceptive environmental claims. Consumers, now more than ever, are becoming increasingly aware of greenwashing, with many questioning the sincerity of corporate sustainability initiatives. This growing awareness has sparked a wave of skepticism toward companies that engage in superficial or exaggerated claims, ultimately eroding brand loyalty. Silva et al. (2020) note that this skepticism varies across different economies, shaped by factors such as consumer education, regulatory frameworks, and cultural context. In regions where regulatory oversight is stronger, consumers are more likely to demand verifiable proof of sustainability claims, which in turn pressures firms to adopt more transparent practices.

The psychological effects of greenwashing, as discussed by Panigyraki and Polyportis (2024), reveal that skepticism can have lasting impacts on consumer behavior. The erosion of trust can lead to increased scrutiny of corporate practices, making it harder for companies to maintain a positive image. Transparent and verifiable communication regarding sustainability is essential to counteract this skepticism and foster consumer confidence. Brands that fail to provide clear, substantiated evidence of their environmental and social commitments risk losing their customer base and damaging their long-term reputation.

The implementation of ESG frameworks has become a central aspect of corporate sustainability assessments. Agnese et al. (2024) demonstrate that when firms effectively integrate ESG practices, it can lead to better financial performance and increased trust among stakeholders. However, Sætra (2024) offers a cautionary perspective, critiquing the politicization of ESG metrics and the potential for their superficial application. Superficial adherence to ESG standards can create the illusion of sustainability while allowing companies to continue harmful practices behind the scenes, contributing to the problem of greenwashing.

The reliability of ESG metrics, especially in emerging markets, remains a concern. Banerjee and David (2024) argue that although ESG scores are increasingly incorporated into investment strategies, their validity hinges on robust reporting and verification mechanisms. The manipulation of ESG scores through selective disclosure or selective reporting of positive outcomes can mislead investors and distort market dynamics. This is where AI technologies can play a pivotal role in enhancing the transparency of ESG data. Rehman and Umar (2024) stress that Industry 5.0 technologies, including AI, offer significant potential for improving the accuracy and consistency of ESG reporting, ensuring that claims are substantiated by reliable data.

In this context, AI can also enhance green accounting practices, helping firms to better align their financial performance with sustainability goals. Khan and Gupta (2024) illustrate how AI can boost the efficacy of green accounting by moderating the relationship between sustainability initiatives and firm performance. AI technologies can automate sustainability reporting processes, reduce human error, and provide real-time data analytics, which helps organizations maintain higher accounting quality. This reduces the risk of greenwashing by ensuring that sustainability efforts are monitored, validated, and reported in a more standardized and verifiable manner.

Disruptive technologies, such as AI and industrial robots, are also shaping how companies manage their environmental responsibilities. Luan et al. (2024) demonstrate how industrial robots, particularly in the Chinese manufacturing sector, contribute to corporate environmental governance by enhancing operational efficiency and reducing environmental impact. These technologies not only improve productivity but also facilitate greater adherence to environmental standards, making it easier for companies to substantiate their sustainability claims. Such advances in corporate governance and environmental stewardship can deter greenwashing by fostering a more rigorous approach to sustainability.

While AI offers promising solutions for improving the accuracy and transparency of sustainability practices, its adoption in ESG reporting raises ethical concerns, particularly in terms of data privacy and algorithmic bias. As noted by Capaldi (2023), there is a need for a principled approach to CSR and ESG practices. Ensuring that AI applications are aligned with ethical standards and regulatory frameworks is essential to mitigate the risks associated with the misuse of data and algorithmic decision-making. The use of AI in ESG reporting must be carefully regulated to maintain its legitimacy and effectiveness.

Overall, the integration of AI into shared economy business models and ESG frameworks holds the potential to revolutionize how companies report and manage their sustainability efforts. By providing real-time data analysis, enhancing transparency, and reducing the opportunities for greenwashing, AI technologies can play a critical role in promoting genuine corporate sustainability. However, to fully realize this potential, businesses must invest in robust AI systems that align with ethical principles, ensuring that the data generated is not only accurate but also used responsibly. As noted by Haski-Leventhal (2020), the future of higher education and corporate sustainability will depend on the effective integration of these technologies, fostering a more sustainable and ethically grounded business environment.

The combination of AI, green accounting, and ESG frameworks provides a powerful toolkit for enhancing corporate sustainability practices, but its effectiveness will depend on the careful alignment of technological innovations with ethical, regulatory, and transparency standards. As companies continue to adopt these technologies, it is essential that they remain committed to fostering genuine sustainability rather than engaging in greenwashing practices that ultimately undermine their credibility and long-term success.

Banerjee and David (2024) provide insights into the relevance of ESG metrics in investment decision-making, particularly in emerging markets like India. They argue that while ESG scores are increasingly factored into investment strategies, their reliability depends on robust reporting and verification mechanisms. Rehman and Umar (2024) emphasize the role of Industry 5.0 technologies in advancing ESG practices, advocating for the use of AI and other digital tools to enhance data accuracy and transparency.

AI offers significant potential in detecting greenwashing by analyzing large datasets to identify discrepancies between corporate claims and actual performance. de Villiers et al. (2024) propose a conceptual framework for AI-driven sustainability reporting, highlighting its ability to streamline data processing and uncover inconsistencies in ESG disclosures. Their work aligns with McBride et al. (2022), who examine AI's impact on corporate governance and financial markets, emphasizing its role in promoting accountability and reducing information asymmetry.

Chen and Zhang (2024) explore the implications of AI applications for ESG performance, demonstrating that AI-driven digital transformation can enhance corporate sustainability by improving operational efficiency and reducing environmental impact. Similarly, Khan and Gupta (2024) discuss the moderating effects of AI and accounting quality on green accounting, arguing that AI can strengthen internal controls and ensure the accuracy of sustainability reports.

Digital transformation and the move toward a circular economy, which prioritizes waste reduction and resource efficiency, are closely related. A thorough analysis of circular economy techniques is given by Maguire and Robson (2023a), who also emphasize how digital technology supports sustainable company models. Their work emphasizes how crucial it is to incorporate AI and other digital tools to improve sustainability reporting and resource management.

de Silva et al. (2024) explore the impact of digital knowledge integration on sustainable accounting and reporting, emphasizing the need for advanced digital skills to leverage AI effectively. Their findings suggest that digital transformation can enhance the reliability of sustainability data, reducing the risk of greenwashing.

The deployment of AI in greenwashing detection raises important regulatory and ethical considerations. Pagallo et al. (2022) examine the environmental challenges of AI within the European Union's regulatory framework, highlighting the need for policies that balance innovation with environmental protection. Their analysis of the Artificial Intelligence Act (AIA) illustrates the complexities of regulating AI to ensure it supports sustainable development goals (SDGs) without exacerbating environmental harm. Ure (2024) discusses the role of civil society in achieving the SDGs, advocating for stronger regulatory frameworks and stakeholder collaboration to enhance corporate accountability. Their work complements the findings of Sharma et al. (2024), who emphasize the need for integrated sustainability measures to promote well-being and social equity.

Understanding consumer behavior is crucial for addressing greenwashing in shared economy models. Mahama Braimah et al. (2023) examine the relationship between green perceived value and consumer attitudes, revealing that consumers in developing economies are increasingly valuing sustainability in their purchasing decisions. Their study highlights the potential for shared economy platforms to capitalize on this trend by adopting genuine sustainability practices.

The transition toward a circular economy, characterized by resource efficiency, waste reduction, and sustainability, is intricately connected to the ongoing digital transformation in various industries. Maguire and Robson

(2023a) present a detailed overview of circular economy practices, emphasizing the transformative role of digital technologies in facilitating sustainable business models. They argue that the integration of digital tools, particularly AI, plays a pivotal role in advancing resource management and enhancing sustainability reporting. The adoption of AI-driven solutions allows businesses to optimize resource usage, reduce waste, and improve operational efficiency—core principles of the circular economy. As a result, businesses can track and measure their sustainability efforts more effectively, ensuring greater transparency and reducing the risk of deceptive practices such as greenwashing.

In the context of sustainability reporting, the integration of AI with digital knowledge management is critical. de Silva et al. (2024) discuss the profound impact that digital knowledge integration has on sustainable accounting and reporting practices. They argue that the incorporation of advanced digital skills—especially in AI and data analytics—can significantly enhance the reliability and accuracy of sustainability data. This technological advancement allows for more robust tracking of environmental impacts and the generation of verifiable, real-time reports that can be used by stakeholders to assess a company's sustainability performance. By leveraging AI, organizations can ensure that their sustainability data is both transparent and trustworthy, mitigating the chances of greenwashing—where companies make misleading claims about their environmental practices. As consumers and investors increasingly demand transparency, AI can play a critical role in reducing misinformation and fostering genuine corporate responsibility.

The application of AI in detecting greenwashing, however, raises significant regulatory and ethical challenges. Pagallo et al. (2022) provide an in-depth analysis of the environmental and regulatory challenges surrounding AI, particularly within the European Union's regulatory framework. Their research highlights the necessity of crafting policies that strike a balance between promoting technological innovation and protecting the environment. The implementation of AI should be guided by frameworks such as the AIA, which aims to regulate AI technologies to ensure they support SDGs without causing unintended environmental harm. This regulatory approach is crucial, as AI, while offering immense potential for improving sustainability practices, could also contribute to unsustainable outcomes if not carefully regulated. Ensuring that AI is deployed in ways that align with the SDGs will require continuous oversight and cooperation among governments, businesses, and stakeholders.

Ure (2024) expands on the importance of civil society's role in achieving SDGs, advocating for stronger regulatory frameworks and collaboration between stakeholders to enhance corporate accountability. Ure argues that achieving sustainability requires not only top-down regulatory measures but also grassroots participation and public oversight. This collaborative approach can foster greater transparency and accountability in corporate practices, ensuring that AI and digital tools are used in ways that genuinely contribute to sustainability. Such frameworks should ensure that AI solutions deployed by companies are thoroughly audited, ethically sound, and aligned with broader societal goals of equity, environmental stewardship, and social well-being.

Mahama Braimah et al. (2023) explore the relationship between green perceived value and consumer attitudes, focusing on developing economies. Their study reveals that consumers in these regions are increasingly prioritizing sustainability in their purchasing decisions, especially when they perceive genuine efforts from companies. Shared economy platforms, which are inherently focused on collaborative consumption and resource sharing, have the potential to capitalize on this growing consumer demand for sustainability. By adopting genuine sustainability practices and incorporating transparent sustainability reporting, these platforms can build trust with consumers and differentiate themselves from companies engaging in greenwashing. This trend is particularly significant in the shared economy model, where trust and transparency are fundamental to consumer decision-making. Mahama Braimah et al.'s findings underscore the importance of aligning business practices with consumer values in order to foster long-term brand loyalty and support for sustainability initiatives.

The convergence of digital transformation, AI integration, and sustainability reporting presents a unique opportunity to address the challenges of greenwashing while advancing circular economy principles. By enhancing the accuracy, transparency, and reliability of sustainability data, AI can help companies maintain consumer trust (CT) and meet regulatory requirements. However, as Pagallo et al. (2022) and Ure (2024) emphasize, this technological potential must be balanced with strong regulatory frameworks to prevent exploitation and ensure that AI is used ethically to further the SDGs. Companies that embrace this balance—leveraging AI for genuine sustainability while adhering to robust regulatory standards—will likely emerge as leaders in the transition to a sustainable, circular economy.

Seyfi et al. (2024) reflect on evolving consumer expectations in the age of Gen Z, noting that younger consumers are more likely to demand transparency and accountability from businesses. Their findings suggest that shared economy platforms must prioritize authenticity in their sustainability efforts to maintain a competitive advantage. The integration of fintech innovations with sustainability initiatives presents new opportunities for enhancing transparency and reducing greenwashing. Baker et al. (2024) explore the implications of fintech for sustainability, highlighting the role of blockchain and AI in improving data integrity and traceability. Trinh et al. (2024) further investigate the intersection of fintech and green finance, demonstrating how digital technologies can support climate risk management and sustainable investment strategies.

Puaschunder (2023b) discusses responsible investment practices in the context of the Great Reset, emphasizing the need for financial markets to align with sustainability objectives. Their analysis underscores the importance of leveraging AI and fintech to promote responsible investment and reduce the prevalence of greenwashing. Despite significant advancements, several research gaps remain in the field of AI-driven greenwashing detection. Samkin et al. (2024) call for the development of a conceptual framework to address the unique challenges of sustainability reporting in the extractive industries. Their work highlights the need for industry-specific approaches to greenwashing detection, considering the diverse environmental and social impacts of different sectors.

Maione (2024) identifies emerging technologies as a key area for future research, advocating for the exploration of AI-driven innovations in sustainability reporting and assurance. Similarly, Sharma, Shishodia, and Gupta (2023) highlight the potential for digital technologies to foster sustainable development, emphasizing the need for interdisciplinary research to address complex sustainability challenges.

RQ1. In what ways can AI-driven tools improve the detection of greenwashing practices in shared economy business models?
RQ2. How does AI-driven transparency in sustainability reporting influence consumer trust and perception of shared economy platforms?

Research Methodology

This study adopts a quantitative research methodology to examine the specified research objectives. A structured survey was conducted, collecting data from 253 respondents in Hyderabad, ensuring diverse demographic representation. The sampling approach was purposive to target individuals familiar with the research context. Data was collected using a well-validated questionnaire structured on a 5-point Likert scale, where responses ranged from "Strongly Disagree" (1) to "Strongly Agree" (5), facilitating precise measurement of variables.

Objectives

- To evaluate the role of AI-driven tools in identifying greenwashing practices in shared economy business models.
- To analyze the effect of AI-driven transparency and ESG compliance on CT in shared economy platforms.

Hypotheses

H1. AI-driven tools enhance the effectiveness of detecting greenwashing practices in shared economy businesses.
H2. Enhanced transparency through AI-driven reporting significantly increases CT in shared economy platforms.

Regression Model

$$\begin{aligned}\text{Consumer Trust (CT)} = \beta 0 &+ \beta 1 \text{ AI-driven Detection Accuracy (ADA)} \\ &+ \beta 2 \text{ Transparency in Sustainability Reporting (TSR)} \\ &+ \beta 3 \text{ ESG Compliance Level (ECL)} + \epsilon\end{aligned}$$

R Studio, a flexible program for data analysis and visualization, was used to do a thorough statistical analysis on the gathered data. While inferential techniques were used to test hypotheses and find correlations between variables, descriptive statistics were used to characterize the demographic features of respondents. Pretesting and internal consistency checks were used in the study to guarantee the validity and reliability of the measuring scale.

Ethical considerations, including informed consent and confidentiality of responses, were strictly adhered to throughout the data collection process. The methodology was designed to capture accurate and comprehensive insights, enabling robust analysis and meaningful conclusions. The use of R Studio ensured efficient data processing, fostering transparency and reproducibility in the analysis. This methodological framework aligns with the research goals and supports the derivation of actionable insights.

Analysis

The demographic analysis of the 253 respondents from Hyderabad provides insights into their gender, age, education, occupation, and income distribution. The sample consisted of 55% males (139 respondents) and 45% females (114 respondents), reflecting a balanced gender representation. In terms of age, the majority of participants, 35% (89 respondents), were aged between 25 and 34 years, followed by 30% (76 respondents) in the 35–44 age group. Respondents aged 18–24 years accounted for 20% (51 respondents), while those above 45 years comprised 15% (37 respondents).

Regarding education, 40% (101 respondents) had a graduate degree, 30% (76 respondents) held a postgraduate qualification, and 20% (51 respondents) had completed higher secondary education. Only 10% (25 respondents) reported other educational qualifications. The occupation profile revealed that 35% (89 respondents) were salaried professionals, 30% (76 respondents) were self-employed, 25% (63 respondents) were students, and 10% (25 respondents) were homemakers.

In terms of income, 30% (76 respondents) earned below ₹50,000 per month, 40% (101 respondents) earned between ₹50,000 and ₹100,000, and 30% (76 respondents) earned above ₹100,000. This demographic distribution highlights a diverse representation across key socioeconomic categories.

With AI-driven Detection Accuracy (ADA), TSR, and ESG Compliance Level (ECL) as independent variables, the regression analysis for CT as the dependent variable offers important insights into the variables affecting CT in greenwashing detection (refer Table 3.1). With an adjusted R-squared of 0.5558, the model shows an excellent overall fit, indicating that the predictors in the model account for around 56% of the variation in customer trust. This implies that, in the framework of the shared economy, the factors chosen—ADA, TSR, and ECL—have a major impact on how consumers perceive sustainability promises. The model is statistically significant, indicating that at least one of the independent variables is a significant predictor of CT, as indicated by the *F*-statistic of 105.7 and a *p*-value less than 2.2e-16. This demonstrates how pertinent the variables in the model are.

Table 3.1. Regression Line for Consumer Trust

Call:

```
lm(formula = CT ~ ADA + TSR + ECL, data = Greenwashing)
```

Residuals:

Min	1Q	Median	3Q	Max
-2.13837	-0.30372	0.04223	0.28435	1.36426

Coefficients:

	Estimate	Std. Error	t value	Pr(>|t|)
(Intercept)	0.59043	0.13118	4.501	1.04e-05 ***
ADA	0.45576	0.05768	7.902	8.98e-14 ***
TSR	0.14232	0.06602	2.156	0.0321 *
ECL	0.11521	0.06078	1.895	0.0592 .

Signif. codes: 0 '***' 0.001 '**' 0.01 '*' 0.05 '.' 0.1 ' ' 1

Residual standard error: 0.5571 on 248 degrees of freedom
Multiple R-squared: 0.5611 **Adjusted R-squared:** 0.5558
F-statistic: 105.7 on 3 and 248 DF **p-value:** < 2.2e-16

Sources: R Studio analysis.

The impact of each independent variable on CT is displayed by the separate regression coefficients. When all predictors are zero, the baseline level of CT is represented by the intercept value of 0.59043. The coefficient for ADA is 0.45576, meaning that, when all other variables are held constant, customer trust tends to rise by 0.456 units as ADA rises. This indicates that one of the main factors influencing customer trust is ADA in identifying greenwashing. Similar to this, TSR has a positive coefficient of 0.14232, indicating that increased sustainability reporting transparency has a positive effect on CT, albeit at the 5% level of significance (p-value = 0.0321).

Conversely, ECL's coefficient of 0.11521 suggests that trust is positively impacted by ECL, but its p-value of 0.0592 is marginally significant, just beyond the 5% cutoff. The average difference between the actual and projected levels of CT is roughly 0.5571, according to the residual standard error of 0.5571. All things considered, the model sheds light on the variables affecting consumers' confidence in sustainability promises and emphasizes the significance of AI, openness, and ESG adherence in preventing greenwashing.

The scatter plot with the regression line in Fig. 3.1 provides a visual representation of the relationship between the dependent variable, CT, and the independent variables: ADA, TSR, and ECL. Each data point represents an individual observation from the dataset, with the regression line indicating the predicted trend. A positive slope in the regression line suggests that as ADA, TSR, and ECL increase, so does CT in detecting greenwashing. The scatter plot helps to visually assess the strength and direction of these relationships and can

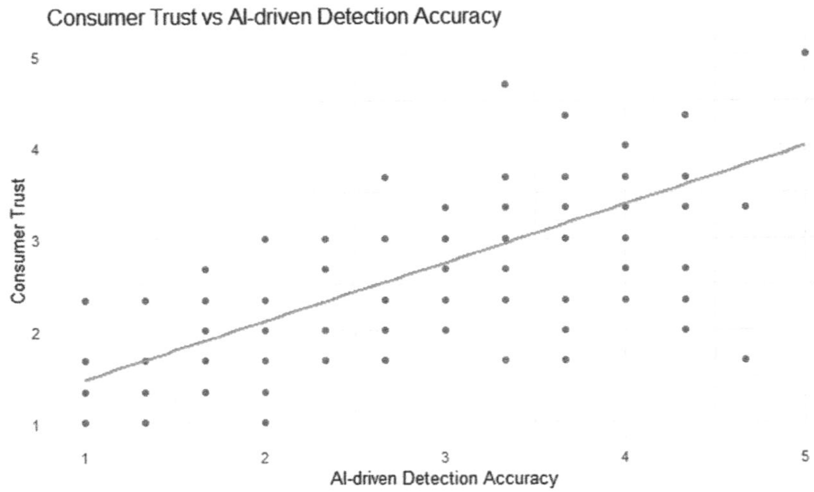

Fig. 3.1. Scatter Plot With Regression Line

also reveal potential outliers or nonlinear patterns that may not be captured by the regression model.

Fig. 3.2 presents the diagnostic plot for the regression model, which is used to assess the assumptions underlying the linear regression analysis. The plot includes key elements such as residuals versus fitted values, a normal Q-Q plot, scale-location, and residuals versus leverage. These plots help identify any potential issues like nonlinearity, heteroscedasticity, or influential outliers. In this analysis, a well-distributed residual plot would suggest that the linear regression

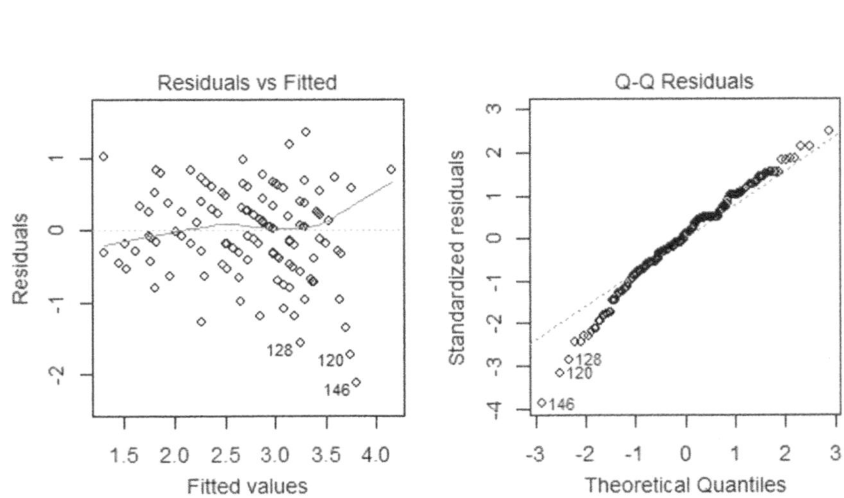

Fig. 3.2. Diagnostic Plot for Regression Model

assumptions hold, with residuals being randomly scattered around the horizontal line. The diagnostic plot provides a crucial check on the reliability and validity of the regression results and ensures that the conclusions drawn from the model are based on sound data assumptions.

Fig. 3.3 displays a correlation plot that illustrates the strength and direction of the relationships between the variables in the regression model. The plot uses color coding and numerical values to show the pairwise correlation coefficients between CT, ADA, TSR, and ECL. A positive correlation is indicated by values closer to +1, and a negative correlation by values closer to −1. This visualization helps in quickly identifying which variables are most strongly correlated with CT. It also provides insight into the interrelationships among the independent variables, which can help in understanding how they collectively contribute to predicting CT in detecting greenwashing.

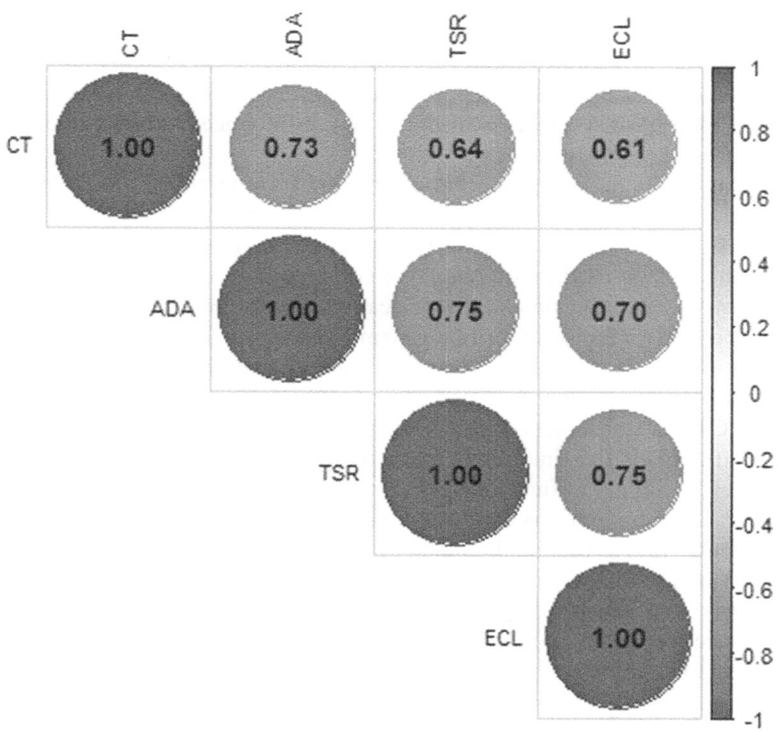

Fig. 3.3. Correlation Plot to Visualize the Relationships Between Variables

Conclusion

This study explores the critical role of AI in detecting greenwashing within shared economy business models, focusing on its potential to enhance CT by improving the accuracy and transparency of sustainability claims. Greenwashing, the practice of making misleading or exaggerated sustainability claims, is a significant challenge for businesses and consumers alike. As sustainability becomes a key criterion for consumer decision-making, ensuring the authenticity of corporate environmental claims has never been more important. AI-driven technologies offer a promising solution to combat greenwashing by enhancing the accuracy of sustainability reporting, improving transparency, and verifying ECLs.

The regression analysis in this study reveals that three key factors—ADA, TSR, and ECL—have a significant positive impact on CT in shared economy business models. Specifically, the study finds that ADA and TSR are the most influential variables in building CT, while ECL, although positively correlated, shows a weaker effect. This suggests that while ESG compliance plays an important role in demonstrating corporate commitment to sustainability, it is the transparency of sustainability reporting and the accuracy of AI-driven detection systems that have a more immediate and pronounced effect on consumer confidence.

The model underscores the importance of transparent sustainability communications and the role of AI in making these communications more accurate and verifiable. AI technologies, such as machine learning and natural language processing, can be used to analyze large volumes of sustainability data, identify discrepancies, and flag potentially misleading claims. By integrating AI-driven tools into sustainability reporting systems, businesses can provide consumers with more reliable, real-time information about their environmental performance. This transparency reduces the opportunity for greenwashing and promotes greater CT, as consumers are increasingly wary of companies that may be exaggerating their sustainability efforts for competitive advantage.

However, while the study's findings are promising, several limitations should be noted. The research was conducted with a relatively small sample size of 253 respondents from Hyderabad, India, which may not fully represent the global diversity of consumer perceptions regarding greenwashing. The focus of the study was also on shared economy platforms, which, although growing in importance, represent only a specific sector of the economy. Future research could expand the sample size to include respondents from diverse geographic locations, sectors, and industries, providing a more comprehensive understanding of global dynamics surrounding greenwashing and CT.

In addition, the study focused primarily on AI as a tool for detecting greenwashing, but other emerging technologies, such as blockchain, could also play a significant role in enhancing sustainability reporting. Blockchain, known for its ability to create secure and immutable records, could be used to track and verify sustainability data, providing an additional layer of transparency. Future studies could explore the intersection of AI and blockchain in sustainability reporting, assessing their combined potential to reduce greenwashing and improve the overall integrity of corporate sustainability claims.

The global implications of this research are far-reaching, as businesses across industries and regions are increasingly under pressure to adopt sustainable practices and provide credible, verifiable evidence of their environmental impact. Consumers, investors, and regulators are demanding higher levels of accountability, and businesses that fail to meet these expectations risk losing CT and market competitiveness. As the study suggests, the integration of AI-driven greenwashing detection systems can be a powerful tool for businesses aiming to maintain transparency and trust. However, it also highlights the need for robust regulatory frameworks to support the widespread adoption of such technologies and ensure that they are used effectively to combat greenwashing.

The scalability of AI-driven detection systems in different regulatory environments and industries is an important area for future research. Regulatory landscapes vary significantly across regions, with some countries having more stringent sustainability reporting requirements than others. Understanding how AI can be adapted to different regulatory environments will be crucial for businesses operating in multiple jurisdictions. This research could explore how AI can be deployed in regions with varying levels of regulatory oversight, examining the challenges and opportunities for harmonizing global standards in sustainability reporting.

Furthermore, future studies could focus on the effectiveness of AI in detecting greenwashing across different industries. While this study focused on shared economy platforms, other sectors, such as manufacturing, retail, and energy, present unique challenges and opportunities for using AI to enhance sustainability reporting. By extending the research to these industries, future studies could provide deeper insights into the sector-specific applications of AI in detecting greenwashing and improving sustainability practices.

As businesses continue to embrace AI and other digital technologies, the global impact of these innovations will be profound. By improving the accuracy and transparency of sustainability claims, AI can help create a more trustworthy, sustainable, and accountable business ecosystem worldwide. The adoption of AI-driven greenwashing detection systems has the potential to revolutionize the way businesses report on sustainability, making it more reliable, accessible, and credible. This, in turn, can lead to greater CT, enhanced corporate reputation, and more sustainable business practices globally

In conclusion, the study provides valuable insights into the role of AI in combating greenwashing within shared economy business models and highlights its potential to enhance CT through improved transparency and accuracy in sustainability reporting. While the research has limitations, the findings have important global implications, suggesting that AI can be a crucial tool for businesses striving to maintain credibility in an increasingly sustainability-conscious market. Future research, focusing on larger, more diverse samples, the integration of AI with blockchain, and the scalability of greenwashing detection systems across industries and regulatory environments, will be essential in shaping the future of corporate sustainability and transparency.

References

Abu Afifa, M. M., Nguyen, T. H., Le, M. T. T., Nguyen, L., & Tran, T. T. H. (2024). Accounting going digital: A Vietnamese experimental study on artificial intelligence in accounting. *VINE Journal of Information and Knowledge Management Systems*. https://doi.org/10.1108/VJIKMS-10-2023-0266

Agnese, P., Carè, R., Cerciello, M., & Taddeo, S. (2024). Reconsidering the impact of environmental, social and governance practices on firm profitability. *Management Decision*. https://doi.org/10.1108/MD-10-2023-1943

Alnoor, A., Bayram, G. E., XinYing, C., & Shah, S. H. A. (Eds.) (2024). Index. In *The role of artificial intelligence in regenerative tourism and green destinations* (pp. 397–406). Emerald Publishing Limited. https://doi.org/10.1108/978-1-83753-746-420241027

Baker, H. K., Filbeck, G., & Black, K. (Eds.). (2024). Index. In *The Emerald handbook of Fintech* (pp. 473–494). Emerald Publishing Limited. https://doi.org/10.1108/978-1-83753-608-520241049

Bandoophanit, T. (2024). Green supply chain management in Thai service organizations. *European Business Review*. https://doi.org/10.1108/EBR-03-2024-0110

Banerjee, S., & David, R. (2024). Does ESG really matter? Accessing the relevance of EsSG in Indian investors' decision-making dynamics. *Qualitative Research in Financial Markets*. https://doi.org/10.1108/QRFM-10-2023-0241

Baycur, G., Delen, E., & Kayişkan, D. (2022). Digital conflicts in marketing and sales. In F. Özsungur (Ed.), *Conflict management in digital business* (pp. 43–61). Emerald Publishing Limited. https://doi.org/10.1108/978-1-80262-773-220221004

Capaldi, N. (2023). The sins of the CSR movement: Errors in CSR. In A. das Gupta (Ed.), *Strategic corporate responsibility and green management* (Vol. 16, pp. 59–68). Emerald Publishing Limited. https://doi.org/10.1108/S2043-905920230000016004

Carter, C. E. (2024). Placemaking and sustainability: Moving from rhetoric to transformative sustainability policies, mindsets, and actions. In D. Higgins & P. J. Larkham (Eds.), *Placemaking* (pp. 91–123). Emerald Publishing Limited. https://doi.org/10.1108/978-1-83753-130-120241011

Chen, R., & Zhang, T. (2024). Artificial intelligence applications implication for ESG performance: Can digital transformation of enterprises promote sustainable development? *Chinese Management Studies*. https://doi.org/10.1108/CMS-11-2023-0653

Choi, J. J., & Kim, J. (Eds.). (2024). Index. In *Responsible firms: CSR, ESG, and global sustainability* (Vol. 23, pp. 245–252). Emerald Publishing Limited. https://doi.org/10.1108/S1569-376720240000023019

Choudhry, M. (Ed.). (2024). Index. In *Professional perspectives on banking and finance* (Vol. 1, pp. 215–225). Emerald Publishing Limited. https://doi.org/10.1108/978-1-83549-334-220241020

Cooper, E., Henderson, C., & Kish, A. (2019). Corporate social responsibility and financial stability: Evidence from the troubled asset relief program. *Managerial Finance*, *45*(8), 1111–1128. https://doi.org/10.1108/MF-09-2018-0458

de Silva, P., Gunarathne, N., & Kumar, S. (2024). Exploring the impact of digital knowledge, integration and performance on sustainable accounting, reporting and assurance. *Meditari Accountancy Research*. https://doi.org/10.1108/MEDAR-02-2024-2383

de Villiers, C., Dimes, R., & Molinari, M. (2024). How will AI text generation and processing impact sustainability reporting? Critical analysis, a conceptual framework and avenues for future research. *Sustainability Accounting, Management and Policy Journal, 15*(1), 96–118. https://doi.org/10.1108/SAMPJ-02-2023-0097

Ferreira, J. J., & Murphy, P. J. (Eds.). (2023). Index. In *Bleeding-edge entrepreneurship: Digitalization, blockchains, space, the ocean, and artificial intelligence* (Vol. 16, pp. 195–201). Emerald Publishing Limited. https://doi.org/10.1108/S2040-724620230000016011

Haski-Leventhal, D. (2020). The way forward in higher education. In *The purpose-driven university* (pp. 133–145). Emerald Publishing Limited. https://doi.org/10.1108/978-1-83867-283-620201011

Khan, S., & Gupta, S. (2024). Boosting the efficacy of green accounting for better firm performance: Artificial intelligence and accounting quality as moderators. *Meditari Accountancy Research.* https://doi.org/10.1108/MEDAR-02-2024-2379

Kumar, S., & Barua, M. K. (2022). Sustainability of operations through disruptive technologies in the petroleum supply chain. *Benchmarking: An International Journal, 29*(5), 1640–1676. https://doi.org/10.1108/BIJ-02-2021-0086

Li, X., & Zhang, Z. (2024). The effects of corporate social responsibility on innovation and performance of firms in China: A structural equation model analysis. *Nankai Business Review International, 15*(4), 660–683. https://doi.org/10.1108/NBRI-04-2023-0038

Luan, F., Qi, W., Zhang, W., & Chang, V. (2024). Do industrial robots matter for corporate environmental governance? Evidence from Chinese firms. *Information Technology & People.* https://doi.org/10.1108/ITP-12-2022-0963

Maguire, S., & Robson, I. (2023a). A review and research agenda for the circular economy. In *Sustainable development through global circular economy practices* (pp. 133–156). Emerald Publishing Limited. https://doi.org/10.1108/978-1-83753-590-320231006

Maguire, S., & Robson, I. (2023b). Index. In *Sustainable development through global circular economy practices* (pp. 157–163). Emerald Publishing Limited. https://doi.org/10.1108/978-1-83753-590-320231008

Mahama Braimah, S., Amoako, G. K., Abubakari, A., Ampong, G. O. A., & Ofori, K. S. (2023). Green perceived value and consumer attitudes in the light of the SDGs: A replication study from a developing economy. *Society and Business Review, 18*(2), 345–362. https://doi.org/10.1108/SBR-03-2022-0088

Maione, G. (2024). References. In *Sustainable innovation reporting and emerging technologies* (pp. 101–127). Emerald Publishing Limited. https://doi.org/10.1108/978-1-83797-739-020241008

McBride, R., Dastan, A., & Mehrabinia, P. (2022). How AI affects the future relationship between corporate governance and financial markets: A note on impact capitalism. *Managerial Finance, 48*(8), 1240–1249. https://doi.org/10.1108/MF-12-2021-0586

Pagallo, U., Ciani Sciolla, J., & Durante, M. (2022). The environmental challenges of AI in EU law: Lessons learned from the artificial intelligence act (AIA) with its drawbacks. *Transforming Government: People, Process and Policy, 16*(3), 359–376. https://doi.org/10.1108/TG-07-2021-0121

Panigyraki, A., & Polyportis, A. (2024). Effects of consumer suspicion: A review and agenda for future research. *Journal of Consumer Marketing*, *41*(6), 610–623. https://doi.org/10.1108/JCM-10-2023-6376

Puaschunder, J. M. (2023a). References. In *Responsible investment around the world: Finance after the great reset* (pp. 195–232). Emerald Publishing Limited. https://doi.org/10.1108/978-1-80382-851-020231011

Puaschunder, J. M. (2023b). Responsibility. In *Responsible investment around the world: Finance after the great reset* (pp. 9–159). Emerald Publishing Limited. https://doi.org/10.1108/978-1-80382-851-020231004

Qayyum, A., Jamil, R. A., & Sehar, A. (2023). Impact of green marketing, greenwashing and green confusion on green brand equity. *Spanish Journal of Marketing - ESIC*, *27*(3), 286–305. https://doi.org/10.1108/SJME-03-2022-0032

Rehman, A., & Umar, T. (2024). Literature review: Industry 5.0. Leveraging technologies for environmental, social and governance advancement in corporate settings. *Corporate Governance: The International Journal of Business in Society*. https://doi.org/10.1108/CG-11-2023-0502

Samkin, G., Mihret, D. G., & Lemma, T. (2024). Accounting in and by the extractive industries: Development of a conceptual framework and avenues for future research. *Meditari Accountancy Research*, *32*(1), 1–41. https://doi.org/10.1108/MEDAR-11-2023-2229

Sætra, H. S. (2024). The ESG backlash: Politics, ideology, and the future of sustainable business. In J. J. Choi & J. Kim (Eds.), *Responsible firms: CSR, ESG, and global sustainability* (Vol. 23, pp. 161–167). Emerald Publishing Limited. https://doi.org/10.1108/S1569-376720240000023009

Seyfi, S., Vo-Thanh, T., & Zaman, M. (2024). Hospitality in the age of Gen Z: A critical reflection on evolving customer and workforce expectations. *International Journal of Contemporary Hospitality Management*, *36*(13), 118–134. https://doi.org/10.1108/IJCHM-01-2024-0035

Sharma, R., Bhardwaj, I., Grima, S., Sachdeva, T., Sood, K., & Özen, E. (Eds.). (2024). Index. In *Sustainable development goals: The impact of sustainability measures on wellbeing* (Vol. 113A, pp. 209–217). Emerald Publishing Limited. https://doi.org/10.1108/S1569-37592024000113A013

Sharma, R., Shishodia, A., & Gupta, A. (Eds.). (2023). Index. In *Fostering sustainable development in the age of technologies* (pp. 359–368). Emerald Publishing Limited. https://doi.org/10.1108/978-1-83753-060-120231025

Sharma, P., Subbarao, P. S., Sane, A., & Biradar, J. (2023). Guest editorial: Innovative practices in business, trade and commerce – Challenges and opportunities. *Journal of Indian Business Research*, *15*(1), 1–8. https://doi.org/10.1108/JIBR-03-2023-384

Silva, M. E., Sousa-Filho, J. M. de, Yamim, A. P., & Diógenes, A. P. (2020). Exploring nuances of green skepticism in different economies. *Marketing Intelligence & Planning*, *38*(4), 449–463. https://doi.org/10.1108/MIP-10-2018-0435

Taneja, S., Kumar, P., Reepu, Balusamy, B., Sood, K., & Grima, S. (Eds.). (2024). Index. In *Sustainability development through green economics* (Vol. 114, pp. 305–315). Emerald Publishing Limited. https://doi.org/10.1108/S1569-375920240000114018

Thivaios, P. (2024). Are we heading towards 'basel V'? Climate, cryptos and other challenges for banks. In M. Choudhry (Ed.), *Professional perspectives on banking and finance* (Vol. 1, pp. 97–121). Emerald Publishing Limited. https://doi.org/10.1108/978-1-83549-334-220241008

Trinh, H. H., Haouas, I., & Tran, T. T. T. (2024). Climate risks, sustainable finance, and green growth: The evolution of fintech. In J. J. Choi & J. Kim (Eds.), *Responsible firms: CSR, ESG, and global sustainability* (Vol. 23, pp. 147–160). Emerald Publishing Limited. https://doi.org/10.1108/S1569-376720240000023008

Unsal, O., & Ozkan, B. (2024). Technologies and emerging trends shaping fintech. In H. K. Baker, G. Filbeck, & K. Black (Eds.), *The Emerald handbook of fintech* (pp. 399–418). Emerald Publishing Limited. https://doi.org/10.1108/978-1-83753-608-520241046

Ure, J. (2024). Civil society (SDGs 5, 9, 10, 12, 16). In *Achieving the United Nations sustainable development goals: Late or too late?* (pp. 115–164). Emerald Publishing Limited.

Chapter 4

The Role of Technology and Social Media in Exposing Greenwashing in the Shared Economy

Abdillahi Mohamoud Sheikh Muse[a], *Abubakar Sadiq Muhammad*[b], *Labaran Isiaku*[a] *and Jana Al Hajj*[a]

[a]Cyprus International University, Turkey
[b]National Information Technology Development Agency, Nigeria

Abstract

This chapter undertakes a critical review of the significant role that technology and social media have played in unmasking greenwashing within the shared economy. Greenwashing refers to the practice by which companies mislead consumers by posing as environmentally friendly though in reality, they are not taking significant measures to be ecologically responsible. In a shared economy where the sharing of resources and peer-to-peer services is promoted, several companies brand themselves based on their so-called environmental benefits to attract consumers; usually, such branding is far from factual. This chapter will elaborate on how blockchain and artificial intelligence (AI) might be used to support the verification of green claims and follow up on the real sustainability performance of shared economy companies. It further explores the role of social media in enabling consumers, activists, and organizations to expose greenwashing by diffusing data, user experiences, and investigative results. This chapter will, through the use of real-life case analysis, show how technology equips consumers to make a difference between genuine sustainability initiatives and deceptive marketing. The discussion will close with guidance for shared economy businesses on ensuring the veracity of their environmental claims, as well as how consumers can use technology to demand genuine accountability in sustainability.

Eco Illusions, 67–89

Published under exclusive licence by Emerald Publishing Limited
doi:10.1108/978-1-83662-782-120261004

Keywords: Greenwashing; shared economy; technology; social media; sustainability

Introduction: Defining Greenwashing and Its Impact on the Shared Economy

Greenwash represents a marketing strategy of deliberately misleading consumers about the environmental benefits of certain goods, services, or companies (De Freitas Netto et al., 2020). This includes exaggeration of the efforts made in sustainable development, making vague or unsubstantiated claims, or fabricating eco-friendly credentials to attract ecologically sensitive customers (Bowen & Aragon-Correa, 2014). Although it is nothing new, with sustainability paramount in consumers' minds, there has been much more greenwashing (Bowen & Aragon-Correa, 2014). In that sense, while environmental considerations largely drive consumer choices, this greenwashing confounds trust in markets and creates real problems for firms that are authentic in their journey toward sustainability.

Sustainability has cropped up as a key driver of consumer behavior, business strategies, and international policy. As such, sustainability has become synonymous with value, integrity, and innovation in the products we consume and the services we use. This paradigm shift has translated into a need for businesses to integrate sustainability into their branding, marketing, and operations. While many companies have genuinely tried to reduce their footprint, others have taken advantage of the "going green" trend through greenwashing. This is a fundamentally misleading practice: It hoodwinks consumers and creates cynicism and confusion in the ecology of genuine environmental progress.

Different forms of greenwashing have been identified to include hidden trade-offs, no proof, vagueness, irrelevance, the lesser of two evils, and frank falsity. A hidden trade-off occurs when firms extol the environmentally friendly dimension of a given product but omit mentioning its worse overall impact. "No proof" refers to claims that lack verification or substantiation. Vagueness: Those claims that are ambiguous or too broad to hold any meaningful significance, using terms like "eco-friendly" without context. Irrelevance: Statements may be made that, though true, relate nothing to the product's sustainability. The lesser of two evils approach will market a product as greener compared to alternatives, even when in actuality, it is environmentally harmful. Outright falsity: Statements that are factually untrue and have to do with a company's environmental practices. All of these methods have contributed to the loss of public confidence and the heightened skepticism toward corporate environmental statements. Activist groups, watchdog organizations, and government agencies have started working harder to keep companies in line. But the persistence of greenwashing underscores the need for constant vigilance and transparency in environmental claims. It is particularly important in the sharing economy, where sustainability is often a major selling factor. The shared economy is a new culture of consumption with businesses and facilitation platforms that are centered on the efficient use of resources, sharing, and access and not ownership. The businesses in the sector include car-sharing businesses, short-stay accommodation websites, and secondhand marketplaces that present themselves as offering environmentally friendly alternatives to traditional consumption practices. The shared economy was in a position to present itself as an ecological alternative to overconsumption through the promotion of efficiency in the use of resources and the minimization of the generation of waste. Such an orientation toward sustainability is often undermined through the practice of greenwashing.

Greenwashing takes on odd senses and forms in the shared economy. A car-sharing scheme, for example, will claim to offset the emissions it produces but not provide the offsetting mechanism or the actual impact of its operations. Short-term letting websites market the decline in the need for new buildings but ignore the environmental price tag on increased energy use, waste generation, and tourism-related pressure on the environment. Secondhand market websites exaggerate the part they play in avoiding waste without considering the environmental price tag on the logistics and shipping operations they engage in. Such strategies not only mar the reputations of businesses but chip away at consumer belief in the shared economy in total.

The impact of greenwashing in the collaborative economy goes beyond loss in reputation: Greenwashing in the guise of the sustainability it claims to represent diverts attention from actual innovation and allocates funds better spent on actual environmental value. A ride-sharing service promoting its "green" credentials in the face of fossil fuel reliance diverts attention away from superior solutions, such as encouraging the use of public transport or active travel like cycling and walking. Such distraction drives momentum toward a global sustainable bottom line through the reinforcement of inefficiency and the erosion of any competitive advantage sustainable businesses enjoy. In addition to this, greenwashing in the collaborative economy trickles down to the consumer, businesses, and legislators. Greenwashing leads to confusion and mistrust among consumers; hence, it becomes even tougher to distinguish between an option that is sustainable and an option that is just faking it. The resulting cynicism then escalates into apathy, where the customers completely switch off any sustainable initiative. The ubiquity of greenwashing is a tough issue for organizations because sometimes the real environmental initiatives get lost or devalued in the process. Firms committed to reducing their environmental footprint may struggle to keep up with competitors who receive the same accolades through misleading strategies. To legislators, greenwashing means the effective regulation and promotion of sustainable initiatives become resource-intensive because there are duplicating efforts in verifying claims and compliance.

The rise in technology and social media has further made the issue of greenwashing in the shared economy even more complex. The platforms have facilitated the ability of consumers and activists to discover and expose false claims. Social media, in particular, has provided a platform for individuals and organizations to share information, raise awareness, and put corporations in the limelight. Social campaigns and online petitions have forced companies to take down false claims, issue apologies, and change practices. On the flip side, the digital era has spearheaded the use of increasingly sophisticated means of greenwashing. Organizations can create compelling but false narratives of sustainability with the help of sophisticated marketing strategies, data analysis, and algorithmic targeting. Technology is also a significant facilitator when it comes to providing evidence for environmental claims and transparency. Blockchain, for example, allows for the creation of unalterable records of sustainability data; hence, the claims become verifiable and trackable. Internet of Things (IoT) devices can track and, hence, report real-time environmental data to validate the various impacts a firm is having on the environment. Artificial intelligence (AI), on the other hand, leverages the capacity to scan humongous amounts of data to recognize patterns in greenwashing and inconsistencies in claims of sustainability. Up to now, the new technology has proved very effective in the battle against greenwashing and promoting accountability in the face of the shared economy.

Social networking is a double-edged sword in the war on greenwashing: On the positive side, it enables customers to demand greater accountability and transparency from companies, and on the negative side, the speed and scale of social media enable it to discover greenwashing and mobilize mass action quickly. Campaigns like #Greenwashing and #EcoFraud have revealed corporate deception and caused boycotts, regulatory action, and reputational damage to the guilty companies. Social media is equally available for companies to use in greenwashing. Employing carefully crafted content, social media influencer partnerships, and targeted advertising, a perception of sustainability may be generated that is difficult to verify on the consumer's part. The dark side of technology, social media, and the sharing economy brings both risk and opportunity. The more advanced these tools are, the greater the potential they have to reduce greenwashing and foster true sustainability. But they raise questions about the role of platforms, regulators, and consumers in ensuring environmental claims are true and meaningful. Grasping the relationship between technology and social media in the detection of greenwashing enables us to develop strategies to foster transparency, accountability, and trust in the sharing economy.

The fight against greenwashing in the shared economy is not merely about holding companies accountable; it's about establishing a culture of transparency where environmental claims are supported with evidence, sustainability programs are effective and measurable, and consumers are empowered to make informed choices. By addressing the root cause of the problem with greenwashing and taking advantage of technology and social media to increase levels of accountability, it's possible to develop an empowering shared economy that fosters a sustainable future. The chapter presents an in-depth analysis of dynamics in the practice of greenwashing in the shared economy with a focus on the strategies, methods, and challenges in detecting and addressing it. We aspire to conceive a world in which the shared economy is genuinely sustainable rather

Fig. 4.1. Process Diagram of the Chapter. *Source:* Authors own work from findings.

than being advertised as environmentally friendly. Fig. 4.1 shows a process diagram that depicts the key areas of the chapter.

Innovative Tech: Leveraging AI and Data Validation Systems for Enhanced Transparency

Within the modern context of sustainability and corporate social responsibility (CSR), AI and data validation systems have emerged as game-changing instruments in enhancing transparency and battling deceitful practices like greenwashing (Fioravante, 2024). This is where such technologies can help corporations support their claims with proof regarding sustainability, building up the trust of stakeholders and encouraging them to care about the environment. This chapter synthesizes insights from various pivotal studies to explore the potential, challenges, and future directions of AI-driven greenwashing detection and transparency enhancement.

AI in Greenwashing Detection

Boedijanto and Delina (2024) show that AI can easily unmask greenwashing in the manufacturing and energy industries. AI algorithms will use machine learning and natural language processing to analyze vast datasets in laying out discrepancies between the declared environmental objectives of companies and real environmental performances. For example, NLP may analyze social media postings and company reports to identify misleading narratives on sustainability.

AI tools track supply chain activities through analysis of manufacturing data, material procurements, and traffic and transportation documents for the observance of sustainability standards. The skill is very important in industries that have a globalized and complex supply chain. The effective deployment of AI faces the following challenges:

- Algorithmic Bias in Algorithms: Sometimes, AI systems' results may get biased by prejudices in the underlying data upon which their training is based.
- Data Integrity: Most of the time, AI is bound by a lack of comprehensive and high-quality information.
- Lack of standardization: The nonexistence of uniform standards hinders implementation and training in AI. The collaboration across disciplines in the creation of reliable data frameworks and global standards for sustainability reporting is very important to overcome such challenges.

Strategic Corporate Responsibility CSR and Responsible AI: The Moral Argument

According to Khan et al. (2024), responsible AI in strategic CSR makes firms more accountable. It is further explained that this should be done using transparent AI systems, which it refers to as Explainable AI or XAI. This builds stakeholders' confidence in an organization to avoid greenwashing in digital forms. Responsible AI, in balancing profitability with ethical consideration, will appeal to green consumers and investors.

AI-Driven Sustainability Evaluations: Enhancing Efficiency and Precision

Khan et al. (2024) suggest an "automated sustainability auditor" using AI to analyze corporate sustainability reports. An AI-driven system would place against the claims made by a company, using publicly available data to minimize cost and add further accuracy to the audit and assurance process. For example, satellite images with geospatial data can be used to verify a claimed emission reduction. A study centered on Chinese companies found that firms aware of AI monitoring were likely to meet their sustainability commitments due to the significantly increased chance of being exposed.

Machine Washing: A Novel Deceptive Strategy

Seele and Schultz (2022) point out that "machine washing" refers to a portfolio of greenwashing camouflaging by using AI to generate a hard-to-read, overly complex, or technical report. This misleading practice renders Providencia's stakeholders unable to ascertain the truth. To combat machine-washing, the authors suggest counterbalancing using AI tools to simplify such documents, or otherwise complex ones, and analyze them in detail, highlighting inconsistencies and unmasking misleading statements. They propose that in the future, research should focus on or develop specific algorithms for identifying and limiting machine washing.

AI as a Greenwashing Deterrent

Li, Zhang, et al. (2024) emphasize the deterrent effect of AI: The presence of AI-based verification systems raises the perceived risk of companies being caught and thus deters them from misbehaving. This effect is even stronger in markets where strict regulations require AI-powered sustainability audits.

AI and FinTech: Encouraging Environmentally Responsible Investments

The study of Si Mohammed et al. (2024) focuses on how AI and FinTech contribute to the promotion of green investments. Advanced approaches include sentiment analysis and natural language processing in identifying greenwashing in investment portfolios based on corporate disclosures, media reports, and public opinion. Further, blockchain technology works with AI in ensuring the irreversibility of claims of sustainability and provides verifiable proof regarding the environmental performance of corporations.

The Role of Blockchain in Addressing Greenwashing in the Shared Economy and Green Finance

In response to the rising customer demand for greening, many firms overclaim or lie about their environmental credentials as a means to gain a competitive advantage. It is here that blockchain technology presents an opportunity by increasing accountability, transparency, and traceability in sustainability commitments. The report draws on results from multiple research studies to analyze the potential for blockchain to mitigate greenwashing across a variety of sectors.

Blockchain's Role in Ensuring Transparency and Traceability

One of the core benefits of blockchain technology is how it can afford an immutable record-keeping system. Blockchain makes verifiable statements of sustainability effort possible by way of ensuring that data cannot be mutable after recording. Li, Chen, et al. (2024) highlighted the relevance of transparency for green financing. Their study assesses how, through blockchain, financial institutions and enterprises are communicating transparently to consumers; hence, reliable green finance practices could be achieved using this technology. Now, imagine blockchain-enabled systems that can prove that funds are being allocated for long-term goals and demonstrate accountability over the investment period. Dong et al. (2023) investigated how blockchain could be applied in logistics outsourcing. Blockchain enables traceability in the supply chain, whereby every step of the process is monitored to see if it follows specific environmental goals. Blockchain can verify that products labelled "eco-friendly" are produced and distributed with sustainability in mind.

Addressing Greenwashing Concerns in Green Credit Markets

While the green credit markets reward firms with good environmental practices, in the absence of a robust verification mechanism, this market is not exempt from different forms of greenwashing. Is blockchain technology, whereby each certification and transaction form is recorded on a distributed ledger. Ling and Wang (2024) discussed how blockchain influences green behavioral strategies in the green credit industry. Their findings indicate that blockchain technology can help reduce deceitful corporate practices whereby green credits are awarded to only those firms that offer stringent environmental criteria. Blockchain-based solutions provide real-time auditing, hence building stakeholders' trust.

Enhancing Consumer Power Through Accurate Information

Consumers make great contributions to sustainability by choosing more environmentally friendly products and services. However, one of the obstacles to making these choices effectively is greenwashing. Blockchain provides open, reliable data about environmental impacts.

Nygaard and Silkoset (2023), on the other hand, studied blockchain's potential in supporting green consumers. It lets customers trace the ecological footprint of their consumption by storing verifiable product lifecycle data. Users are, for example, able to check if the vehicles of a shared platform meet the emission standards or if the packaging of a product is biodegradable.

Combating Greenwashing in the Sharing Economy

In particular, the sharing economy, as generally represented by resource sharing, including tools, accommodation, and transport, demands significant end-user trust. Blockchain can play its role in adding to this further by verifying some of the shared assets' claims about sustainability. Yao et al. (2022) explain that blockchain works against the greenwashing issue on sharing economy platforms. Meanwhile, the blockchain embedded into platforms linked with IoT sensors can present data on resource consumption and environmental consequences in real time. For instance, a car-sharing service could utilize blockchain to validate whether its fleet meets low-emission standards and can be trusted by ecologically sensitive users.

Game Theory and Blockchain-Enabled Regulation

Other applications of blockchain involve regulatory frameworks, wherein it can be used to avoid greenwashing by ensuring a conformance to environmental standards based on game-theory strategic interactions.

Xu and Tian (2023) conducted a study regarding the adoption of blockchain in regulatory systems using evolutionary game theory. In this respect, the results obtained show that blockchain can encourage firms to become genuinely "green" by increasing costs for noncompliance. In other words, given the fact that through blockchain, relevant authorities will be able to observe in real-time the commitment to sustainability, it minimizes any chance of fraud.

Li, Chen, et al. (2024) also applied evolutionary game theory to show that blockchain enables the cooperation of participants in green finance. Blockchain makes the environment transparent, where there is punishment for greenwashing while simultaneously increasing payoffs for mutual effort.

Logistics and Supply Chain Applications

Another frequent problem that supply chain management and logistics have to deal with is greenwashing. The blockchain technology can be used to verify supply chain processes regarding their compliance with the preset environmental objectives. Dong et al. (2023) investigated how blockchain helps prevent greenwashing in logistics outsourcing. The research study shows that the use of blockchain can trace and verify each stage in logistics for environmental promises. Examples might include monitoring blockchain records of raw material sourcing and methods of production that prove a company's claims about using sustainable packaging.

Strengthening Trust in Green Finance

If not regulated, green finance initiatives, like sustainable bonds and climate funds, are often vulnerable to greenwashing. Blockchain technology presents various solutions in the industry for greater transparency and reliability. Yao et al. (2022) examined the part blockchain technology will have in reliable green financing through the provision of an open and immutable record of financial transactions to assist in the realization of the goal. It has helped in minimizing concerns about the misuse of funds and ensuring that money spent on sustainability projects is spent where it is meant to be spent.

Impact of Social Platforms: How Digital Media Networks Contribute to Uncovering Greenwashing Practices Through User Participation and Advocacy

Along with consumers becoming more concerned about the environment, greater interest developed regarding the greenwashing concept: providing false information regarding business operations about a firm's being "green." Social networking sites serve to create awareness regarding greenwashing, mobilize customers, and evoke active participation. According to Long et al. (2024), in the following presentation, social platforms promote these three elements of greenwashing activity.

Consumer Engagement and Greenwashing Exposure

The ability of social media to facilitate the speed at which information is disseminated has dramatically changed how customers view and react to corporate greenwashing. Social media platforms such as Facebook, Instagram, and Twitter have enabled consumers to question and evaluate corporate environmental, social, and governance (ESG) claims, according to Lyon and Montgomery (2013). Companies are increasingly vulnerable to "tweetjacking," a term meaning the practice of customers exposing deceptive environmental claims publicly through corporate social media platforms. These forums make it easier to identify contradictions between corporate green marketing and corporate practices by collectively analyzing these contradictions. This makes it more difficult for firms to engage in unethical behaviors without fear of public censure.

As stated by Fang (2024), environmentally oriented social media has an influence on the ways customers' knowledge about a certain company is changed and on customer perceptions. The use of these media provided an opportunity to compare the level of green commitments announced and what corporates do in business activity. Comparatively, user-generated comments and testimonials unmasked the legitimacy and/or falsification of corporate messages through various methods that consumers did not usually check before buying services. Exposure of business tactics for greenwashing results in loss of consumer trust, which will further bring about changes of priorities toward those providing service maintaining legitimate environmental sustainability standards. Results from Fang have proven the importance of social media in consumer empowerment for holding firms accountable in the case of greenwashing.

Corporate Accountability and Digital Advocacy

Activists utilize social media channels to disseminate information about greenwashing campaigns and exert continuous pressure on companies to be open. Amin et al. (2024) say that, in addition to consumers scrutinizing CSR disclosures on social media platforms like Twitter, activists scrutinize CSR statements for inconsistencies. Online platforms are where activists bring up inconsistencies in (ESG) reports and rally the public in support of their demands for action. Online activism compels companies to prioritize actual environmental actions to defend themselves against the stigma of being greenwashers.

Research carried out by Li et al. (2023) in China revealed that social media pressure can contribute to corporate hypocrisy through the form of companies engaging in cosmetic green behaviors in the interest of placating the public. The same drivers have the capacity to trigger actual changes for the better. The persistence and visibility of social media drive corporations toward the implementation of sustainable practices in the long run. The dynamics illustrate the dual capacity social media has in both preventing greenwashing and triggering actual environmental action.

Impact of Regional and Global Media Coverage

The interaction between traditional and social media heightens the visibility of greenwashing practices. Wei et al. (2023) suggest that local environmental policy and the attention generated through the media largely mitigates the financial effects of greenwashing. The real-time sharing and discussion of traditional news on social media guarantee it is extremely probable that corporate greenwashing will be revealed (Ren et al., 2024). The rapid sharing of such criticism often leads companies to react publicly and, therefore, heighten accountability.

Besides, Zhang et al. (2023) discuss the dilemma between consumer and corporate environmental values, emphasizing the role of social media in this interaction. They argue that consumer engagement with environmental campaigns on social media not only exposes corporate greenwashing but also stimulates genuine green actions. Consumers, through active engagement with and dissemination of environmental campaigns, directly influence corporate behavior, compelling companies to adopt genuine eco-friendly actions to safeguard their reputations. This bidirectional interaction between consumer behavior and corporate responses underscores the imperative role of social media in deterring greenwashing.

The Influence of Social Media and the Risks of Greenwashing

Nazish et al. (2024) bring out both the good and the bad of social media, facilitating the identification of greenwashing activities on the one hand and propagating genuine environmental actions on the other hand. The authors chronicle the way social media empowers consumers with greater clout to question companies more intensely on the one hand and the way it drives the disturbing phenomenon of shallow green actions on the other hand. Social networking websites have customers seemingly interested in engaging in environment-centered discussion with a strong foundation in the shared research and knowledge applied in the myth-busting exercise. The collective exercise not only demolishes the greenwashing action but also disseminates information and encourages others to take the cue. Most companies attempting to misuse social media for greenwashing end up earning prompt criticism when they are questioned.

This then becomes a high-risk situation in which any potential short-term benefits of deceptive environmental marketing are outweighed by the dangers of being labeled a greenwasher. Social media has allowed businesses to be held accountable and consumers to have more transparent information to serve as vital change agents to corporate deception.

Comprehensive Role of Social Media in Greenwashing Dynamics

Social media is a multilayered tool in exposing corporate deception, from greenwashing to promoting genuine environmental causes. This reviewed research points out how social media enables:

More Scrutiny: Lyon and Montgomery (2013) and Fang (2024) argue that social media enables consumers to scrutinize and publicize gaps in corporate environmental claims. Social media platforms become spaces of truth where deceptive practices are systematically exposed and contested through crowds and shared knowledge. Amin et al. (2024) and Li et al. (2023) stressed how social media enables activists to consistently press firms for genuine environmental improvement. Advocates scale minor critiques into large-scale advocacy campaigns, compelling corporations to become greener in their behavior and more transparent. Greater Media Impact: Wei et al. (2023) and Zhang et al. (2023) provide evidence that social platforms amplify traditional media both in the discovery of greenwashing and in forming environmental attitudes of consumers and businesses. Social media connects the local and the global for audiences, and corporate missteps become visibly accountable to all.

Consumer Empowerment: Where consumers, in their active uses of content in social media, challenge “greenwashing” for authenticity. This transforms the role that customers play into one from a traditionally passive client to an active actor in this fight against corporate “deceit” (Nazish et al., 2024).

Case Studies: Instances of Greenwashing in the Shared Economy and How Technology Aids in Its Exposure

From freelance job platforms and car-sharing services to apps for vacation rentals, the gig economy is turning out to be an eye-catching feature of economic activity today. Many of them market themselves as innately green because of their focus on efficient resource use, reduced waste and environmental care. But there is also, in this sharing economy, a widespread practice of what’s called greenwashing: a term describing how businesses make spurious or exaggerated claims about the environmental benefits of a product. For the sharing economy to genuinely *aid* in avoiding the eco-illusion, it must move beyond simply promoting shared access and actively embrace deeper circular economy principles and robust ESG integration. To genuinely avoid the eco-illusion, the sharing economy must prioritize maximizing asset utilization, design for circularity, actively mitigate rebound effects, conduct thorough lifecycle assessments, and integrate ESG principles holistically (Long et al., 2024).

This section will review some real examples of greenwashing, as well as how technology helps to reveal and reduce these mischievous practices. In the context of the sharing economy, greenwashing occurs by misrepresentations or exaggeration of their environmentally friendly credentials that appeal to greener consumers. Sharing economy organizations differ from others in their “access over ownership” business model, which naturally positions them as friendly to the environment. However, most of these claims have been proven to mask hazardous externalities such as increased emissions, depletion of resources, and social exploitation. According to De Freitas Netto et al. (2020), greenwashing may be presented in several ways, including:

Concealed Compromises: Favoring one environmental benefit while neglecting others.

Ambiguity: Employing terms like "eco-friendly" without substantiating evidence.

Negligibility: Emphasizing those features that do not make any significant contribution to sustainability.

Outright Lies: Providing completely incorrect information about environmental practices.

These tactics are spread across industries in gig economy services, car-sharing, and vacation rentals, extending to consumer-to-consumer shipping.

Car-Sharing Services: The Illusion of Decreased Carbon Footprint

Most car-sharing companies advertise that they reduce emissions and decrease car ownership. However, a study by Hazel and Brittany (2020), entitled "Greenwashing in the Information Industry," says otherwise. For instance:

Empty Runs: The majority of car-sharing journeys comprise empty drives without passengers, adding to the pollution problem.

Stimulated usage: car-sharing increases total trip-making by substitution of public transit and nonmotorized modes of transportation.

The studies using location and traffic information unwound claims of emissions or congestion reduction from car-sharing, showing that urban traffic volumes have increased as a result.

Peer-to-Peer Accommodation Services: Promoting Sustainable Travel or Exacerbating Overtourism?

Most of the P2P accommodation providers advertise their services as an environmentally friendly option to hotels because they use fewer resources and bring business to local communities. However, Choudhury et al. (2024) discovered that such marketing masks several negative impacts:

- Excessive Tourism: The increase in short-term letting both in cities and rural areas is putting additional pressure on local ecosystems and infrastructure.
- Resource Use: Short-term letting tends to have higher water and energy consumption per customer, as opposed to professional hospitality establishments which apply efficiency measures.

Circular Economy Claims: Inaccurate Portrayal of Resource Reuse

Many sharing economy platforms market a line that their activities accord with the circular economy through encouraging the sharing of resources and prevention of waste. Kopnina (2019) researched in the area of greenwashing and business education, showing how these claims are often unsubstantiated. Food delivery services, for example, highlight their use of recyclable packaging as a sustainability practice while excluding the emissions related to inefficient routing.

Alignment With Sustainable Development Goals (SDGs)

Pimonenko et al. (2020) discussed in their study on greenwashing and SDGs how companies use the general appeal of SDGs to increase environmental legitimacy. Shared economy platforms mostly boast about minor sustainability initiatives taken by them, such as collaboration with any environmental NGO and the use of renewable sources of energy, while avoiding any discussion of the actual environmental impact of their overall operations.

Advocacy on Social Media Platforms

Social media has dramatically altered the way exposure and confrontation of greenwashing have been carried out. Kopnina (2019) highlights the role of hashtags such as #GreenwashingAlert in extended campaigns that promote awareness, advance boycotts, and eventually force companies to adopt sustainable behavior. Direct evidence against the exaggerated claims in the form of user-generated content in videos and photographs is often found. Public outcry and regulatory action have followed the social activists' and social media influencers' accusations of greenwashing in car-sharing apps.

Real-World Examples of Technology's Impact

Volkswagen Emissions Case: Setting a Precedent

One of the most glaring examples of technology-enabled greenwashing is the Volkswagen emission scandal. It utilized software just to cheat the outcome of emission testing when it made unsubstantiated claims about the environmental footprint of its diesel vehicles. The environmental credentials of the vehicles were immediately invalidated by the fact that they emitted pollutants in much larger quantities than legal limits during actual use on the roads. This example illustrates how technology can serve a dual purpose in greenwashing; initially facilitating deception, advanced diagnostic tools and software analysis ultimately exposed the manipulation. The episode underscored the imperative for enhanced regulatory oversight and independent audits to ensure transparency. It also showed how technology can make companies accountable by exposing the discrepancy between their environmental regulations and marketing claims (Siano et al., 2017).

Ride-Hailing Services: Carbon Footprint Assessments

Investigative studies based on data collected from applications proved that the claims of reduced congestion with ride-sharing systems were unfounded.

Researchers proved that the tracking of emissions and journey trends contributes to increased urban congestion.

Yang et al. (2020) assert that the majority of the time, such companies advertise themselves as being ecologically responsible because they say that shared rides reduce emissions as well as the number of vehicles that people own. However, case studies have shown exactly the opposite to be true; overall, vehicle use is increased, and congestion and emissions are exacerbated by "dead mileage," those trips where drivers operate without any passengers. To appear green, some platforms even advertise partnerships with electric vehicle projects while they do not tackle much larger operational inefficiencies. Technologies that measure real-world impacts, such as data analytics and pollution tracking systems, are essential to expose these disparities. This transparency forces firms to address the gap between their environmental commitments and the actual ecological impacts of their operations.

Analysis of Logistics in Food Delivery Services

According to Choudhury et al. (2024), "Greenwashing and its role in hindering the transition towards the circular economy and sustainability." These websites highlight how they focus on sustainability, with options including carbon-neutral delivery and biodegradable packaging. Many of those claims are not true, however. Packaging often needs commercial composting plants, which a lot of places do not have, and ends up in landfills. Similarly, while route optimization algorithms are said to reduce emissions, these benefits are usually offset by the surge in the frequency of delivery and single-use packaging.

An international food delivery company announced carbon neutrality via offset programs but failed to consider its full emissions production. The service used such claims to position itself as green-conscious instead of dealing with inherent problems like huge waste generation and inefficiency in operations. Verification of product lifecycles by verifying the actual environmental impacts is an important contribution of technologies like blockchain and AI-powered carbon tracking to unmask greenwashing and push corporations beyond superficial claims.

Obstacles and Prospects: Validating Genuine and Credible Environmental Assertions

In the sharing economy, where eco-friendliness is often touted as a primary selling point, businesses are under increasing pressure to prove their environmental claims. Indeed, the sharing economy often touts sustainability as a central selling feature and that has come with increased scrutiny of businesses' green claims. This is driven by increased awareness and scrutiny by consumers, watchdog organizations, and regulatory authorities. Greenwashing claiming more in sustainability than actual performance is getting worse and presents a serious menace to business through undermining customer trust. Therefore, from a business perspective that is keen on keeping up with the times and staying competitive, it is necessary to break away from apparently shallow claims to transparent and verifiably testable environmental practices validated for their accuracy. Such a transition is, of course, plagued with a variety of issues; first and foremost among these are the fact that they are the products of complex supply chains and scarce financial resources and shifting regulatory climates. While all this is important, emerging technologies and collaborative approaches represent enormous new opportunities for businesses in securing the veracity of their environmental claims.

Challenges in Ensuring Authentic Environmental Claims

The major challenges for the shared economy include the intricate nature of supply chains. Most businesses depend on complex networks of suppliers, partners, and middlemen, which makes it very hard to gauge the environmental impacts throughout the operational stages. To put this into perspective, a car-sharing platform might use electric vehicles at the core of its claims of sustainability. On the other hand, the company's overall sustainability claim may be at variance with the higher environmental impact associated with the production of EV batteries, the mining of rare earth materials, or the acquisition of electricity used for charging. When these inconsistencies come to the fore, there is a possibility of reputational damage, considering that consumers and watchdog groups are becoming very sensitive to false or misleading claims in recent times.

But then again, things are not going to be made that much easier by a lack of standards underlying the definition of sustainability performance. Different industries, often in different locations, use their definitions and standards for measuring environmental performance; this makes the establishment and dissemination of commonly accepted measures of sustainability difficult for any enterprise. Because standards do not exist, internal environmental impact tracking and reporting are problematic while consumers are perplexed by a host of claims that defy distinction between fact and advertising hyperbole. The dilemma that pits sustainability against profitability is indeed a thorny challenge. Sustainability will no doubt enhance the brand image of a firm and also make it attractive to socially responsible consumers, but many such programrs do require considerable investments on the front line. There is a need to deploy new technologies or redo current processes, or obtain various certifications, all of which come with a lot of cost implications. Small firms may have severe resource constraints to invest in these transformations. So there is the risk for others to greenwash themselves as a profitable but not very sustainable opportunity. A shared house website would be carbon neutral but would not account for the customer or affiliate-generated emissions correctly, for instance. Another issue is the regulatory problem. With the increasing numbers of governments and international organizations requiring companies to be greener, there is the need for an increasing range of rules and norms with which companies need to comply. Noncompliance will have penalties, litigation and damage to reputation.

Navigating such a regulatory environment is especially complicated for companies with operations in multiple jurisdictions where various legislation and enforcement arrangements may deter compliance initiatives.

Opportunities for Ensuring Authentic Environmental Claims

Despite these limitations, there are a few ways in which the legitimacy and validity of the environmental statements of the firm may be strengthened. Dong et al. (2023) present a set of technological innovations in the domain of blockchain and AI as effective tools for monitoring, verification, and sharing their sustainability practices. Blockchain technology is effective in establishing transparent and unaltered records in association with the life cycle of any commodity; for example, with the use of blockchain technology, a firm would be in a position to trace an environmental footprint associated with its operation in the most comprehensive way possible from raw material extraction to the breakdown in the environment. Such records establish credibility for the environmental claims and provide a strong basis for compliance with global standards on sustainability. AI-based innovations strengthen the same in ways in which companies would be in a position to explore long and complex sets of carbon footprints, energy consumption, and waste disposal. For instance, machine learning algorithms can detect inefficiencies in supply chains, optimize resource utilization, and predict the environmental impacts of various operational decisions. Companies that integrate AI into their sustainability strategies will move beyond anecdotes to real data-driven proof of their performance in the environment. Besides that, digital platforms run by the might of AI and blockchain will avail a channel of communication through which consumers can find out in real time the effort a company has made in terms of sustainability and hold companies accountable.

The shared economy also offers enormous opportunities for collaboration. Together with independent certifying organizations, environmental NGOs, and sustainability experts, companies can check their claims and reduce greenwashing risks. Third-party certification through organizations like the FSC or LEED acts as a signal that a company is genuinely committed to sustainability. In addition, partnerships with NGOs and academic institutions can provide groundbreaking research, best practices, and expertise for improving companies' environmental performance. Sharing economy businesses will also benefit from transparent partnerships that engage consumers in sustainability efforts. Educating consumers on what to look for in terms of sustainability and encouraging them to think critically about environmental claims creates a sense of shared responsibility. It can also show the consumers' carbon footprint from every trip made on ride-sharing; alternates can be given to reduce such emissions through some accredited programs. Also, in accommodation-sharing, users can be incentivized for their ecologically positive actions, such as going easy on energy use or choosing eco-friendly travel alternatives.

Policy advocacy and participation in industry-wide initiatives allow companies to overcome regulatory challenges and shape new sustainability standards. Joint work with policymakers and contribution to the development of environmental regulations contribute to the fact that new measures will be strict but achievable. Industry coalitions and sustainability alliances provide organizations with the opportunity to pool resources, share experience, and collaborate on complex issues, such as supply chain transparency and standardization.

Building a Culture of Authenticity and Trust

For the truth of environmental claims to be ensured, firms should be able to embed sustainability into their core operations and principles. This requires a lifecycle approach that considers environmental impacts throughout the business cycle, from design and sourcing through marketing and to end-of-life disposal. Equally important is clear communication. Businesses should provide more clear, accurate, and accessible information about their sustainability performance and avoid vague or exaggerated claims that might undermine consumer confidence. The leadership's role in promoting a culture of authenticity is very important. The executives and managers should consider sustainability as a strategic objective and allocate the necessary resources and establish quantifiable targets. It ensures the targets on awareness are met through internal audits and third-party assessments while reporting often builds accountability and transparency.

The emergence of sustainability as a consumer priority has turned into both a challenge and an opportunity for firms operating in the shared economy. By using technology, fostering collaboration, and being transparent, organizations can efficiently handle supply chain challenges, overcome budgetary constraints, and work within regulatory conditions. In this way, companies do not only protect their reputation but also contribute to making the future more sustainable. Watchdog organizations and educated consumers will hold corporations accountable, and those leading with authenticity and confidence in their environmental promises will be the frontrunners in the shared economy and beyond.

Conclusion: Leveraging Technology and Social Media to Combat Greenwashing and Foster Authentic Sustainability

New technology and the pervasiveness of social media are rebuilding commotion on sustainability into strong protection of greenwashing practices. Instead of today's informed and increasingly demanding consumers, companies fully realize that deep environmental claims bereft of proof can no longer justify their benefits. Social media and technology are key levers in establishing transparency, debunking myths, and fostering real, sustainable performance.

But most critically, it integrates blockchain, AI, and IoT devices to keep the war against greenwashing in check. Blockchain brings traceability in chains where supply is not easily traced back to its origins, a component that will, therefore, be capable of enabling customers and regulators to verify claims with ease regarding sustainability. Blockchain provides irrefutable evidence of environmental behavior since it records every step and transaction in a chain of supply to establish corporate responsibility. Such traceability is greatly beneficial in such fields as fashion, agriculture, and electronics where unethical behavior and violations against the environment have been greatly prevalent. Alternatively, AI-based analysis is capable of detecting inconsistencies in environmental reports, identifying patterns in misrepresentation, and tracking real-time environmental footprints. For instance, AI programs can check large sets of data to find inconsistencies in carbon offsetting claims or inconsistencies between claimed and actual emissions. IoT devices contribute even more to the sustainability push with accurate real-time data on the consumption of resources and emissions and establishing a culture of accountability. The network of connected technology enables companies to validate environmental claims and not misrepresent or exaggerate the same and hence avoid greenwashing. Social media contributes to the democratization of information and the amplification of consumer voices.

Social media platforms like Twitter, Instagram, and TikTok have become places for greenwashing exposure and the recognition of genuine initiatives. Viral campaigns, influencer endorsements, and consumer feedback create a chain reaction that encourages companies to put action into action when it comes to sustainability. Social media added transparency into the forefront with companies willing to be transparent about sustainability initiatives having a better chance to build consumer confidence and loyalty. The interactive nature of social media allows consumers to engage and interact with brands directly and, in the process, allows them to question, ask for explanations, and question them directly an aspect of the real world reversing power and balance towards ensuring enterprises promote reality rather than rhetoric. Technology and social media will continue evolving in the future, and it will increasingly be difficult for companies to engage in greenwashing. Increased access to information will continue to strengthen consumers, and businesses will find themselves compelled toward genuine sustainability initiatives. It will have far-reaching implications in the form of corporate policy and regulatory climates and trickle down to consumer behavioral changes.

Implications of Technology and Social Media on Sustainability

The use of new technology and social media in the practice of sustainability will have a few significant implications. First and foremost, the companies will have to be more transparent in their approach. Companies will no longer have to react to consumer backlash or regulatory action but will have to be open in the publication of their key sustainability metrics and independently verifying the same. The transparency will redefine CSR from a voluntary goodwill action to an absolute business necessity.

It hence opens completely new avenues to use environmental standards on various issues by regulators and policymakers both. For example, when verifiable data start arriving with such technology as blockchain and AI, the regulatory tool it is accompanied with gets stronger, maybe mandates may be implemented with tracking their carbon footprint for all major polluting sectors through blockchains, or have artificially intelligent-based audited reports on the sustainability particular to firms. Besides scolding and leaving the guilt of greenwashers in limbo, there also surfaces innovation-led, encouraging sustainable performances.

Third, consumer behavior stands at the threshold of a paradigm shift. As consumers become more aware and empowered, their purchasing decisions will increasingly reflect their greener values. This heightened awareness could spur demand for products and services that demonstrate genuine sustainability. Companies failing to make this transition risk losing market share and suffering damage to their brand reputation.

Finally, the cultural narrative of sustainability will shift. Social media has proved it can reshape public discourse, and sustainability is no exception. Social media can create a sense of accountability by showcasing success stories and exposing malpractices, which in turn may spur people into collective action. Such a cultural mind-shift will likely trickle down beyond the individual consumer level to the community, organization, and state levels and more inclusive and collaborative behavior on the care of the environment.

Future Research Directions

The current research underlines the transformative potential of technology and social media concerning greenwashing, but other segments call for more detailed research. An exciting area for further research might be the interaction between blockchain technology and consumer behavior. In such a case, research could investigate the impact of blockchain-forced transparency on trust and loyalty in consumers, perhaps especially in industries that involve complex supply chains. Further research can be done in investigating the scalability and cost efficiency in deploying blockchain systems among SMEs, mostly those that often do not possess resources as compared to large companies.

Another important field is the role of AI in improving regulatory frameworks. While AI-driven analytics have shown some promising results in the detection of greenwashing, few explorations have surfaced regarding the use of AI in policymaking. Future research will look into the incorporation of AI in the rule-making procedure in order to accelerate checks on compliance and identify novel environmental threats. It may also look into the ethics of AI and sustainability in the context of data protection and algorithmic bias.

One rich area for investigation is the influence of IoT devices on sustainable practices. Although IoT technology provides valuable information on the use of resources and emissions, there remains uncertainty regarding the energy use and environmental footprint of IoT devices themselves. Future research may explore ways to reduce the environmental footprint of IoT devices and increase their usefulness of IoT devices in advancing sustainability.

The most promising direction would be the impact on customers' attitudes toward sustainability via social media. It would involve a comparison of the most effective social media strategies in shaping customers. It would judge top-down campaigns with influencer champions as more or less effective in generating demand for sustainable products in comparison with grassroots consumer campaigns. Future research will be directed towards the ways social media algorithms will be utilized to promote or suppress content on issues regarding sustainability and will discover a few information-spreading secrets in cyberspace.

Lastly, interdisciplinary studies would be able to yield the greatest insights into the global effects of technology and social media on sustainability. Combining the understanding of environmental science, sociology, and information technology, researchers would be able to develop comprehensive models for understanding and tackling greenwashing. One would be able to research the effect of cultural differences on the use and success of technology-based sustainability programs and provide valuable insights to international business corporations and international politicians.

Conclusion

Where technology and social media intersect lies a very different landscape, one in which new solutions to the pervasive problem of greenwashing are possible. Blockchain technology, AI, and IoT devices allow companies to substantiate claims with verifiable fact and promote a culture of transparency and accountability, and social media levels the playing field and empowers consumers with a strong voice as a viable counterbalance to corporate misuse.

The widespread consequences: businesses must adopt transparency as a strategy, regulators have new levers to enforce the rules, and consumers are ever more empowered to make conscious decisions. Together, these shifts amount to a new cultural story about cooperation and honesty for sustainability.

The relationship between technology and social media will be even stronger in the future and will have both challenges and opportunities along with it. Keeping in view the fact that new applications and implications of such technology are still being unveiled through studies and researches, it is perhaps the right time for all the stakeholders in different segments to sit together and harness these tools in the name of true sustainability. More studies on scalability, ethics, and cultural specifics need to be directed toward making the technology effective and just in use.

Sincerity is the key to long-term success in the shared economy. We would be a more open and sustainable society if businesses, governments, and individuals all used the transformative capacity of technology and social media to help each other. Along with solving the pressing issue, such a paradigm shift would be fertile ground for long-term innovation and resilience in addressing the environmental challenges we are confronted with globally.

References

Amin, M. H., Ali, H., & Mohamed, E. K. A. (2024). Corporate social responsibility disclosure on Twitter: Signalling or greenwashing? Evidence from the UK. *International Journal of Finance & Economics*, *29*(2), 1745–1761. https://doi.org/10.1002/ijfe.2762

Boedijanto, F. J. O., & Delina, L. L. (2024). Potentials and challenges of artificial intelligence-supported greenwashing detection in the energy sector. *Energy Research & Social Science*, *115*, 103638. https://doi.org/10.1016/j.erss.2024.103638

Bowen, F., & Aragon-Correa, J. A. (2014). Greenwashing in corporate environmentalism: Research and practice: The importance of what we say and do. *Organization & Environment*, *27*(2), 107–112. https://doi.org/10.1177/1086026614537078

Choudhury, R. R., Islam, A. F., & Sujauddin, M. (2024). More than just a business ploy? Greenwashing as a barrier to circular economy and sustainable development: A case study-based critical review. *Circular Economy and Sustainability*, *4*(1), 233–266. https://doi.org/10.1007/s43615-023-00288-9

De Freitas Netto, S. V., Sobral, M. F. F., Ribeiro, A. R. B., & Soares, G. R. D. L. (2020). Concepts and forms of greenwashing: A systematic review. *Environmental Sciences Europe*, *32*(1), 19. https://doi.org/10.1186/s12302-020-0300-3

Dong, C., Huang, Q., Pan, Y., Ng, C. T., & Liu, R. (2023). Logistics outsourcing: Effects of greenwashing and blockchain technology. *Transportation Research Part E: Logistics and Transportation Review*, *170*, 103015. https://doi.org/10.1016/j.tre.2023.103015

Fang, Z. (2024). Greenwashing versus green authenticity: How green social media influences consumer perceptions and green purchase decisions. *Sustainability*, *16*(23), 10723. https://doi.org/10.3390/su162310723

Fioravante, R. (2024). Beyond the business case for responsible artificial intelligence: Strategic CSR in light of digital washing and the moral human argument. *Sustainability*, *16*(3), 1232. https://doi.org/10.3390/su16031232

Hazel, S., & Brittany, M. (2020). Greenwashing in the information industry. *The iJournal: Graduate Student Journal of the Faculty of Information*, *5*(2). https://doi.org/10.33137/ijournal.v5i2.34413

Khan, M. K., Huo, C., Zahid, R. M. A., & Maqsood, U. S. (2024). The automated sustainability auditor: Does artificial intelligence curtail greenwashing behavior in Chinese firms? *Business Strategy and the Environment*, *33*(8), 9015–9039. https://doi.org/10.1002/bse.3961

Kopnina, H. (2019). Green-washing or best case practices? Using circular economy and cradle to cradle case studies in business education. *Journal of Cleaner Production*, *219*, 613–621. https://doi.org/10.1016/j.jclepro.2019.02.005

Li, S., Chen, R., Li, Z., & Chen, X. (2024). Can blockchain help curb "greenwashing" in green finance? - Based on tripartite evolutionary game theory. *Journal of Cleaner Production*, *435*, 140447. https://doi.org/10.1016/j.jclepro.2023.140447

Li, W., Li, W., Seppänen, V., & Koivumäki, T. (2023). Effects of greenwashing on financial performance: Moderation through local environmental regulation and media coverage. *Business Strategy and the Environment*, *32*(1), 820–841. https://doi.org/10.1002/bse.3177

Li, D., Zhang, Z., & Gao, X. (2024). Does artificial intelligence deter greenwashing? *Finance Research Letters*, *67*, 105954. https://doi.org/10.1016/j.frl.2024.105954

Ling, X., & Wang, H. (2024). Green behavior strategies in the green credit market: Analysis of the impacts of enterprises' greenwashing and blockchain technology. *Sustainability*, *16*(11), 4858. https://doi.org/10.3390/su16114858

Long, L., Wang, C., & Zhang, M. (2024). Does social media pressure induce corporate hypocrisy? Evidence of ESG greenwashing from China. *Journal of Business Ethics*. https://doi.org/10.1007/s10551-024-05747-3

Lyon, T. P., & Montgomery, A. W. (2013). Tweetjacked: The impact of social media on corporate greenwash. *Journal of Business Ethics*, *118*(4), 747–757. https://doi.org/10.1007/s10551-013-1958-x

Nazish, M., Khan, Z., Khan, A., Naved Khan, M., & Ramkissoon, H. (2024). Green intentions, green actions": The power of social media and the perils of greenwashing. *Journal of Global Marketing*, 1–20. https://doi.org/10.1080/08911762.2024.2429517

Nygaard, A., & Silkoset, R. (2023). Sustainable development and greenwashing: How blockchain technology information can empower green consumers. *Business Strategy and the Environment*, *32*(6), 3801–3813. https://doi.org/10.1002/bse.3338

Pimonenko, T., Bilan, Y., Horák, J., Starchenko, L., & Gajda, W. (2020). Green brand of companies and greenwashing under sustainable development goals. *Sustainability*, *12*(4), 1679. https://doi.org/10.3390/su12041679

Ren, J., Wu, P., & Hou, L. (2024). Social media attention and corporate greenwashing: Evidence from China. *Corporate Social Responsibility and Environmental Management*, *31*(6), 5446–5465. https://doi.org/10.1002/csr.2875

Seele, P., & Schultz, M. D. (2022). From greenwashing to machinewashing: A model and future directions derived from reasoning by analogy. *Journal of Business Ethics*, *178*(4), 1063–1089. https://doi.org/10.1007/s10551-022-05054-9

Si Mohammed, K., Serret, V., Ben Jabeur, S., & Nobanee, H. (2024). The role of artificial intelligence and fintech in promoting eco-friendly investments and non-greenwashing practices in the US market. *Journal of Environmental Management*, *359*, 120977. https://doi.org/10.1016/j.jenvman.2024.120977

Siano, A., Vollero, A., Conte, F., & Amabile, S. (2017). "More than words": Expanding the taxonomy of greenwashing after the Volkswagen scandal. *Journal of Business Research*, *71*, 27–37. https://doi.org/10.1016/j.jbusres.2016.11.002

Xu, L., & Tian, T. (2023). Blockchain-enabled enterprise bleaching green regulation banking evolution game analysis. *Environment, Development and Sustainability*, *26*(11), 27457–27483. https://doi.org/10.1007/s10668-023-03768-y

Yang, Z., Nguyen, T. T. H., Nguyen, H. N., Nguyen, T. T. N., & Cao, T. T. (2020). Greenwashing behaviours: Causes, taxonomy and consequences based on a systematic literature review. *Journal of Business Economics and Management*, *21*(5), 1486–1507. https://doi.org/10.3846/jbem.2020.13225

Yao, S., Liu, Y., & Shi, X. (2022). Suppliers' corporate social responsibility efforts with greenwashing concerns: Can blockchain help? *IFAC-PapersOnLine*, *55*(10), 1986–1991. https://doi.org/10.1016/j.ifacol.2022.09.690

Chapter 5

Greenwashing in the Age of Digital Media: An Empirical Study

Mahnoor Sahrash[a], *Soumya Nedunuri*[a], *Sumayya Fatima*[a] *and Anvita Chitrapu*[b]

[a]St. Francis College for Women, India
[b]University of Michigan, USA

Abstract

Of late, 'Sustainability' and 'Eco-friendly' have become the new buzz words in the marketing arena, thanks to the growing awareness and eco-consciousness of consumers. As the demand for green products rises, companies continue to devise creative marketing techniques to capture the imagination of the consumers. This has gradually resulted in greenwashing or deceitful marketing practices that deceive consumers about the true nature of the environmental activities of a company or its products and services and lead to the detriment of the environment.

With the emergence of digital platforms, greenwashing has become more widespread. This study aims to analyze the practice of greenwashing in the context of digital media by understanding the visual and textual content strategies used by companies and to evaluate the authenticity of their claims against their actual environmental performance. This paper intends to investigate consumer perceptions of genuine sustainability as opposed to greenwashing. Such analysis is especially crucial in the Indian context, which is emerging as a potential market for green products.

Thus, this study also aims to highlight the impacts of greenwashing on business practices, as well as its broader implications on the relevant legal and regulatory authorities in India such as the Advertising Standards Council of India (ASCI), which can shape the future of green marketing in India in the coming years.

Eco Illusions, 91–108

doi:10.1108/978-1-83662-782-120261005

Keywords: Greenwashing; green marketing; visual analysis; textual analysis; digital media

Introduction

Greenwashing was first coined in the 1980s by the renowned environmentalist Jay Westerveld, modelling on the word 'whitewashing', to refer to the deceitful marketing practices used by organizations to mislead consumers about the true nature of the environmental impact of their activities or of their products and services. It often involves the use of marketing tactics, visual branding and textual content.

This makes the study of greenwashing more relevant than ever, especially in the context of digital media. Advertisements have the power to not only influence targeted consumer purchase behaviours but also shape the attitudes and behaviours of society as a whole (Budinsky & Bryant, 2013). Digital platforms – such as social media and websites – through which these online advertisements are disseminated, have become an increasingly common medium of communication between consumers and companies, especially since the latter can now influence and reach wider audiences more effectively than ever before. While these platforms enable companies to communicate sustainability initiatives and appeal to environmentally conscious consumers, they have also facilitated the increase of greenwashing in recent years. It has hindered genuine green marketing initiatives (even leading to the emergence of 'green-blushing' where companies downplay and fail to promote their environmentally responsible initiatives for fear of being accused of greenwashing), and it has a significant impact on consumer trust, loyalty, purchasing decisions and perceptions of corporate ethics. Studying it is crucial for identifying deceptive practices and helping regulators and consumers make informed choices.

The demand for eco-friendly or 'green' products has grown over the years due to increasing consumer awareness and consciousness regarding environmental sustainability. So companies often engage in greenwashing as a way to attract these consumers, to enhance brand reputation, gain a competitive edge or even to mitigate criticism or regulatory scrutiny.

This can occur at the product level, where individual products are marketed as eco-friendly without adequate evidence (TerraChoice, 2009). To address and categorize these practices, the TerraChoice Group developed the 'Seven Sins of Greenwashing', which explain common misleading strategies:

(1) Sin of Hidden Trade-Off: Highlighting one positive environmental attribute while ignoring significant negative impacts. For instance, energy companies may promote 'clean energy' but continue environmentally damaging oil drilling, harming natural habitats and biodiversity.
(2) Sin of No Proof: Making claims without evidence, such as stating a product contains a percentage of recycled material without credible proof.
(3) Sin of Vagueness: Using unclear or overly broad terms like 'sustainable' or 'natural', which lack concrete definitions. An example is fast fashion brands

claiming 'sustainable collections' without addressing their unsustainable business models.

(4) Sin of Worshipping False Labels: Using fake certifications or labels to appear credible, such as 'guaranteed ethical product' without third-party verification.

(5) Sin of Irrelevance: Making true claims that do not matter, like stating a product is 'CFC-free' when CFCs are already banned by law.

(6) Sin of Lesser of Two Evils: Promoting a product as eco-friendlier than others in its category while ignoring the broader environmental harm, such as calling SUVs 'fuel-efficient'.

(7) Sin of Fibbing: Making outright false statements, such as claiming a product is '100% recycled' when it is not.

Contreras-Pacheco and Claasen described greenwashing strategies at the company level:

(1) Dirty Business: Companies with overall unsustainable practices highlight small sustainability efforts to distract from the harm caused by their core operations.

(2) Ad Bluster: Shifting focus to achievements unrelated to the major sustainability issues they should address.

(3) Political Spins: Manipulating government policies to favour their business under the guise of sustainability.

(4) It's the Law, Stupid!: Promoting actions required by law as voluntary environmental initiatives.

(5) Fuzzy Reporting: Using incomplete or unclear sustainability reports to paint a misleadingly positive image.

Béatrice Parguel, Florence Benoit-Moreau and Cristel Antonia Russell introduced a newer form, Executional Greenwashing, which does not rely on explicit claims but uses nature-evoking elements like green colours, nature sounds or images of wildlife and landscapes to create an illusion of environmental responsibility which primarily influences non-expert consumers, who are more likely to associate such visuals with eco-friendliness.

The history of greenwashing in India reveals a trajectory influenced by globalization, economic reforms and the digital revolution. Over the past few decades, as environmental awareness has grown in India, so has the tendency of businesses to exploit this awareness through greenwashing. In response to this trend, regulatory bodies like the Advertising Standards Council of India (ASCI) have introduced guidelines to address misleading environmental claims (ECs). These guidelines aim to promote honesty, transparency and substantiation in advertisements to safeguard consumer interests.

Greenwashing is particularly prevalent in industries such as consumer goods, fashion, energy, automotive and real estate, where sustainability has become a competitive differentiator. These sectors often leverage sustainability claims to appeal to environmentally conscious consumers, even when their operations remain far from eco-friendly.

Objectives

(1) Systematically analyze the visual and textual strategies used in green ads to convey sustainability messages in social media.
(2) Assess Indian consumer perceptions of sustainability claims in ads from companies accused of greenwashing.
(3) Evaluate the alignment of social media marketed green claims and the companies' known environmental practices in India.
(4) Explore the implications of greenwashing on Indian regulatory frameworks and green marketing.

Approach and Methodology

The paper uses a two-part study, which was found to be effective for understanding how digital media is used to promote sustainable activities and to attain a deeper understanding about the depiction of greenwashing and its subsequent perception. A mixed approach of qualitative and quantitative analysis has been taken. The qualitative approach was taken as a primary approach, with critical discourse analysis being used to analyze and interpret the advertisements and posts, along with the help of existing literature, and this was accompanied with a comprehensive visual semiotic analysis to understand the visual elements of the content. A quantitative approach was conducted with a survey to evaluate consumer perceptions, which was then analyzed and used to support the qualitative data.

Critical discourse analysis is a form of content analysis. It analyzes how specific actors formulate claims and how these claims fit into broader social practices. It helps understand the types of claims that the actors want to establish as self-evident and accurate. It points out the rhetorical strategies used to communicate those realities in a convincing, effective or natural way. It shows how their assertions and the frameworks of meaning that the actors rely on, spread through communication practices.

Data Collection

A variety of companies and brands were selected across many broad categories, based on the criteria that they all must have a digital presence (be it in the form of Google advertisements or social media presence), communicate their sustainability activities and products and have a revenue of more than 1,000 crores in FY 2023. This included brands and companies such as Nestle India, Raymond Group, Himalaya Wellness Company, H&M, Godrej Group (which includes the Good Knight brand), Hindustan Unilever (HUL) (which includes the Surf Excel brand) and Fabindia.

Advertisement Search Platforms

The advertisements and social media posts analyzed were sourced from Instagram, Facebook, Google advertisements and Amazon storefronts. Instagram was particularly favoured due to its rising popularity and ability to support diverse formats such as posts and reels.

Sample Selection Technique

The simple random sampling method was used to select respondents for the survey, ensuring a fair representation of consumer perceptions.

Company Profiles

Nestlé India

Nestlé India began operations in 1961, introducing products that have become household staples. It offers diverse options across categories like dairy, beverages and ready-to-cook meals. Maggi, launched in the 1980s, is one of its most popular offerings. Today, Nestlé holds a strong position in the Indian FMCG market, with a significant share in instant noodles, infant nutrition and confectionery. Its focus on innovation and health-centric products keeps it a leader in the market.

Himalaya Wellness Company

The Himalaya Wellness Company, established in 1930, is synonymous with herbal healthcare. Known for blending Ayurveda with modern science, it delivers solutions in personal care, pharmaceuticals and wellness. Its flagship product, Liv.52, revolutionized liver care globally. In India, the company is a trusted name for skincare, hair care and baby care products, with a wide reach across urban and rural areas.

H&M

H&M entered the Indian market in 2015, bringing global fashion trends to local customers. It operates through a mix of physical stores and an online platform, offering affordable and stylish clothing for all age groups. With its commitment to sustainability, H&M's Conscious Collection is gaining attention. The brand caters to the fast-fashion segment, competing with other global players and appealing to a young, fashion-forward audience.

Godrej Group

The Godrej Group, founded in 1897, has a legacy that spans across industries like appliances, real estate, consumer goods and agriculture. From launching

India's first indigenously produced locks to becoming a trusted name in soaps with brands like Cinthol, Godrej has grown immensely. Today, it enjoys a loyal customer base and a reputation for quality and innovation.

Hindustan Unilever

HUL, with roots in India since 1933, is one of the country's largest FMCG companies. Its vast portfolio includes iconic brands such as Dove, Surf Excel and Kwality Wall's. HUL's products are found in nearly every Indian household, spanning personal care, home care and food and beverages. The company has made significant strides in sustainable practices, contributing to its strong brand image.

Fabindia

Fabindia, established in 1960, celebrates India's rich artisan heritage. It works with rural craftsmen to offer a wide range of handcrafted apparel, home furnishings and organic products. The brand's emphasis on natural materials and traditional techniques has won it a unique place in the market. With stores across major cities, Fabindia is a go-to destination for those seeking ethnic and sustainable products.

Any existing allegations of greenwashing against some of these companies and brands were obtained from case studies and research articles.

In accordance with Eisenhardt's (1989) recommendation of selecting between four and ten cases, six digital advertisements and social media posts from these companies and brands were chosen for the survey from the company's official social media handles (Instagram and Facebook, most were obtained from Instagram due to its increasing usage and popularity and its ability to support a wide variety of formats such as posts and reels), advertisements from Google and Amazon storefronts. More than a 100 responses were recorded.

Literature Review

There has been substantial research conducted with regard to the advertising and marketing communication used by brands to influence consumer perception. The colour, image, logo and font and their relationship with green semiotics have been explored in detail, and it has been observed that there is a predominantly negative association between green semiotics and consumer perceptions (Worakittikul et al., 2024). Thus, challenging the assumption that eco-friendly branding can be used to positively influence consumer perception. Green advertising, while using nature-evoking elements, can also be seen as misleading, and its impact on the brand' ecological image can be positive on non-expert consumers, while expert consumers can be less influenced (Parguel et al., 2015). It was further observed in the same study that providing only environmental performance information is not enough to counteract the lack of a positive consumer perception, and a basic labelling system was found to be much more effective in creating a more positive image of the brand for experts and non-experts alike. Social media marketing, with its ever-evolving series of strategies, has been looked at in detail for its relevance to the Fast Fashion Industry to understand where does one draw the line between whether a brand is sustainable or just being greenwashed. A content analysis using the social media platform, Instagram, by renowned fast-fashion brands – ZARA, H&M, Shein and Mango – was conducted to understand the various strategies that these companies use to promote sustainability efforts. Vague information, lack of proper proof of sustainability claims and generalization of efforts stood out as strategies that typically define greenwashing. However, it was interesting to note that data collected on consumer perception largely showed a positive outcome for brands – consumers were positively inclined to perceive the brands as more eco-friendly after viewing the Instagram posts, while also recognizing the broad and misleading nature of the green communication (Schwenk Lagun, 2022). A deeper analysis with regard to greenwashing across digital platforms revealed that greenwashed posts, presented in visual or textual formats, were perceived as less credible compared to non-greenwashed ones, with text-based posts generally receiving higher credibility ratings than visual ones (Laukas, 2023). In the Indian context, a research study on the prevalence of greenwashing in Indian English print advertising found that 51.7% of the claims were greenwashed, with a significant portion being vague or ambiguous (67%), and most claims lacking specificity (60%). Image-related claims dominated, comprising 60% of the advertisements, and only 3.3% utilized certifications to substantiate their claims (Fernando et al., 2014). An experimental study on the role of colour – specifically a comparison of green and red – was conducted, and it was found that the colour green enhanced positive evaluations and conceptual fluency when associated with ECs, while the colour red failed to produce the same effect. It was also found that the positive impact of green could mislead consumers regarding the environmental superiority of products, highlighting the potential for greenwashing, thus posing risks of consumer deception if not used carefully (Joon Yong Seo, 2007). It is observed that the level of understanding of greenwashing significantly affects the relationship between receptivity to green advertising and green purchase behaviour, such that those with a higher awareness of greenwashing were more likely to respond positively to green advertising messages, leading to increased green purchase behaviour. It is also observed that income levels impacted the relationship between environmental consciousness and green purchase behaviour where higher-income consumers displayed greater environmental consciousness, which positively affected their green purchase behaviour (Jog & Singhal, 2020). It was observed that consumers with higher greenwashing awareness were more discerning in their purchases, indicating a growing consumer consciousness regarding ECs. Using a mixed-methods approach, it was observed in another study that significant percentage of consumers failed to identify greenwashing claims, and many expressed a favourable attitude towards misleading advertisements. Observations indicated that most respondents recognized the 'sins' of greenwashing, such as hidden trade-offs and lack of proof (Katait, 2017).

Research on corporate appropriation of environmental discourses through green washing and green capitalism – with a focus on three brands – revealed that these advertisements made vague and unexaggerated claims that often misled consumers by promoting the idea that purchasing green products could solve environmental issues, while simultaneously obscuring the larger systemic problems associated with consumerism and corporate practices. The study concluded that such advertising practices reinforce neoliberal ideologies and individualism, detracting from the need for collective action for meaningful environmental change (Budinsky & Bryant, 2013).

It was revealed in a study that while news stories significantly influenced public concern, photographs were found to be more effective in mobilizing public support for specific policy action. It was observed that text in advertisements could directly change opinions and influence the importance of underlying values, whereas photographs did not have the same effect on opinion change (Jenner, 2005).

Companies whose business models are in ecologically sensitive sectors, such as food and oil, are increasing recognizing in the need to have a favourable consumer perception towards its practices. The BP Oil Spill, which continues to remain one of the biggest ecological disasters, saw BP working hard to undo the damage it started causing its brand image. Research on the strategies employed by BP focused on the use of visual imagery to manage its reputation. By utilizing a visual semiotic approach and systematically tracking changes on BP's website from 2006 to 2014 with a focus on its Environment page, the study revealed that BP strategically shifted from a text-heavy presentation to a more visually driven approach, adopted a 'horizontal triptych' format that separated the 'ideal' (BP's aspirations and commitments) from the 'real' (the actual practices and outcomes) practices and noted the use of vibrant colours like green, the use of specific symbols and images, such as its logo (the sun or Helios) and photographs of scientists and engineers at work, effectively perpetuating greenwashing practices (Kassinis & Alexia Panayiotou, 2017).

Conceptual Model of the Study

The current study aims at understanding consumer awareness regarding greenwashing, the importance of sustainability for a consumer and the overall perception of greenwashing that consumers have towards ECs that companies make (refer Fig. 5.1).

Data Analysis and Interpretation

A survey questionnaire was administered to 114 respondents with the following profile, to understand consumer perception towards the marketing communication of the brands in question.

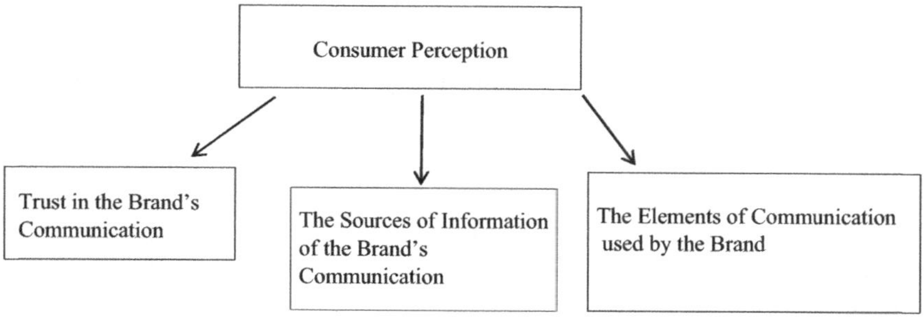

Fig. 5.1. Elements Influencing Consumer Perception.

An analysis of data revealed insights into consumer perception towards greenwashing, while also understanding the extent to which consumers perceive positively, the sustainability claims of companies.

Demographic Profile of Respondents

As per the survey conducted (refer Table 5.1), in terms of gender, 58.8% are female, and 41.2% are male. Most respondents (71.1%) belong to the 18–25 age group, with smaller proportions in older categories. Regarding education, 62.3% have completed undergraduate studies, followed by 16.7% with postgraduate degrees and smaller shares at other levels (refer Table 5.1). Occupation-wise, 60.5% are students, 21.1% are job holders, and the rest include homemakers, entrepreneurs and others. Together, these show a predominantly young, educated and student-heavy respondent base.

As per the survey conducted (refer Fig. 5.2), social media and product labels were chosen as the main information sources, with TV being least used at just

Table 5.1. Demographic Profile (*N*-114).

Variable	Frequency	Percentage (%)
Gender		
Male	47	41.2
Female	67	58.8
Age		
18–25	81	71.1
26–35	14	12.3
36–45	7	6.1
46 and above	12	10.5

(Continued)

Table 5.1. *(Continued)*

Variable	Frequency	Percentage (%)
Occupation		
Student	69	60.5
Entrepreneur	5	4.4
Homemaker	13	11.4
Job holder	24	21.1
Others	3	2.6
Education		
Matriculation	5	4.4
Intermediate	13	11.4
Under-graduation	71	62.3
Post-graduation	19	16.7
Doctorate	6	5.3

Source: Authors' compilation of data collected.

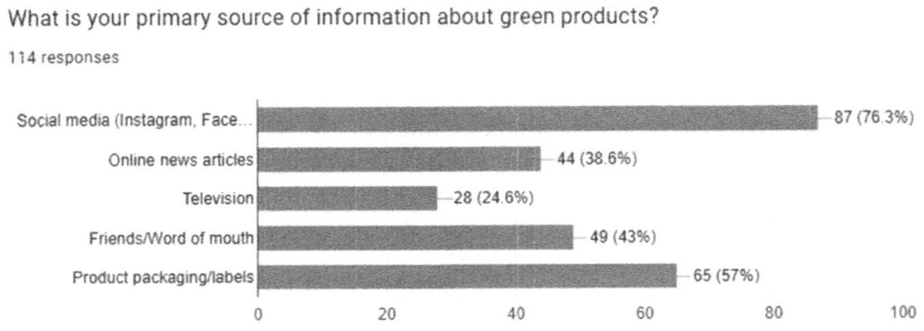

Fig. 5.2. Respondents' Primary Sources of Information About Green Products.

208%. Half the respondents mentioned that they valued sustainability and felt misled by claims, citing ambiguous language, misleading images and vague labels as top greenwashing tactics and also believed Indian companies lack accountability (refer Fig. 5.3). 54.4% found testimonials as the most influential social media content on ECs. Transparent communication and trusted certifications (74.6% each) were seen as key to building trust, while independent audits ranked lowest (45.6%) (refer Fig. 5.4).

Subsequent questions evaluate the consumer responses towards specific advertisements for greenwashing, and the responses for the same have been elaborated in the following section with their respective companies.

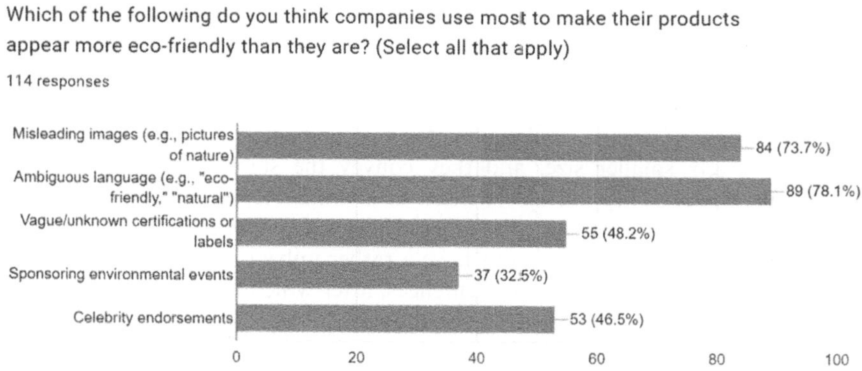

Fig. 5.3. Respondents' Perception of Use of Type of Marketing Content Companies Use to Exaggerate Eco-Friendliness of Products.

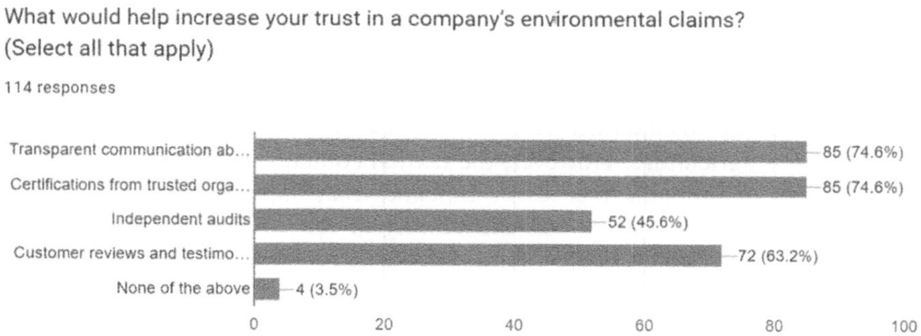

Fig. 5.4. Respondents' Preference of Marketing Strategy That Might Increase Trust in a Company's Environmental Claims.

Analysis of Consumer Perception to Social Media Marketing

Nestle India

A series of seven posts were posted on Nestle's official Indian Instagram handle, nestle.india, on 5 December 2020.

Another series of six posts were posted on Nestle's official Indian Instagram handle, nestle.india, on 9 December 2020. In 2020, Break Free From Plastic published its annual report, naming Nestle as one of the world's top plastic polluters for the third year in a row.

Short yet bold phrases are used in the posts. In both these post series, the phrase 'We will reach NET ZERO by 2050' occupies a slide, carrying considerable emphasis as a bold pledge and commitment. It conveys an aspirational tone, and it is written in an active voice, portraying a sense of determination. Similarly, the phrase 'Tackling CLIMATE CHANGE can't wait and neither can we'. occupies half a slide in the first series, but has its own slide in the second series. This phrase has also been written in an active voice, and its wording portrays a sense of urgency and action. The text phrases in the other slides are in a comparatively smaller size, and they convey the steps Nestle is taking to achieve its pledge. They are also written in a similar tense and are all accompanied by images that dominate the slides. There are no literary devices identified in the textual content. The captions have a rather upbeat and inspirational tone and are limited to just one or two sentences, after which a link of the company website is provided, followed by the hashtags.

In terms of the visuals, Nestle employed a bright green colour scheme, perhaps to signify eco-friendliness and nature, and used it for its backgrounds, text colours and even to highlight terms like 'Reducing Waste', 'Zero' and 'Sustainable Feed'. Images such as cattle fields and solar panels occupy the majority of the slides as carousels and seem to emphasize the connection to sustainability, and the images of the workers and scientist seem to portray credibility, action and innovation. A sans serif font is used for the text, with the keywords written in caps in a brush font, adding simplicity, hierarchy and emphasis.

The posts have a simple design layout that are made as carousels, giving it a smooth and narrative flow. The themes that could be derived from these post series were related to climate action, renewable energy and energy efficiency and eco conscious agriculture. However, the textual content of these posts does not mention any quantifiable metrics or timelines that support the vague claims made. Moreover, the current unsustainability of the core operations (such as water and plastic pollution) remains unaddressed, and this points towards greenwashing.

The survey results for Nestle's second post series received mixed reactions regarding its sustainability claims. While 31.6% of respondents had a positive first impression, a significant 33.3% remained neutral, indicating varied opinions. Regarding Nestlé's claim of being 'sustainable', 45.6% of respondents believed it, 33.3% were uncertain and 21.1% rejected it, reflecting some scepticism. Elements like nature-associated visuals (53.5%) and terms like 'sustainable' (50%) were the most trusted features, while only 39.5% trusted the ad due to the level of detail provided. Interestingly, familiarity with the brand's environmental efforts influenced just 16.7% of respondents, and 21.1% found no elements convincing. This suggests that while visual cues and buzzwords are impactful, the lack of specific details and broader credibility concerns may limit the advertisement's overall effectiveness.

Himalaya Wellness Company

Digital campaigns were run on Himalaya's official Instagram handle, himalaya_facecare, on 24 July 2024 and 26 September 2023, respectively. The posts are an advertisement for the Himalaya Purifying Neem Face Wash.

In the first post, the text is rather short and simple. The claim '100% Recyclable Tube'. is made, followed by the text 'A Greener Planet With Every Wash', which seemingly suggests that every use of the product contributes towards the 'greening' of the planet. The caption also reflects this same optimistic tone, saying that while the skin stays protected with the facewash, so does the planet, followed by a few hashtags in the end. In the second post, the text 'WE DON'T LEAVE ANY TRACE BEHIND' is prominently displayed and gives two meanings: It does not leave any pimple marks behind and does not leave any trace of the product behind, suggesting that the product is biodegradable; hence in this way, this text uses a pun as a literary device. This is followed by the claim '100% recyclable Pack', and the claim of no pimple marks. These same claims are emphasized in the caption of the post as well and are followed by more hashtags.

In the first post, the product is centrally aligned in the post and seemingly placed on a rock, against a blurry green foliage background, thus giving the post a natural setting. Due to its positioning and size compared to the text, it stands out as a dominating element. In the second post, the product is set against a prominent green background with neem leaves around it, and is positioned in the right, and here too, due to the size and position, the product stands out the most. Both these posts utilize a green colour scheme in different ways, again signifying the connection of its product to nature. The logos are placed in the upper right-hand corner of the post. The font used for the text in both these posts is sans serif, and it is bolded for emphasis in the second post's tagline, thus adding emphasis and hierarchy while maintaining simplicity.

Both these posts have a minimalistic and simple design layout, and overall themes that can be found in them are related to skincare and recyclability. However, despite the repeated focus on the latter, both the posts failed to clarify how the 'tube' or 'pack' is recyclable, especially since it appears that the product is made of plastic. Moreover, their implied claim of leaving no trace of product behind is incorrect, since recyclability does not in itself necessarily mean the product is biodegradable. In addition, there seems to be no clear evidence or disclaimers given to back the claims made.

The survey results for the second post also received mixed perceptions of the advertisement's sustainability claims. While 37.7% of respondents had a positive first impression, a significant 36.8% remained neutral, indicating divided opinions. Regarding the Himalaya's claim of the pack/tube being 'recyclable', 31.6% believed it, 39.5% were uncertain and 28.9% rejected it, highlighting potential scepticism and a lack of clarity. Elements like nature-associated visuals (52.6%) and terms like 'recyclable' (53.5%) were the most trusted features, whereas only 28.9% trusted the ad due to detailed information. 36.8% were influenced by familiarity with the brand's environmental efforts, but 13.2% did not find any elements convincing. Thus, while nature imagery and buzzwords are effective, the lack of concrete proof seemingly reduced the overall credibility of the post.

H&M

H&M ran a campaign for a collection titled 'Conscious' during 2019. In November the same year, ads consisting of clothing made from sustainably sourced materials were showcased across different media and H&M provided in-store recycling bins where customers can drop off their old clothes and receive a redeemable coupon in return.

The same year, the Consumer Authority investigated H&M under Norway's Marketing Control Act and lawsuits were filed in Missouri and New York against H&M's Conscious line. I:CO (short for I:Collect), which runs H&M's garment-collecting scheme – mentioned that only 35–45% of the collected textile was recycled, while failing to provide transparency about the recycling process, production methods or the carbon footprint of its products. It was found that H&M's Conscious line contained a higher percentage of harmful synthetic materials compared to its main line, and once recycled plastic is transformed into clothing, it cannot be recycled again, leading to these items ultimately ending up in waste.

For the campaign, the text is short and does not contain any additional details. They are written in an active voice, which gives a sense of motivation and also acts as a call to action. In all these images, recyclability is greatly emphasized upon. The name of the campaign itself, 'Conscious', seems to be used to create an association with H&M being environmentally conscious or eco conscious, and the tagline 'Sustainable fashion future' also seems to support the same. Additionally, phrases such as 'Close the loop' as a metaphor not only refer to the production of garments itself but also seem to imply the closing of the circular fashion supply chain by the recycling of old garments to manufacture new garments. The tone used in the third picture is appreciative and positive, claiming that old garments will get a new life, and stating the incentive of 15% discounts.

The themes that could be derived from the images are of recyclability and circular economy. However, just like in Nestle's case, not only does this particular initiative contribute to environmental degradation but it also ignores the overall unsustainability of H&M as a business towards the environment.

The survey results showed that the images received a majority of positive impressions (71.1%), with 47.4% rating it as positive and 23.7% as very positive, while 25.4% were neutral. 50.9% of respondents believed the brand's claims of being 'recyclable' or 'conscious', 30.7% were uncertain and 18.4% outright rejected the claims. The most trusted element was the use of terms like 'conscious' or 'recyclable' (48.2%), followed by nature-associated visuals (42.1%), detailed environmental information (41.2%) and familiarity with the brand's initiatives (36.8%). Notably, only 13.2% found no element convincing.

Godrej Group

The images of 'Protekt handwash' and 'Goodknight Mosquito repellant' were observed on Godrej's digital storefronts on Amazon and Flipkart, respectively.

In 2015, Godrej Consumer Products Limited faced scrutiny and was fined Rs. 15 lakh by the ASCI for misleading claims regarding its Godrej No. 1 soap, which was marketed as '100% natural', 'biodegradable' and 'eco-friendly', despite containing synthetic ingredients. Similarly, in 2012, Godrej Industries was fined Rs. 5 lakh by the ASCI for falsely advertising its Good Knight Fast Card mosquito repellent as '100% natural' and 'chemical-free'.

The ads have a very simple design layout overall. The major theme that can be derived from them is naturalness. And despite the immense emphasis on it, the ads fail to adequately clarify the actual implication that it meant to convey with use of the phrases 'naturally derived' or 'natural actives', and they also ignore the overall environmental impact of the product. Moreover, there is no valid evidence, certification or endorsement given to substantiate the claims made.

The survey result of the second ad showed a predominantly neutral response (48.2%) in terms of first impressions, with only 35.1% in total expressing positivity and 15.8% reacting negatively. A significant majority (55.3%) did not believe the ad's natural claims, while 31.6% were uncertain, leaving only 13.2% convinced. While trust in the ad was mainly driven by the use of terms like 'natural' (39.5%) and elements associated with nature (27.2%), the majority 40.4% found no element trustworthy, highlighting scepticism. The lack of detailed, verifiable information and overreliance on vague language likely contributed to perceptions of greenwashing and distrust in the brand's sustainability claims.

Hindustan Unilever

An advertisement published on 13 September 2021, closely coinciding with the celebration of World Cleanup Day, which was held annually on 20 September, was closely observed. The same ad led HUL, in 2019, being fined Rs. 10 lakh by the Central Pollution Control Board after the Ministry of Environment and Forests filed a case against them for falsely advertising its Surf Excel Easy Wash detergent as '100% natural' and 'environment-friendly', despite containing synthetic ingredients and harmful chemicals.

The tagline text in the ad tells that the product has '...100% ECO FRIENDLY BIODEGRADABLE ACTIVES...', and the other text near the bottles mentions '100% RECYCLABLE BOTTLE', all to indicate that the product is eco-friendly. The tone is optimistic and upbeat, and there are no literary devices used.

The ad uses a storytelling narrative to positively promote its product. And the major themes that can be seen are eco-friendliness and environmental activism. However, the ad fails to provide any legitimate proof to back its claims of biodegradability and does not clarify how the bottle is '100% recyclable'. It fails to address the harm caused by its production or manufacturing as well as the harm caused by the company's core operations on the environment.

Trust was most influenced by the use of terms like 'biodegradable' or 'eco-friendly' (53.5%) and nature-related visuals (38.6%), though fewer trusted the ad based on the level of detail provided (26.3%) or familiarity with the brand's environmental track record (26.3%). Notably, 22.8% found no convincing elements.

Fabindia

A series of posts on Fabindia's official Instagram handle, fabindiaofficial, between March and June 2023, coincided with World Environment Day celebrated annually on 5 June. The posts are an advertisement for Fabindia's sustainability initiative, 'Shunya'.

The overall themes derived from these series are sustainability and recycling. However, the posts seem to lack any credible data or certifications to back up its claims. The post also fails to address the environmental impact of the manufacturing process of recycling Polyethylene Terephthalate into the products or the impact of the potential end-of-life issues of the products on the environment. Terms like 'Zero carbon footprint' are ambiguous and vague as well. Overall, while these posts may not seem to directly point at greenwashing, it risks the potential of having it.

The survey results of these posts show a generally positive response, with 64.9% having a positive or very positive first impression and 48.2% trusting its claims. Key trust factors included the use of terms like 'sustainable' (59.6%) and detailed information (48.2%), while 36% cited associations with nature. However, 28.9% were uncertain about the claims, and 14.9% found no trustworthy elements, highlighting a need for clearer communication.

The Legal Perspective

The Consumer Protection Act, 2019, plays an important role in addressing greenwashing practices in India. It defines unfair trade practices as those employing deceptive methods to market goods or services and thereby includes greenwashing practices. In order to prevent misleading marketing practices that make false ECs, it gives the Central Consumer Protection Authority (CCPA) the power to issue necessary guidelines to prevent unfair trade practices and protect the interests of the consumers.

In January 2024, the Central Authority issued the draft guidelines for the prevention and regulation of greenwashing. These guidelines apply to all advertisements, service providers, product sellers, advertisers or agencies involved in promoting specific goods or services. The guidelines state that ECs should be clear and unambiguous and that such claims should be adequately substantiated. It also states that ECs should avoid using generic terms such as 'clean', 'green', 'eco-friendly' and '100% organic' without adequate explanation, substantiation or disclosures. The draft guidelines also state that while using any technical terms, the meaning and implications of such terms should be clearly explained. Also, it states that all ECs should be truthful and accurate.

The Consumer Protection Act also empowers consumers to file complaints against deceptive practices enabling individuals to fight against greenwashing. Consumers can file complaints with the District, State or National Consumer Disputes Redressal Commission.

Key Findings

The brands chosen have been found to use visual and textual strategies, including green imagery and eco-friendly buzzwords, to make sustainable claims, raising concerns about misleading consumers. Overall, the survey results reveal mixed consumer perceptions, with visual elements and buzzwords seemingly fostering initial trust but scepticism emerging due to vague or unsupported claims. Regulatory bodies like the ASCI and the CCPA are addressing these issues by issuing guidelines to counter the same.

Conclusion

As digital media becomes an integral part – in shaping consumer responses and business functioning – the line between genuine sustainability and deceptive representation blurs, within which lies the uncertainty, where businesses will not only have to contend with shifting consumer expectations but also deal with the increasing level of consumer awareness and the evolving regulatory scrutiny, all while operating in an increasingly unpredictable world marked with climate change and resource constraints.

Businesses must shift from false messaging to evidence-based practices that encourage transparency and engagement, not short-term gains through greenwashing that can potentially lead to loss in consumers' trust and legal repercussions. The regulatory system needs robust guidelines, transparent reporting and collaboration with third parties for credible certifications to address this practice.

Sustainability must go beyond marketing tactics – it must be integrated in the very core operations of a business itself.

Limitations and Scope for Further Research

The study relied on a single post (or post series) per brand and company, risking generalization and bias, and was mainly focused on the FMCG industry. Future studies can include multiple social media platforms in its sample and analyze engagement metrics like likes and comments. Additionally, incorporating audio analysis and video formats and examining brand communication strategies immediately before and after greenwashing scandals could provide deeper insights into consumer perceptions of Corporate Social Responsibility advertising and greenwashing.

References

Budinsky, J., & Bryant, S. (2013). "It's not Easy being green": The greenwashing of environmental discourses in advertising. *Canadian Journal of Communication, 38*(2), 207–226. https://doi.org/10.22230/cjc.2013v38n2a2628

Eisenhardt, K. M. (1989). Building theories from case study research. *The Academy of Management Review, 14*(4), 532–550. https://doi.org/10.2307/258557

Fernando, A. G., Sivakumaran, B., & Suganthi, L. (2014). Nature of green advertisements in India: Are they greenwashed? *Asian Journal of Communication, 24*(3), 222–241. https://doi.org/10.1080/01292986.2014.885537

Jenner, E. (2005). *Greenwashing: Visual communication and political influence in environmental policy*. The Manship School of Mass Communication.

Jog, D., & Singhal, D. (2020). Greenwashing understanding among Indian consumers and its impact on their green consumption. *Global Business Review*. https://doi.org/10.1177/0972150920962933

Katait, S. K. (2017, February). Green washing in India: An alarming issue — Misleading and deceptive environmental claims in advertising. *International Journal of Commerce and Management Research, 3*(2), 91–97. https://www.managejournal.com/assets/archives/2017/vol3issue2/3-1-46-626.pdf

Kassinis, G., & Panayiotou, A. (2017). Visuality as greenwashing: The case of BP and deepwater horizon. *SAGE*, 1–23. https://doi.org/10.1177/1086026616687014

Laukas, M. O. (2023). *Navigating the intricacies of greenwashing across digital formats: An examination of non-greenwashing and greenwashing posts in visual and textual contexts* [MA Thesis]. BI Norwegian Business School in Oslo.

Parguel, B., Benoit-Moreau, F., & Russell, C. A. (2015). Can evoking nature in advertising mislead consumers? The power of 'executional greenwashing'. *International Journal of Advertising, 34*(1), 107–134. https://doi.org/10.1080/02650487.2014.996116

Schwenk Lagun, C. (2022). *Sustainable or greenwash? An analysis of how fast fashion brands use social media marketing* [Dissertation]. Universidade Católica Portuguesa.

TerraChoice Group Inc. (2009, April). *The Seven Sins of Greenwashing: Environmental claims in consumer markets, summary report (North America)*. http://www.sign-sofgreenwashing.org. https://www.scribd.com/document/14475597/The-Seven-Sins-of-Greenwashing

Worakittikul, W., Saenwerm, C., & Naruetharadhol, P. (2024). Unlocking the secrets of green semiotics: The revolutionary power of eco-symbols in transforming consumer perceptions and catalyzing behavioral shifts in emerging markets. *PLoS One*, 1–39.

Yong Seo, J. (2007). *The role of color in environmental messages and claims: Green can be both beneficial and misleading* [Dissertation]. The University of Utah.

Chapter 6

Eco-Stories: How Companies Interact in the Digital Age

Narinder Kaur[a], *Dheeraj Nim*[b] *and Sanjay Bahl*[c]

[a]Maharishi Markandeshwar (Deemed to be University), India
[b]Oriental University, India
[c]Indus International University, India

Abstract

This chapter focuses on innovative marketing policies and its transformation in ecosystem mushrooming in India. As the country experiences rapid modernization, technological advancements and evolution of consumer habits, corporate and industrial sectors have adopted new marketing approach to facilitate and accelerate sustainable growth, ensuring green promotion. This chapter explores in what methods businesses are coupling with the environmentally aware consumer through the digital marketing, influencer mixtures, data testing, and useful marketing. It also highlights the importance of community-based marketing, social media activism, and eco-labeling in influencing purchases and fostering corporate responsibility to environmental goals. This chapter analyzes successful examples from green and sustainable industries in India to demonstrate how these strategies are not only helping to build an ecosystem to scale up sustainability but also how such consumption models are preserving biodiversity while also creating economic benefits for the future. This chapter highlighted the place of market and environmental stewardship integration across the price in scores of holistic and sustainable growths in growing Indian market landscape.

Keywords: Ecosystem growth; artificial intelligence; sustainability; innovative marketing strategies; personalization; social media

Eco Illusions, 109–132

doi:10.1108/978-1-83662-782-120261006

Introduction

The ecosystem has evolved as a put in which the primary system of association movement and appendage pith in the modern readymade goods. An e-ecosystem is a network of interconnected technologies, data, and users that interact to create value, and controls are the means by which this ecosystem is managed, secured, and navigated (Sinha & Park, 2017). A concept of business ecosystem refers to a network of a business, partners, customers, and more stakeholders in a business environment, which are shared together to generate and maintain value in a specified business domain (Sattari & Mehrabi, 2016). Yes, the uplifting of an ecosystem for your space or even specific companies can be crucial and critical at the same time as industries tend to grow upwardly interdependent as they age. While expansion is the more common context for discussing the makeup of the ecosystem by the company, adapting and optimizing its relationships with the nodes encompassing it in the network to fuel the success of the company and the other is an important facet of ecosystem growth (Jia et al., 2022). Ecosystem-based companies benefit from pooling resources, harnessing complementary proficiencies, and rapidly scaling-up to meet changing market demands (Stefan, 2024). And thus, the development of these ecosystems is an emergent variable of long-term business success.

Multiple elements intensify the demand for ecosystem expansion in today's competitive landscape. In the same way, digital transfiguration means that companies must continually spike reliance on reciprocal partnerships; expectations being raised on the other side are perhaps the tougher ask, is understandable (Hensmans, 2021). Organizations cannot rely on past competitive strategy frameworks, such as cost leadership or item separation; they must create value by establishing an ever-evolving ecosystem that (3) promotes invention, (4) enables cooperation, and (5) triggers value for everything associates (Nim et al., 2024). Through science creating within these ecosystems, corporations can unlock opportunities for boom and ensure ongoing competitive advantage (Mohammadi et al., 2024).

It is nothing but the fuel that accelerates the growth in the ecosystem. Traditional principles suggest that marketing defined a function, serving primarily to promote a firm's products and services to external customers in an attempt to create awareness (Guha et al., 2021). Ecosystem development is far beyond that as far as marketing goes. It not just works on promotion related but also works on relationship making and shared value as well. Marketing continues to building trust with many partners and other ecosystem investors. Through marketing policies (Lettner et al., 2022), it defines the brand look, partners, and joint work in the ecosystem.

Enterprises can establish awareness, impact the relevant stakeholders, and strengthen the relationships fueling the growth of the ecosystem through creative marketing efforts (Juma et al., 2023). Content marketing, co-branding marketer partnerships and communities can help position companies as main players within an ecosphere. Marketing oriented toward customer experience and engagement perspective also creates end value building ecosystem stewards making ecosystems a real value to the participants (Kumar et al., 2025).

The aim of this chapter is to explore creative marketing, which is beneficial in ecosystem development. It brings into light how innovative marketing has a supporting act in growth-driven new, creative ideas that are found on the platform with the most lucrative partnerships being established for life. The key objectives are investigation of the role of marketing policies in building of healthier ecosystems, identification of best practices in raising collaboration, and discussion of the impact of marketing innovation on long-term validity of ecosystems. From these conclusions, the chapter will provide a broad comprehension of the essential part of marketing in creating maintainability and accomplishing focused advantages within the advanced trade environment.

Understating of Ecosystem Growth

Definition of Ecosystem Growth

Business ecosystem development is the expansion and evolution of connected networks of organizations (or individuals) in collaboration to deliver value and enhance innovation. The ecosystems: electronic, trade, and innovation-based digital ecospheres can be proposed as a network of tech firms, and software comes together with their users and platforms to link with each other to drive digital transformation in particular companies or industries. In contrast, trade ecosystems involve the cooperation of firms in a system functioning in a similar market environment, often impacting one another's success. Innovation ecosystems emphasize the pipe forming and practicing of new ideas, products, or services by uniting together multiple actors from researchers, startups, investors, and the likes (Rifa'i et al., 2023).

Ecosystem Elements

An ecosystem contains process in parallel that is integral to its growth movement and sustainability (Fig. 6.1). These include:

Stakeholders: In this context, stakeholder is any person who has an interest in the ongoing of the organization. These host enterprises, consumers, investors, regulators, or other players that add value to or receive value from an ecosphere. To manage innovation and ensure their ecology yields benefits stakeholders often coalesce into association or partnerships (Khanna, 2024).

Resources: The resources are both tangible and intangible assets that fuel the growth of the ecosystem. These include capital, IP, brain power, and manpower. For successful interpretation of ecosystem sustainability, balanced allotment and proper utilization of resources are very significant.

Platforms: A platform is the foundation or network that makes an interaction possible between different components. In the field of electronics, a platform is in the form of market places, online, cloud services, and social media system. In the context of business ecosystems, platforms refer to technological or physical environments that enable businesses to interact for business transactions. They serve as station to connect the participants to each so that they can exchange information and partnership and provide services.

Business Ecosystem: The Business Ecosystem is defined as all the connected relations between the entities of the ecosystem; organizations there are large networks. It consists of the goods of customer support, e-rivalry, supply line direction, and tool sharing. Strong networks enable swift information sharing, partnership building, and innovation or agile problem-solving.

Growth of Ecosystem: Why Does It Matter?

For an ecosystem to thrive over the long term, it must be nurtured and supported. A mature ecosystem allows businesses and other participants to tap into numerous revenue opportunities:

Adaptation and Innovation: As the ecosystem grow from maturity, there are high rise of innovation. Participants have such diversity that inspires new ideas, in particular, product and service invention. Ecosystem is more agile to growth and can march ahead to adopt the changes in market environment, technology, or in consumer conduct (ElZarrad et al., 2022).

Resource Optimization: As ecosystems where, the exchange of resources whether org-related knowledge, collaborate in capital or technology sharing become more prevalent. This sharing of business resources diminishes oversupply and forces the businesses to capitalize on one another's assets, thus raising productivity and functional cost reducing (Obrenovic et al., 2023).

Contention's Value, Advantages: Globalized and completely ready environment of the companies adds significantly to the contention merits for organizations since a solid net of accomplices and players gets made. It offers a host of advantages as it enhances customer relationship, improves supply chain management, and expands market reach.

Old School vs New School Marketing Tactics

Classical Marketing Approaches

In the traditional marketing, sales were the main key factor of each business. It was considered that the best way to reach consumers is through mass media, advertising in TV and newspaper, and communication where only one side of the

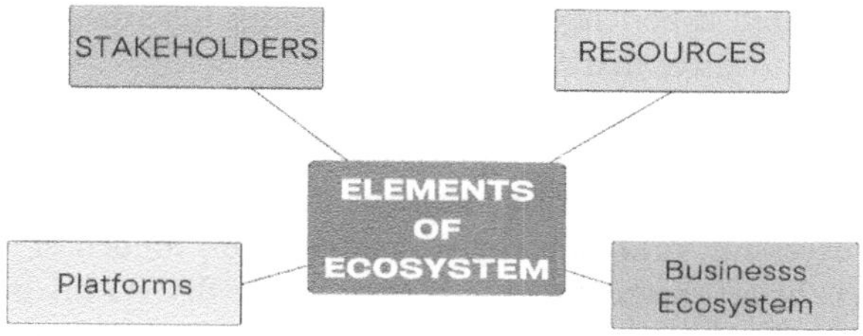

Fig. 6.1. Elements of Ecosystem. Source: Author's Compilation.

conversation happens, with no feedback. These have usually been bolted onto large crowds through traditional pathways—television, radio, print commercials, billboards, and being there in person. So, some of the key features of traditional marketing are as follows:

Direct Sales: The salesperson directly reaches out to the end customers to sell products or services. This approach creates personal ties with service, but this is extremely expensive strategy. This strategy needs a number of customers for direct sale, and also the rate of maintaining market is limited, hence limiting scalability (Wirtz & Kowalkowski, 2023).

One-Way Communication: Marketing is a one-way street for the producer to deliver his product to the customer. There is no way for the end customers to respond or give feedback to the business on the product. There can be no interaction and trust-building due to one-way communication.

Mass Media: You can also reach the masses through advertising, such as television, radio, newspapers, and magazines. These are all ways to engage large audiences. But this strategy has disadvantages as well, like mass media, wasting resources because the message is spread to a in general as opposed to target audiences.

Despite its widespread applicability, traditional marketing comes with many caveats, particularly in the context of ecosystem expansion. For instance, sales people cannot be everywhere to do direct sales and cannot target niche customers, which results in the business's ability to reach potential customers in an effective way. This does not create customer engagement or build a customer relationship, which is why the one-way model is not a practical marketing tactic—there is no customer feedback.

Innovative Marketing Strategies

The adoption of innovative marketing strategies makes businesses more dynamic, creative, and interactive so that they leverage digital techniques, data-based information, and customer-centered strategies (Rosário & Dias, 2023). The objective of strategies is to engage customers in more smooth ways, enhance personalized experiences, and build loyalty towards brand. The main components of innovative marketing include:

Originality: Novel marketing is all about thinking beyond the horizon and feeding unique and stimulating content that makes sense to the audience such as excessive viral campaigns, gamification, influencer partners, and these sorts of off-the-beat methods that simply BANG hit attention.

Digital Tools: The emergence of the digital platforms changed the way marketing was carried out completely. Best social media, Search Engine Optimization, and email campaigns all target niche audiences as precisely as possible. Websites, apps, and interactive platforms create an immersive experience that is out of the horizon of traditional media avenues.

Deriving Insight from Data Source: The bedrock of contemporary marketing is the utilization of advanced analytical methods and big data. It helps a company record customers' actions, interests, and engagement trends, so it can adjust its advertising strategies to achieve the maximum effect. With predictive analytics and artificial intelligence (AI), businesses can predict customer needs and develop customized marketing journeys (Singh & Kaunert, 2024).

Two-Way Communication: Real-time interaction with customers via social media and other digital tools creates opportunities for feedback, dialogue, and deeper engagement, empowering the customers to be able to voice opinions, ask questions, and engage in brand-building processes.

Innovational marketing aims through higher retention rate, loyalty, and advocacy not only how to get people in the front door but how to keep them through the back door. Hence, these would be more scalable and adaptable as they will have high degree of dependence on technology and data. This means that businesses can adapt to any change in market and consumer behavior instantaneously.

Transitioning From Conventional to Contemporary Marketing

Evolution of the Market: The change in the marketing industry is due to the shift from traditional marketing to ingenious marketing strategies. This affects by some factors as follows:

Technological Development: Digital technologies have completely transformed the way business interacts with consumers. As the internet, mobile devices, and social media became integral to life, businesses were forced to use creative marketing tactics in order to keep up in a networked world.

Changing Customer Expectations: Customers today expect brands to communicate in a very personalized and real-time manner. They won't tolerate general advertising anymore; they expect content that speaks directly to their needs, their wants, and their values. New expectations call for more tailored and engaging experience, which is where creative marketing comes in.

Market Saturation: Traditional marketing strategies are insufficient to differentiate brands as markets become increasingly crowded and competitive. Teaching through Innovative Marketing which focuses on creativity and customer engagement gives businesses new solutions to compete from one another in a crowded marketplace.

Purposeful Intent: The modern marketing-centric approach is less expensive compared to traditional marketing, especially mass media campaigns. That's because digital platforms, social media, and content marketing are less expensive and provide more personalized, measurable reach. The data-driven aspect also allows companies to be able to optimize campaigns for the highest return as possible.

Globalization and Real-time Interaction: In the modern world, brands would have to deal with customers of various cultures and countries. Hence, new trends in marketing, which is obviously, real-time social networking, can help companies to transform the customer to interact with them in real-time platforms that traditional campaigns may not offer.

Technology, data, and creativity have radically transformed this marketing landscape. In some scenarios, traditional strategies still hold their territory, but business growth for the ecosystem is tilted towards innovative approach. Such approaches are the key to engagement, personalization, and adaptability. While ensuring it can meet shifting expectations of consumers, these behaviors will allow companies to differentiate themselves from their competition and form deeper connections with their audience.

Innovative Marketing Strategies to Boost the Ecosystem

In the interconnected world of today, business ecosystems are slowly emerging as the foundation of success. It entails the mutualistic connections among brands, stakeholders, partners, and influencers, and the leveraged strategic marketing approach can drive their growth (Purchase & Volery, 2020). Here are some of the most creative ecosystem expansion/tactical marketing strategies, including content marketing, influencer and community marketing, data-driven personalization, partnerships, agile marketing, and experiential campaigns.

Learn More About Content Marketing and Thought Leadership

Content marketing can be one of the primary tactics any brand can employ to position itself as the thought leader in the ecosystem. Thus, by regularly sharing helpful, meaningful and appropriate content, brands can show expertise as well as develop trust in the process. It will attract partners and customers around the brand, placing the brand at the hub of the ecosystem.

Example

Inbound marketing of HubSpot is an outstanding example of inbound marketing. It has established a massive content ecosystem of blogs, webinars, eBooks, and online courses to assist customers and partners. It enables the marketing software leadership does attract the clients and the strategic partners through this content and the alignment of the clients with the company's value and objectives (Warrior Smiling, 2024).

Microsoft Partner Network—Another example. Microsoft's partner-driven motion with its broad partner network is content-led. The firm bolsters its ecosystem via resources, thought leadership articles, and exclusive events to inspire innovation and promote the adoption of Microsoft technologies while enabling partners to develop.

These examples also highlight the content marketing strategy of engaging and maintaining a mix of customers, partners, and influencers that go to bat for growth in an ecosystem.

Influencer and Community Marketing

Influencers and communities are critical for ecosystem growth, especially with regards to reach and building trust. Influencers can help brands reach new audiences, especially those that have similar values (Aguilar & Arbaiza, 2021). Social networks or specialized forums can serve to disseminate the brand message and promote brand loyalty.

Example

GoPro: GoPro has effectively leveraged influencer and community marketing by harnessing user-generated content, sharing social media posts featuring their product. The brand pulls on a worldwide network of explorers and sports fans who film and shareable videos on GoPro products. This helps not just in creating brand messages but also helps in making community (University of Brighton, 2020).

Marketing and Personalization With Data

Leveraging big data, AI and machine learning (ML) will devise personalized marketing strategies for individual members of the ecosystem humanly. Understanding customer behavior helps in delivering customized content, products and services to different stakeholders.

Example

Amazon: Data-driven marketing at Amazon provides customers with a personalized shopping experience. Whether recommending products based on past purchases or tailoring email campaigns to the individual, Amazon leverages ML to make each user feel uniquely addressed. This customized ecosystem feels and potential for rewards create customer loyalty and drive ongoing usage (Majury, 2024).

Partnerships and Co-Creation

Expansion of business ecosystems is driven by strategic partnerships and joint ventures. By working with other organizations, brands can harness the strengths of each other to pool ideas, expertise and resources together and create new products, services, or solutions that ultimately help everyone involved. In this manner, it goes beyond just expanding the brand's reach, creating tighter bonds in the ecosystem.

Co-creation Example

Nike-Athletic Trainer: This app is a collaboration with Apple; it provides an excellent athletic trainer to Nike, and the app is recommended running sync with apple fitness ecosystem This partnership not only improved the ecosystems of both brands but also provided a seamless user experience that was appealing to fitness enthusiasts and tech-savvy consumers (Winay, 2024).

Brands not only benefit by mutual shared resources, technologies, and networks but also grows their ecosystem by their contribution as they work together to create unique offering.

Agile and Adaptive Marketing

As the business surrounding ecosystem has always been dynamic, they must swiftly adapt to these changes because you also have a (very short) attention span.

Example

***Spotify An Example Of Agile Marketing*:** The brand curates its playlists according to user preferences and seasonality. Moreover, Spotify adapts its promotional strategies per local preferences to ensure that its messaging remains relevant across diverse markets (pplco.in, 2024).

Event Organization and Experiential Marketing

Experiential marketing is focused on creating highlights of experiences that engage customers and partners on an emotional level. They range from events to interactive displays to immersive campaigns that foster physical touchpoints within the ecosystem and drive deeper exploration.

Example

Coca-Cola's 'Share A Coke' Experience: Coca-Cola's 'Share a Coke', in which a name was printed on a bottle, was a new relationship that created interaction with the customer experience, which they could then share on social media. Fostering such an ecosystem added another layer of brand loyalty and engagement to the brands ecosystem (Coca-Cola, 2025).

Such innovative marketing strategies that create meaningful connections between brand and customers, partners, influencers, and other stakeholders serve as effective tools to build the business ecosystem and gain extensive growth. Strategies like Ecosystem Growth Marketing, Content Marketing, Influencer Marketing, Data-Driven Personalization, Partnerships, Agility and Experiential Campaigns. Such marketing strategy ensures market domination as well as allowing forming a long-term relation with the company affiliates, maintaining the life of an ecosystem.

Innovation in Marketing: Technologies and Tools

The rise of advanced technologies and digital tools has revolutionized marketing, enabling businesses to connect with customers in more personalized, data-driven and impactful ways. Through augmented reality and virtual reality, companies can create interactive experiences that allow consumers to engage with products or services in a simulated environment, fostering emotional connections and driving sales. Additionally, social media platforms, automation tools, and influencer marketing have reshaped the way brands talk to audiences, enabling on-demand engagement and viral spread. AR/VR technology: These revolutionary technologies allow virtual product testing and storytelling. Moreover, customer relationship management (CRM) software, email marketing platforms, and search engine optimization (SEO) tools contribute to a more effective process and foster broader outreach. These breakthroughs are improving customer journeys and delivering tangible results and ROI for brands across verticals.

As the digital marketing industry continues to evolve, technology is facilitating the expansion of ecosystems through the development of new opportunities, better audiences, and improved efficiency. Now, there is a wide array of tools and platforms that allow businesses to scale their marketing activities while keeping the experience personalized and ensuring proper engagement. Digital platforms, automated marketing tools, AI , ML and blockchain are the key enablers of this transformation. These go hand in hand, creating a more dynamic and efficient marketing ecosystem, be it a business or consumer-centric.

Digital Platforms: New Ecosystem Expansion

The basis of the modern approaches that enable businesses to reach out to people at an affordable price while being efficient is all based on the digital marketing platform. These channels offer social media platforms like Facebook, Instagram, LinkedIn, and many more, a unique chance for brands to connect with their communities in real time, thus managing direct communication and hence providing an effective feedback loop to improve customer relationships (Kumar et al., 2023; Saini et al., 2025). They enable targeting of certain demographic groups, thereby assisting businesses to promote their products to appropriate audiences with right messages (Barykin et al., 2020).

Another pillar of digital platforms, especially those that have already established their business online, is email marketing, in which businesses keep in touch with their current customers by sending them personalized content, promotions, and news. With SEO, businesses can drive traffic to their websites and these two can work together for better traffic on resources, i.e., Google search. SEO helps provide better user experience by providing relevant, helpful content that matches user queries, leading to more qualified leads. Taken together, these web platforms create business ecosystems where customers, partners, and influencers engage with the brand and develop their own cycles of engagement and growth.

Artificial Intelligence and Machine Learning

AI and ML techniques revolutionizing the marketing strategies by bringing forth data-derived intelligence, improving targeting accuracy, and optimizing content delivery. AI algorithms are capable of splitting the audience of companies in a very accurate way to ensure that the companies' marketing message reach the most relevant people. An example can be predictive analytics, where AI predicts customer behavior, and the business alters its strategy according to the prediction leading to increased conversion rates and customer satisfaction.

Along with audience targeting, AI and ML are also improving content optimization. Creating personalized, engaging content for customers is the best way for marketers to go about it, and tools like ChatGPT (which uses AI for content generation) help them get it right and get it fast! ML algorithms are especially useful for analyzing massive amounts of data to understand which content strikes a chord with various customer demographics, allowing businesses to make real-time adjustments to their campaigns (L. Ma & Sun, 2020).

Another set of tools that are becoming essential to sales and marketing ecosystems within companies are AI-driven chatbots. Providing instant, round-the-clock customer service support, and personalized recommendations enriches customer service and enhances brand loyalty. These AI models learn constantly from interactions and improve their ability to cater to the customer needs, which makes marketing strategies more dynamic and effective.

Blockchain and Trust: Increasing Transparency

Blockchain technology (primarily linked to cryptocurrencies) is slowly but surely becoming the next heavy-hitter in establishing trust and transparency in marketing ecosystems (Tyagi & Khanna, 2025). It is because blockchain provides a transparent, immutable ledger of transactions and helps ensure data authenticity and integrity. In the case of advertisements, for example, blockchain technology can track real-time ad impressions, clicks, and conversions to enable marketers to pay just for valid interactions.

Technology has transformed marketing by offering powerful tools that enable a business to connect with customers, scale its operations, and build trust in its ecosystems. Digital platforms enable direct engagement while tools to automate marketing make the efforts streamlined and effective. The use of AI and ML is driving changes in targeting and content optimization to provide greater insights and a better experience for customers (Vashishth et al., 2024). Unlike this, blockchain adds transparency as well as trust, which allows businesses to function with a clean image. Yet, these technologies must continuously drift towards granting a more relevant marketing strategies framework aimed to guide the sustainable attributes of the entire ecosystem (Peres et al., 2023).

Evaluation of Ecosystem Growth due to Marketing Strategies

Marketing strategies are accounted for the development of business ecosystems at an increasing pace. Not only do these strategies further drive brand awareness and customer acquisition, they also enable the collaborative creation of the value between several stakeholders, from suppliers and partners to customers and even competitors. The marketing practices of 2023 aren't mere punched tickets anymore that you buy at a counter, waiting for the ride to begin, but they're rather a batch of personalized interventions with targeted customers at each touchpoint to ensure success—data-based personalization, influencer partnerships, co-branding, experiential marketing, digital storytelling, community building, etc. These approaches, in turn, allow an entity to establish deeper connections with their customers and drive organic growth which can lead them to build an ecosystem. The digital transformation in marketing has increased businesses' ability to reach broader audiences with campaigns based on social media platforms, SEO, and more optimized content at lower costs, for example. This creates value for so many other players in the ecosystem including logistics operators, digital platforms, or offering complementary services. This interconnection fosters faster ecosystem growth.

Furthermore, co-creation of value is a marketing strategy of the ecosystem, where customers and partners add to ideas, feedback, and innovations. As such, it allows companies to tweak offerings instantly, allowing for shorter time to market and better product–market fit. Amazon and Airbnb, for example, have leveraged user-generated content and peer-to-peer reviews to build trust and facilitate buy-in, which has accelerated the growth of their respective ecosystems exponentially. In these types of models, marketing add on marketing and promotion is not only correlative for the markets. At the same time, performance-based marketing that aligns interests between parties such as with affiliate programs or influencer relationships incentivizes cooperation between parties. This combination amplifies the volume of marketing messages while also enhancing their trustworthiness and contextuality, resulting in better conversion rates and contributing to organic growth across the ecosystem.

Data analytics and AI in marketing strategies is another crucial aspect of ecosystem growth. Today, companies use consumer behavioral data as their foundation to segment markets, customize messaging, and forecast trends. Such predictive capabilities allow businesses to respond to consumer needs proactively, improving user experience and satisfaction in turn. This acts as a cycle, as the more data being created and analyzed, the more intelligent and responsive to the needs of the ecosystem. Also, marketing alliances ensure organizational strategic alliances which help enter new markets and help leverage each other's strengths. For example, co-marketing campaigns allow brands to leverage one another's customers to create a mutual growth path. This interdependence is rewarding for sustainable growth in the digital economy.

Moreover sustainability- and social impact-focused marketing strategies are increasingly affecting ecosystem dynamics. Consumers will prefer to buying a product of companies with some ethics and social responsibility. By making sure their marketing messages are aligned with societal values, companies can attract like-minded partners and customers and build a purpose-driven ecosystem. Such value-aligned strategies yield customer loyalty and fuel advocacy leading to a more resilient ecosystem. It also establishes a strong emotional connection from community-based marketing, which fosters user interaction, peer support, and shared experiences with the brand. Not only does this drive-up customer lifetime value, but it also turns users into active participants within the ecosystem.

To sum up, marketing strategies very much contribute to growth within the ecosystem through better visibility, collaboration, technology leverage, and synergies with customers' values. We are now operating in a world that has moved beyond linear value chains to market ecosystems where strategic marketing has transitioned to become a core engine for creating and managing complex systems of value creation and delivery. This fusion leads to a system that is dynamic, robust, and self-sustaining, enhancing collective development and innovation for all its stakeholders.

Marketing policies fuels the success and continuity of ecosystems. Hence, measuring the key performance indicators (KPIs) becomes very important, which will give one an idea about the health and the potential of the ecosystem. These metrics allow businesses to evaluate how effectively their marketing efforts contribute to cultivating growth, engagement and long-term value.

Metrics and KPIs

Data on KPIs are significant to gauge the effectiveness of marketing strategies. Some of the KPIs that they consider are as follows:

- ***Engagement Rates:*** The engagement metrics, including likes, shares, comments, and time spent on content, help to determine how effectively the audience is interacting with marketing efforts (Shahbaznezhad et al., 2021).
- ***Network Growth:*** How much does an ecosystem thrive as new partners, customers, or contributors join?
- ***Customer Acquisition and Retention:*** The ROI of the entire ecosystem is crystallized by measuring the speed at which new customers or users are acquired and how well existing ones are retained in the long term (Allioui et al., 2023).
- ***Brand Loyalty:*** Brand loyalty, commonly tracked by repeat purchases or long-term involvement, is an indicator of how well the ecosystem has enabled enduring relationships (Hossain et al., 2024).

Feed-Back Loops and Continuous Improvement

AI can also help in the analysis of feedback loops to refine and optimize marketing approaches (Rad et al., 2022). Ecosystem growth is not only a process—it is a continuous ecosystem assessment towards market adaptation. The gap can also be identified by seeking feedback from stakeholders, including customers, partners, or influencers, to fill the gap in the strategy and find new opportunities for engagement. Analyzing user behavior, gathering survey data, and measuring performance metrics can produce actionable insights to improve content, refine messaging, and adjust tactics.

Lasting vs Immediate Effect

Effect of marketing strategies on the growth of an ecosystem can be analyzed from short-term as well as long-term perspectives. Metrics over short periods of time, like the upswings in sales or visits to websites, only offer a glimpse of how successful marketing campaigns are when it comes to delivering quick wins. These results are crucial to maintain momentum while onboarding initial users or partners into the ecosystem (Wu et al., 2017).

However, the long-term impact is more important for sustainable growth (Ortiz-de-Mandojana & Bansal, 2016). Building accretive layers of trust, loyalty, and brand recognition is a process that takes time and consistency and strategy—ecosystem development is not built in a day. Sustainability in an ecosystem is best measured by long-term KPIs, such as customer lifetime value, market penetration, and network resilience (Micheli & Muctor, 2021). Growing ecosystems will experience steady increases in active users, partnerships, and value co-creation over time. In fact, the long-term perspective enables this ecosystem to stay relevant, adaptable, and able to thrive when market dynamics shift.

Real-World Case of Creating Ecosystem Through Marketing

Apple—Creating A Digital Ecosystem via Seamless Integration

Some of the leading forces that built a strong and prosperous digital ecosystem using brilliant marketing strategies are tech companies, one of them is Apple. Key to Apple's success has been its emphasis on an integrated user experience that spans its product ranges, from iPhone, iPad, Mac and Apple Watch to software and services, including iCloud and Apple Music.

The company pitches its products not so much as stand-alone gadgets but as essential components of an integrated digital ecosystem. Apple's advertising draws attention to how the utility of these products is easily coordinated with one another. "Ecosystem of Apple" is presented itself as "Luxuary" high end experience to make more desirable brand (Patov, 2024).

One vital strategy that Apple employed is in the form of a 'closed-loop' ecosystem in which consumers are encouraged to buy additional Apple devices as those devices work together. Implementation of strategic pricing, value-added packages like Apple One and committing to a platform with software like iOS and macOS helps in retain customer base. This makes reach and trust bigger in association with the brand, as it is not sold only through actively promoting it but bought through word of mouth (Patov, 2024).

Greenwashing in Innovative Marketing Policies Within Environmental, Social, and Governance (ESG) and SDG Frameworks

Over the past decade, though, ESG criteria and the SDGs of the United Nations have been gaining traction worldwide as frameworks for corporate responsibility and sustainable development. With the trend of companies aligning their business models and marketing strategies with ESG and SDGs, an increased attention has been driven on greenwashing—the misleading of consumers and stakeholders into believing a company's products and policies are environmentally friendly or that they are taking meaningful steps to be responsible based on tick-box and not real business practice (Todaro et al., 2024). Greenwashing as one of the new marketing ploys has now become developed as a complex and systemic issue, especially when it comes to firms that use the most updated technologies to invent so-called green campaigns to show the public the corporate socially responsible image, yet without executing any real and also visible sustainability activities (de Freitas Netto et al., 2020). Although ESG and SDG integration seeks to strengthen responsible management and positive environmental and societal impacts, the usage in a manipulated way of these structures for branding and profit reduce their credibility and the progress toward actual sustainability.

Modern marketing is advanced by digital transformation, AI-based personalization, influencer culture, and data-driven storytelling. Brands can use these to create a strong narrative around sustainability even when there is little to no follow through. For example, businesses can use terms like "eco-friendly", "green", or "carbon-neutral" without clear verification or third-party certification. While these promises are appealing to sustainability-minded consumers, they may hide unsustainable practices such as overuse of resources, labor exploitation in the supply chain, or weak commitment to carbon offsetting. Additionally, marketing material can carefully provide favorable information while omitting vital specifics about the company's overall environmental footprint. This incomplete picture, however, not only misinforms investors about consumer attitudes but also obscures and distorts the contribution that ESG disclosure could make to informing stakeholders such as investors and regulators about the true risk involved in investing in or otherwise doing business with certain companies.

This coupling between brand identity and SDG targets (i.e., sustainable consumption (SDG 12), climate (SDG 13), decent work (SDG 8)) has emerged as a norm in marketing. Most corporations advertise and promote their commitment to these goals, on their websites, in their sustainability reports, and on social media—usually with insufficient audit mechanisms (Lashitew, 2021). For instance, a fashion brand might promote a range of clothing made from recycled materials as its contribution to SDG12 and overlook the broader environmental vandalism and waste generated by the rest of its fast fashion supply chain. This selective engagement is certainly beneficial for a brand like Vans, which gets to enjoy a sustainable image, without actually implementing systemic changes in its business operations. The risk is not just reputation but eroding public confidence.

At the same time, the lack of common, enforceable frameworks across jurisdictions for ESG and SDG marketing have also enabled greenwashing. ESG reporting is still mostly voluntary and is produced in spurts that have different metrics and methodologies across companies and industries. Though some jurisdictions such as the EU have tightened disclosure requirements through the initiatives such as the Corporate Sustainability Reporting Directive (CSRD), many markets do not yet have robust enforcement regimes in place. This regulatory void makes it a fertile field for use by companies to commodify ESG frameworks as reputational capital in name, not in reality. Lacking numerical targets, deadlines, and the means to verify results, companies will be able to say they are responding to the SDGs without anyone being able to hold them to account, reducing the universal goals to little more than advertising's moral washing line (Y. Ma et al., 2024).

What's more, the proliferation of ESG-branded investment products has given companies more reason than ever to go greenwash. As ESG factors become commonplace in the portfolios of institutional investors and asset managers, companies are under pressure to look like they are ESG compliant and sustainable. This financialization of ESG performance in turn increases the pressure to greenwash to make sustainability credentials look good for marketing. The funds themselves can also be guilty of greenwashing; ESG classifying funds might still hold companies with shady practices because they score a high mark elsewhere on the ESG criteria, sparking a false narrative of ethical investing. The outcome is a vicious circle in which superficial sustainability reporting meets investor demand without spurring actual change.

The advantage of digital platforms and social media creates the power behind greenwashed messaging. Digital influencers, content creators, and sponsored posts can be at the helm of corporate sustainability initiatives and claims—even when the purveyor is unaware. For example, a beauty influencer with millions of followers may promote a "clean-beauty" line because they were given specific talking points by a corporate public relations person without doing their due diligence on how ingredients were obtained, whether labor was ethical, or if the product line is safe for the environment. Yet due to the immersive nature of digital storytelling and the emotional connection it can evoke, consumers may find it more challenging to differentiate between authentic marketing offerings and performative efforts (Nobanee, 2024). Additionally, algorithmic echo chambers that only serve specific types of sustainable content can mislead consumers into believing false narratives are proven true simply due to the frequency of being presented (Cownie & Rutherford, 2024).

Yet although the phenomenon of greenwashing seems to permeate practically every corner of the market, various tools and frameworks exist to mitigate the risk and restore legitimacy to ESG- and SDG-based marketing. First, third-party certifications go a long way to substantiate claims; B Corp, Fair Trade, Cradle to Cradle, and LEED serve as mandatory approvals that validate efforts. Second, transparent reporting—the GRI, SASB, and TCFD—provides a vetting process for successful ESG endeavors; however, safety in numbers does not rely on social sentiment but instead on other regulatory agencies to render disclosures about GRI-, SASB-, and TCFD-approved metrics—or lack thereof—mandated and uniform across industries. Finally, institutions of government and non-profits can serve as a watchdog with the potential for partnership to expose greenwashing through dedicated investigation, campaigns for community awareness, and even litigation.

Ultimately, corporate accountability depends on creating a culture of trust and transparency from within. Chief marketing officers must communicate with chief sustainability officers and interdepartmental teams to ensure that whatever is communicated to the external public is accurate about current assets, as opposed to aspirational SWOT assessments. Companies that have shortcomings will have a better chance of survival if they acknowledge where they are currently falling short and where they hope to improve over time, providing a plan versus an inaccurately perfect facade with no truth behind it. Over time, consumers will appreciate unvarnished enterprises more than those hiding behind deception.

Eco-Illusion in Innovative Marketing Policies

Eco-illusion, a term for marketing under the banner of sustainability the underbelly of modern marketing in India's rapidly growing modern marketplace is coming under the grip of innovative strategies and increasingly putting up the fig leaf of sustainability. This is greenwashing on steroids, where businesses promote themselves as green when at their core they're not, you risk breaking consumer trust and tricking the ecosystem to grow (Edwards, 2019). As India faces an explosion of ecosystem mushrooming especially in digital and consumer play platforms, such shenanigans can displace stakeholder efforts, detract from genuine sustainable innovation pathways, and create a greenwashing culture (Ernestivita & Kumar, 2004). The revolution of marketing gangways must then be grounded in transparency, measurable impact and authenticity. Solutions to the greenwashing problem include strict regulation, the creation of external auditing groups to monitor sustainability claims, and consumer education to facilitate recognition of legitimate, trustworthy green claims (Parguel & Johnson, 2022). Additionally, any new startups or companies that reinforce real impact (proven environmental impact) can help transform the ecosystem towards genuine growth. Moreover, for India to go ahead, right placement along with innovative marketing under accurate sustainability principles must be done in order to build a strong, competitive and ethical business ecosystem. Here are number of ways to cut greenwashing. To break through greenwashing in the realm of new marketing policies, corporate communications should focus on the pillars of transparency, authenticity, and accountability (Crime, 2023). In terms of more specific, general claims, those that are both clear and third-party certified can encourage marketers to be "truthful and substantiated" when it comes to the environmental performance of a product. Life cycle assessments and transparency around supply chains help consumers to make more informed decisions and brands more responsible for the environmental impact, including stakeholder engagement (e.g., NGOs, sustainability pundits or community opinions) in the marketing plan, as it also adds to credibility. Further, by instituting internal controls—like sustainability audits and ethics committees—it can be more effective to oversee and correct misleading behaviors. Equally important is education and training for the marketing team on environmental issues and ethical communication.

Conclusion

In this chapter, we discussed how innovative marketing strategies play a vital role in the ecosystem development. For instance, we first talked about how traditional marketing models have had to give way to more dynamic, interactive, and consumer-centric approaches. The incorporation of digital tools and platforms, such as social media, content marketing, and influencer partnerships, has immensely bolstered companies' capabilities to interact with their audiences on a more profound level (Singha, 2024). We insisted that we focus on data-driven marketing in which companies can demonstrate how consumer behavior affects their decisions and how their strategies are now tailored to different needs.

Collaborative marketing is a key concept for the ecosystem growth (Graça & Camarinha-Matos, 2021). So instead of competing, businesses are uniting forces to increase their joint impact. With the help of partnership, co-branding or joint ventures, organizations get access to new markets and business opportunities that would be impossible to reach in their own. Moreover, the importance of sustainability in marketing is growing, as consumers are more aware of the environmental and social impact of their purchase decisions (Font & McCabe, 2017). In this scenario, ethical brands willing to undergo sustainability receive a competitive advantage in both congratulating and loyalty.

We talked about new technological advancements impacting on marketing practices, how AI would change marketing, to mechanize businesses and more crucially, to conveniently learn more about the preferences and behavior of customers (Jayawardena et al., 2022). Last but not least, the new virtual ecosystem, perhaps best known in its most recent form as the technology "metaverse," as well as virtual reality or VR would open new possibilities for businesses to deliver immersive customer experiences in ways heretofore unimaginable (Golf-Papez et al., 2022).

Now, as we look into the future, we can anticipate several burgeoning trends to capture the global marketing landscape to reshape marketing strategies at large and subsequently their contribution to the growth of the ecosystem. However, as AI technology continue to advance, it is expected to become an increasingly significant contributor to tailoring customer experiences (Flavián et al., 2019; Jayawardena et al., 2022). Above, marketers will have ML algorithms that will continue to improve the targeting as well as the messaging of their campaigns, which might lead to more personalized content for consumers (Bhardwaj et al., 2024).

This can be further seen in the trend of creating the digital twins of physical items as businesses seek to adopt this innovation, thereby blurring the line between digital and physical ecosystems. For example, the connection between physical and AR environments will facilitate a more immersive relationship with consumers by brands that will enhance ecosystem engagement and growth (Cowan et al., 2024). According to Biggemann et al. (2014), these consumers are seeking sense of responsibility on the part of the brands along with transparency in the value chain; thus, sustainability and ethics continue to be dominant in the marketing arena of business.

This is where business needs to realize the disruptive potential of new ways for marketing and leading ecosystems. Marketers in the future will need to adapt to the inevitable development of technology, build partnerships, and engage consumers in meaningful relationships to succeed in the new economy. With recent trends and tools in place, companies can also create sustainable ecosystems that not only offer improvements in their revenues but also helps better society and environment. This call to action is evident: with the growth in this space, businesses must adopt new marketing methods, stay ahead of the curve in an evolving market landscape, and ultimately lay the foundation for long-term growth.

References

Aguilar, D., & Arbaiza, F. (2021). The role of fitness influencers in building brand credibility through distorted imagery of healthy living on Instagram. In *Iberian Conference on Information Systems and Technologies*. CISTI. https://doi.org/10.23919/CISTI52073.2021.9476251

Allioui, H. ;, Mourdi, Y., Allioui, H., & Mourdi, Y. (2023). Exploring the full potentials of IoT for better financial growth and stability: A comprehensive survey. *Sensors, Vol. 23*(19), 8015. https://doi.org/10.3390/S23198015

Barykin, S. Y., Kapustina, I. V., Kirillova, T. V., Yadykin, V. K., & Konnikov, Y. A. (2020). Economics of digital ecosystems. *Journal of Open Innovation: Technology, Market, and Complexity*, *6*(4), 124. https://doi.org/10.3390/JOITMC6040124

Bhardwaj, S., Sharma, N., Goel, M., Sharma, K., & Verma, V. (2024). Enhancing customer targeting in E-commerce and digital marketing through AI-driven personalization strategies. In *Advances in digital marketing in the era of artificial intelligence* (pp. 41–60). https://doi.org/10.1201/9781003450443-4/ENHANCING-CUSTOMER-TARGETING-COMMERCE-DIGITAL-MARKETING-AI-DRIVEN-PERSONALIZATION-STRATEGIES-SUYASH-BHARDWAJ-NIRMESH-SHARMA-MAUSMI-GOEL-VANDANA-KIRTI-SHARMA-VINEETA-VERMAVandana

Biggemann, S., Williams, M., & Kro, G. (2014). Building in sustainability, social responsibility and value co-creation. *Journal of Business and Industrial Marketing*, *29*(4), 304–312. https://doi.org/10.1108/JBIM-08-2013-0161/FULL/XML

Coca-Cola. (2025). *Share A Coke memory maker experience | Coca-Cola*. Coca-cola. https://www.coca-cola.com/us/en/brands/coca-cola/share-a-coke-memory-maker

Cowan, K., Plangger, K., & Javornik, A. (2024). Insights for advertisers on immersive technologies the future of ads using VR, AR, MR and the metaverse. *Journal of Advertising Research*, *64*(3), 249–254. https://doi.org/10.2501/JAR-2024-023

Cownie, F., & Rutherford. (2024). *Sustainable digital advertising and greenwashing* (pp. 65–80). Taylorfrancis.Com. https://doi.org/10.4324/9781003168485-6/SUSTAINABLE-DIGITAL-ADVERTISING-GREENWASHING-RUTHERFORD-FIONA-COWNIE

Crime, G. M. (2023). Abuse of consumer trust in the digital market and the green market: The case of green washing in the Italian legal system. *Journal of Financial Crime*, *30*(6), 1692–1705. https://doi.org/10.1108/JFC-10-2022-0242/FULL/HTML

de Freitas Netto, S. V., Sobral, M. F. F., Ribeiro, A. R. B., & Soares, G. R. D. L. (2020). Concepts and forms of greenwashing: A systematic review. *Springer*, *32*(1). https://doi.org/10.1186/S12302-020-0300-3

Edwards, C. (2019). *Corporate greenwashing in online marketing*. University of Derby. https://www.researchgate.net/profile/Hannah-Chan-Edwards/publication/341323809_Corporate_Greenwashing_in_Online_Marketing/links/5ed785ed92851c9c5e74d12d/Corporate-Greenwashing-in-Online-Marketing.pdf

ElZarrad, M., Lee, A., & . . . R. P.-C. and translational, and 2022, undefined. (2022). Advancing an agile regulatory ecosystem to respond to the rapid development of innovative technologies. *Wiley Online Library*, *15*(6), 1332–1339. https://doi.org/10.1111/cts.13267

Ernestivita, G., & Kumar, V. (2004). *Beyond greenwashing: Genuine use of corporate social responsibility in digital marketing*. Grenze International Journal of Engineering and Technology. https://search.ebscohost.com/login.aspx?direct=true&profile=ehost&scope=site&authtype=crawler&jrnl=23955287&AN=181690776&h=INEwrqNVJ4oXwskOVGradfxl50j61%2BvWFw8tQ5OCG1BRUINvH6mO%2BGWfAwmdgZto2pjH6PbMEm5c1H3sFU8aWA%3D%3D&crl=c

Flavián, C., Ibáñez-Sánchez, S., & Orús, C. (2019). The impact of virtual, augmented and mixed reality technologies on the customer experience. *Journal of Business Research, 100*, 547–560. https://doi.org/10.1016/J.JBUSRES.2018.10.050

Font, X., & McCabe, S. (2017). Sustainability and marketing in tourism: Its contexts, paradoxes, approaches, challenges and potential. *Journal of Sustainable Tourism, 25*(7), 869–883. https://doi.org/10.1080/09669582.2017.1301721

Golf-Papez, M., Heller, J., Hilken, T., Chylinski, M., de Ruyter, K., Keeling, D. I., & Mahr, D. (2022). Embracing falsity through the metaverse: The case of synthetic customer experiences. *Business Horizons, 65*(6), 739–749. https://doi.org/10.1016/J.BUSHOR.2022.07.007

Graça, P., & Camarinha-Matos, L. M. (2021). Assessment of sustainable collaboration in collaborative business ecosystems. *Computers, 10*(12), 167. https://doi.org/10.3390/COMPUTERS10120167

Guha, S., Mandal, A., & Kujur, F. (2021). The social media marketing strategies and its implementation in promoting handicrafts products: A study with special reference to Eastern India. *Journal of Research in Marketing and Entrepreneurship, 23* (2), 339–364. https://doi.org/10.1108/JRME-07-2020-0097/FULL/XML

Hensmans, M. (2021). How digital fantasy work induces organizational ideal reversal? Long-Term conditioning and enactment of digital transformation fantasies at a large alternative bank (1963–2019). *Organization, 28*(1), 132–163. https://doi.org/10.1177/1350508420968185

Hossain, M., & H. K.-J. of S. S., and 2024, undefined. (2024). Exploring the evolution of brand loyalty in the age of social media. *Stm.E4journal.Com, 17*, 219–247. https://doi.org/10.4236/jssm.2024.173011

Jayawardena, N. S., Behl, A., Thaichon, P., & Quach, S. (2022). Artificial intelligence (AI)-based market intelligence and customer insights. *Artificial Intelligence for Marketing Management*, 120–141. https://doi.org/10.4324/9781003280392-10

Jia, H.(Michael), Wang, Y., Tian, Q., & Fan, D. (2022). Marketing innovations and sustainable development for the future ecosystem. *Journal of Cleaner Production, 372*, 133295. https://doi.org/10.1016/J.JCLEPRO.2022.133295

Juma, N., Olabisi, J., & Griffin-EL, E. (2023). External enablers and entrepreneurial ecosystems: The brokering role of the anchor tenant in capacitating grassroots ecopreneurs. *Strategic Entrepreneurship Journal, 17*(2), 372–407. https://doi.org/10.1002/SEJ.1462

Khanna, P. (2024). *Dark gamification: A tale of consumer exploitation and unfair competition* (Vol. 138–147). Igi-Global. https://doi.org/10.4018/979-8-3693-0724-3.CH008

Kumar, P., Dadwal, S., Verma, R., & Kumar, A. (2025). Prelims. *Digital Transformation for business Sustainability and Growth in emerging markets*, i–xxi. https://doi.org/10.1108/978-1-83549-109-620251014

Kumar, P., Oberoi, S., & Jaitly, R. (2023). *Impact of social media influencers on consumer engagement and its consequences in the emerging environment of metaverse* (pp. 225–240). https://doi.org/10.4018/978-1-6684-8898-0.CH014

Lashitew, A. A. (2021). Corporate uptake of the Sustainable Development Goals: Mere greenwashing or an advent of institutional change? *Journal of International Business Policy*, *4*(1), 184–200. https://doi.org/10.1057/S42214-020-00092-4/METRICS

Lettner, N., Wilhelm, S., Güldenberg, S., & Güttel, W. (2022). Customers as knowledge partners in a digital business ecosystem: From customer analytics towards knowledge partnerships. *Journal of Digital Economy*, *1*(2), 130–140. https://doi.org/10.1016/J.JDEC.2022.08.001

Ma, Y., Feng, G. F., Yin, Z. jia, & Chang, C. P. (2024). ESG disclosures, green innovation, and greenwashing: All for sustainable development? *Sustainable Development*, *33*(2), 1797–1815. https://doi.org/10.1002/SD.3210;SUBPAGE:STRING:ABSTRACT;WEBSITE:WEBSITE:PERICLES;WGROUP:STRING:PUBLICATION

Ma, L., & Sun, B. (2020). Machine learning and AI in marketing – connecting computing power to human insights. *International Journal of Research in Marketing*, *37*(3), 481–504. https://doi.org/10.1016/J.IJRESMAR.2020.04.005

Majury, A. (2024, August 3). *(78) AI case study Saturday: Personalised shopping experience - Amazon | LinkedIn*. https://www.linkedin.com/pulse/ai-case-study-saturday-personalised-shopping-amazon-alastair-tdqme/

Micheli, P., & Muctor, G. (2021). The roles of performance measurement and management in the development and implementation of business ecosystem strategies. *International Journal of Operations and Production Management*, *41*(11), 1761–1784. https://doi.org/10.1108/IJOPM-05-2021-0317/FULL/XML

Mohammadi, N., Maghsoudi, M., & Soghi, M. (2024). Innovation ecosystems in retail: Uncovering technological trends and collaboration networks through patent mining. *IEEE Access*. https://doi.org/10.1109/ACCESS.2024.3515290

Nim, N., Pedada, K., & Hewett, K. (2024). Digital marketing ecosystems and global market expansion: Current state and future research agenda. *International Marketing Review*, *41*(5), 872–885. https://doi.org/10.1108/IMR-04-2024-0108/FULL/XML

Nobanee, H. (2024). Digital entrepreneurship and greenwashing: Addressing ethical challenges in sustainable business. *SSRN*. https://papers.ssrn.com/sol3/papers.cfm?abstract_id=5073927

Obrenovic, B., Godinic, D., & Njavro, M. (2023). Sustaining company performance during the war-induced crisis using sourcing capability and substitute input. *Environment, Development and Sustainability*, *26*(12), 30001–30026. https://doi.org/10.1007/S10668-023-03892-9

Ortiz-de-Mandojana, N., & Bansal, P. (2016). The long-term benefits of organizational resilience through sustainable business practices. *Strategic Management Journal*, *37*(8), 1615–1631. https://doi.org/10.1002/SMJ.2410

Parguel, B., & Johnson, G. (2022). Beyond greenwashing: Addressing 'the great illusion' of green advertising. *Responsible Organization Review*, *16*(2), 59–66. https://shs.cairn.info/journal-responsible-organization-review-2021-2-page-59?lang=en&tab=texte-integral

Patov, A. (2024, September 4). *How apple elevates customer experience (CX) through ecosystem integration*. https://www.renascence.io/journal/how-apple-elevates-customer-experience-cx-through-ecosystem-integration

Peres, R., Schreier, M., Schweidel, D. A., & Sorescu, A. (2023). Blockchain meets marketing: Opportunities, threats, and avenues for future research. *International Journal of Research in Marketing*, *40*(1), 1–11. https://doi.org/10.1016/J.IJRESMAR.2022.08.001

pplco.in. (2024, November 21). *Case study: Agile transformation at Spotify – PPLCO.IN | Product Management | Strategy and Innovation | Leadership and Stakeholder Management | Agile Insights | User Research and Customer Insights | Design Thinking and UX*. https://pplco.in/case-study-agile-transformation-at-spotify/

Purchase, S., & Volery, T. (2020). Marketing innovation: A systematic review. *Journal of Marketing Management*, *36*(9–10), 763–793. https://doi.org/10.1080/0267257X.2020.1774631

Rad, F. F., Oghazi, P., Palmié, M., Chirumalla, K., Pashkevich, N., Patel, P. C., & Sattari, S. (2022). Industry 4.0 and supply chain performance: A systematic literature review of the benefits, challenges, and critical success factors of 11 core technologies. *Industrial Marketing Management*, *105*, 268–293. https://doi.org/10.1016/j.indmarman.2022.06.009

Rifa'i, A., Raharja, S. J., Rivani, R., & Purbasari, R. (2023). Three decades research in the field of business ecosystem. *Cogent Business & Management*, *10*(2). https://doi.org/10.1080/23311975.2023.2234143

Rosário, A. T., & Dias, J. C. (2023). How has data-driven marketing evolved: Challenges and opportunities with emerging technologies. *International Journal of Information Management Data Insights*, *3*(2), 100203. https://doi.org/10.1016/J.JJIMEI.2023.100203

Saini, H., Kumar, P., & Verma, R. (2025). *Social media and its influence on travel decision making* (pp. 261–282). https://doi.org/10.4018/979-8-3693-3972-5.CH011

Sattari, B., & Mehrabi, J. (2016). Model of marketing innovative strategies in international entrepreneurship: A global business environment. *Asian Social Science*, *12*(10), 76–91. https://doi.org/10.5539/ASS.V12N10P76

Shahbaznezhad, H., Dolan, R., & Rashidirad, M. (2021). The role of social media content format and platform in users' engagement behavior. *Journal of Interactive Marketing*, *53*, 47–65. https://doi.org/10.1016/J.INTMAR.2020.05.001

Singh, B., & Kaunert, C. (2024). Future of digital marketing: Hyper-personalized customer dynamic experience with AI-based predictive models. In *Revolutionizing the AI-digital landscape: A guide to sustainable emerging technologies for marketing professionals* (pp. 189–208). https://doi.org/10.4324/9781032688305-14/FUTURE-DIGITAL-MARKETING-HYPER-PERSONALIZED-CUSTOMER-DYNAMIC-EXPERIENCE-AI-BASED-PREDICTIVE-MODELS-BHUPINDER-SINGH-CHRISTIAN-KAUNERT

Singha, S. (2024). Navigating the social media maze: Strategies for effective digital marketing in a fragmented landscape. *Services.Igi-Global*, 84–106. https://doi.org/10.4018/979-8-3693-3767-7.CH005

Sinha, S. R., & Park, Y. (2017). Building an effective IoT ecosystem for your business. In *Building an effective IoT ecosystem for your business* (pp. 1–278). https://doi.org/10.1007/978-3-319-57391-5/COVER

Stefan, A. (2024). *Digitalization of entrepreneurial ecosystems and smart specialization: The importance of place specific factors.* http://pea.lib.pte.hu/handle/pea/45508

Todaro, D., & R. T.-C. S. R., and 2024, undefined. (2024). *From greenwashing to ESG washing: A focus on the circular economy field.* Wiley Online Library. https://doi.org/10.1002/CSR.2786and

Tyagi, R., & Khanna, P. (2025). A comprehensive review of digital transformation for sustainable development in emerging markets: Vis-a-vis blockchain and gamification. *Digital Transformation for Business Sustainability and Growth in Emerging Markets*, 223–246. https://doi.org/10.1108/978-1-83549-109-620251009/FULL/XML

University of Brighton. (2020, March 6). *The million dollar challenge: A case study of how GoPro creatively leverages user-generated content marketing | Jinnie's.* https://blogs.brighton.ac.uk/vanj/2020/03/06/the-million-dollar-challenge-a-case-study-of-how-gopro-creatively-leverages-user-generated-content-marketing/

Vashishth, T. K., Vikas Sharma, K. K., Kumar, B., Chaudhary, S., & Panwar, R. (2024). Enhancing customer experience through AI-enabled content personalization in E-commerce marketing. *Advances in Digital Marketing in the Era of Artificial Intelligence*, 7–32. https://doi.org/10.1201/9781003450443-2/ENHANCING-CUSTOMER-EXPERIENCE-AI-ENABLED-CONTENT-PERSONALIZATION-COMMERCE-MARKETING-TARUN-KUMAR-VASHISHTH-VIKAS-KEWAL-KRISHAN-SHARMA-BHUPENDRA-KUMAR-SACHIN-CHAUDHARY-RAJNEESH-PANWAR

Warrior Smiling. (2024, March 27). *Inbound marketing strategy: HubSpot's case study | by Smiling Warrior | Medium.* https://medium.com/@every1lovesyeni/inbound-marketing-strategy-hubspots-case-study-b8f99b258468

Winay, N. (2024, September 30). *(78) The power of collaboration: Nike and Apple's strategic partnership - a success story | LinkedIn.* https://www.linkedin.com/pulse/power-collaboration-nike-apples-strategic-partnership-winay-n–utc9c/

Wirtz, J., & Kowalkowski, C. (2023). Putting the "service" into B2B marketing: Key developments in service research and their relevance for B2B. *Journal of Business and Industrial Marketing*, *38*(2), 272–289. https://doi.org/10.1108/JBIM-02-2022-0085/FULL/XML

Wu, L., Subramanian, N., Abdulrahman, M. D., Liu, C., & Pawar, K. S. (2017). Short-term versus long-term benefits: Balanced sustainability framework and research propositions. *Sustainable Production and Consumption*, *11*, 18–30. https://doi.org/10.1016/J.SPC.2016.09.003

Chapter 7

Moderating Role of Demographic Variables in the Link Between Greenwashing Perception, Attitude, and Green Purchase Intention

Kritika Gupta

Chandigarh University, India

Abstract

The current research explores how consumer-specific variables (e.g., education, income) impact the relationship between greenwashing perceptions and attitudes on green purchase intentions and how this may provide useful information and/or recommendations for marketers and policymakers related to Sustainable Development Goal (SDG) 12: Responsible Consumption and Production. The research study adopts a descriptive research design to examine consumer responses to greenwashing in the fast-moving consumer goods (FMCG) context. The data collection process involved a self-administered online survey that was subsequently analyzed using the Smart PLS software package to test the proposed hypotheses. The results indicate that education and income are significant moderating variables of the association between greenwashing perception and green purchase intention and in the relationship between attitude toward green washing and green purchase intention. This study provides actionable insights for marketers and policymakers to promote sustainable consumption by addressing the moderating effects of education and income. Tailored green marketing strategies and targeted educational initiatives can help rebuild consumer trust and align with SDG 12 goals. The research uniquely highlights the role of education and income in shaping green purchase intentions amidst greenwashing perceptions, offering a fresh perspective on consumer behavior in the FMCG sector and bridging a key gap in sustainability studies.

Eco Illusions, 133–158

Published under exclusive licence by Emerald Publishing Limited
doi:10.1108/978-1-83662-782-120261007

Keywords: Greenwashing; greenwashing perception; eco-illusion; education; income; sustainable development; demographic variables; green purchase intention; attitude toward green products

Introduction

The increased emergence of greenwashing, or deceptive claims relating to environmental benefits, has become a prominent issue in consumer behavior research. As businesses continue to engage in legitimate eco-promotional and marketing practices, it will be important to understand the ways demographic variables moderate the relationships between consumer attitudes, greenwashing, and environmental purchase intentions to help clarify the "eco-illusion". The environmental movement that began in the 1960s represents a significant shift in global consciousness about pollution and environmental degradation, uniting scientific research, public awareness, and community activism into an unprecedented awareness of ecological threats to a planet. Over the decades, awareness of these threats has grown into organized movements leading to sustainability activism at the business, policy, and people levels.

The Genesis of the Environmental Movement

The 1960s and 1970s represented incredible moments in our environmental history, which created modern environmentalism. The publication of Rachel Carson's Silent Spring (1962) highlighted the devastating impacts of pesticides on ecosystems, with specific focus on DDT. Carson's research generated public awareness and regulatory changes, ultimately resulting in the creation of the United States Environmental Protection Agency (EPA).

The first Earth Day, celebrated on April 22, 1970, was the encapsulation of the then emerging environmental awareness. Initiated by Senator Gaylord Nelson, Earth Day brought millions of Americans together to engage in environmental awareness and activism. Moreover, the success of Earth Day led to significant policy reform, including the Clean Air Act and Clean Water Act, illustrating how collective action could influence environmental policy.

The Rise of Green Consumerism

As people's awareness of environmental issues continued to grow, their actions began aligning with their beliefs, and they were increasingly choosing eco-friendly products and practices. Between the years 2009 and 2010, the prevalence of green products doubled, indicating a shift toward sustainable consumption because of growth in public awareness of environmental problems and a desire to reduce their personal ecological impact.

The United Nations Sustainable Development Goals (SDGs), adopted in 2015, provided a worldwide plan for dealing with environmental issues. Specifically, SDG No.12, which is to "ensure sustainable consumption and production patterns", requires societies to reconsider how they produce and consume goods. Rather than simply minimizing resource use, people are encouraged to reduce their ecological footprint in line with a belief that every element of the product's lifecycle can impact the environmental and social welfare of our planet.

Most consumers respond favorably to companies they believe are addressing environmental issues (Carlson et al., 1993) and some in the green consumer segment are suspicious of corporate motives. Many green consumers are skeptical of corporate intentions and distrust advertising, which means it is difficult for companies to build trust in their green marketing efforts. This skepticism erodes consumer confidence" because consumers look to and trust companies to help inform their purchases (Gupta & Singh, 2024a; Singh et al., 2022). As trust is undermined, consumers are left confused about who or what to believe. They are, therefore, more skeptical toward these companies that exploit environmental trends through greenwashing as it relates to corporate messaging to inform their purchase (Pomering & Johnson, 2009).

Greenwashing is derived from "whitewash" and describes a relatively common phenomenon in advertising and marketing. It involves an instrumentally strategic use of green public relations (PR) and marketing tools, so it strategically means illegal misrepresentation by conveying a supposedly caring attitude toward the environment regarding an organization's products, objectives, and policies (Sandeen, 2009; Simon, 2000).

In 2017, Terra Choice, the independent organization par excellence in testing and ensuring transparency, published the first edition of the seven sins associated with greenwashing. It is these moral transgressions brought under a single banner of immoralities of greenwashing, representing the several deceptions some marketers embrace to fool consumers. The following list of seven sins illustrates how readily customers fall victim to these kinds of tactics:

- The "*Sin of Hidden Trade-off*" is a marketing approach that, while touting the positive environmental trait of a product, ignores the greater environmental consequences in the larger context of the product's lifecycle. As consumers increasingly seek sustainable attributes in products, businesses create marketing strategies that focus on one or two factors while ignoring the vast majority of environmental harm associated with the product lifecycle. This can be an ultimately misleading approach based on limited knowledge and trust consumers have in being sustainable. For example, a company may market its paper as "green" because it uses trees that are sustainably harvested, thus presenting a message of sustainability. However, the greater environmental harm associated with the production of the product, such as greenhouse gas emissions, water pollution from chemical processes, and energy used in the manufacturing process, is ignored. The goal of highlighting the sustainability of the paper relies upon the perception that if one aspect is sustainable, then the rest must be too. In other words, while the product may have a sustainable attribute, that attribute is only one criterion in measuring the environmental impact of the product. In situations like these, business practices reinforce the image of being environmentally conscious while not revealing the true environmental impact of the product on the issue of sustainability.

- The *"Sin of No Proof"* is a misleading marketing tactic that enables companies to make environmentally friendly claims without offering significant proof or independent evidence to support their statements. Companies gain an unfair advantage because consumers have no way to verify the claims' validity and are left to base their faith entirely on the company's information. Companies profit from not being transparent by gaining the customer's trust without providing independent certification, test data, or documents on the site. For instance, a company may market its tissue papers as "recyclable" but not publish any third-party validation to support the claim. It may not offer certification from a recognized environmental organization or any scientific evidence to demonstrate that tissue paper is recyclable. Consumers typically lack access to the same resources or ability to check the claims, thus assuming the company has purposefully made a clear and unambiguous claim. This uncertainty benefits marketers under the assumption that consumers will make a purchase based on assumed socially and environmentally responsible characteristics, even if unsubstantiated. The "Sin of No Proof" doesn't just frustrate efforts toward real sustainability, it dilutes the credibility of trustworthy eco-labels and certifications. It establishes a market context where false and exaggerated green claims can prosper, creating a barrier for consumers to identify which products are truly sustainable and which ones claim to be sustainable. This circumstance also emphasizes the need for stronger regulations, third-party certifications, and transparent reporting standards, which provide companies with the ability to back up environmental claims while better informing consumers.
- The *"Sin of Vagueness"* has arisen when any environmental claims by a company are ambiguous, not clearly defined, or open to differing interpretations that can easily confuse and, at worst, mislead consumers. The vagueness of these statements is frequently used to give the impression of being "green" but without specifying what "green" actually means. This resulted in consumers being unable to understand the environmental attributes of the product, leading to potential misjudgments, and ultimately deceiving the consumer. For example, if a company labels its product "all-natural," on the face of it sounds good, environmentally friendly, and safe. But "natural" is an indefinable word that does not necessarily mean it is safe or sustainable. For instance, there are many substances which are "natural" (mercury, arsenic, uranium, etc.) that are toxic and harmful to humans and the environment. When there is a lack of definitions, or context for potential meaning, consumers are led to believe that "all-natural" means the product is safe to consume, sustainable for the environment, or superior to a synthetic alternative when in fact that may not be the case. This sin takes advantage of the lack of standardizing and regulation of eco-labels and "green" terminology. In generalities and vagueness, companies can say what they want for accountability while benefiting from consumers' preference toward more sustainable

products. Such practices undermine confidence in legitimate environmental claims and create confusion among consumers hoping to make informed, responsible choices. When faced with the "Sin of Vagueness," we need clear definitions, sound standards, and third-party certifications to provide factual and verifiable claims about a product's environmental impacts. Transparency and specificity in marketing language can enable consumers to distinguish between true sustainability and vague claims that evoke harms while benefitting from meaningful eco-friendly marketing.

- The *"Sin of Irrelevance"* occurs when companies communicate environmental benefits which, while true, are minor or unrelated to the environmental impact of the product and mislead consumers into thinking the product is more environmentally friendly than it is. Irrelevant benefits often highlight past performances or compliance with regulations already mandated as opposed to any true environmental gain. For instance, a manufacturer may describe its refrigerators as "chlorofluorocarbon-free." This is true, but it is irrelevant since chlorofluorocarbons have been banned globally for decades. As a selling point, this experience offers no true value to consumers nor does it demonstrate any added environmental citizenship. This sin plays on consumers' lack of understanding of regulatory norms, creating the false appearance of an actual sustainable product. By creating irrelevant claims, companies are camouflaging other significant environmental issues related to their product. True sustainability efforts would include clarity about their product and activities that contribute to its sustainability efforts rather than simply highlighting outdated or required norms.
- The *"Sin of Lesser of Two Evils"* occurs when companies tout a product's minor environmental benefit while conveniently ignoring the larger impact of the product's use. This approach is detrimental to consumers because it gives the illusion of marketing a particular positive aspect in the category that distracts from the large risk or negative associated with the product itself. For example, organic cigarettes may be considered "green" because the cigarettes are made from organic ingredients. While this is true, it completely ignores the negative health effects associated with the product and the environmental damage associated with cigarettes, such as the ecological (and health-related) concerns of tobacco farming, poisonous gases released by smoking. While talking about "organic" cigarettes may be a step forward, the company is clearly trying to veil the fact that the product is a harmful product. This is a "sin" because it exploits the consumer's willingness to attempt better choices within a product category that is ultimately harmful. This creates the illusion that consumers may be ethically or eco-friendly consumers while in fact sustainability requires considering the full impact of the product instead of making surface level improvements that change nothing about the underlying risk of using the product.
- The *"Sin of Fibbing"* is the rarest but tedious examples of greenwashing where a company embellishes or downright lies to customers about what they are doing environmentally. This can mean providing false data to purposely make customers believe that the company or its products are more environmentally

aware. For example, a company could claim emissions are reduced by 1,000 pounds when emissions actually increased. A company could claim its products are certified by a reputable eco-certification entity but actually are not registered or approved. This type of sin creates a perception that consumers are being deceived when that is not the case, thus questioning the integrity of legitimate sustainable actions and certifications.

- The *"Sin of Worshipping False Labels"* is when a company presents a product or packaging with deceptive imagery or wording to imply that it is endorsed or certified by a third party. This would lead the customers to believe there was a reputable entity that verified the claims and findings, which the company is not registered or had endorsement. As an example, a product may have a seal or logo that the company created that look and sound official, suggesting approval. However, these are not approved eco-labels from a certification organization. This action exploits consumer trust to try and suggest that the product is of higher environmental performance than it is.

Understanding the seven sins of Greenwashing is useful, and necessary, for a consumer's ability to navigate the marketplace and make decisions. With this information, it allows consumers to interrogate green claims and demand a certain level of transparency within companies. This, in turn, creates a more sustainable and accountable business ecosystem where the consumer can make choices aligned with their values, ultimately supporting a more sustainable future.

Challenges in Achieving Sustainable Consumption

The challenge of achieving sustainable consumption continues, even with SDG 12 having been endorsed. Challenges such as food waste, overconsumption, and unsustainable and inefficient resource use remain an issue for the environment. As a point of reference, roughly one-third of the food produced globally is either lost or wasted, wasting all the associated greenhouse gas emissions as well as the natural resource inputs.

The circular economy has become increasingly popular as a business model and is a sustainable model for a business. In contrast to the linear model, which focuses on taking, making, and disposing of things, the circular economy emphasizes designing goods to last, to be repaired, and to be recycled. For example, IKEA provides a range of services that allow for product leasing and take back schemes in line with their commitment to circular economy to sustainably reduce waste and increase resource efficiency.

The Corporate Shift Toward Sustainability

Due to an increase in consumer and regulatory demand, businesses have increasingly looked to incorporate sustainability into their daily activities.

Companies have initiated environmentally friendly practices, such as decreasing their carbon footprint, adopting renewable energy sources, and waste reduction. Organizations are implementing these changes for not only ethical purposes but also because sustainable practices are also recognized by organizations to lead to long-term financial stability (cost saving and reputational value).

The development of environmental, social, and governance (ESG) was developed in part due to changing behaviors in corporate conduct. Investors were willing to either invest or allow investment only when identifying companies making decisions that adhered to one of the three guidelines. As corporate actors were also being influenced by this, organizations began adhering to these guidelines, resulting in recognizing more transparent and responsible behavior by corporate. This is representative of a societal shift toward a growing value of sustainability and ethical behavior by corporate actors.

The Sharing Economy and Collaborative Consumption

The sharing economy has created new consumption models that focus on access instead of ownership. The sustainability of services that facilitate taping into items and services you use infrequently (such as car-sharing, accommodation-sharing, and tool-lending libraries) make these platforms fantastic options that have boomed as substitutes for traditional consumption models. These platforms lessen the need for people to own things they seldom use, lowering resource consumption and waste generation.

The sustainability of the sharing economy concept can be understood in terms of the circular economy framework as a means of lowering the amount of resources ultimately required and the environmental toll of manufacturing and disposal. By reusing and sharing, these platforms are a resource-efficient and sustainable way to consume.

The Role of Policy and Regulation

Government policies are vital in establishing patterns of consumption and production that are sustainable. Regulations that create incentives for energy efficiency, reduction of waste and use of renewable resources are critical to creating systemic change. The European Union's extended producer responsibility (EPR) schemes hold manufacturers accountable for their products' lifecycles. Many countries follow suit vis-a-vis EPR requirements for disposal and in part related to recycling products when they are at the end of life.

International agreements and frameworks have purposefully engaged various levels of governmental and nongovernmental actors, like the Paris Agreement on climate change, that set targets for a reduction of emissions and that aim to incentivize commitment to shared sustainability goals.

Looking ahead: the Path to Sustainable Futures

The path to sustainable consumption and production is dynamic and multidimensional. There has been progress since the 1960s, yet we still face hurdles to accomplish the ambitious targets set out in SDG 12. Sustained action from governments, businesses, and consumers is necessary to enable a global culture of sustainability.

Education and awareness are two essential ingredients in this process. Helping people realize how their choices impact the environment and motivating them to embrace sustainable behaviors will enable societal contributions towards achieving sustainability. Furthermore, technological advances and innovations in sustainable practices are exciting ways in which we can support resource efficiency and reduce environmental footprint. Companies often utilize greenwashing communication strategies with the intention of distancing themselves from environmental action or the environmental action of their suppliers (Gupta & Singh, 2024c; Pizzetti et al., 2021). Companies use such strategies to construct a positive public perception of caring for the environment, concealing or masking the actual behavior, misrepresenting to consumers, and distracting consumers from ecological transgressions. Gupta and Singh's research (2024b) demonstrate how perceived greenwashing acts as a mediator between consumer attitudes and their intentions to purchase green products.

While there is extensive research on the impact of demographic variables on consumer behavior toward green products, less research has examined the perceptions of greenwashing (Halverson, 2018). This research study is addressing that gap by examining how demographic factors (gender, age, income, occupation, education) influence perceptions of greenwashing (the perceived dishonesty or misleading environmental claims by companies). By investigating these relationships, the research study provides valuable insights into the role demographic characteristics play in shaping greenwashing perceptions, thereby contributing to a deeper understanding of this underexplored area of consumer behavior.

This chapter addresses the following key questions concerning this matter:

RQ1: Which demographic variables (age, gender, education, occupation and income) have moderating impact in the relationship between greenwashing perception and the intention to purchase green fast moving consumer goods (FMCGs)?

RQ2: Do demographic variables (age, gender, education, occupation and income) play the moderating role in the link between consumer attitudes and the intention to buy green FMCGs?

The structure of this research paper proceeds as follows: a review of the literature, an explanation of the research design and methods, presentation of findings, and finally, a conclusion.

Literature Review

Diverse findings have emerged from many studies regarding the effect of demographic variables on consumer behavior and intention to purchase green products. Canöz (2022) stated that gender, marital status, income, age, and education greatly influence the green product buying behavior with singles and people from the wealthy section being more environmentally conscious and ready to pay for green products. Dangelico et al. (2022) indicated that there has been a tremendous shift in the behaviors of consumers due to the pandemic, where females were more receptive to sustainable consumption than males. Das (2015) reported that older married private employees and middle-income earners displayed greater environmental responsibility whereas gender made no significant impact. To echo this, D'Souza et al. (2007) concurred that there was moderate dissatisfaction with product labeling among older and middle-aged consumers whereas Halverson (2018) indicated that older consumers were more trusting and less cynical about greenwashing than younger consumers.

Also, education is another significant variable in affecting green behavior. Kerber et al. (2023), Shamsi & Siddiqui (2017), Meet et al. (2024) and Nath et al. (2015) discovered education to have a positive impact on environmental consciousness, attitudes, and green purchase intentions. Patharia et al. (2022) also observed that "age and income affected green purchase behavior positively" while Rezai et al. (2013) showed how socio-demographic factors, such as education, income, age, and marital status, operating together, contribute to a person's perceptions about green concepts. Royne et al. (2016) suggested that demographic variables like gender, ethnicity, and age, along with concerns about waste and environmental technology, influenced sustainable behaviors across various categories.

The varying responses of age and education could have possible effects on consumers' intentions to purchase a green product whereas the opinions directed toward buying green products were thought to possess some sort of degree of harmony with other factors. Sun et al. considered variations in attitude and intention based upon personality traits and demographic subgroups, such as age, gender, and birthplace. Interestingly, Trivedi and Sharma observed no significant differences in consumer perception based on demographics such as education, income, and age, indicating some demographic influences may be limited in influencing green purchase behavior in certain contexts. Taken together, they have all highlighted the undivided and challenging relationship between demographic variables and green consumer behavior.

Research Design and Method

This study conducts descriptive research to find out how and what cause consumers' perceptions about greenwashing to lead to their green product attitudes. This research study aims to help understand these perceptions in the decision-making of consumers. The field research in this study relied on a targeted recruitment, focusing on consumers in North India, to assure that the data gleaned is both representative and reliable, as respondents were expected to belong to a knowledgeable and well-informed population. In this light, the region becomes a focal point as it provides researchers with insights from people who are more likely to have higher awareness and exposure to greenwashing practices.

Data collection was conducted primarily through an online survey. Its purpose was to obtain detailed backgrounds and respondents' perceptions of greenwashing. Following the guidelines suggested by Chen et al. (2014), it was made clear to the participants that they should only take part in the study if they had prior knowledge of or experience with the practices of greenwashing. This would ensure that there were accurate, relevant and meaningful answers obtained from the responses, thus enhancing the validity of the findings of the given study. Questions in the survey clearly focused on FMCG products simply because these kinds of goods are bought frequently and repeatedly. These products typically reflect day-to-day household needs, providing a convenient reference point for assessing the attitudes and behaviors of consumers. Since they represent a considerable part of consumers' daily purchases, FMCG products provide the best category for studying how greenwashing affects consumers' purchasing decisions. This would allow the researchers to gather contextually relevant content while revealing the implications of addressing practices of greenwashing within a sector that directly affects sustainable consumption patterns.

The existing literature has been referred to developing the framework in which relationships between consumers' greenwashing perceptions and their green purchase intentions are moderated by demographic variables. The research study focuses on how consumer-specific characteristics affect the relationship between attitude towards the green products and green purchase intention. Therefore, the proposed conceptual model expressed further, shown in Fig. 7.1, consists of these components for a better understanding of the complexities of green practices for purchase by the consumers and their effects on their sustainable consumption purchase behaviors.

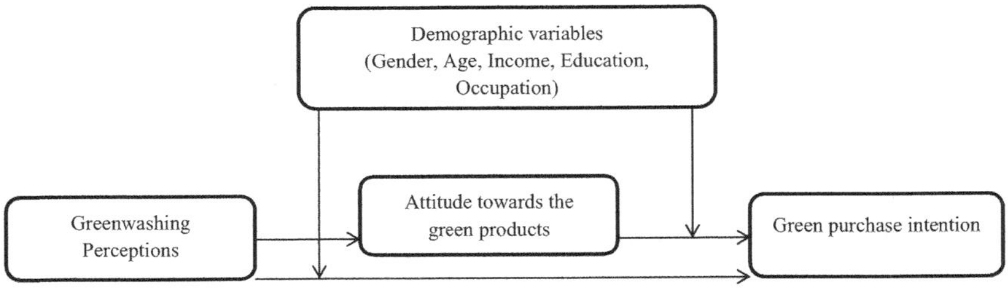

Fig. 7.1. Conceptual Framework of the Study.

Findings

Demographic Details of the Respondents

The detail of demographic analysis of a sample population based on gender, age, education, income, and occupation are given below. In terms of gender, males represent 53.18% (418 individuals) while females account for 46.82% (368 individuals), making a total of 786 participants. Regarding age, the largest group belongs to the 26–35 years category (32.9%), followed by those aged 36–45 years (30.9%), 46 years and above (25.8%), and 18–25 years (10.4%). Education-wise, the majority of the population has completed undergraduate studies (34.9%) or postgraduate studies (32.6%) while 25.8% hold professional degrees, and only 6.7% have education up to the higher secondary level. When it comes to income, 42.8% of the population earns between ₹500,001 and ₹10,00,000 annually, followed by 25.2% earning less than ₹250,000, 19.5% in the ₹250,001–₹500,000 range, and 12.5% earning over ₹10,00,001. Lastly, in terms of occupation, salaried employees make up the largest group (38.9%), followed by students (33.5%), businesspersons (25.4%), and retired individuals (2.02%). Overall, the data provides insights into the population's gender balance, age distribution, educational qualifications, income levels, and occupational diversity.

Moderation Analysis of Demographics Characteristics Between Greenwashing Perceptions (GWP) and Green Purchase Intention (GPI)

In an analysis of the moderation effects of demographics characteristics between GWP and GPI were examined. The results are reported in Table 7.1 (Fig. 7.2).

Analyzing the hypothesis H1a, H1b, H1c, H1d, and H1e examines whether gender, income, age, education and occupation moderate the relationship between GWP and GPI. The interaction effects of GWP with Gender ($\beta = -0.021$, $p = 0.414$), Income ($\beta = -0.153, p < 0.001$), Age ($\beta = 0.009, p = 0.778$), Education ($\beta = -0.115$, $p < 0.001$), and Occupation ($\beta = -0.022$, $p = 0.488$) were examined. Among these, only the interaction term Income x GWP with GPI ($\beta = -0.153, p < 0.001$) and Education x GWP showed a significant negative relationship with GPI ($\beta = -0.115$, $p < 0.001$), indicating that the impact of GWP on green purchase intentions is moderated by income and education. Hence, hypothesis H1b and H1d are significant. Other hypotheses H1a, H1c, and H1e were insignificant.

The findings suggest that higher-income individuals typically have more financial flexibility, allowing them to prioritize eco-friendly purchases despite higher costs, and they are more likely to have access to resources that enhance their ability to recognize greenwashing. This awareness encourages them to avoid greenwashed products and choose genuinely sustainable alternatives. Similarly, individuals with higher education levels are more aware of environmental issues, including greenwashing, and are more adept at critically evaluating product claims, making them more likely to reject misleading products in favor of those that are genuinely sustainable. In contrast, individuals with lower income or education may face financial constraints that limit their ability to prioritize

Table 7.1. Moderation Analysis of Demographics Characteristics Between GWP and GPI.

Hypothesis	**Path**	**Original Sample (O)**	**Sample Mean (M)**	**Standard Deviation (STDEV)**	**T Statistics (|O/STDEV|)**	***P* Values**	**Results**
H1a	Gender x GWP - > GPI	−0.021	−0.021	0.026	0.817	0.414	Insignificant
H1b	Income x GWP - > GPI	−0.153	−0.153	0.028	5.547	0.000	Significant
H1c	Age x GWP - > GPI	0.009	0.010	0.033	0.282	0.778	Insignificant
H1d	Education x GWP - > GPI	−0.115	−0.115	0.028	4.084	0.000	Significant
H1e	Occupation x GWP - > GPI	−0.022	−0.023	0.031	0.694	0.488	Insignificant

Source: Author's findings through Smart PLS.

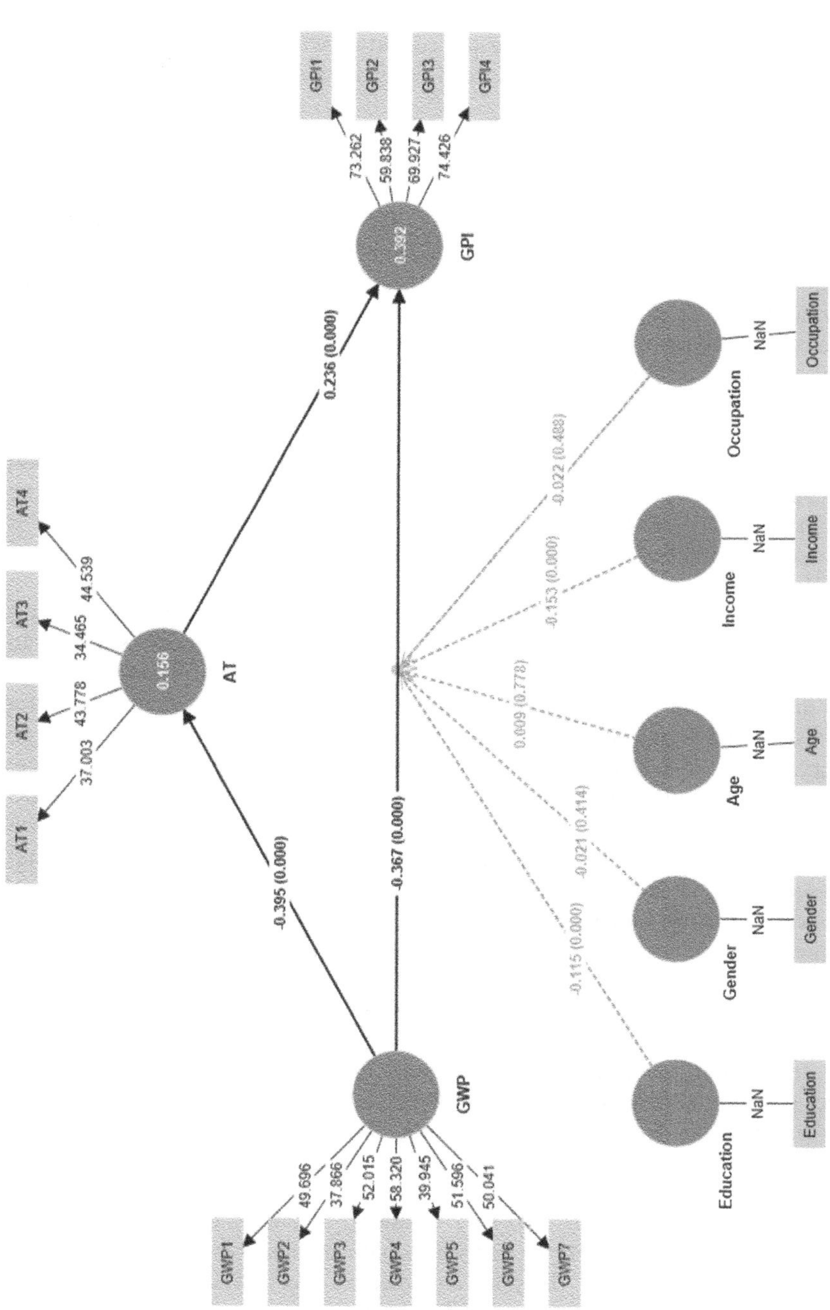

Fig. 7.2. Moderation Analysis of Demographics Characteristics Between GWP and GPI. Source: Author's findings through Smart PLS.

eco-friendly purchases, and their awareness of greenwashing may be lower, making them more susceptible to deceptive claims. Overall, these findings suggest that the interaction between income and education with greenwashing perception plays a significant role in forming green purchase intentions.

PLS Predict

In evaluating the predictive relevancy of the structural model, determination coefficients R^2 and adjusted R^2 are employed (Hair et al., 2017). The R^2 coefficient ranges between 0 and 1 and signifies the extent of the variance in the internal construct explained by all of the correlated external constructs. When the model involves an array of constructs, the adjusted R^2 is computed to control for the model's complexity. According to Chin (1998), an R^2 value of 0.67 or higher shows a strong relationship while an R^2 between 0.33 and 0.67 suggests a moderate relationship. An R^2 of 0.19 or higher indicates a weak relationship. Also, we evaluate Cohen's f^2, explaining the influence of a specific external construct on the R^2 of an internal construct. The basic guideline for calculating effect sizes with Cohen's f^2 is as follows: an effect size is considered small if f^2 is less than or equal to 0.02, medium if f^2 falls between 0.15 and 0.35, and large if f^2 is 0.35 or greater (Cohen, 1988).

The predictive power of the model in Partial Least Squares Path Modeling is further tested through the Q-square statistic measuring the model's ability to predict future observations. This statistic is described by Henseler et al. (2009) as "the difference between the predictive accuracy of the PLS model and that of a simplistic model that uses the mean value of the response variable for all observations." If a Q-square value is positive, it implies the model was more accurate in its predictions than a naïve model; for a Q-square of zero, the model would be equally accurate as the naïve model; and the model did not perform well if there is a Q-square value that is negative. The standard benchmark is that a Q-square value above 0.25 is considered robust, suggesting a construct has significant predictive relevance, and if it is below 0.25, it indicates limited utility for predicting new observations (Tenenhaus et al., 2005).

The structural model was assessed to explain the variance in AT and GPI, using R^2, Q^2 predict, and f^2 effect size values (See Table 7.2). The f-square values indicate the effect size of each predictor. According to Cohen (1988), values of 0.02, 0.15, and 0.35 indicate small, medium, and large effects, respectively. For direct effects, the results showed that the effect of AT on GPI was significant ($f^2 = 0.075$), suggesting a small to "Medium effect size" The effect of Age on GPI was negligible ($f^2 = 0.000$), indicating no effect. Education had a very small effect on GPI ($f^2 = 0.013$). The effect of GWP on AT was moderate ($f^2 = 0.184$) while its effect on GPI was small ($f^2 = 0.127$). Gender ($f^2 = 0.004$), Income ($f^2 = 0.019$), and Occupation ($f^2 = 0.001$) all had very small to negligible effects on GPI.

For interaction effects, the analysis revealed that the interaction between Gender and GWP on GPI was negligible ($f^2 = 0.001$). The interaction between Income and GWP on GPI showed a small effect ($f^2 = 0.033$). The interactions of

Table 7.2. Predictive Relevance.

Path	*f*-square	Effect	Construct	R^2	Q^2	Adjusted R^2
AT - > GPI	0.075	"Small effect size"	**AT**	**0.156**	**0.151**	**0.155**
Age - > GPI	0.000	"Small effect size"	**GPI**	**0.392**	**0.325**	**0.383**
Education - > GPI	0.013	"Small effect size"				
GWP - > AT	0.184	"Small effect size"				
GWP - > GPI	0.127	"Small effect size"				
Gender - > GPI	0.004	"Small effect size"				
Income - > GPI	0.019	"Small effect size"				
Occupation - > GPI	0.001	"Small effect size"				
Gender x GWP - > GPI	0.001	"Small effect size"				
Income x GWP - > GPI	0.033	"Small effect size"				
Age x GWP - > GPI	0.000	"Small effect size"				
Education x GWP - > GPI	0.019	"Small effect size"				
Occupation x GWP - > GPI	0.001	"Small effect size"				

Source: Author's findings through Smart PLS.

Age x GWP (f^2 = 0.000), Education x GWP (f^2 = 0.019), and Occupation x GWP (f^2 = 0.001) on GPI were all negligible to very small. The *R*-square values of the AT and GPI to the predictor(s) indicate by what percentage of variance those values are explained. The *R*-square for AT was 0.156, which means that 15.6% of variance in the dependent AT is explained by the predictors, and the *R*-square for GPI was 0.392 meaning that 39.2% of the variance in GPI is explained by the predictors. The Q^2 predict values, a test for predictive relevance of a model, showed that predictive relevance for AT was 0.151 and GPI was

0.235 where both indicate moderate predictive relevance of both constructs. Overall, the results highlight that while some predictors like AT and GWP have small to moderate effects on GPI, other factors like Age, Gender, Income, and Occupation, as well as their interactions with GWP, have negligible impacts. The model shows a significant portion of the variance in GPI and has moderate predictive relevance.

Moderation Analysis of Demographics Characteristics Between AT and GPI

Analyzing the hypotheses H2a, H2b, H2c, H2d, and H2e examines whether occupation, gender, education, age, and income moderate the relationship between AT and GPI. The Table 7.3 displays (see Fig. 7.3) the moderating effects of individual characteristics and interactions on the relationship between Attitude towards green products (AT) and GPI. The key results are detailed as follows: The moderating effects of Gender x AT, Occupation x AT, Income x AT, Age x AT, and Education x AT on the relationship between AT and GPI were investigated. The moderation effects of Gender x AT (β = −0.013, p = 0.609), Occupation x AT (β = 0.053, p = 0.055), Income x AT (β = 0.164, $p < 0.001$), Age x AT (β = −0.061, p = 0.034), and Education x AT (β = 0.131, $p < 0.001$) were also examined. The Income x AT and Education x AT demonstrated significant interactions, indicating that the relationship between AT and GPI is moderated by income and education levels. Hence, hypotheses H2c and H2e are significant. Other hypotheses H2a, H2b and H2d were insignificant.

These findings suggest that a person's income and education significantly impact how their positive attitudes toward green products are translated into actual buying decisions. Higher income allows individuals to afford eco-friendly products, making it easier for their positive attitudes to lead to purchases. Similarly, higher education provides individuals with more knowledge about environmental issues and the benefits of green products, which can strengthen their intention to buy. Therefore, while having a positive attitude is crucial, income and education levels can influence whether that attitude results in purchasing green products.

PLS Predict

In evaluating the predictive relevancy of the structural model, determination coefficients R^2 and adjusted R^2 are employed (Hair et al., 2017). The R^2 coefficient ranges between 0 and 1 and signifies the extent of the variance in the internal construct explained by all of the correlated external constructs. When the model involves an array of constructs, the adjusted R^2 is computed to control for the model's complexity. According to Chin (1998), an R^2 value of 0.67 or higher shows a strong relationship while an R^2 between 0.33 and 0.67 suggests a moderate relationship. An R^2 of 0.19 or higher indicates a weak relationship. Also, we evaluate Cohen's f^2, explaining the influence of a specific external construct on the R^2 of an internal construct. The basic guideline for calculating

Table 7.3. Moderation Analysis of Demographics Characteristics Between at and GPI.

Hypothesis	Path	Original Sample (O)	Sample Mean (M)	Standard Deviation (STDEV)	T Statistics (|O/STDEV|)	*P* Values	Results
H2a	Gender x AT - > GPI	−0.013	−0.013	0.026	0.512	0.609	Insignificant
H2b	Occupation x AT - > GPI	0.053	0.053	0.027	1.919	0.055	Insignificant
H2c	Income x AT - > GPI	0.164	0.164	0.027	6.049	0.000	Significant
H2d	Age x AT - > GPI	−0.061	−0.061	0.029	2.121	0.034	Insignificant
H2e	Education x AT - > GPI	0.131	0.131	0.028	4.731	0.000	Significant

Source: Author's findings through Smart PLS.

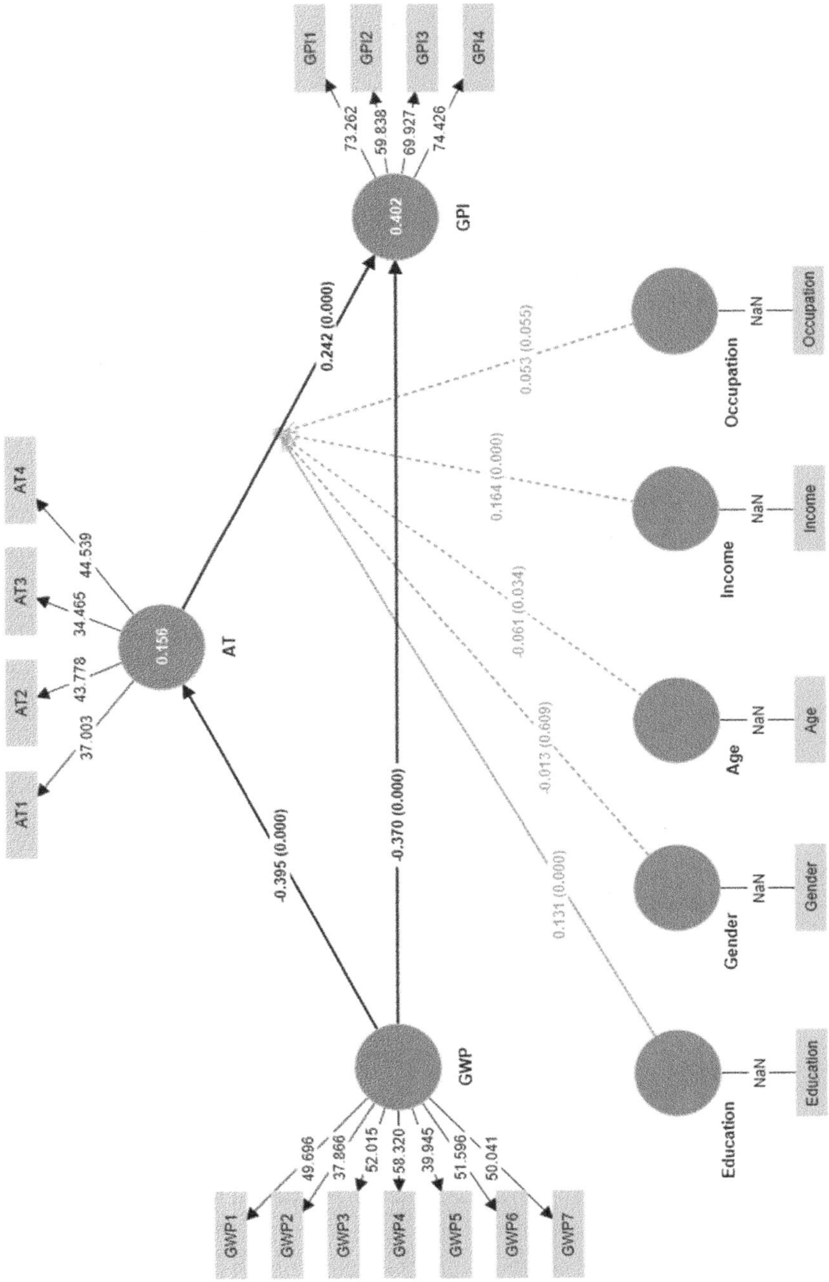

Fig. 7.3. Moderation Analysis of Demographics Characteristics Between at and GPI. Source: Author's findings through Smart PLS.

effect sizes with Cohen's f^2 is as follows: an effect size is considered small if f^2 is less than or equal to 0.02, medium if f^2 falls between 0.15 and 0.35, and large if f^2 is 0.35 or greater (Cohen, 1988).

The predictive power of the model in Partial Least Squares Path Modeling is further tested through the Q-square statistic measuring the model's ability to predict future observations. This statistic is described by Henseler et al. (2009) as "the difference between the predictive accuracy of the PLS model and that of a simplistic model that uses the mean value of the response variable for all observations." If a Q-square value is positive, it implies the model was more accurate in its predictions than a naïve model; for a Q-square of zero, the model would be equally accurate as the naïve model; and the model did not perform well if there is a Q-square value that is negative. The standard benchmark is that a Q-square value above 0.25 is considered robust, suggesting a construct has significant predictive relevance, and if it is below 0.25, it indicates limited utility for predicting new observations (Tenenhaus et al., 2005).

The structural model was assessed to explain the variance in AT and GPI, using R^2, Q^2 predict, and f^2 effect size values (See Table 7.4). The f-square values indicate the effect size of each predictor, where values of 0.02, 0.15, and 0.35 suggest small, medium, and large effects, respectively (Cohen, 1988). For direct effects, AT had a small effect on GPI (f^2 = 0.080). Age had no effect on GPI (f^2 = 0.000) while Education had a very small effect (f^2 = 0.010). The impact of GWP on AT was moderate (f^2 = 0.184), and its effect on GPI was small to medium (f^2 = 0.133). The effects of Gender (f^2 = 0.003), Income (f^2 = 0.019), and Occupation (f^2 = 0.001) on GPI were very small. In terms of interaction effects, the interaction between Gender and AT had no effect on GPI (f^2 = 0.000). The interactions of Occupation x AT (f^2 = 0.004), Age x AT (f^2 = 0.005), and Education x AT (f^2 = 0.025) with GPI had very small effects while the interaction between Income and AT on GPI had a small effect (f^2 = 0.037). The values of R-square reflect the proportion of variance that is explained by the predictors. The R-square for AT is 0.156, meaning that 15.6% of the variance in AT is explained by its predictors. The R-square for GPI is 0.402, meaning that 40.2% of the variance in GPI is explained by its predictors. The values of Q^2 predict, which assess the predictive relevance of the model, showed predictive relevance for AT of 0.151 and for GPI of 0.314, suggesting moderate predictive relevance for both constructs. In conclusion, the findings suggest that while factors like AT and GWP have meaningful effects on GPI, other variables such as Age and Occupation, along with their interactions with AT, have negligible impacts. The model accounts for a significant portion of the variance in GPI and demonstrates moderate predictive relevance.

Discussion

Demographic factors such as age, gender, education, income, and culture have implications for how consumers see greenwashing, which in turn affects their attitudes and purchase intentions. These characteristics are likely to accentuate

Table 7.4. Predictive Relevance.

Path	f-square	Effect	Construct	R^2	Q^2	Adjusted R^2
AT - > GPI	0.080	"Small effect size"	**AT** ***GPI**	**0.156** **0.402**	**0.151** **0.314**	**0.155** **0.393**
Age - > GPI	0.000	"Small effect size"				
Education - > GPI	0.010	"Small effect size"				
GWP - > AT	0.184	Medium size effect				
GWP - > GPI	0.133	"Small effect size"				
Gender - > GPI	0.003	"Small effect size"				
Income - > GPI	0.019	"Small effect size"				
Occupation - > GPI	0.001	"Small effect size"				
Gender x AT - > GPI	0.000	"Small effect size"				
Occupation x AT - > GPI	0.004	"Small effect size"				
Income x AT - > GPI	0.037	"Small effect size"				
Age x AT - > GPI	0.005	"Small effect size"				
Education x AT - > GPI	0.025	"Small effect size"				

Source: Author's findings through Smart PLS.

or diminish consumers' perceptions of greenwashing. In general, younger consumers, particularly Millennials and Gen Z consumers, are more engaged with environmental protection and skeptical of green claims than older generations. However, younger consumers will likely have fewer experiences to draw upon to assess the credibility of green claims is even greater than older consumers. In general, education is correlated with environmental awareness and skepticism towards unsubstantiated green claims. Educated consumers with knowledge about supporting evidence will scrutinize eco-friendly claims closer and are more likely to question their authenticity. Consumers with higher disposable income may be more comfortable paying a premium for true sustainable products. The eco-illusion occurs if a consumer believes that a product is environmentally friendly if they rely on cues, such as green labels or imagery with a nature-based connection. Demographic factors are a major influencer in the creation or diminishment of the illusion.

Amplification of the Eco-Illusion

Consumers with less education and less knowledge about science and the environment are more likely to rely on heuristic cues for products, like colors or package designs, leading to the eco-illusion. For example, they may see that a product has green packaging or images related to nature, and assume the product is environmentally friendly without substantiated claims.

Mitigation of the Eco-Illusion

Consumers who are more educated or have a higher amount of environmental concern are more likely to engage in more critical thinking around a green claim. They look for information like certified environmental labels, audits by third-parties, and opportunities to consider supply chain transparency, resulting in less likelihood of being fooled by greenwashing. The current research involved empirical exploration of the mediating effects of "consumer attitude towards green products" on "green purchase intention" triggered by "greenwashing perception". Jain et al. (2023) examined how income plays a role in the relationship between predicted behavior and actual behavior. This could mean that individuals with more income may consider green claims and products and may also be more likely to actualize their environmentally friendly preferences. This goes along with the findings that education increases environmental awareness and pro-environmental behavior (Meet et al., 2024; Sharma et al., 2021). Those with higher education tend to be more aware of environmental issues and more critical of misleading green claims, which lead to more informed, intentional green purchasing (Shamsi & Siddiqui, 2017).

Practical Implications

This research study will also be useful to green marketers and eco-conscious decision-makers. The findings demonstrate that novel green communication strategies and product offerings are more likely to resonate with agreeable consumers if they involve the dimensions of honesty, environmental consciousness, and sustainability. These dimensions are endorsements and will resonate with agreeable persons. Companies need to understand the values and motives of customers in terms of both outcomes in and out of the purchasing process and analysis the personalities and behaviors of the customer in order to engage them in these ways. In the case of green marketing, for example, taking into account the linkage among conscientiousness from personality attributes, greenwashing perceptions, and perceived sustainability, it is obvious that the way current marketing strategies are embedded into the green environment in the sequential development of products is important. We can infer from this research study that the ties between the personality of the customer, the perception of greenwashing, and the perception of green products are complex. Therefore, the relevant policing/regulatory bodies and companies should take into account consumers' contextual needs in decision-making strategies to mitigate greenwashing views and influence more people to increase ecological living habits. As the latest technology evolves, based on customer and species standards, to engage their target market about sustainable consumption practices and develop more sustainable consumption routines, society will be better off, and the future will be a bit more sustainable.

For managers, the implications are significant. A decline in the uptake of sustainable products due to greenwashing can impede progress towards *SDG- 12,* aimed at promoting sustainable consumption and production practices. This underscores the need for not just raising awareness but also fostering genuine sustainability knowledge and consumption values among consumers, particularly in the FMCG sector. Bridging the gap between consumers awareness and actual green purchasing behavior requires more than educational efforts alone. Implementing policies such as subsidies and taxes can be crucial in motivating firms to adopt and promote sustainable practices, thereby advancing sustainability goals and encouraging responsible consumption and production. For managers who want to support legitimate sustainability instead of creating an "eco-illusion," it is essential to grasp the moderating role that demographic factors may play in the relationships between greenwashing perception, consumer attitudes toward brands, and green purchase intentions. Managers can make sense and meaning of this understanding in multiple ways:

- Specialized Marketing Plans: Consumers' perceptions of greenwashing are likely informed by their demographic factors, such as age, education, income, and cultural background. Tailor marketing messages to the demographic segments of interest and emphasize transparency and authenticity so that consumer trust can be invoked.
- Improved Disclosure and Transparency: In Canada, consumers with high levels of environmental concern and higher education are more likely to carefully assess eco-claims made by brands. Managers should consider providing information on verified and verifiable environmental practices as well as environmental certifications, in a timely manner, so they can meet consumer expectations around what for these consumers is necessary information being provided.
- Managing Brand Credibility: Managers can plan for brand credibility while also managing consumer expectations and possibly overcome skepticism with educated, socially responsible consumers by investing in third-party certifications and providing transparent reporting of nonmarket, environmentally

focused business decisions. They can dampen the impacts of greenwashing perception by demonstrating legitimation for legitimacy.

- Consumer Education: Managers can develop or partner with credible programs that educate consumers through providing important information in recognizing when they are purchasing authentic green products or greenwashed eco-claims. This will enable consumers to make better informed purchasing decisions and will reduce the eco-illusion.

By adopting these tactics, managers can manage the complexities surrounding green marketing, while also ensuring their sustainability initiatives are taken as real and beneficial efforts, and reducing the potential for the eco-illusion to endure.

For different *businesses*, the research study will provide the company with a unique opportunity to improve marketing strategies. By the use of these inputs, companies can verify their environmental credentials, which are supported by the evidence and are clearly communicated, and thus avoid the charge of greenwashing. According to the study, the run-up of green is the result of actual sustainability approaches that are essential for the adoption of genuine principles and the abandonment of the announcement style. The discovery shows that dealing with perennial greenwashing problems gives businesses the opportunities to gain consumer trust, develop credibility, and differentiate themselves from the rest by being honest and by third-party verification. By recognizing the moderating role of demographic variables, companies can customize their marketing strategies for different consumer groups in the following ways:

- Customized Communication: Companies can tailor a marketing message to a particular demographic group by appealing to ${\it transparency}$ or ${\it authenticity}$ in their marketing to build trust.
- Educational Campaigns: Companies can share information about environmental certifications or sustainable practices of suppliers, so that consumers can make an informed decision, while also being less vulnerable to greenwashing.
- Product Transparency: Given an educated, environmentally conscious consumer, companies can provide as much information as possible regarding the sourcing of the product, manufacturing processes, and environmental impact of the product.

Future Research Directions and Conclusion

This study emphasizes the importance of consumer-specific factors, such as education and income that moderate the relationship between perceptions of greenwashing, attitudes, and green purchase intention within the FMCG sector. The findings reveal that education and income are important factors shaping consumer perceptions of greenwashing and subsequent intentions to purchase green products. These insights provide key evidence in favor of tailored green marketing strategies and educational programs to regain consumer confidence and promote consumption sustainability. Future research can study the impact of brands image, trust, customer satisfaction and price of the product on greenwashing perception of the consumers. Moreover, the moderating role of these variables can also be studied between greenwashing perception and green purchase intention. In addressing these moderators, marketers and policymakers can better align efforts with SDG 12, thus promoting sustainable consumption and production practices. This research study makes a valuable and original contribution to understanding consumer behavior in the context of sustainability and makes practical suggestions for improving the effectiveness of green marketing and policy interventions. The findings provide a basis for companies to understand how to align their claims about green practices with consumer expectations and thereby encourage sustainability in purchasing behavior and increased customer loyalty. Demographic variables significantly influence how consumers perceive greenwashing and their attitudes towards green products.

In recognizing these moderating effects, businesses can create strategies that are part of true sustainability and also help consumers make sense of ecologically sound marketing, all in an effort to minimize the eco-illusion.

References

Canöz, F. (2022). Tourists' attitudes toward green product buying behaviors: The role of demographic variables. *Tourism & Management Studies*, *18*(4), 7–16.

Carlson, L., Grove, S. J., & Kangun, N. (1993). A content analysis of environmental advertising claims: A matrix method approach. *Journal of Advertising*, *22*(3), 27–39.

Chen, Y. S., Lin, C. L., & Chang, C. H. (2014). The influence of greenwash on green word-of-mouth (green WOM): The mediation effects of green perceived quality and green satisfaction. *Quality and Quantity*, *48*, 2411–2425.

Chin, W. W. (1998). The partial least squares approach to structural equation modeling. In G. A. Marcoulides (Ed.), *Modern methods for business research* (pp. 295–336). Lawrence Erlbaum Associates.

Cohen, J. (1988). *Statistical power analysis for the behavioral sciences* (2nd ed.). Lawrence Erlbaum Associates.

D'Souza, C., Taghian, M., Lamb, P., & Peretiatko, R. (2007). Green decisions: Demographics and consumer understanding of environmental labels. *International Journal of Consumer Studies*, *31*(4), 371–376.

Dangelico, R. M., Schiaroli, V., & Fraccascia, L. (2022). Is Covid-19 changing sustainable consumer behavior? A survey of Italian consumers. *Sustainable Development*, *30*(6), 1477–1496.

Das, M. (2015). Consumer demographics and environmental responsibility: An empirical investigation of the consumers' of Tripura, a state in North-East India. *Prabandhan: Indian Journal of Management*, *8*(5).

Gupta, K., & Singh, N. (2024a). A systematic review of literature on Greenwashing. *Sustainability Development through Green Economics*, *114*, 75–90.

Gupta, K., & Singh, N. (2024b). Greenwashing perception and attitude-intention relationship towards green products purchase: A mediating model. *Environment, Development and Sustainability*, 1–24.

Gupta, K., & Singh, N. (2024c). Visualization of global research trends and future research directions of greenwashing by using bibliometric analysis. *Environment, Development and Sustainability*, 1–21.

Hair, J. F., Hollingsworth, C. L., Randolph, A. B., & Chong, A. Y. L. (2017). An updated and expanded assessment of PLS-SEM in information systems research. *Industrial Management and Data Systems*, *117*(3), 442–458.

Halverson, R. (2018). *Consumer perceptions of greenwashing: Understanding awareness, trust, and effectiveness*. (Undergraduate honors thesis, University of Colorado Boulder). University of Colorado Boulder. https://www.scribd.com/document/678347390/consumerPerceptionsOfGreenwashingUnderstandingAware-nessTr

Henseler, J., Ringle, C. M., & Sinkovics, R. R. (2009). The use of partial least squares path modeling in international marketing. In *New challenges to international marketing* (pp. 277–319). Emerald Group Publishing Limited.

Jain, V. K., Gupta, A., Verma, H., & Anand, V. P. (2023). Embracing green consumerism: Revisiting the antecedents of green purchase intention for millennials and moderating role of income and gender. *International Journal of Sustainable Agricultural Management and Informatics*, *9*(3), 213–231.

Kerber, J. C., de Souza, E. D., Fettermann, D. C., & Bouzon, M. (2023). Analysis of environmental consciousness towards sustainable consumption: An investigation on the smartphone case. *Journal of Cleaner Production*, *384*, 135543.

King, A., & Lenox, M. (2002). Exploring the locus of profitable pollution reduction. *Management Science*, *48*(2), 289–299.

Meet, R. K., Kundu, N., & Ahluwalia, I. S. (2024). Does socio demographic, green washing, and marketing mix factors influence Gen Z purchase intention towards environmentally friendly packaged drinks? Evidence from emerging economy. *Journal of Cleaner Production*, *434*, 140357.

Nath, V., Agrawal, R., Gautam, A., & Sharma, V. (2015). Socio–demographics as antecedents of green purchase intentions: A review of literature and testing of hypothesis on Indian consumers. *International Journal of Innovation and Sustainable Development*, *9*(2), 168–187.

Patharia, I., Rastogi, S., & Vinayek, R. (2022). Determining green purchase behaviour towards electronic products in an emerging economy: Theory and evidence. In *Environmental sustainability in emerging markets: Consumer, organisation and policy perspectives* (pp. 69–94). Springer Nature.

Pizzetti, M., Gatti, L., & Seele, P. (2021). Firms talk, suppliers walk: Analyzing the locus of greenwashing in the blame game and introducing 'vicarious greenwashing. *Journal of Business Ethics*, *170*, 21–38.

Pomering, A., & Johnson, L. W. (2009). Advertising corporate social responsibility initiatives to communicate corporate image: Inhibiting skepticism to enhance persuasion. *Corporate Communications*, *14*(4), 420–439.

Rezai, G., Teng, P. K., Mohamed, Z., & Shamsudin, M. N. (2013). Is it easy to go green? Consumer perception and green concept. *American Journal of Applied Sciences*, *10*(8), 793–800.

Royne, M. B., Thieme, J., Levy, M., Oakley, J., & Alderson, L. (2016). From thinking green to buying green: Consumer motivation makes the difference. *Journal of Business Strategy*, *37*(3), 37–43.

Sandeen, C. (2009). It's not easy being green: Green marketing and environmental consumerism in continuing higher education. *Continuing Higher Education Review*, *73*, 93–113.

Shamsi, M. S., & Siddiqui, Z. S. (2017). Green product and consumer behavior: An analytical study. *Pertanika Journal of Social Sciences and Humanities*, *25*(4), 1545–1554.

Sharma, M., Trivedi, P., & Deka, J. (2021). A paradigm shift in consumer behaviour towards green cosmetics: An empirical study. *International Journal of Green Economics*, *15*(1), 1–19.

Simon, D. R. (2000). Corporate environmental crimes and social inequality: New directions for environmental justice research. *American Behavioral Scientist*, *43*(4), 633–645.

Singh, N., Gupta, K., & Kapur, B. (2022). Greenwashed word of mouth (GWWOM): A vibrant influence on customer green behaviour. *Journal of Global Responsibility*, *13*(4), 472–487.

Sun, Y., Wang, S., Gao, L., & Li, J. (2018). Unearthing the effects of personality traits on consumer's attitude and intention to buy green products. *Natural Hazards*, *93*, 299–314.

Tenenhaus, M., Vinzi, V. E., Chatelin, Y. M., & Lauro, C. (2005). PLS path modeling. *Computational Statistics & Data Analysis*, *48*(1), 159–205.

TerraChoice. (2010). *The sins of greenwashing, home and family edition*. https://sinsofgreenwashing.com/. Accessed on April 21, 2019.

Trivedi, P., & Shrama, M. (2018). An empirical study on the perception of consumers about green products in Delhi. *International Journal of Engineering and Technology*, *7*(2.11), 41–47.

United Nations. (2017). *Progress Towards the sustainable development goals* (report of the Secretary-general). https://www.un.org/ga/search/view_doc.asp?symbol=E/2017/66&Lang=E

Chapter 8

Beyond the Green Facade: New Challenges in Detecting and Preventing Greenwashing in Indian Companies

Ram Singh[a], *Vinay Pal Singh*[b], *Rohit Bansal*[c] *and Fazla Rabby*[d]

[a]Symbiosis University of Applied Science, India
[b]Quantum University, India
[c]Vaish College of Engineering, India
[d]Stanford Institute of Management and Technology, Australia

Abstract

The increasing demand for environmentally sustainable products has led to adoption of green marketing strategies by many Indian companies. The green marketing strategies aimed at appealing to environmentally conscious consumers. While this trend reflects a positive side of environmental awareness, it has also given rise to the practice of *greenwashing*, which is a deceptive tactic where businesses falsely present their products or services as environmentally friendly. Greenwashing not only erodes consumer trust but also negatively affects the genuine efforts towards sustainability. The chapter focuses on the environment issue of detecting and preventing greenwashing in today's era. By investigating the methods some companies misrepresent their sustainability claims, this study emphasizes on the challenges faced by regulators, consumers, as well as the organizations striving to uphold authentic sustainable practices. A qualitative research approach is being done in this study. It examines the documented cases of greenwashing across various industries by using secondary data from scholarly articles, reports, and the regulatory frameworks. Furthermore, this study anticipates the increasing complexity of the greenwashing techniques, which is making them more difficult to identify. It is expected to reveal significant gaps in existing regulatory frameworks and to emphasize the need for stronger and at the same time, more effective standards. The research also

Eco Illusions, 159–180

doi:10.1108/978-1-83662-782-120261008

highlights the importance of an informed and rational consumer base in holding companies accountable for their sustainability claims.

Keywords: Greenwashing; sustainability; consumer trust; environmental regulation; corporate transparency

Introduction

Greenwashing refers to the deceptive practice in which companies falsely claim to follow environmentally friendly practices to create a positive public image. It often involves making unverified or exaggerated statements about their sustainability efforts to attract customers who value eco-friendly products. The concept of greenwashing was popularized in the 1980s, and from then onwards, this concept has expanded to include various unfair tactics like using ambiguous language and showing eco-labels that are not certified (Lyon & Montgomery, 2015). Such deceptive marketing strategies can go from little overstatements to major lies and manipulations, which makes it even harder to detect such practices. Due to the growing focus on sustainability as well as environmental stewardship, the business houses are embracing the concept of green marketing to take a step towards environment conservation and become socially responsible. But with the popularity in green marketing, there has been a significant rise in greenwashing wherein companies fake themselves to be environmentally responsible just to gain a competitive advantage. And for that sake, they mislead the customers while undermining the genuine sustainability efforts and also complicating the pursuit of environmental justice (Delmas & Burbano, 2011; D'Souza & Taghian, 2005). In India, where sustainability awareness is growing, greenwashing has become an increasingly significant concern, especially with the rise of corporate social responsibility (CSR) initiatives and governmental regulations aimed at promoting sustainable business practices (Narula & Upadhyay, 2021). The Indian economy has witnessed a significant economic growth and development and with this, the environment concerns too are rising at a rapid pace. The environment concerns related to over utilization of resources, emergence of harmful pollutants mainly due to activities followed in agriculture and allied sector, manufacturing and textiles are growing significantly (Saxena, 2020). Due to this, many Indian companies are paving the way to move towards green marketing practices to promote environment sustainability and to become socially responsible. However, in many cases such efforts are just superficial, i.e. these practices are being followed just to portray a fake image in the minds of people (Bala et al., 2022). Another reason why greenwashing is significantly rising is because the regulations in India require the companies to follow green practices due to which people are opting to show them are socially responsible although that's not their true image. The regulatory framework in India to avoid the greenwashing practices is still at the early stages of development. This proves that in India, people are more vulnerable to fall in the trap of these marketing strategies and deceptive claims. The guidelines for CSR and environment reporting have been published by the Ministry of Corporate Affairs, but they are still limited in scope due to which the companies grab the opportunity to use loopholes and exploit the customers as well as the environment (Gandhi & Sharma, 2021). The Securities Exchange Board of India (SEBI) makes it compulsory for the large companies to disclose their ESG (Environmental, Social and Governance) practices, but their verification still is not done consistently. As a result of this, the customers who wish to contribute to environmental sustainability by using sustainable products fall under the trap of greenwashing. There are various studies that show that customers are becoming aware about sustainability and some are even ready to pay premium price to buy products that are environment friendly and foster sustainability (Lim et al., 2023). But because of lack of regulatory framework and appropriate measures, the customers are unable to differentiate between environment friendly products and misleading claims that are made by the companies.

Greenwashing and Eco-Illusion

Greenwashing refers to the deceptive practice where companies falsely portray their products, policies, or operations as environmentally friendly to appeal to sustainability-conscious consumers. This strategy misleads the public and undermines genuine environmental efforts. Closely related is the concept of *eco-illusion*, where firms use vague or exaggerated claims, such as labels like "natural," "eco-safe," or "biodegradable," without scientific validation. According to a 2023 study by the European Commission, 42% of green claims made by companies were exaggerated, false, or deceptive. In India, a 2022 report by TERI revealed that nearly 60% of consumers could not differentiate between real and fake green certifications. Such practices hinder sustainable development by creating confusion and reducing accountability, and these practices emphasize the urgent need for stricter regulatory standards and transparent eco-labelling systems to uphold consumer trust and environmental integrity (Table 8.1).

The growing prevalence of *greenwashing* and *eco-illusion* calls for a critical debate around corporate accountability and consumer awareness in sustainability claims. Eco-illusion, where companies craft deceptive perceptions of being eco-friendly through symbolic gestures like green packaging, unverified certifications, or vague terms, poses a serious threat to genuine sustainable practices. This illusion not only misleads consumers but also distorts market competition, making it difficult for truly sustainable businesses to thrive. The lack of stringent ESG norms and regulatory oversight enables such practices, undermining the broader goals of Sustainable Development Goals (SDGs), particularly SDG 12 (Responsible Consumption and Production) and SDG 13 (Climate Action). It is thus crucial to debate the role of policy-makers, industry, and civil society in dismantling these illusions and creating mechanisms for accountability and transparency. One way to counter eco-illusion is by promoting and integrating the *sharing economy*, which focuses on circularity, shared usage, and resource optimization. Platforms that facilitate shared mobility, rental housing, co-working spaces, and collaborative consumption reduce the environmental footprint and reflect core principles of ESG and circular economy. Unlike eco-illusion, where the focus is on appearance, the sharing economy is inherently functional and outcome-oriented minimizing waste and maximizing asset utilization. For instance, companies like Ola and Zoomcar promote car-sharing, which reduces the need for individual ownership and ultimately lowers emissions and resource usage. By embedding traceability and measurable impact in business models, the sharing economy can offer a transparent, authentic path to sustainability helping avoid the pitfalls of eco-illusion while advancing genuine progress towards SDGs.

Preventing Greenwashing in Indian Companies

Preventing greenwashing in Indian companies requires a multi-pronged approach involving regulatory enforcement, corporate accountability, and consumer awareness. With the Securities and Exchange Board of India (SEBI) mandating Business Responsibility and Sustainability Reporting (BRSR) for the top 1,000 listed firms from FY 2022–23, companies are now compelled to disclose verifiable ESG metrics. However, many firms still rely on vague or exaggerated eco-friendly claims. To address this, Indian companies must adopt credible certifications such as ISO 14001, Eco-mark, and GRI Standards while leveraging technologies like blockchain and QR codes to ensure supply chain traceability and transparent reporting. Consumer awareness is equally vital initiatives like GRIHA and awareness campaigns can help people identify genuine sustainability efforts. Moreover, promoting the sharing economy and circular business models such as EV-sharing services (e.g., BluSmart) and rental platforms (e.g., Rentomojo) reduces overconsumption and offers measurable impact, thereby kerbing eco-illusion and aligning corporate actions with SDGs like SDG 12 (Responsible Consumption) and SDG 13 (Climate Action).

Table 8.2 highlights how Indian companies can prevent greenwashing by adhering to strict frameworks, adopting traceable technologies, involving third-party audits, and promoting consumer transparency, thus fostering authentic contributions to sustainable development.

Review of Literature

The study of Delmas and Burbano (2011) emphasized on the economic as well as the organizational forces that encourage greenwashing practices and deceptive tactics. They highlighted how these practices lead to a feeling of distrust among customers and pose challenge to the authenticity of green initiatives. By understanding such drivers, we develop an understanding of why the companies choose these deceptive marketing practices to show that they are environmentally responsible just to meet the regulatory compliance is. Chen and Chang (2013) also highlighted about the consequences of greenwashing on trust and faith of customers and how it affects their behaviours. The main focus was on the

Table 8.1. Greenwashing and Eco-Illusion.

Aspect	Greenwashing	Eco-Illusion
Definition	Misleading portrayal of environmental responsibility	Psychological trick using vague terms/images to appear eco-friendly
Common Tactics	False labels, unverifiable claims, hiding true impact	Use of earthy colours, fake certifications, "green" buzzwords
Impact on Consumers	Erodes trust, misguides purchase decisions	Confuses ethical choices and misinforms public perception
Example	A company claims "zero emissions" while outsourcing pollution	A plastic bag labelled "biodegradable" without lifecycle assessment
Data Highlight	42% of green claims are false (Lyons et al., 2022)	60% of Indian consumers misled by false green tags (Glaser et al., 2022)

Source: Authors' compilation.

role of green trust, which represents the reliability in the authenticity of environmental claims. This study highlighted how such deceptive greenwashing practices and claims can break trust of the customers and increase skepticism (Prasad & Thomas, 2019; Sharma & Raina, 2021). This brings a challenge for the credible efforts of sustainability. One of the key consequences of greenwashing is customer distrust in green-labelled products due to increasing greenwashing tactics, leading to a huge demand from the side of customers for transparency, accountability, and verification along with strict regulations.

Lyon and Montgomery (2015) extend this exploration by categorizing greenwashing tactics. In the study the author focused on developing a theoretical framework that highlighted the different motivations behind greenwashing practices used by the corporates, which involves creating a fake image in the mind of customers and regulatory authorities and build up their reputation as environmentally responsible companies for cost cutting and other benefits. This study also highlighted that there are certain companies which employ superficial green measures without making a meaningful change. For instance, some companies put emphasis on eco-friendly packaging without making changes in areas in waste reduction and carbon emissions. It also highlights the increasing complexity of greenwashing practices and how the advancement in such areas is making it difficult for the customers and regulatory bodies to distinguish between deceptive practices and genuine green initiatives. A study conducted by Marquis et al. (2016) highlighted how societal scrutiny and the cultural norms have an influence on environmental disclosures of companies that operate in different countries and also revealed that companies generally adopt greenwashing

Table 8.2. Preventing Greenwashing in Indian Companies.

Aspect	Details/Description	Real Data/Examples (India)
Definition	Greenwashing is when companies falsely market products or policies as environmentally friendly	As per *Consumer VOICE India* (2023), 57% of consumers in urban areas are unable to verify eco-claims on products
Regulatory Frameworks	Mandatory ESG disclosures, BRSR (Business Responsibility and Sustainability Reporting) by SEBI	SEBI made BRSR reporting compulsory for top 1,000 listed Indian firms from FY 2022–23
Voluntary Certifications	Eco-mark, ISO 14001 (Environmental Management), Fair Trade, GRI Standards	Only about 200 Indian firms are ISO 14001 certified (BIS, 2022). Eco-mark uptake is under 5% in FMCG sector
Industry Best Practices	Use of lifecycle assessments (LCAs), third-party environmental audits, carbon transparency reporting	Tata Power reports verified emissions and uses LCAs in renewable projects; Infosys conducts annual sustainability audits
Consumer Awareness Programs	Public education, eco-label literacy, Green Rating for Integrated Habitat Assessment (GRIHA)	GRIHA has certified over 1,600 building projects across India promoting green construction awareness
Use of Technology	Blockchain for supply chain traceability, AI to verify green claims, QR codes for sustainability disclosures	ITC uses blockchain for agri-supply chains; FabIndia uses QR codes to display environmental footprint
Corporate Penalties	Imposing fines for misleading green claims, cancelation of false certifications, media disclosure	In 2023, ASCI flagged over 300 ads in India for misleading sustainability claims, 40% from the textile sector
Role of Sharing Economy	Encouraging platforms for shared consumption (e.g., EV rentals, furniture leasing)	ZoloStays and Rentomojo promote circular consumption; BluSmart

Table 8.2. *(Continued)*

Aspect	Details/Description	Real Data/Examples (India)
	reduces false consumption claims	offers verified electric ride-sharing services
Link to SDGs	Aligns with SDG 12 (Responsible Consumption), SDG 13 (Climate Action), SDG 9 (Industry, Innovation, Infrastructure)	NITI Aayog's SDG Index (2023): India scored 66/100 for SDG 12, with improvement needed in sustainable consumption

Source: Authors' compilation.

practices just to meet the perceptions and expectations. They also highlighted that greenwashing is not only a corporate issue but is also a cultural and societal one. This complex relationship between cultural norms and corporate behavior puts emphasis on the need of globally coordinated regulations that are needed to address greenwashing practices, which pose an obstacle to sustainable development.

Dauvergne and Lister (2012) highlighted the sustainability governance challenges that are faced by MNCS, highlighting on the fact that many large companies project themselves to be the leaders in sustainability, the commitments made by them are often limited to profitability and regulatory requirements. The compliance towards sustainability measure by such companies towards sustainability measures is merely for law's sake. They maintain an image of being socially responsible while making least efforts towards achieving sustainability. Terra Choice (2010) introduced the concept of "The sins of greenwashing." This concept classified the misleading claims of the companies to display themselves as environment friendly. The classification included the categorization of such tactics into sins of vagueness (wherein companies use unclear language) and sins of irrelevance (where claims don't hold genuine environment significance). This classification has helped out the consumers as well as the regulatory bodies to identify and understand the greenwashing tactics which contributes to greater awareness and skepticism for the green claims and take a step towards meeting environment goals.

Consumer behavior plays a key role both in encouraging and discouraging greenwashing. Grimmer and Bingham (2013) highlighted on these factors that shape how the consumers respond to deceptive claims that are made by companies. As per their study, environmentally conscious consumers have a tendency to look into the authenticity of such claims and challenge unverified claims. Therefore, the urgent need for education and awareness campaigns should be addressed in order to equip the consumers with the ways to recognize and resist the deceptive marketing practices that are being followed by the corporates.

Chen et al. (2016) conducted a research study in which they highlighted that a strong commitment to CSR can help to a significant extent in reducing inclination of the corporates to engage in greenwashing practices. Their study also put emphasis on the fact that organizations, which have a well-established CSR framework, are less likely to overstate and brag about their environmental efforts and are more likely to pursue genuine and authentic sustainability initiatives. This suggest that integrating CSR initiatives deeply into corporate culture can help to avoid greenwashing and can also foster alignment between business objectives and SDGs that have been laid down by the United Nations.

The role of transparency has also been emphasized in several studies for the purpose of addressing greenwashing. For instance, Ramachandran and Mehta (2022) emphasize that honest and transparent reporting mechanisms are very important for minimizing the practice of greenwashing, especially in the emerging markets where regulatory frameworks may be less strict. They stressed upon the challenges that Indian companies would face due to the greenwashing practices because they need to navigate the global expectations and at the same time must also meet the local requirements to adhere to sustainability standards. Creating a balance between global and local standards could be challenging for the Indian companies. Singh and Chandra (2023) have also explored how the blockchain technology could be used to track the authenticity of environmental claims, which would allow consumers to verify the origins and impact of products. This technology has the potential for increasing the accountability and reducing deceptive green marketing. Bowen and Aragon-Correa (2014) also provided information on the global view of greenwashing and corporate transparency with a specific reference to the importance of global organizations in developing the guidelines for environmental reporting. Global harmonization proponents argued that the use of sustainability standards throughout the world would reduce the inducement for management directors to engage in selective disclosures just for meeting the legal requirements with no intent to make authentic efforts for sustainability and consequently, introduce a global standard for environment reporting around the world, which would ultimately enable less opportunity for greenwashing. With this global trend, Narula and Upadhyay (2021) noted that although CSR is being followed in India and the companies remain legally bound to their CSR framework, but some companies use the name of CSR for the sole purpose of making profits without any sustainability intention, in which they create only symbolic gestures not real commitments to sustainability.

Though digital media has advanced green marketing opportunities through new channel opportunity, it has also brought greenwashing opportunities with them. As per Rexhepi and Ramadani (2021), the firms make use of social media platforms to greenwash many of the products in the market, and due to the nature of social media marketing, this study establishes that digital literacy should be practiced by the consumers. The third-party eco-labels are a very positive thing in the war against greenwashing as it can help to combat the deceptive practices and make the consumers aware about the misleading promotion of unsustainable products as environment friendly, which is done through targeted advertisement. Lin and Chang (2012) explore ways in which fair trade and energy star certification systems serve as tools of making consumer decisions. They also acknowledged that the abuse of such labels is an issue of greenwashing whereby the companies falsely use the certifications. Bansal and Clelland (2018) studied how ESG metrics can indirectly reduce greenwashing practices that are followed by the companies. The finding of their study is that companies with high ESG scores are less likely to follow greenwashing because they are more under the scrutiny of investors who invest in sustainable practices and the investors are likely to verify their claims. The intersection between greenwashing and consumer awareness is an emerging field. According to Johnson and Fujita (2020), those who are deeply against deceptive claims react to greenwashing differently than environmentally conscious consumers as their response often results in a consumer boycott and bad word of mouth marketing which cause damage to corporate reputation. Jain and Goyal (2022), in their research gave a review of the impact of greenwashing on corporate reputation. As per their research, in the long term, greenwashing loses its brand value and customer loyalty as consumers keep up the pressure on the companies, and they stand behind to start being accountable. Finally, these studies emphasize the multi-dimensional nature of greenwashing and the fact that robust policies, technological tools along with consumer awareness are essential to combat greenwashing, and each study adds to our growing understanding of how companies can be made to be accountable and the consumers better protected from misleading environmental claims whether through emerging technologies or through the regulatory frameworks that enable them.

Research Gap

Various researches concerning greenwashing have been conducted in the past, but there are many areas where it is possible to cover its true potential especially in the growth market of India. In previous studies related to greenwashing, subjects are primarily associated with western nations, leaving greenwashing in developing nations relatively unexplored. As social media is used for greenwashing and use of these practices are being done by companies for portraying themselves as environment friendly, researches have also highlighted how we can differentiate between green marketing and greenwashing. However, there remains limited study to assess the effectiveness of the new technologies that have recently appeared such as blockchain for combating greenwashing. These gaps mean that more region-specific research needs to be done on different economies to provide more effective ways of combating greenwashing and enhancing customer confidence in sustainability claims. Despite of the extensive research on greenwashing, several gaps remain in understanding its implications, especially within emerging markets like India which are needed to be addressed to enhance consumer trust in sustainability claims.

Objectives and Methodology

The chapter aims to explore the issues that are emerging in detection and prevention of greenwashing in Indian companies. By examining the tactics used in greenwashing, this chapter highlights the challenges due to greenwashing that are faced being consistently faced by regulatory bodies, consumers and businesses that are committed to sustainable practices. Qualitative research approach is employed in this chapter, which aims at analyzing the cases of companies accused of greenwashing across various industries. It also reviews the latest literature and regulatory policies that have an objective of mitigating greenwashing. The secondary data will also be compiled and used for the analysis.

Emerging Issues in Detecting Greenwashing in Indian Companies

Identifying greenwashing cases of Indian organizations is a complex process due to various emerging issues with its rapidly evolving political and economic systems and cultural contexts of sustainability management. While environmental claims are being featured continuously in corporate marketing communication, it is becoming important to determine which ones are real and what is just hype. There have been developments in greenwashing verification for Indian firms, including the relevance of legislation, cultural influences, social media, and digital impact along with the verification methods restrictions.

Regulatory and Policy Gaps: A major problem in identifying greenwashing is the fragmentation of the regulatory environment of India. Still, CSR legislation is minimal. Although India passed Section 135 of the Companies Act, 2013 that requires specific companies to spend a particular percentage of their net profits on social and environmental projects, still it is not being followed authentically by many companies. According to Gandhi and Sharma (2021), these CSR mandates have triggered some environmental programs but are they still insufficient to avoid practices being utilized in greenwashing. Moreover, the lack of universally acceptable and enforceable environment reporting policies makes it easy for companies to fake environment reports, particularly when relevant environmental indexes are provided only in a selective and biased manner (Marquis et al., 2016).

Cultural Factors that influence customer awareness: The second factor that is of essence in determining the practices of greenwashing in India is that the awareness of the environmental problems is not uniform across the country. Research shows that cultural beliefs have a strong influence on consumers perceptions of environmental messages, particularly regarding product sustainability, most consumers in India are more concerned with the cost and product utility than the environmental issues (Ramachandran & Mehta, 2022). This minimal consumer understanding means that even though firms may make ambiguous or overstated sustainability labels, the customers who don't have deep rooted environment concerns would not be taking a step towards combat greenwashing. For instance, Narula and Upadhyay (2021) find that most consumers in emerging markets such as India do not have enough knowledge or information regarding sustainability at the individual level to distinguish between mere deceptive claims and actual sustainability initiatives by these corporations.

Social media in greenwashing: In recent years, social networks have extended corporate communication to the next level as it is now easier for a company to get more people on the sustainability claims made through these platforms. This has also resulted in enhanced greenwashing because the firms have started using these platforms for fake green affirmations on the digital media without sufficient scrutiny. Rexhepi and Ramadani (2021) argue that social media is a double-edged sword in the context of greenwashing because although these platforms create spaces for messaging about sustainable development, it lacks the instruments that would ensure that the message advertised as sustainable is authentic and reliable too. Since the consumers are head over heels for social media platforms especially in India, they are time and again coming across the sustainability messages which have no solid sources for following a check for being real and are rather just promoting more of the green wash (Jain & Goyal, 2022).

Limitations of third-party certifications: Energy star and fair trade are good examples of third-party eco-labels that are common in green marketing. But in the whole of India, there are issues with regard to the compliance with these certifications to the general issue of consistency in the implementation of the set certifications. Therefore, Lin and Chang (2012) argue that things cannot improve where there is way of improving transparency through certifications and vice versa if the firms fail to meet the set standard in the labels that they display. Whereas in India the legal entities and third parties do not possess sufficient authority to compel compliance with certification, the companies can misuse the certifications in marketing pit without following the procedures specified in the certification standards (Grimmer & Bingham, 2013).

Technological Gaps in claim verification: For verification of green claims, blockchain can be used. The use of blockchain technology enhances the credibility of environmental reports because they provide ways of monitoring supply chain operations in real time. However, the adoption of such technology is still limited across firms, especially the small firms in the India because of its high costs and weak base infrastructures. Singh and Chandra (2023) have explained that while from theoretical perspective, blockchain could eliminate greenwashing since it provides extensive information about the products and their effects to the customers, this is not feasible in the present technological landscape in India. Thus, fair verification technology has not been created and environmental information remains rather difficult to reveal as being falsified even if it is greenwashing.

Consumer Mistrust: This suggests that just like greenwashing the problem of "green advertisements" also increases the level of consumer mistrust in advertisement messages. Chen and Chang (2013) pointed out that if the consumer is frequently exposed to information concerning green claims that are being made by corporates in the market, he or she gets used to it and becomes indifferent to true and false information that is represented on environmentally friendly issues.

In India, this problem is increasing due to the inefficient mechanism of verification of references of green products, which in effect reduces the impact of authentic green marketing. This mistrust does not only harm the companies that are part of the sustainability initiatives but also impact the usefulness of green consumerism by leaving consumers less capable and willing to distinguish between the true and deceptive practices.

Emerging Issues in Preventing Greenwashing in Indian Companies

Analyzing the problem of combating greenwashing that prevails in India reveals all the aforementioned issues emerging due to the specific conditions of the regulatory environment, characteristics of the market, and the tendencies in people's behaviour. When focusing environmental issues in the corporate world, sustainability claims in the products or services offered by firms in India are increasing. However, with the help of managers manipulating the truth, greenwashing is being possible as companies make false claims about being environment friendly. This has become a tough nut to beat, especially when it comes to ensuring accountability and preventing deception. One of the major problems of tackling greenwashing in India is the absence of a set of strict rules regulating various sustainable issues in companies. Although India has set the discourse of sustainability through the Section 135 of the Companies Act, 2013, these measures have proved to be inadequate in reversing the trend of greenwashing because the CSR Act isn't compulsory and has weak measures of enforcement. Greenwashing is being followed in India because Indian laws do not require companies to provide information about their real environmental impacts. Thus, regulatory deficiencies have shown to be failed to affect the necessary prevention and exposure of greenwashing, thereby allowing firms to yield to sustainability declarations without warrant. Increase in the interest in environmental issues makes it even more important to look up into the regulations to include requirements for environmental disclosures. Market regulators, like SEBI, have tried to implement change through colorful innovations like BRSR, which is a guide for reporting social responsibilities. However, this is voluntary for most companies, and as such, its adoption continues to be sporadic (Ramachandran & Mehta, 2022). The difficulty however is in enhancing these regulations and making certain that the current requirements for corporate reporting are consistent. Also, a lack of consumer consciousness and lack of awareness about the environment is one of the main challenges that hinders campaign against greenwashing in India. Despite the awareness being spread by the west markets is touching greater heights, the Indian customers remain at risk of embracing these so called "green" claims. Stukhart (2019) gives examples after analyzing the study of Narula and Upadhyay (2021), where it was found out that mobile consumers are unable to distinguish between sustainable and unsustainable initiatives because they lack enough information and because sustainability branding is complex. Such knowledge deficit is worsened by the fact that there is growing incidence of green marketing scams more so in the era of the internet advertising. Greenwashing can therefore be prevented through consumer education. The authors also point out that potential consumers who possess more information about the impacts of environmental declarations are susceptible to frauds. Emerging from global markets including India where majority of the population is still ignorant about environmental issues, it is important that awareness of greenwashing be created through public campaigns and sensitization. In addition, increasing overall environmental awareness among consumer segments of different socio-economic status will prevent those segments from engaging in ineffective use of greenwashing strategies.

Indian companies don't receive straightforward incentives while ensuring adequate, genuine sustainable measures in their organization. However, the multinational corporations have responded to sustainable rules and regulations due to environmental activism, policies from international bodies and increasing demand for green products while only a few SMEs are financially prepared to invest heavily on sustainable assets. That is why there is an ideological disposition in companies to engage greenwashing as an inexpensive approach. For example, Singh and Chandra (2023) reported that firms/orgs that are in such an environment where the latter is not penalized for greenwashing and customers do not know about penalties for deception tend to bear low financial/reputational costs even when they do not practice what they claim. Scholars must therefore search for a way towards improving the connection between the companies' incentives and the sustainable practice to ensure that they do not engage in greenwashing. As one of the possible references, there is a provision of tax credit, subsidies, and other motivational stimuli for certified sustainability, and mostly, SME companies embrace environmentally sound official systems since they have higher hurdles to support environmental technologies. Furthermore, a setup of the measures which can verify such sustainability statements as accurate will improve corporate governance and prevent firms from using such approaches. Bowen and Aragon-Correa (2014) focused on the establishment of link between integrity of corporate image and factually correct and truthful environmental performance as creating fit for real sustainability in place of just hype or green deception.

Technological Solutions for Transparency: New technologies provide solutions on how to fight greenwashing since consumers can easily validate a company's sustainability claims through tech-driven services. Blockchain as a technology has the potential to offer a system or a chain of blocks for managing the environmental footprint of the products while they go through their life cycle. Singh and Chandra (2023) have highlighted that blockchain has a capability of enhancing the flow of information within the supply chain. It can also allow for real time tracking of the origin of a produced product, energy consumption and disposal of wastes in an effort to curb on the incidences of greenwashing by providing the consumer with real-time information. Nevertheless, only a limited number of companies have embraced these innovations, and more specifically, this type of solution is still not popular among small enterprises, also in those that have no possibilities for integrated digitalization. In addition, the rule- and law-making requirements for the application of blockchain in sustainability reporting are under construction. Therefore, it is required to invest in technology infrastructure and support from the government and other industrial bodies for the further penetration with such technologies in India.

Social Media in Combating Greenwashing: Social media is being used as a means of greenwashing and environmental communications at the same time. Although many firms operationalize green marketing communication through digital media, the same media provide consumers with a strong platform for verification of corporate claims. Several consumers instigated social media activisms are rising all over the world like Boycott Greenwashing or Sustainable Brands, and similar instances are being noticed in India. These deep efforts seem to be most useful where regulatory bodies cannot enforce the management to take accountability on fake and misleading information. Rexhepi and Ramadani (2021) also claimed that those who are into greenwashing can be controlled because social media are means for consumers to share information and experiences about brands. However, the freedom that lets the consumer expose the greenwashing is also being used for sharing of information that contains half-truths due to poor regulation of the sites. Preventing greenwashing in Indian companies requires a more comprehensive approach that addresses regulatory as well as market challenges. Strengthening regulatory frameworks, improving consumer education, and aligning corporate incentives with genuine could help in leveraging emerging technologies; therefore, these are very essential steps towards curbing deceptive environmental claims.

Environmental Awareness and Greenwashing

The subject of environmental awareness and greenwashing in India and its relation to the formation of the consumer image of corporate sustainability is intertwined. The trend of greenwashing in India is seen to be increasing. It involves making disingenuous or flat out lies about environmental responsibility to make the company seem cleaner than they are:

Environmental Awareness in India: During the last decade, there has been a growing concern of the Indian population towards the environment, caused by the global climate change, pollution and the depletion of natural resources. With the help of continuous media campaigns, education programs, and other environmental organizations like Swachh Bharat Abhiyan (Clean India Mission), questions of environment have gained deeper exposure in the society. Also, change in global sustainability trends and international environmental regulation has gained significant popularity among Indian consumers, and there is a growing tendency of demanding environmentally friendly products and services. A study conducted by Jain and Goyal in the year 2022 reveals that the Indian consumer, especially the urban ones, are now getting sensitive to sustainable consumption, and this has brought pressure on the companies to brand their marketing efforts in this line. Realizing the global rising importance on environmental concerns, several Indian companies have started advertising their environmentally sensitive "green" credentials through seal and claims associated with CSR and lesser carbon footprint. For instance, today several big corporate houses, including Tata Group, ITC and Mahindra & Mahindra, have come with sustainable development as an integral part of their strategy and advertisement strategies. Still, this shift towards sustainability came with a significant increase in greenwashing, as some companies pretend to bring solutions that meet growing consumer demand for all things through produced that are labelled as "eco-friendly." The companies in India have increasingly turned to "green" marketing strategies to cater to this demand. However, this trend has also given rise to greenwashing, i.e. misleading or false environmental claims intended to portray companies as more eco-friendly than they actually are.

The Growth of Greenwashing in India: The limited legal requirements and insufficient information on the sustainability of products have made a problem in Indian organizations. Greenwashing involves deliberate manipulation of the general public over the false claims regarding a particular product or company. It is possible that a company greenwashes their product intentionally; however, there are many other firms that may participate in the process due to ignorance of sustainable practices or regulation. The most ideal example of "Greenwashing" can be experienced with the firms operating in the food and beverage industry in India most of whom incorporate labels such as "Organic," "Natural," and "Eco-Friendly" although these statements lack proof of the same. Here, Ramachandran and Mehta (2022) demonstrate that this largely owes to the reality that numerous corporations can indeed use falsified claims for "greenness" because clients often cannot assess the legitimacy of these claims due to deficient legal frameworks. This is especially the case when the consumer themselves within a given market are not yet sufficiently and adequately informed of the environmental questions and appropriate consumption norms. Another area in which one can detect the signs of greenwashing is in the fashion industry. Various brands of fast fashion companies in India as well as others around the world have labelled their products as sustainable and eco-friendly, but in reality, they do not disclose sufficient information concerning the procurement of raw material and manufacturing of the clothing products. This is a big issue because now the fast fashion around the world is facing the pressure to become sustainable. However, instead of doing that, many companies make what is known as green wash instead (Grimmer & Bingham, 2013).

Consumer Awareness and its Role: There has been an increase in cases of misleading green claims from the Indian firms. On the one hand, increased concern for the environment results in the call for the promotion of sustainability and to make companies more honest about their sustainability efforts. On the same note, a low level of engagement in sustainable products and services and the ability of Indians to distinguish between truthful messages and marketing scams generates conditions for such manipulations. A recent study showed that Indian consumers are often unaware of how they can tell if a company is being truly sustainable or if they are faking it. Narula and Upadhyay (2021)'s findings depict that despite of the heightened awareness of the environment, consumers don't possess the ability to fully assess credibility of green marketing claims;

hence, the confusion appears in the market. For example, terms such as "eco-friendly" or "green" are gradually gaining acceptance, but there is no universally acceptable definition. In addition, there has also been an influx of disclosure of misleading or fake information through the social media platforms. Although the information is helpful in increasing people's awareness of their environments, but they are also helping disseminate fake information making it even harder for the average person to discern between reality and social media hype (White et al., 2012). The general illiteracy and misunderstanding surrounding environmental concerns have to be addressed for consumers in India. These include guided consumer self-protection, which involves explaining the criteria for recognizing the authenticity of claims stating ecological friendliness, the meaning of certification and the methods for determining the environmental friendliness of specific products. Another approach to minimizing greenwashing is consumer education, as evidenced by Chen and Chang (2013) when they presented their work highlighting how a more informed consumer would reject firms that make misleading green claims for greenwashing prevention third-party certifications and independent verification systems should be used. Some eco-labels and sustainability certifications exist in India like IGBC and the Fair Trade through which consumers can directly know which products is environmentally friendly. However, Lin and Chang (2012) indicate that there are difficulties with enforcement. It is critical to set measurable standard of certification that should be compulsorily required where ever environmental claims are made. Companies should be required to provide accurate and authentic information about their sustainability policies. Singh and Chandra elucidated that the use of blockchain technology can enhance the transparency as the consumers would be able to trace the effects of relevant products on the environment. It is noteworthy that India has developed a new consciousness towards environment that in turn has led to an increasing demand for "green" products; but like everything else, it also came with an impressive partner in the form of "Going Green Scam." Since consumer awareness has the potential of eradicating greenwashing, it is evident that there is still unawareness and legal jurisconsults that facilitate false environmentally friendly declaration by companies. In this regard, there is need to enhance the consumer consciousness, enhance the credibility of certifications and, of course, to introduce higher levels of critical accountability that would force companies to accept sustainable orientation. Only then India has a chance to eradicate greenwashing and prepare the ground for consumers to trust actual green claims that firms make.

Challenges: Regulatory Bodies, Consumers, and Businesses

Challenges Faced by Regulatory Bodies: In India, the two main governmental agencies that have a large role to play in putting in place rules of sustainability of business and at the same time, a crucial role of monitoring violators of environmental laws are SEBI and MoEFCC. However, the following challenges make it difficult for these bodies to enforce the regulations:

Inconsistent Enforcement of Sustainability: There is inconsistent enforcement of sustainability regulations, and many organizations particularly those in the unorganized sector are unable to afford full compliance with reporting requirements. A survey conducted by the SEBI in 2022 revealed that only 35% of large-cap Indian firms provide information on sustainability practice in full and there remains a significant gap in data assurance (SEBI, 2022). Currently, there are little consequences for failure to disclose such information and methods of checking disclosures are normally insufficient resulting to questionable information. The financial constraints on regulatory bodies are another significant challenge. According to the World Bank report (2021), it is evident that financing is a major problem that weakens the environmental regulatory organizations in India. For instance, the CPCB, the board that oversees pollution and environmental standards across the country, has recently had its budget cut because of measures that aimed at constraining expenditure across ministries and departments. Sadly, these organizations receive little funding that limits their ability to conduct basic audits regarding sustainability initiatives and adhesion to regulations.

Challenges Faced by Consumers: The same goes with the engagement with the sustainable businesses and products by the customers in India. Despite the fact that awareness to sustainability issues is increasing, there are hurdles in making well informed purchase decisions. Lack of transparency on sustainability claims is one of the main challenges with which consumers struggle today. Without clearly verifiable data, it's hard for consumers to differentiate between products that are sustainable and those that use greenwashing tactics. According to Kantar Group (2020)'s survey, 52% Indian consumers were confused whether brands were truly practicing sustainable practices or simply said they were. This further compound the confusion following the proliferation of "eco-friendly and" "green" kind of terms, without proof. Also, companies face higher cost to source from more eco-friendly materials and are required to pay the workers ethically at the same time are also required to conduct low-cost carbon production. Due to this, sustainable products are priced higher than the conventional products. The report by PwC India (2021) states that although Indian consumers are becoming more conscious about it, 48% consumers consider cost to be the most important factor when making a purchase. And in price sensitive markets, for most consumers, the higher price tag of "sustainably produced" goods are a barrier. Lack of availability of sustainable products is another challenge as the products are not readily available, or available at all, especially in rural communities or smaller towns. Many retailers and businesses around sustainability only focus on urban markets and leave rural consumers with fewer options.

Challenges Faced by Businesses Committed to Sustainability: Many Indian businesses are committed to adoption of sustainable practices, but certain barriers exist that prevent them from using such practices, especially in manufacturing, textile and agriculture industries. In order to operate in a sustainable manner, heavy investment is required in new technologies, eco-friendly materials, and renewable energy sources. As per a CII (Confederation of Indian Industry)

(2020) study, 67% of Indian companies cited high initial costs as the biggest barrier for sustainability initiatives. For instance, companies that adopt solar panels for renewable energy sources, or even companies who are switching to sustainable packaging, require very high capital costs that may take years to recoup. In addition, collection and reporting of financial data related to sustainability is a challenge to businesses. It is resource intensive to collect accurate energy usage, emissions, waste management, and other environmental data. The World Economic Forum (2022) reported that only 30% of companies in India could measure their carbon footprint accurately because there were no standardized data collection methods and adoption of advanced environmental monitoring systems was expensive. Profitability vs sustainability is something with which many companies and even SMEs have a hard time juggling with. Since profit margins are small in a highly competitive market, this price sensitivity would be a challenge. As per a report released by McKinsey & Company (2020), 55% of Indian companies cited maintaining profitability with a commitment to sustainability as one of its biggest challenges. But there has been much more uptake in green financing although many businesses in India still find it difficult to access capital for sustainable projects. As per the Reserve Bank of India (RBI) 2020 report on green finance, less than one fourth of Indian banks' lending portfolio goes to environmentally sustainable projects. The challenges faced by regulatory bodies, consumers, and businesses in India in their pursuit of sustainability are multi-faced and require a comprehensive approach to overcome. Regulatory bodies must strengthen enforcement mechanisms and should also aim to provide adequate resources and at the same time should also develop standardized sustainability reporting frameworks to tackle greenwashing. Consumers need more transparency, better education and more affordable options to make informed, sustainable choices. Businesses, on the other hand, face financial constraints in transitioning to sustainable practices but can overcome these challenges by leveraging innovative technologies, accessing green finance, and aligning sustainability with profitability. As sustainability continues to gain importance in India, it is essential for all stakeholders' regulators, businesses, and consumers to collaborate in overcoming these challenges.

Findings and Suggestions

Findings

There are various agencies at the government level such as SEBI and MoEFCC that play an important role in implementing sustainability norms. Despite that, there are many areas without sufficient regulation and supervision. While various guidelines have been established, the sustainability reporting still remains incomplete making it difficult to confirm sustainability information. Lack of a standard regime or special penalties for non-compliance has made it possible for some organizations to exploit regulatory requirements thereby leading to high cases of greenwashing. Reports point to a lack of a comprehensive, centralized and efficient platform for developing and validating corporate sustainability data and information for more transparency (SEBI, 2022; World Bank, 2021).

Consumers in India are becoming sensitive to environmental issues although there is still misunderstanding as to the credibility of greenwashing. A survey conducted by Kantar Group in 2020 found that more than half of Indians remain skeptical about green claims because of terms like biodegradable, recyclable, and compostable as their verifiability remains ambiguous and there is inadequate certification system in place. Consequently, most consumers are likely to fund firms that practice greenwashing, which may erode consumer confidence in the long run. As the present study suggests, filling this transparency gap by harmonizing labelling and claims is imperative for improving consumers abilities to choose sustainably.

Challenges to implementing sustainable business models of production depend largely on the availability of eco-materials, costs of renewable energy sources and low emission manufacturing systems. The problem is further worsened by the scarcity of green financing which hampers the funding required to support green investment. Thus, yielding to true sustainable efforts, incentives or subsidies are the types of policy intervention that could help to reduce these financial disparities significantly.

Eradicating all those financial constraints and factors affecting the profitability will bring about a significant change in the Indian businesses and would help to take a step towards sustainable development and the development of a green economy. Everyone needs to make a change – governments, companies and the public should take actions to foster versatile real change across the economy. Consequently, the nation can set an example of a sustainable way of development for other countries to emulate.

Suggestions

With regard to reducing greenwashing in India, the following strategic suggestions might be given to help the regulatory authorities, consumers, and environmentally responsible organizations. It is hoped that these recommendations would provide a solid framework to tackle greenwashing issues.

Indian regulatory entities, like SEBI and MoEFCC, must look into the policies of the standardized ESG reporting at every industry. Reporting can be made more accountable by requiring third-party audits for sustainability reports, which could also minimize greenwashing. Another way in which transparency could be increased is through creation of a centralised online repository that is accessible to the regulators and consumer (World Bank, 2021). Regulators could also intervene to see the matters in which firms make false sustainability claims and impose fines on them and at the same time provide incentives for companies that have made actual measurable improvements. The former could establish penalties for non-compliance such as fines for greenwashing while the latter includes rewarding efforts achieved through phenomenon such as tax reductions for organizations operating beyond acceptable thresholds of sustainability indices. Such an approach would make more business establishments complied with the provision and funded sustainable practices (SEBI, 2022).

A sound governmental supported and enforced eco-certification system could greatly increase consumer confidence. The use of labels such as "SEBI approved Eco-Certified" or "Green Label India" would allow consumers to determine whether a product or firm is truly a sustainable one or not within the blink of an eye. Adherence to cleaner production criteria should be done with much fewer doubts originating from greenwashing (Kantar Group, 2020).

Consumers would be able to make better decisions regarding products which are friendly to the environment if knowledge relating to such products is enhanced. Sustainability reports should be made easily understandable to consumers; thus, organizations should be mandated to post simple summaries of these sustainability reports on the internet. Such simplification of the presented environmental impact data would help consumers make informed choices, on par with local levels of greenwashing, which is higher in industries like consumer goods and fashion.

The access to green financing options can be expanded by Indian banks if they open a special credit line or some special financial product to support credible green initiatives of the companies. The RBI could explore on promoting corporate credit facilities that are directed to environmentally friendly projects (RBI, 2020). SMEs with higher risk have financial restrictions, and they would prefer having green fund necessary to finance their green projects. This could be made through collaboration between government, financial institutions, and development organizations.

A sound government supported and enforced eco-certification system could greatly increase consumer confidence. The use of labels such as "SEBI approved Eco-Certified" or "Green Label India" would allow consumers to determine whether a product or firm is truly a sustainable one or not within the blink of an eye. Adherence to cleaner production criteria should be done with much fewer doubts originating from greenwashing (Kantar Group, 2020).

Conclusion

Combatting greenwashing in firms in India requires a complex approach, which includes regulation, sensitization, enforcement of accountability, and provision of funding to support green initiatives. There is a common-sense value-added for regulatory agencies to require reporting standardization coupled with external audit to ensure consistency between the stated declaration on green activities and action. Besides, making the messages and communication about environmental practices clear and transparent to the customers will allow eliminating the concept of overemphasized "green" statements. Such measures could go a long way in the process of reconstructing consumer confidence with a proper market for organic food that is safe for the environment. Help to these "Green friendly" businesses is essential and can be provided by "Green money," financial grants from the government, and special tax incentives. While adopting sustainable methods DECL for organizations, they are likely to gain, for example, increased trust among their publics, better positioning in the marketplace, and greater long-term stability. By going after the root cause of greenwashing and designing a cultural and economic climate of authenticity, India can proceed in its goal of fostering sustainable practices, thus helping not only the preservation of the global environment but the Indian economy as well.

References

Bala, S., Sharma, M., Dashora, K., Siddiqui, S., Diwan, D., & Tripathi, M. (2022). Nanomaterials based sustainable bioenergy production systems: Current trends and future prospects. *Nanofabrication*, *7*, 314–324.

Bansal, P., & Clelland, I. (2018). Investor influence on environmental, social, and governance factors: Implications for corporate greenwashing. *Journal of Business Ethics*, *149*(2), 349–364.

BIS. (2022). *Environmental management and voluntary certification statistics in India*. Bureau of Indian Standards.

Bowen, F., & Aragon-Correa, J. A. (2014). Greenwashing in corporate environmentalism: Forging links between regulation, environmental impacts, and business responsibility. *Business & Society*, *53*(2), 107–129.

Chen, L., Lai, P., & Wen, C. (2016). The influence of green organizational identity on green innovation: The mediating role of corporate environmental ethics. *Sustainability*, *8*(5), 397.

Confederation of Indian Industry (CII). (2020). *Corporate sustainability: The next frontier*. CII.

D'Souza, C., & Taghian, M. (2005). Green advertising effects on attitude and choice of advertising themes. *Asian Pacific Journal of Marketing and Logistics*, *17*(3), 51–66.

Dauvergne, P., & Lister, J. (2012). Big brand sustainability: Governance prospects and environmental limits. *Global Environmental Change*, *22*(1), 36–45.

Delmas, M. A., & Burbano, V. C. (2011). The drivers of greenwashing. *California Management Review*, *54*(1), 64–87.

Gandhi, A., & Sharma, V. (2021). The evolving role of SEBI in ESG compliance: A case of greenwashing in India. *Journal of Financial Regulation and Compliance*, *29* (1), 67–84.

Glaser, J. A., Sahle-Demessie, E., & Teri, L. R. (2022). Are reliable and emerging technologies available for plastic recycling in a circular economy? Waste material recycling in the circular economy-challenges and developments. IntechOpen.

Grimmer, M., & Bingham, T. (2013). Company environmental performance and consumer purchase intentions. *Journal of Business Research*, *66*(10), 1945–1953.

Jain, M., & Goyal, S. (2022). Impact of greenwashing on corporate reputation and consumer loyalty. *International Journal of Business Research and Development*, *11* (3), 205–218.

Johnson, C., & Fujita, R. (2020). Consumer green identity and responses to corporate greenwashing. *Environmental Psychology Review*, *10*(4), 467–490.

Kantar. (2020). Who cares, who does? A global study of sustainability attitudes and actions (India insights). https://www.kantar.com

Lim, W. M., Kumar, S., Pandey, N., Verma, D., & Kumar, D. (2023). Evolution and trends in consumer behaviour: Insights from Journal of Consumer Behaviour. *Journal of Consumer Behaviour*, *22*(1), 217–232.

Lin, C., & Chang, D. (2012). Eco-labeling in green marketing: Consumers' perception of the green label. *International Journal of Business and Social Science*, *3*(2), 74–81.

Lyon, T. P., & Montgomery, A. W. (2015). The means and end of greenwash. *Organization & Environment*, *28*(2), 223–249.

Lyons, L., Lecomte, E., Georgakaki, A., Letout, S., & Mountraki, A. (2022). *Clean energy technology observatory: Heat pumps in the European Union-2023 status report on technology development, trends, value chains and markets*. Publications Office of the European Union.

Marquis, C., Toffel, M. W., & Zhou, Y. (2016). Scrutiny, norms, and selective disclosure: A global study of greenwashing. *Organization Science*, *27*(2), 483–504.

McKinsey & Company. (2021). *India's sustainable future: Driving green growth*. McKinsey & Company.

Narula, S., & Upadhyay, S. (2021). Corporate social responsibility in India: Recent trends and implications. *Management of Environmental Quality*, *32*(4), 933–945.

Prasad, K., & Thomas, M. (2019). Corporate greenwashing in India: A consumer perspective. *Indian Journal of Marketing*, *49*(2), 15–25.

PwC India. (2021). *Sustainable business practices in India: Consumer trends and insights*. PwC India.

Ramachandran, M., & Mehta, P. (2022). Transparency and greenwashing in India: A regulatory perspective. *Environmental Policy and Law*, *52*(3), 187–194.

Reserve Bank of India (RBI). (2020). *Green financing report*. RBI.

Rexhepi, G., & Ramadani, V. (2021). Green marketing and social media: New pathways in digital business models. *International Journal of Sustainable Economy*, *13*(2), 156–169.

Saxena, A. (2020). Environmental policies and practices in India: A critical overview. *International Journal of Environmental Studies*, *77*(6), 946–963.

SEBI. (2022). *Business responsibility and sustainability report (BRSR) annual report*. Securities and Exchange Board of India.

Sharma, R., & Raina, M. (2021). Green marketing and consumer awareness: A study in the Indian context. *Journal of Business and Retail Management Research*, *15*(2), 128–135.

Singh, R., & Chandra, M. (2023). Blockchain and sustainable supply chains in India: Addressing greenwashing concerns. *Journal of Sustainable Supply Chain Management*, *8*(1), 34–45.

Stukhart, G. (2019). Greenwashing and consumer perception: Challenges in identifying sustainable practices. *Journal of Sustainable Business*, *7*(2), 45–58.

Terra Choice. (2010). *The sins of greenwashing: Home and family edition*. Environmental Marketing Claims in North America.

White, K., MacDonnell, R., & Ellard, J. H. (2012). Belief in a just world: Consumer intentions and the "green" response. *Psychology and Marketing*, *29*(9), 632–639.

World Bank. (2021). *Environmental regulation and monitoring in India*. World Bank.

World Economic Forum. (2022). Decarbonizing India: Pathways to sustainable growth. https://www.weforum.org

Chapter 9

Unmasking Greenwashing and Building Social Trust: Role of Social Media Influencer

Pinnika Syam Yadav[a], *P B Narendra Kiran*[a], *M Ruben Anto*[a], *G N P V Babu*[a], *Ankitha Sharma*[c] *and Arun Kumar*[b]

[a]Christ University, India
[b]Mianz International College Malé, The Republic of Maldives
[c]Lovely Professional University, India

Abstract

The current study aims to understand the role of social media influencers (SMIs) in promoting awareness of greenwashing. Over the last 10 years due to an increase in environmental awareness, the majority of consumers are trying to switch their daily routine to purchase more green products. The current study tries to understand the role of SMIs in the promotion of educating greenwashing via the mediating role of social trust. Through quantitative data, the study has collected data from a total of 423 respondents in the metropolitan city of New Delhi. The vast majority of the individuals in this specific region are educated and have purchased and promoted green products more than anyone. Through SmartPLS, the analyzed results indicate that SMIs have a significant role in promoting greenwashing. Furthermore, social trust has a stronger influence on greenwashing. Social trust has a significant mediating role in between SMIs to greenwashing. The study is first in nature trying to understand the role of SMIs in promoting greenwashing on social media platforms. The study results will help in enhancing consumers to make better informed decisions to purchase green products and expand the existing literature review.

Eco Illusions, 181–201

doi:10.1108/978-1-83662-782-120261009

Keywords: Social media influencers; social trust; level of awareness; SmartPLS; greenwashing; greenwashing education; frequency of purchase

Introduction

Over the last few years, it's been clear that people are paying attention to the environment, and these behavioural changes have made them much more aware of their purchases (De Falco et al., 2019). As public concern for the environment is rising, everybody is playing their part in the protection of the environment. Not just one sector, food, fashion, cosmetics and logistics, each sector has played a significant role in contributing and promoting (Badar et al., 2024) green Shield 'Green policies and technologies in production line' to protect the environment (Schmidt & Donsbach, 2012). Studies and policies have claimed to care about the environment (Badar et al., 2024), attitudes seldom translate into behavioural changes (Badar et al., 2024; Breves & Liebers, 2022; Pimonenko et al., 2020). The use of single-use plastic products has been a common practice in our society despite having sustainable alternatives (Schmuck et al., 2018). To engage eco-conscious consumers and drive sales by branding a product with a green label and emphasizing its environmental benefits (Badar et al., 2024) that include unsubstantiated and misleading statements that cannot be considered sustainable and green-friendly (Schmuck et al., 2018) or environmentally friendly. In context, marketers play deceitful tactics most known as greenwashing Torelli et al. (2020) and Martínez-López and López (2018). By hiding alternative motives, these brands try to present themselves as green brands so that customers try to engage with these brands. Marketers are genuinely paying much more attention to modifying the consumer attitude towards green consumption (Olbermann & Reis, 2024; Qayyum et al., 2023; Zhao & Lee, 2024). Through the circulation of green-masked products in society, individuals might regard them as critical and unable to understand the ulterior motives, which harms consumers' attitudes towards products that are advertised under the green label (Eng et al., 2021). Through these activities, consumers would be reluctant to adopt green consumption behaviour and unable to use sustainable product alternatives (Ende et al., 2023).

Existing studies have primarily examined the constructs, practices, and specific instances of greenwashing (Beppato, 2024). The studies focus on the influencer's role in educating and building social trust towards green products (Lyon & Montgomery, 2015), or the extent to which consumers (Zhang et al., 2018) are willing to learn about environmentally friendly (Zhang et al., 2018) products or services (Newton et al., 2015). Studies have stated that consumers are willing to fulfil their role with a good intention to protect the environment known as 'social responsibility' (Grimmer & Bingham, 2013) and some are even willing to pay a higher premium to products (Leblebici Kocer et al., 2023). Through education of greenwashing consumers tend to stop engaging in green activities which has an insignificant intention on consumers' trust (Chen et al., 2024).

In the digital landscape, social media influencers (SMIs) as brand endorsers play a vital role in marketing activities. It has been observed that last few years significant rise in online marketing activities, and e-commerce has picked up from 1.7 to 13.8 billion dollars in 2021 and at present 60 billion dollars officially mentioned on the India Brand Equity Foundation e-commerce industry report 2024. Studies have also noticed that SMIs have gained huge popularity, and a considerable number of articles have been published in 2018 (Hudders et al., 2021). Scholarly studies have stated that influencers have a significant impact on advertising activities, through the activities of influencers, number of followers, credibility, reliability, and advertising disclosure (De Veirman et al., 2017; Eisend et al., 2020), some studies have even worked on the agreement between SMIs and endorsed brand products (Breves et al., 2019; De Veirman et al., 2017). The relationship between the influencers and their followers is generally termed a parasocial relationship and has been recognized to explain the cognitive (Yuan & Lou, 2020), the current study has identified that none of the studies have focused on the SMI in unveiling non-green products, popularly known as greenwashing (Hwang & Zhang, 2018; Reinikainen et al., 2020).

Literature Review

Social Media Influencer

The use of real people as instruments of influence to sell and produce content in a way that persuades the public has long been explored by the literature of celebrity endorsements (Yuan & Lou, 2020). More recently, with the widespread adoption of the Internet and the emergence of digital social networks, a new breed of celebrity, the 'influencer', has become the subject of study (Llamas, 2024). These social media personalities are credited with having large online followers who value their opinions while modulating these opinions in line with the interests of commercial stakeholders. Influencers form part of a wider set of promotional forces employed by brands and small businesses that use social media to reach diverse segments of the public (Zaid et al., 2022). They produce content that can inform, persuade, entertain, shape tastes, and help their followers feel part of a specific community (Goanță & Ranchordás, 2020). SMIs play the role of trendsetters, curator of tastes and distributors of messages (Nuji et al., 2023). They create and deliver original and engaging content produced in different forms, owning narratives of different dimensions while maintaining a storytelling format. Influencers use channels such as written blogs, photo blogs and video blogs with content formatted to either entertain or instruct and to drive consumer engagement. These platforms are typically used in a lifestyle context, which can include food and fashion, health and fitness, beauty, travel, parenting and pets, among other themes (Goanță & Ranchordás, 2020). As a form of advertising, SMIs affect the power of persuasion and the building of a personal image. Studies show that celebrity endorsements can stimulate attitude change and revalue a brand's image. Based on their followers and readers, sponsors see influencers as the ideal candidates to segment the female market and access other social media niches, such as young fashion-interested male consumers (Tartaraj et al., 2024).

Prajapati (2023) Marketing scholars have extensively employed numerous theoretical frameworks to understand SMI marketing. Social proof explains how consumers imitate the behaviours of others in an attempt to undertake reasonable actions (Jin et al., 2019). Such content seems more trustworthy, leading to increased purchase intentions. Source credibility is the extent of trustworthiness and expertise associated with the source of information (Arora et al., 2019). It influences the effectiveness of the SMI in trying to elicit an attitude shift or behaviour change, applying the principle of liking or homophily, which is also associated with source-related variables (Chivandi et al., 2019). The Elaboration Likelihood Model explains that there are a number of variables that can help marketers assess which route to persuasion (Ayob et al., 2023) is more beneficial, depending on various situational factors as they relate to the SMI and their ability to persuade their followers. Recent conceptual examinations of SMIs have proposed the application of the congruence concept referred to in the literature as brand fit. Following the principles of Attribution Theory (Joshi et al., 2023), consumers are more favourable to a brand fit endorser as they see that person as being genuinely congruent with the product being endorsed and so more tightly link the paired entities. Therefore, superior marketing outcomes are expected when the manager considers this variable Consumer's trust (Vukmirović et al., 2020) and engage (Mim et al., 2022).

Several studies have been undertaken through the application of eWoM to identify what shapes consumer-influencer relationships in this digital milieu. Family brand and family user modelling are based on studies where the SMI recorded in the marketing context is a friend or family member (Goanță & Ranchordás, 2020; Zniva et al., 2023). This research has typically been framed through the general SMI literature to try to generalize as to what works, what does not, and what is consumer sentiment concerning using this form of advertising strategy (Wellman et al., 2020). Many of these studies look at the top two most used social media sites. The family Facebook research has reported on a range of issues such as gender differences in response to SMIs, the impact of brand in this forum, the issue of authenticity in a world of fake ads and paid influencers, the psychology of friends (or familiarity) of the SMI (Goanță & Ranchordás, 2020; Vukmirović et al., 2020) as a way to connect and have product influence in purchase, and the modelling of consumption promoted through SMI marketing (Kovalevski et al., 2020). The Instagram family brand work has framed research questions looking at consumer attitudes to SMIs on the platform, as well as how they have been impacted by fraudulent users, which has questioned the authenticity of (Chew, 2025) eWoM in this domain and how it impacts social media indirect-to-consumer marketing. This preceding work has adopted a family (Zniva et al., 2023) of concepts relating to this subfield of consumer influencer marketing and has developed a range of measures in this area; for example, family brand engagement (Dwivedi et al., 2021), relationship equity, and others, all designed for a domestic consumption view. A macro view of eWoM has adopted a different modelling than the micro consumer-influencer relationships noted above.

SMI to Social Trust

The preferential field of the research is SMIs and their function in building communal confidence and uncovering greenwashing (Lacerda, 2022; McCole et al., 2009). In contemporary years, some brands have been accused of utilizing greenwashing advertising approaches, and YouTube influencers have the prospective to unmask these greenwashing activities to their followers (Erdem & Harrison-Walker, 2006; Wu & Lin, 2016). The trust in brands has a noteworthy function for consumers, while they preferentially prefer to purchase from trustworthy and authentic brands and are more likely to suggest these brands to their households and pals. In this sense, brand reliability is linked with trust in a brand (McCole et al., 2009; Unsal & Ozkan, 2024; Xu, 2014). Social trust is the mutual reliance on one another between individuals and communal trust is collective and disintegrated across the society, referring to the confidence in each other (Unsal & Ozkan, 2024). At the societal level, the trust is communal and a nation may have diverse quantities of social trust depending on the communal context. Social trust has the enhancing function to neutralize communal disorder and to make simple affairs in community and it can further improve the public spheres and preference to follow the laws and rules (Xu, 2014). This social dynamic can be significantly influenced by SMIs, who possess the ability to shape perceptions and foster relationships among community members.

Such benefits can yield social trust as those consumers are motivated to positively interact and contribute to social norms (Kim & Kim, 2021; Liu & Lee, 2024; Ohanian, 1990) due to increased transparency and authenticity that such influences bring to the game. This, in turn, builds a community where members feel appreciated and cared for, leading to a supportive ecosystem that enables mutual support and principles. However, as trust is established between SMIs and their audience, studies considered that a balance was supposed to be maintained between SMIs and their audience to maintain authenticity and transparency (Lowry et al., 2013; McCole et al., 2009). This has a significant impact on brands by establishing a sustainable outlook via influencer promotion and information (Rizzo et al., 2023; Zniva et al., 2023). Previous studies stated that influencer amplifies their followers via their content to heighten the sense of sustainable practices, furthermore, fostering a culture of transparency and ethical consumerism (Kim et al., 2021; Kim & Kim, 2021).

Besides, the exchange not only encourages people to improve their behaviour but also helps to maintain a community that shares sustainable practices. Influencers are change agents who help brands to get identity among consumers and vice versa, by using social media as a convenient platform to promote sustainable brands (Lacerda, 2022). Specifically, social trust has a positive and direct relationship with consumer adoption. Consumers are likely to follow these influencers' content on a virtual platform by engaging with social audiences and enabling them to invest in the influencer's content (Erdem & Harrison-Walker, 2006; Wu & Lin, 2016). However, some studies suggested that SMIs lack authenticity and trust, as many consumers don't have confidence in the content promoted by the influencers. Social trust plays a pivotal role in influencing the Unmasking greenwashing operations, and it is analyzed that exposure of influencer content will strengthen on promotion of education on green products to avoid greenwashing (Lacerda, 2022).

SMI to Greenwashing

Greenwashing is the deceptive use of environmental claims to sell products to consumers. Masks reference the deceptive facade of green claims vis-á-vis product content (Delmas & Burbano, 2011; Dwivedi et al., 2021). Wrong use of green mask may mislead consumers about a product's biodegradability (Long et al., 2024). Green masks, such as packaging, can additionally falsely suggest that a product itself is green.

Recent studies on Green masking (Li et al., 2022) stated that setting a product mask and virality masks and greenwashing make a hidden and viral mask of the greenwashed image (Delmas & Burbano, 2011) formed the basis for such deception. Masks, prevalent empirical research is referenced as evidence for three controversial relationships with greenwash products and for the mechanisms connecting greenwashing with these relationships (Dutta et al., 2024). These relationships reveal the unintended role of influencers in perpetuating false narratives surrounding sustainability, thereby complicating the trust framework between consumers and brands (Delmas & Burbano, 2011; Nyilasy et al., 2014). Studies analyzing the Digital technologies, particularly the role of SMIs in constructing conceptions of environmental responsibilities, should also not be overlooked (Nazish et al., 2024).

SMIs play a significant role in the promotion of environmental discussions. Studies stated that promoting sustainability can be quite unintentional and end up fuelling greenwashing (Pimonenko et al., 2020; Sailer et al., 2022). The significant reach of influencers allows them to eco eco-friendly products, though it also stirs doubts about whether what they say is truly legit (Zhang & Liansheng, 2024). Which has been addressed in Fig. 9.1 Conceptual Framework, carefully shape their online images, these differences can promote environmental care, and just slick marketing gets a bit blurry-often eroding trust among consumers. In most cases, this so-called 'greenwashing' makes people believe they support real sustainable practices, while, in reality, they're just being drawn in by smart, sometimes even cheeky, promotional tactics (Netto et al., 2020).

Influencers find themselves in a tangled digital scenario where they must be straight forward about their brand ties and genuinely show care for environmental causes (Ktisti et al., 2022). Taking this Route generally boosts trust and in many cases helps audience start to notice the difference between real eco-actions and plain marketing actions (Pimonenko et al., 2020). When they back companies that truly invest in sustainability, they often play a big part in

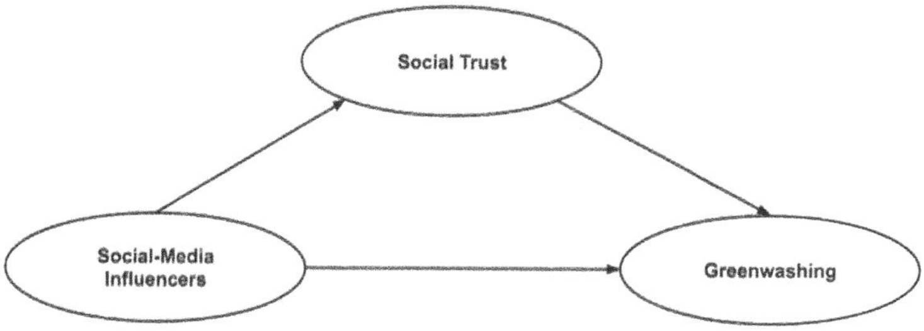

Fig. 9.1. Conceptual Framework.

curbing greenwashing and even spark fresh debates on what environmental responsibility really means (Kwon et al., 2023), a move that both spotlights genuine brands and consumers' influence towards more careful choices. Influencers can channel sneaky risks of greenwashing, to questioning and hands-on eco-friendly pitches (Chew, 2025). This kind of clarity, in most of cases, hands over power to consumers hands gradually pushing companies to adopt truly sustainable practices. Dropping hints about the tricks of greenwashing, they help foster an air of transparency and accountability in the current market scenario (Eng et al., 2021; Liu et al., 2023; Sailer et al., 2022). Studies suggested that brands sometimes overstate their green claims and in turn, fuel a habit of closer scrutiny about sustainability (Fang, 2024). Some influencers take money to produce advertising content. Examples of influencer advertising can be seen on various platforms. These may be declared advertising, but often the paid-for nature of the post is vague or hidden. A meta-analysis of experiments finds varying effects on trust when viewers can infer a financially motivated bias, but on average, this reduces trust. Optionally paid cooperation of influencers can be a kind of promotional activity, including greenwashing. Cases of greenwashing promoted by influencer cooperation are discussed based on their own research in the context of theoretical models. Social trust is an important consideration for maintaining consumers with a business, especially in new and dynamic contexts (Dutta et al., 2024; Pimonenko et al., 2020).

Research Methodology

To analyze people's perception of greenwashing among Indian consumers, the study has collected data from online chat rooms, social activity platforms, and social media platforms, where social media influencers are more active in creating and engaging with content. The study gathered quantitative data from SMIs, Social Trust, and Greenwashing constructs through Google Forms. A total of 452 participants have been actively considered for the final evaluation; a total of 128 respondents have been excluded from the study via screening questions. The data demographics are as follows:

The gender distribution Table 9.1 presents a detailed representation of data breakdown by gender. Out of 452 respondents, 259 respondents have been identified as male, consisting of a total of 57.3% of the data set, and 193 respondents as female, consisting a total of 42.7% of the data set.

Similarly, in Table 9.2, Age presents a detailed breakdown of respondents' age as follows: Out of 452 respondents, 15 respondents are less than 18 years old, consisting of a total of 3.3% of the data set, and 41 respondents are between 18 and 30 years old, with 9.1% of the data set. One hundred and fifty-eight respondents are between 30 and 40 years old, with 35% of the data set; 208 respondents are between 40 and 50 years old, with 46% of the data set; and a total of 30 respondents are more than 50 years with 6.6% of the entire population.

Similarly, in Table 9.3, Education presents a detailed breakdown of respondents' education as follows: Out of 452 respondents, 22 respondents have an education level of 'High School of less', consisting of a total of 4.9% of the data set, and 72 respondents have an education level up to 'Plus 12', consisting of a total of 15.9% of the data set. One hundred and eighty-six respondents were educated up to graduation, consisting of a total of 41.2% of the data set; 153 respondents have a 'Post-graduation degree', consisting of a total of 33.8% of the data set; and a total of 19 respondents are at the 'PhD level', consisting of a total of 4.2% of the entire population.

Table 9.1. Gender Frequency Distribution.

Gender	**Frequency**	**Percent**
Male	259	57.3
Female	193	42.7
Total	452	100.0

Table 9.2. Age Frequency Distribution.

Age	**Frequency**	**Percent**
>18	15	3.3
18–30	41	9.1
30–40	158	35.0
40–50	208	46.0
<50	30	6.6
Total	452	100.0

Table 9.3. Education Frequency Distribution.

Education	Frequency	Percent
High school or less	22	4.9
Plus 12	72	15.9
Graduation	186	41.2
Post-graduation	153	33.8
PhD or higher	19	4.2
Total	452	100.0

Table 9.4. Level of Awareness Frequency Distribution.

Level of Awareness	Frequency	Percent
Not at all aware	16	3.5
Slightly aware	60	13.3
Somewhat aware	169	37.4
Moderately aware	184	40.7
Extremely aware	23	5.1
Total	452	100.0

Similarly, in Table 9.4, Level of Awareness presents a detailed breakdown of respondents' level of awareness as follows: Out of 452 respondents, 16 respondents are 'Not at all aware', consisting of a total of 3.5% of the data set, and 60 respondents 'Slightly aware', consisting of a total of 13.3% of the data set. One hundred and sixty-nine respondents are 'Somewhat aware', consisting of a total of 37.4% of the data set; 184 respondents are 'Moderately aware', consisting of a total of 40.7% of the data set; and a total of 23 respondents are 'Extremely aware', consisting of a total of 5.1% of the entire population.

Similarly, in Table 9.5, Frequency of Purchase presents a detailed breakdown of respondents' Frequency of Purchase as follows: Out of 452 respondents, 11 respondents are 'Never', consisting of a total of 2.4% of the data set, and 68 respondents are 'Rarely', consisting of a total of 15% of the data set. Two hundred and six respondents are 'Sometimes', consisting of a total of 45.6% of the data set; 147 respondents are 'Often', consisting of a total of 32.5% of the data set; and a total of 20 respondents are 'Always, consisting of a total of 4.4% of the entire population.

Table 9.5. Frequency of Purchase.

Frequency of Purchase	Frequency	Percent
Never	11	2.4
Rarely	68	15.0
Sometimes	206	45.6
Often	147	32.5
Always	20	4.4
Total	452	100.0

Analysis

The collected data were analyzed using SmartPLS to test the hypotheses through Structural Equation Modeling–Partial Least Squares. Although the proposed model was relatively simple, SmartPLS was selected due to its covariance-based estimation approach. The research investigates the effect of SMIs on greenwashing education, incorporating social trust as a mediator in the analytical framework in the Fig. 9.2 PLS Model. Furthermore, the study has taken the frequency of purchases and level of awareness as moderators in the study.

The study evaluates the constructed model through the PLS algorithm using SmartPLS, outer loading, the average variance extracted (AVE), the composite reliability (CR) and the Rho factor, which will be used by us all along the process of doing the reliability investigation. Table 9.6; Construct Model has provided a detailed explanation of the constructs with outer loadings more than 0.7, composite reliability, and Cronbach Alpha values are more than 0.7, and the AVE

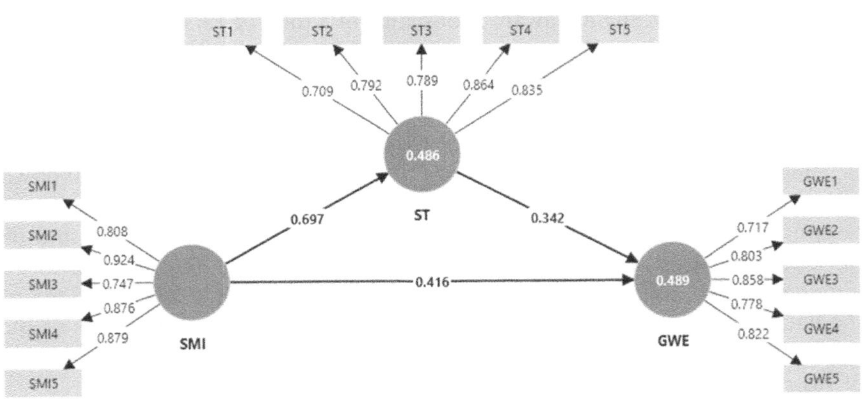

Fig. 9.2. PLS-Model.

Table 9.6. Construct Model.

Construct Model						
Construct	**Item**	**Outer Loading**	**AVE**	**CR**	**Cronbach's Alpha**	**rho_A**
Social media influencer	*SMI1*	0.808	0.721	0.928	0.907	0.902
	SMI2	0.924				
	SMI3	0.747				
	SMI4	0.876				
	SMI5	0.879				
Social trust	*ST1*	0.709	0.639	0.898	0.874	0.859
	ST2	0.792				
	ST3	0.789				
	ST4	0.864				
	ST5	0.835				
Greenwashing education	*GWE1*	0.717	0.635	0.897	0.866	0.856
	GWE2	0.803				
	GWE3	0.858				
	GWE4	0.778				
	GWE5	0.822				

values are more than 0.5. Through the following results, the study concludes that data has a high degree of internal consistency, showing reliability.

To assess the construct validity, the study has utilized discriminant validity through HTMT and the FLC to assess the data discriminant validity of the instruments. Through Table 9.7, Discriminant Validity, it could be observed that HTMT values are less than 0.875, indicating that the data are discriminant, and similarly in the FLC tables, the adjacent values from top to bottom and right to left are in descending order, confirming that the data are discriminately valid.

Throughout the study effort, the R2 and Q2 values were used to assess the model's performance and improve the accuracy of its predictions. In Table 9.8, Predictive Model Assessment demonstrates that these metrics were used to assess the model (He et al., 2024) and its ability to make accurate predictions. Given that the R2 value of the research is lower than 0.5, it may be concluded that the model has a limited impact. The give obtained values are assessed based on the previous studies of Hair, Sarstedt, & Ringle (2019). The Stone-Geisser Q2 was used to assess the predictive (Hair, Risher, et al., 2019) importance of the model, as shown by Khan et al. (2019) and Shmueli et al. (2019). Both Stone (1977) and Pandey and

Table 9.7. Discriminant Validity.

Discriminant-Validity							
HTMT				**FLC**			
	GWE	*SMI*	*ST*		*GWE*	*SMI*	*ST*
GWE				*GWE*	**0.797**		
SMI	0.738			*SMI*	0.654	**0.849**	
ST	0.716	0.777		*ST*	0.632	0.697	**0.799**

Note: Latent variables are highlighted in bold to emphasize their role as unobserved theoretical constructs in structural models. This formatting distinguishes them from observed indicators, enhances clarity in tables or diagrams, and guides readers' attention to key components of the analysis, especially when interpreting factor loadings or evaluating model relationships.

Table 9.8. Predictive Model Assessment.

Endogenous Latent Constructs	**R-Square**	**R-Square Adjusted**	**Q^2_Predict**	**RMSE**	**MAE**
GWE	0.489	0.487	0.423	0.765	0.522
ST	0.486	0.485	0.482	0.723	0.512
Value effect size: 0.02, Small; 0.15, Medium; 0.35, Large					

Source: Author's own calculations.

Yadav (2023) said that the model demonstrated a significant level of predictive significance in their respective conversations.

The study moves to test the hypothesis through Bootstrapping via SmartPLS with 5,000 sub-samples. The hypothesized model can be observed in Fig. 9.3; Hypothesized Model.

The study tried to test the direct effect technique, which states in the following way that 'X has a direct effect on Y' (Mitchell & Maxwell, 2013). If the study has identified that X does or does not have a direct effect on Y (Chen et al., 2013), then via the mediation effect through indirect effect, the study is going to affect X on Y with M in between as a mediator. To assess the hypothesis, the study will utilize the T values and p values as a general construct to assess the hypothesis. From the above Fig. 9.3, it could be observed that all the direct construct paths have significant relationships.

A total of 4 hypotheses have been proposed to assess the model; 3 Direct and 1 indirect path were proposed and presented in the above Table 9.9, Hypothesis Assessment. All 4 proposed hypotheses have significant relationships. Hypothesis H1: There is a significant relationship between SMIs and social trust have a significant relationship (T = 22.033; P = 0.00). Hypothesis H2: There is a significant relationship between social trust and greenwashing education (T = 6.432;

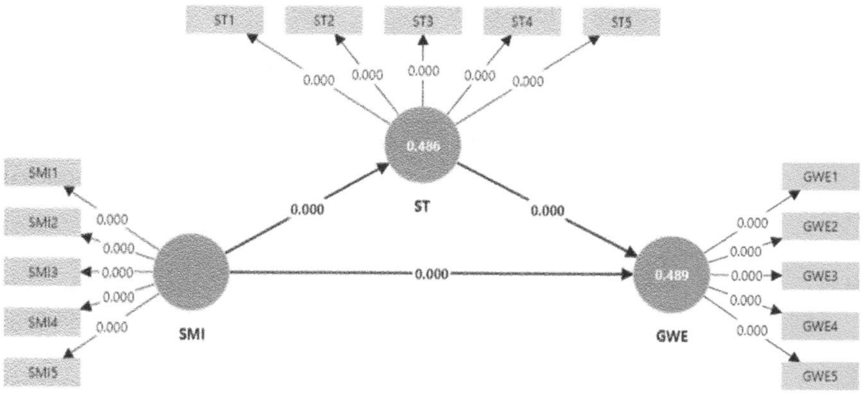

Fig. 9.3. Hypothesized Model.

Table 9.9. Hypothesis Assessment.

Hypothesis	Path	Path Coefficient	SE	*t*-Statistics	*p* Values	Decision
H1	SMI → ST	0.698	0.032	22.033	0	Supported
H2	ST → GWE	0.342	0.053	6.432	0	Supported
H3	SMI → GWE	0.416	0.051	8.137	0	Supported
H4	SMI → ST → GWE	0.239	0.038	6.321	0	Supported

Source: Author's own calculations.

P = 0.00). Hypothesis H3: There is a significant relationship between SMIs and greenwashing education (T = 8.137; P = 0.00), and Hypothesis H4: There is a significant mediation effect of Social Trust between social media influencers and Greenwashing Education (T = 6.321; P = 0.00).

Furthermore, the study has conducted a moderating effect using the Level of awareness and Frequency of purchase to effect the SMIs to greenwashing education presented in Table 9.10; Moderating Effect Table and Fig. 9.4; Moderating Model.

From the above table study concludes that there is no moderating role of Level of awareness and Frequency of purchase. All the construct paths have shown significant negative relationships.

Discussion and Conclusion

The results of the research show that the Social Media Flow has a significant, positive and mediating effect on green purchase intention (Yesiloglu &

Table 9.10. Moderating Effect Table.

Hypothesis	Path	Path Coefficient	SE	t-Statistics	p Values	Decision
H1a	LA × SMI → ST	−0.024	0.051	0.536	0.592	Not supported
H2a	LA × ST → GWE	0.075	0.06	1.378	0.168	Not supported
H3a	LA × SMI → GWE	−0.055	0.063	1.017	0.309	Not supported
H4a	LA × SMI → ST → GWE	−0.008	0.017	0.531	0.595	Not supported
H1b	FP × SMI → ST	0.023	0.052	0.567	0.571	Not supported
H2b	FP × ST → GWE	0.037	0.059	0.492	0.622	Not supported
H3b	FP × SMI → GWE	−0.029	0.061	0.279	0.78	Not supported
H4b	FP × SMI → ST → GWE	0.008	0.018	0.566	0.571	Not supported

Source: Author's own calculations.

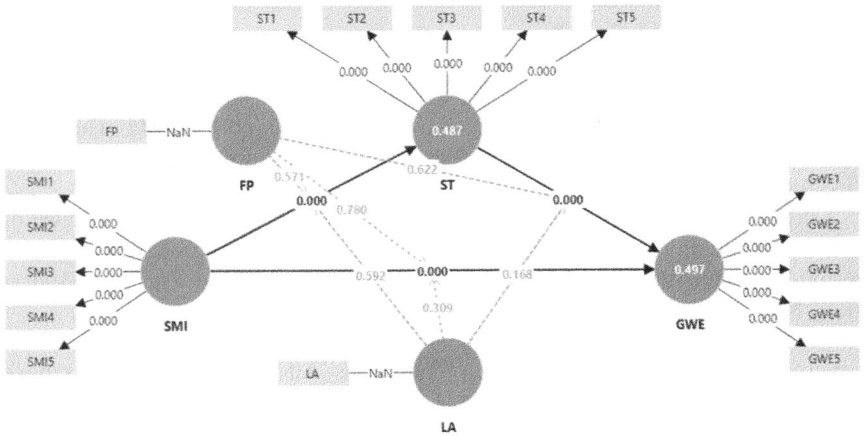

Fig. 9.4. Moderating Model.

Costello, 2020). Greenwashing is the insincere act of wrongfully representing an organization or product as environmentally beneficial. It supports eco illusion, where consumers genuinely think they are making resourceful choices, but they are misled into the fabrication of brand images. This has to be debated, as corporate greenwashing could undermine current practical sustainability efforts. The sharing economy, which includes all circular usage models, Environmental, Social and Governance (ESG) principles, and Sustainable Development Goals (SDGs), provides an opportunity and a challenge when considering the building of greenwashing. While circular economic practices enhance resource efficiency and ESG principles promote corporate accountability, businesses may also adopt these frameworks superficially, resulting in sustainability efforts that project an eco-friendly image rather than delivering meaningful environmental mitigation. When considering the emerging sharing economy, the impacts on sustainability ultimately rest on transparency, consumer knowledge and regulatory enforcement: calling customers' bluff, so to speak, and making sure it results in real impact and real change and not just marketing stories. In reality, without the enforcement of real transparency within this space, businesses can easily use sustainability narratives to passively mislead consumers instead of to advance systemic environmental change. Therefore, to diminish greenwashing, we need critical dialogue around corporate accountability and consumer awareness while working against eco illusion and shifting this to tangible progress in sustainability.

A scale measuring the Social Media Flow in the context of sustainable environment activities that are sponsored by companies, by the green parties organizing communities is developed and validated. The operationalization of the Social Media Flow in the context of environmental activism is new and adds to the existing body of research. It is expected that these findings will be beneficial and contribute to businesses and organizations, especially in designing and delivering messages that improve the followers' positive responses towards an environmentally sustainable behaviour on social media (Segumpan & Zahari, 2022). Last but not least, it is highly likely that businesses and organizations will generate a new perspective in utilizing social media as a means to communicate the brand in order to reach out and influence potential customers. This shift not only emphasizes transparency but also aligns with consumer expectations for authenticity. As social media continues to evolve, influencers will play a crucial role in holding brands accountable, fostering a culture of honesty and integrity.

SMIs and brands have a positive relationship to amplify their impact on greenwashing, those misleading claims accompanied with brands about being eco-friendly. By being transparent and authentic, they can help people make smarter decisions. The study results indicate that SMIs have a real influence. By prioritizing transparency and ditching empty claims, we can push for a future where 'going green' means actual action, not just a trendy hashtag.

References

Arora, A., Bansal, S., Kandpal, C., Aswani, R., & Dwivedi, Y. K. (2019). Measuring social media influencer index- insights from Facebook, Twitter and Instagram. *Journal of Retailing and Consumer Services*, *49*, 86. Elsevier BV. https://doi.org/10.1016/j.jretconser.2019.03.012

Ayob, N. A., Kamaruddin, N. A., & Zaidi, M. Z. H. M. (2023). Social influencer factors that affect young adult buying behaviour. *International Journal of Academic Research in Business and Social Sciences*, *13*(1). https://doi.org/10.6007/ijarbss/v13-i1/14610

Badar, M. A, Gupta, R., Srivastava, P., Ali, I., & Cudney, E. A. (Eds.). (2024). *Handbook of digital innovation, transformation, and sustainable development in a post-pandemic era*. CRC Press.

Beppato, C. (2024). *Greenwashing and sustainability: People's perception, awareness, and behavior* (Master's thesis). Universidade NOVA de Lisboa.

Breves, P., & Liebers, N. (2022). #Greenfluencing. The impact of parasocial relationships with social media influencers on advertising effectiveness and followers' pro-environmental intentions. *Environmental Communication*, *16*(6), 773–787.

Breves, P. L., Liebers, N., Abt, M., & Kunze, A. (2019). The perceived fit between Instagram influencers and the endorsed brand: How influencer–brand fit affects source credibility and persuasive effectiveness. *Journal of Advertising Research*, *59* (4), 440–454.

Chen, J. T., Beckfield, J., Waterman, P. D., & Krieger, N. (2013). Can changes in the distributions of and associations between education and income bias temporal comparisons of health disparities? An exploration with causal graphs and simulations. *American journal of epidemiology*, *177*(9), 870–881.

Chen, L., Ma, Y., Feng, G. F., & Chang, C. P. (2024). Does environmental governance mitigate the detriment of greenwashing on innovation in China? *Pacific-Basin Finance Journal*, *86*, 102450.

Chew, F. P. (Ed.). (2025). *Global dialogue on media dynamics, trends and perspectives on public relations and communication: Proceedings of the international conference on public relations and media communication, (PRMC 2024)*, June 28–30, 2024, Beijing, China (1st ed.). CRC Press. https://doi.org/10.1201/9781003564966

Chivandi, A., Samuel, M. O., & Muchie, M. (2019). Social media, consumer behavior, and service marketing. In *Consumer behavior, and service marketing*. IntechOpen. https://doi.org/10.5772/intechopen.85406

De Falco, F., Di Pace, E., Cocca, M., & Avella, M. (2019). The contribution of washing processes of synthetic clothes to microplastic pollution. *Scientific Reports*, *9*(1), 6633.

de Veirman, M., Cauberghe, V., & Hudders, L. (2017). Marketing through Instagram influencers: The impact of number of followers and product divergence on brand attitude. *International Journal of Advertising*, *36*(5), 798–828.

Delmas, M. A., & Burbano, V. C. (2011). The drivers of greenwashing. *California Management Review*, *54*(1), 64–87. https://doi.org/10.1525/cmr.2011.54.1.64

Dutta, S., Rocha, Á., Dutta, P. K., Bhattacharya, P., & Singh, R. (2024). *Advances in data analytics for influencer marketing: An interdisciplinary approach*. Springer.

Dwivedi, Y. K., Ismagilova, E., Hughes, D. L., Carlson, J., Filieri, R., Jacobson, J., Jain, V., Karjaluoto, H., Kefi, H., Krishen, A. S., Kumar, V., Rahman, M. M., Raman, R., Rauschnabel, P. A., Rowley, J., Salo, J., Tran, G. A., & Wang, Y. (2021). Setting the future of digital and social media marketing research: Perspectives and research propositions. *International Journal of Information Management*, *59*, 102168.

Eisend, M., Van Reijmersdal, E. A., Boerman, S. C., & Tarrahi, F. (2020). A meta-analysis of the effects of disclosing sponsored content. *Journal of Advertising*, *49*(3), 344–366.

Ende, L., Reinhard, M. A., & Göritz, L. (2023). Detecting greenwashing! The influence of product colour and product price on consumers' detection accuracy of faked bio-fashion. *Journal of Consumer Policy*, *46*(2), 155–189.

Eng, N., DiRusso, C., Troy, C. L. C., Freeman, J. R., Liao, M. Q., & Sun, Y. (2021). 'I had no idea that greenwashing was even a thing': Identifying the cognitive mechanisms of exemplars in greenwashing literacy interventions. *Environmental Education Research*, *27*(11), 1599–1617. https://doi.org/10.1080/13504622.2021.1976732

Erdem, Ş., & Harrison-Walker, L. J. (2006). The role of the Internet in physician–patient relationships: The issue of trust. *Business Horizons*, *49*(5), 387. https://doi.org/10.1016/j.bushor.2006.01.003

Fang, Z. (2024). Greenwashing versus green authenticity: How green social media influences consumer perceptions and green purchase decisions. *Sustainability*, *16*, 10723. https://doi.org/10.3390/su162310723

Goanță, C., & Ranchordás, S. (2020). The regulation of social media influencers: An introduction. In *The regulation of social media Influencers*. Edward Elgar Publishing. https://doi.org/10.4337/9781788978286.00008

Grimmer, M., & Bingham, T. (2013). Company environmental performance and consumer purchase intentions. *Journal of business research*, *66*(10), 1945–1953.

Hair, J. F., Risher, J. J., Sarstedt, M., & Ringle, C. M. (2019). When to use and how to report the results of PLS-SEM. *European Business Review*, *31*(1), 2–24. https://doi.org/10.1108/EBR-11-2018-0203

Hair, J. F., Sarstedt, M., & Ringle, C. M. (2019). Rethinking some of the rethinking of partial least squares. *European Journal of Marketing*, *53*(4), 566–584. https://doi.org/10.1108/EJM-10-2018-0665

He, J., Li, W., Zhao, W., Shen, H., Chang, Y., Liu, B., He, Q., Yu, H., Wang, Y., Shi, L., & Cai, X. (2024). Potential of lncRNAs to regulate cuproptosis in hepatocellular carcinoma: Establishment and validation of a novel risk model. *Heliyon*, *10*(2).

Hudders, L., De Jans, S., & De Veirman, M. (2021). The commercialization of social media stars: A literature review and conceptual framework on the strategic use of social media influencers. *Social Media Influencers in Strategic Communication*, 24–67.

Hwang, K., & Zhang, Q. (2018). Influence of parasocial relationship between digital celebrities and their followers on followers' purchase and electronic word-of-mouth intentions, and persuasion knowledge. *Computers in Human Behavior*, *87*, 155–173.

Jin, S. A., Muqaddam, A., & Ryu, E. (2019). Instafamous and social media influencer marketing. *Marketing Intelligence & Planning*, *37*(5), 567. https://doi.org/10.1108/mip-09-2018-0375

Joshi, Y., Lim, W. M., Jagani, K., & Kumar, S. (2023). Social media influencer marketing: Foundations, trends, and ways forward. *Electronic Commerce Research*. https://doi.org/10.1007/s10660-023-09719-z

Khan, G. F., Sarstedt, M., Shiau, W. L., Hair, J. F., Ringle, C. M., & Fritze, M. P. (2019). Methodological research on partial least squares structural equation modeling (PLS-SEM): An analysis based on social network approaches. *Internet Research*, *29*(3), 407–429. https://doi.org/10.1108/IntR-12-2017-0509

Kim, J., Giroux, M., & Lee, J. C. (2021). When do you trust AI? The effect of number presentation detail on consumer trust and acceptance of AI recommendations. *Psychology and Marketing*, (*38*(7), 1140. https://doi.org/10.1002/mar.21498

Kim, D. Y., & Kim, H.-Y. (2021). Trust me, trust me not: A nuanced view of influencer marketing on social media. *Journal of Business Research*, *134*, 223. https://doi.org/10.1016/j.jbusres.2021.05.024

Kovalevski, V. V., Reinikainen, S. P., Reinikainen, V., Rozhkova, V. S., & Sihvonen, T. (2020). Shungite rocks of varying genesis in innovative water treatment technologies. *Transactions of KarRC RAS*, *6*, 97–105.

Ktisti, E., Hatzithomas, L., & Boutsouki, C. (2022). Green advertising on social media: A systematic literature review. *Sustainability*, *14*, 14424. https://doi.org/10.3390/su142114424

Kwon, K., Lee, J., Wang, C.-K., & Diwanji, V. S. (2023). From green advertising to greenwashing: Content analysis of global corporations' green advertising on social media. *International Journal of Advertising*, *43*, 97. https://doi.org/10.1080/02650487.2023.2208489

Lacerda, M. (2022). Contra o comunismo demoníaco: o apoio evangélico ao regime militar brasileiro e seu paralelo com o endosso da direita cristã ao governo Bolsonaro. *Religião & Sociedade*, *42*(1), 153–176.

Leblebici Kocer, L., Senturk Ulucak, Z., & Delice Akca, T. (2023). The role of environmental concern in purchasing decision on organic food and the link to greenwashing. *Environment, Development and Sustainability*, 1–24.

Li, W., Li, W., Seppänen, V., & Koivumäki, T. (2022). Effects of greenwashing on financial performance: Moderation through local environmental regulation and media coverage. *Business Strategy and the Environment*, *32*, 820. https://doi.org/10.1002/bse.3177

Liu, F., & Lee, Y. H. (2024). Virtually authentic: Examining the match-up hypothesis between human vs virtual influencers and product types. *The Journal of Product and Brand Management*, *33*(2), 287–299.

Liu, Y., Li, W., Wang, L., & Meng, Q. (2023). Why greenwashing occurs and what happens afterwards? A systematic literature review and future research agenda. *Environmental Science and Pollution Research*, *30*, 118102. https://doi.org/10.1007/s11356-023-30571-z

Llamas, M. (2024). *Blogging mastery: Analyzing the key strategies behind successful blogs* (Doctoral dissertation). Pepperdine University.

Long, L., Wang, C., & Zhang, M. (2024). Does social media pressure induce corporate hypocrisy? Evidence of ESG greenwashing from China. *Journal of Business Ethics*, 1. https://doi.org/10.1007/s10551-024-05747-3

Lowry, P. B., Wilson, D. W., & Haig, W. (2013). A picture is worth a thousand words: Source credibility theory applied to logo and website design for heightened credibility and consumer trust. *International Journal of Human-Computer Interaction*, *30*(1), 63. https://doi.org/10.1080/10447318.2013.839899

Lyon, T. P., & Montgomery, A. W. (2015). The means and end of greenwash. *Organization & Environment*, *28*(2), 223–249.

Martínez-López, F. J., & López, D. L. (2018). *Advances in digital marketing and eCommerce, second international conference, 2021*. Springer Cham. https://doi.org/10.1007/978-3-030-76520-0

McCole, P., Ramsey, E., & Williams, J. (2009). Trust considerations on attitudes towards online purchasing: The moderating effect of privacy and security concerns. *Journal of Business Research*, *63*(9), 1018. https://doi.org/10.1016/j.jbusres.2009.02.025

Mim, K. B., Jai, T., & Lee, S. (2022). The influence of sustainable positioning on eWOM and brand loyalty: Analysis of credible sources and transparency practices based on the S-O-R model. *Sustainability*, *14*(19), 12461. https://doi.org/10.3390/su141912461

Mitchell, M. A., & Maxwell, S. E. (2013). A comparison of the cross-sectional and sequential designs when assessing longitudinal mediation. *Multivariate Behavioral Research*, *48*(3), 301–339.

Nazish, M., Khan, Z., Khan, A., Khan, M. N., & Ramkissoon, H. (2024). "Green intentions, green actions": The power of social media and the perils of greenwashing. *Journal of Global Marketing*, 1. https://doi.org/10.1080/08911762.2024.2429517

Netto, S. V. de F., Sobral, M. F. F., Ribeiro, A. R. B., & Soares, G. R. da L. (2020). Concepts and forms of greenwashing: A systematic review. *Environmental Sciences Europe*, *32*, 1. https://doi.org/10.1186/s12302-020-0300-3

Newton, J. N., Briggs, A. D., Murray, C. J., Dicker, D., Foreman, K. J., Wang, H., Naghavi, M., Forouzanfar, M. H., Ohno, S. L., Barber, R. M., Vos, T., Stanaway, J. D., Schmidt, J. C., Hughes, A. J., Fay, D. F. J., Ecob, R., Gresser, C., McKee, M., Rutter, H., ... & Davis, A. C. (2015). Changes in health in England, with analysis by English regions and areas of deprivation, 1990–2013: A systematic analysis for the global burden of disease study 2013. *The Lancet*, *386*(10010), 2257–2274.

Nuji, M. N. N., Ali, A., Noordin, W. N. W., Thaheer, B. A. N. M., & Mathiew, V. (2023). Of trust and influence: A look at social media influencers and brand promotion. *International Journal of Academic Research in Business and Social Sciences*, *13*(6). https://doi.org/10.6007/ijarbss/v13-i6/15444

Nyilasy, G., Gangadharbatla, H., & Paladino, A. (2014). Perceived greenwashing: The interactive effects of green advertising and corporate environmental performance on consumer reactions. *Journal of Business Ethics*, *125*, 693–707. https://doi.org/10.1007/s10551-013-1944-3

Ohanian, R. (1990). Construction and validation of a scale to measure celebrity endorsers' perceived expertise, trustworthiness, and attractiveness. *Journal of Advertising*, *19*(3), 39. https://doi.org/10.1080/00913367.1990.10673191

Olbermann, Z., & Reis, M. (2024). It's a match: The impact of influencer-message congruence and recipients identity on perceptions of rainbowwashing. *Journal of Promotion Management*, 1–29.

Pandey, M., & Yadav, P. S. (2023). Understanding the role of individual concerns, attitude, and perceived value in green apparel purchase intention; the mediating effect of consumer involvement and moderating role of generation Z&Y. *Cleaner and Responsible Consumption*, *9*, 100120.

Pimonenko, T., Bilan, Y., Horák, J., Starchenko, L., & Gajda, W. (2020). Green brand of companies and greenwashing under sustainable development goals. *Sustainability*, *12*(4), 1679. https://doi.org/10.3390/su12041679

Prajapati, N. (2023). Effect of influencer marketing on consumer buying behavior: A comprehensive analysis. *International Journal For Multidisciplinary Research*, *5*(4). https://doi.org/10.36948/ijfmr.2023.v05i04.5996

Qayyum, A., Jamil, R. A., & Sehar, A. (2023). Impact of green marketing, greenwashing and green confusion on green brand equity. *Spanish Journal of Marketing-ESIC*, *27*(3), 286–305.

Reinikainen, H., Munnukka, J., Maity, D., & Luoma-aho, V. (2020). 'You really are a great big sister' – Parasocial relationships, credibility, and the moderating role of audience comments in influencer marketing. *Journal of Marketing Management*, *36*(3–4), 279–298. https://doi.org/10.1080/0267257X.2019.1708781

Rizzo, G. L. C., Berger, J., & Villarroel, F. (2023). *What drives virtual influencer's impact?* Cornell University. https://doi.org/10.48550/arXiv.2301.09874

Sailer, A., Wilfing, H., & Straus, E. (2022). Greenwashing and bluewashing in black Friday-related sustainable fashion marketing on Instagram. *Sustainability*, *14*, 1494. https://doi.org/10.3390/su14031494

Schmidt, A., & Donsbach, W. (2012). „Grüne“ Werbung als Instrument für „schwarze“ Zahlen. *Publizistik*, *1*(57), 75–93.

Schmuck, D., Matthes, J., & Naderer, B. (2018). Misleading consumers with green advertising? An affect–reason–involvement account of greenwashing effects in environmental advertising. *Journal of Advertising*, *47*(2), 127–145.

Segumpan, R. G., & Zahari, J. S. A. (Eds.). (2022). *Mixed methods perspectives on communication and social media research*. Routledge.

Shmueli, G., Sarstedt, M., Hair, J. F., Cheah, J. H., Ting, H., Vaithilingam, S., & Ringle, C. M. (2019). Predictive model assessment in PLS-SEM: Guidelines for using PLSpredict. *European Journal of Marketing*, *53*(11), 2322–2347.

Stone, M. (1977). An asymptotic equivalence of choice of model by cross-validation and Akaike's criterion. *Journal of the Royal Statistical Society*, *39*(1), 44–47.

Tartaraj, A., Avdyli, D., & Trebicka, B. (2024). Accessing the TikTok influencer marketing on consumer behavior: An econometric examination. *Journal of Educational and Social Research*, *14*.

Torelli, R., Balluchi, F., & Lazzini, A. (2020). Greenwashing and environmental communication: Effects on stakeholders' perceptions. *Business Strategy and the Environment*, *29*(2), 407–421.

Unsal, O., & Ozkan, B. (2024). Technologies and emerging trends shaping Fintech. In *The Emerald handbook of Fintech* (pp. 399–418). https://doi.org/10.1108/978-1-83753-608-520241046

Vukmirović, V., Kostić-Stanković, M., & Domazet, I. (2020). Influencers as a segment of digital marketing communication: Generation Y attitudes. In *Marketing* (Vol. 51(2), p. 98). Srpsko udruženje za marketing. https://doi.org/10.5937/markt2002098V

Wellman, M. L., Stoldt, R., Tully, M., & Ekdale, B. (2020). Ethics of authenticity: Social media influencers and the production of sponsored content. *Journal of Media Ethics*, *35*(2), 68. https://doi.org/10.1080/23736992.2020.1736078

Wu, T.-Y., & Lin, C. A. (2016). Predicting the effects of eWOM and online brand messaging: Source trust, bandwagon effect and innovation adoption factors. *Telematics and Informatics*, *34*(2), 470. https://doi.org/10.1016/j.tele.2016.08.001

Xu, Q. (2014). Should I trust him? The effects of reviewer profile characteristics on eWOM credibility. *Computers in Human Behavior*, *33*, 136. https://doi.org/10.1016/j.chb.2014.01.027

Yesiloglu, S., & Costello, J. (2020). *Influencer marketing: Building brand communities and engagement*. https://doi.org/10.4324/9781003434498

Yuan, S., & Lou, C. (2020). How social media influencers foster relationships with followers: The roles of source credibility and fairness in parasocial relationship and product interest. *Journal of Interactive Advertising*, *20*(2), 133–147.

Zaid, B., Fedtke, J., Shin, D., Kadoussi, A. E., & Ibahrine, M. (2022). Digital Islam and Muslim millennials: How social media influencers reimagine religious authority and Islamic practices. *Religions*, *13*(4), 335. https://doi.org/10.3390/rel13040335

Zhang, L., Li, D., Cao, C., & Huang, S. (2018). The influence of greenwashing perception on green purchasing intentions: The mediating role of green word-of-mouth and moderating role of green concern. *Journal of Cleaner Production*, *187*, 740–750.

Zhang, Y., & Liansheng, Y. (2024). In the clash between consumer green values and company green values, who will win? The role of greenwashing and involvement in environmental campaigns on social media. *Journal of Cleaner Production*, *480*, 144103. https://doi.org/10.1016/j.jclepro.2024.144103

Zhao, Y. N., & Lee, C. C. (2024). The impact of vertical environmental regulation mechanism on greenwashing. *Journal of Cleaner Production*, *475*, 143637.

Zniva, R., Weitzl, W., & Lindmoser, C. (2023). Be constantly different! How to manage influencer authenticity. *Electronic Commerce Research*, *23*(3) 1485. https://doi.org/10.1007/s10660-022-09653-6.

Chapter 10

Unmasking Greenwashing in the Outdoor Sporting Industry: The Illusion of Sustainability in the Shift to a Circular Model

Avtar Singh[a], *Rahul Sharma*[a] *and Dalwinder Kaur Dhillon*[b]

[a]Lovely Professional University, India
[b]Manipal GlobalNxt University, Malaysia

Abstract

The sports industry is faced with challenges in managing demand for products in an eco-efficient manner and is relying on so-called circular economy (CE) concepts to kerb environmental damage. Even though circular economy (CE) strategies are actively advocated by business and retailers as their sustainability strategies, the claims are viewed skeptically due to the extensive knowledge about the possibility of greenwashing. This study investigates the claims of the outdoor sporting goods industry regarding the implementation of CE strategies in comparison with the actual practices of brands and dares to theorize the illusion of sustainability the industry operates under. Conducting expert interviews, this research investigates the multifaceted obstacles and catalysts to a concerted adoption of CE and reveals disarray between marketing rhetoric and sustainability in practice. Areas of analysis include product design for durability and repair, consumer perception and behaviour and recycled content use. The results indicate on the balance an over-emphasis on promotive sustainability narratives compared to tangible operational change, exposing how circulate economy principles may be frayed and speak more to branding than environmental impact. The study findings reveal the current narratives about the corporate sustainability by offering the basis for ensuring transparency and accountability during the implementations of the CE. Such insights will certainly assist industry tycoons, policymakers and sustainability advocates

Eco Illusions, 203–228

Published under exclusive licence by Emerald Publishing Limited
doi:10.1108/978-1-83662-782-120261010

since they understand and combat instances of greenwashing occurrence in the outdoor sporting industry.

Keywords: Circular economy; sustainability in sports industry; greenwashing; eco-efficiency; consumer perception and sustainable product design

Introduction

The outdoor sporting industry as a segment of the recreational industry has always been characterized by a respect for the environment. However, the activities performing and undergoing within this industry are not compatible with such values because the production and consumption occur at the cost of the environment. The current lifecycle of gears from the extraction of raw materials to the generation of wastes at the post-consumer stage exposes the industry to numerous negative sustainability factors erroneously famed as the 'take-make-dispose' or linear economy (LE) model (Ellen MacArthur Foundation, 2013). Thus, the switch to a circular economy (CE) concept represents a radical shift in the idea based on the use of resources, minimization of waste production and product lifecycle prolongation. Such transition complies with the principles of sustainable development and has the potential of bringing both economic and reputational benefits to business within the sector.

Sustainability is a topic that is under extensive research currently and with practical application across commercial firms and other forms of literature, although resource scarcity and pollution are doubtlessly a critical issue in today's society. This conversation is accompanied by the concept of CE, which has attracted attention because of the purported benefits to the environment and economy (Geissdoerfer et al., 2017; Merli, Preziosi, & Acampora, 2018). Along with such positive attitudes, these studies have also highlighted potential implementation challenges; concerns regarding the enactment of many circular economy attributes have been voiced by Masi et al. (2017) and Bressanelli et al. (2019) among others. As for this tension, practitioners need to be aware of both the benefits and pitfalls of CE notion in the pursuit of the CE practices within their companies.

Textiles is one industry where CE concept is discussed in detail (Jia et al., 2020). As for individual elements, the actors in this area that belong to the sporting particularly outdoor sports items industry are recognized as pioneers more often (Bocken, Albareda, et al., 2016; Ellen Macarthur Foundation, 2017; Holtstrom et al., 2019). However, this sector has only recently been analyzed in a systematic manner regarding CE implementation; our findings have been published in this journal only recently (Fuchs & Hovemann, 2022). The obstacles and facilitators of these CE practices within the outdoor sporting goods sector remain underexplored even though the study focused on practices that are currently in use among the outdoor brands and merchants. Thus, this plan is expected for this paper to expand on the first by venturing more broadly in the topic by assessing the enablers and inhibitors of CE practices to encounter as identified based on the review of literature. Furthermore, we will evaluate the possibility that CE procedures are specific to textile and can be employed in numerous industries. We also would like to get more insights of which CE strategies are compatible with the outdoor sporting items through this. This work contributes new knowledge to the CE body of knowledge as it presents data from the industry perspective. In this way, it attempts to provide clarification to the claims and counterclaims of benefits and challenges to its applicability. Furthermore, it helps managerial staff to apply CE components and assist in the appreciation of the practical applications. The outdoor sporting industry is built on the need to provide equipment for excitement, but all too often the equipment is abandoned once it is no longer useful. It is where a CE comes handy, as it addresses the take-make-dispose model and extends useful life of products and material. This introduction positions you to answer the question of whether the outdoor sporting industry can embrace a CE.

Used tents stacked up, bicycles collecting dust in garages and hiking shoes grouped together awaiting disposal make the environmentally sensitive traveller worry about the future. As the outdoor sporting industry gears up for the next generation of adventurers, it faces a crucial challenge—can it transition toward a truly circular model with minimal waste and environmental impact? Moving away from the conventional approach, which emphasizes take-make-dispose, a CE can be seen as a way to reduce negative environmental effects as well as a chance to discover new revenue streams and attract more customers who are beginning to care about the planet's future.

Since its inception, the outdoor sporting industry has nurtured the spirit of adventure by delivering high-quality equipment that enables people to explore mountains, rivers, and trails. The passion for adventure which young people hold appears secondary during this time. The natural environment suffers from the accumulation of used and damaged travelling tents together with worn-out rock-climbing harnesses and countless pairs of shoes which eventually end up taking up space in enormous dumping grounds. Becoming leaders of exploration requires the outdoor sporting sector to establish its commitment to the circular economy. A holistic comprehension of environmental sustainability allows the development of this idea which promises future generations will enjoy clean and sustainable outdoor experiences.

The outdoor sporting sector, which previously aimed to protect nature, now harms the environment because it follows the LE take-make-dispose model. The gap between sustainability marketing by companies and their actual implementation of circular economy principles becomes increasingly noticeable when we examine deeper into their operations. Brand campaigns that present CE initiatives through green marketing strategies frequently show inadequate execution in practice. Greenwashing deceives consumers through false sustainability narratives therefore creating wrong perceptions about environmentally responsible consumption. Research shows multiple difficulties exist in implementing CE practices across industries and production sectors even though they generate increasing industrial attention. The implementation faces obstacles from supply chain complexities and production costs together with consumer disengagement and insufficient business cooperation.

Some outdoor brands adopt circular-based strategies, while others keep the sustainability factor as their tool to market themselves in spite of following the traditional practices. Unused bicycles and worn-out hiking gear piling up in landfills reflect the widening gap between sustainability claims and actual environmental practices. Therefore, this research significantly evaluates whether the outdoor sporting industry is prominent in leading to a circular economy or by just playing mind mapping as their organizational strategy. This study has discovered the enablers and inhibitors that further expose the idea of greenwashing in the industry and whether the industry is actually committed to sustainability or merely capitalizes on demand from the consumer based out of greener alternatives.

Problem with the Linear Model

The traditional LAE (also referred to as *Linear Economy Approach*) is characterized by a heavy dependence on virgin materials and profound waste production. For instance, sporting gears for recreation on the outdoors include: tents, back packs, apparels, among others, which have fabric materials that include polyester and nylon originating from non-renewable fossil fuels. These materials are highly energy consuming to manufacture, and they also have low recyclability as they remain in landfills for at least 30 years (Bocken, Albareda, et al., 2016). Additionally, since there is always increasing pressure for companies to develop the new product and deal with the new products at certain seasons, this makes resource consumption and waste generation to be out of control.

The environmental effects are intensified by the procuring sector, which has long chains and contributes to greenhouse gas (GHG) emissions, water pollution and loss of biodiversity. According to the European Outdoor Group (2021), the dependency on the natural resource and product recyclability for the outdoor industry remains as significant challenges to sustainability. The following practices are clearly contradictory to an industry that portrays itself as the protector of the natural environment.

CE as a Solution

Such problems can be solved using the approach provided by the CE model. It aims at closing the loop by designing products and systems for which few inputs are required materials and few outputs are generated. Design for producibility, ease of disassembly, maintenance, and upgrade are essential principles in developing circular products (Kirchherr et al., 2017). Based on the reference to the outdoor sporting goods industry using innovations, it could mean designing taking measures like: the gear's modularity that makes it easy to repair, take-back schemes means for reprocessing of used gear and the usage of recycled resources during their manufacture. For instance, through the 'Worn Wear' campaign, Patagonia provides an excellent example of applying circular strategy by promoting the repair and reuse of the products people primarily use for outdoor activities. Not only does this programme effectively minimize wastage but it also enhances patrons' loyalty in addition to the brand's association with the right cause (Patagonia, 2020). Likewise, Arc'teryx's 'ReBird' programme entails upcycling of already used products and integration of recycled material in newer products proving that circular economy ideas are feasible economically (Arc'teryx, 2021).

Economic and Social Benefits

While adopting the CE model of production and consumption is a wonderful way of solving environmental issues, it has great economic and social benefits as well. This is since the company will take longer to order for the raw materials, hence cutting on expenses, and also since the products will have a longer life span; this means that the company has less frequency in disposing of the products hence saving on expenses on product disposal. Further, circular practices, such as repair services and rental programmes, may help develop new business models and employment possibilities (Stahel, 2016). According to a report by the Ellen MacArthur Foundation based on a market analysis, the global economy might benefit from an overall improvement in circular operations to the tune of up to 4.5 trillion dollars by 2030.

In a social aspect, topicality is driven, and circulation of product or service ensures responsible consumption level. Outdoor users are beginning to realize that there are sustainable variables in the market, and according to Gleim and others, customers have the willingness to spend more for an item that has an environmentally friendly consideration. Thus, meeting of the above demands enables firms to increase brand value and improve their commitment to clients with an interest in environmental conservation. However, the transformation towards a circular model is far from smooth sailing, as presently will be shown. The change needs capital expenditures in R&D, investment over new processes and consumer canvassing. Lastly, the current regulatory environment in most ecosystems is not adequate in encouraging circularity practices due to existing challenges (Geissdoerfer et al., 2017). These challenges require firms to engage their stakeholders throughout the value system and lobby for the right regulatory measures. It elaborates the circular economy concept by reviewing literature on obstacles and facilitators for CE pertaining to the industry based on textiles, of which our research questions are formed. Then, we lay down our process of doing things or our workflow. Lastly, there is a discussion and conclusion in which we describe the theoretical contribution, practical implications, limitations and possible future research.

While the outdoor sporting industry promotes a circular economy as a sustainability initiative, a closer look reveals that marketing often outpaces genuine, large-scale implementation. Despite programmes like Patagonia's Worn Wear and Arc'teryx's ReBird, many brands continue to depend on resource-heavy production and struggle to achieve widespread circularity. The survey shows that while circular approaches offer social and economic benefits, 'greenwashing' dilutes their impact. To ensure sustainability, radical operational reforms, stakeholder engagement and stricter regulatory schemes are needed. The survey reveals that businesses often prioritize sustainability-focused branding over actual adoption of circular manufacturing, continuing linear methods. While circular practices offer benefits like job creation and cost savings, widespread 'greenwashing' undermines their potential. Meaningful operational changes, stakeholder engagement and stronger regulations are crucial to ensure sustainability claims reflect genuine environmental impact.

Literature Review

After political adoption in China (Circular Economy Promotion Law in 2009) and the European Union (EU) (Closing the Loop: There was an EU Action Plan for the Circular Economy, developed in 2015, with a revision completed in 2020 under the European Green Deal), the idea of a CE has gained popularity in the private business sector and in literature since 2015. CE, according to the European Parliament, is an economy that keeps resources in the economy for as long as possible by reusing, repairing, refinishing or recycling them into new products. This description sets CE apart from the linear production model commonly associated with the 'takemake-consume-throw away' paradigm (European Parliamentary Research Service, 2022). Global textile industry ranks as one of the highest polluting industries in terms of carbon emissions, water use and waste output and is responsible for around one fifth of the globe's carbon emissions (Ellen MacArthur Foundation, 2017). As global sustainability pressures increase, shifting from the LE paradigm towards CE has become more and more necessary. The textile CE seeking enhanced environmental and economical sustainability involves extending product lifecycles, remanufacturing and minimizing waste (Geissdoerfer et al., 2017). The following literature review aims to pinpoint key challenges and supports for implementing CE practices in the textile industry based on the findings of empirical and theoretical research.

The outdoor sporting industry, long a symbol of adventure and exploration, faces a growing challenge reducing harm to the overall environment in which it operates. Although there has been improvement in the use of technical fabrics and wear-gear that inflamed our love of the outdoors, this product has created more waste. A 2022 study by Patagonia a global apparel brand – demonstrates considerable environmental harm from used gear, suggesting that the circular economy is an effective way to address it. The concept of a circular economy in which products are built to last longer and be easily repairable, with reuse at their end of their lifecycle, promotes an excellent solution for the outdoor industry.

The area of concern in the outdoor sporting industry – a key sector for adventure tourism – is sustainability. The recent developments and new equipment have helped us to expand our interest and love for nature but have done so by creating more waste. A 2021 study by The Research Institute for Textiles and Apparel (RITA) at The Hong Kong Polytechnic University ([The CE notion in the OSGI: Confronting Current Practices and Exploring Challenges & Facilitators among Brands and Retailers], published in MDPI in 2021), discusses the difficulties brands face when trying to implement a circular economy approach because the items they sell are diverse. However, there is no doubt that such opportunities exist. On the back of its latest lifecycle assessment (LCA) report for the year 2022, the woes of used gear are painting a grim picture. A circular economy, where products with long lifecycle and inherent reparability and recyclability are employed, presents a solution. Such an approach explored by ISPO, the world's leading sports business platform, is not only a way to reduce waste but also to open new opportunities for business that are aligned with consumers' changing values and preferences.

The circular economy has been observed and proved to contain multiple positive impacts to the environment, economical and societal front by cutting down the cost of disposal of waste, reducing GHG emissions and basically making a healthier society due to less polluted closed loops. The limitations of such a concept as increased fixed costs, especially reverse logistics costs, have not been given adequate attention (Sehnem et al., 2019). Hence, it was also suggested that barring a few, other circular economy methods may face difficulty in overcoming the entrenched linear model financially (Uhrenholt et al., 2022). But Geissdoerfer et al. (2017) stated that a circular economy is a useful concept in improving sustainability indices. Research further also elaborated the notion as other ideas that ensure higher sustainability.

Textile Industries' CE Practices: Obstacles and Facilitators

Many greater problems have been identified, and many of them are also sub-divided into practical sub-issues. First, internal affairs that challenge companies are poor managerial support, improper or short-term managerial approaches, ambiguous or a complete absence of performance indicators (Jia et al., 2020), and a scarcity of knowledgeable staff members (for example, designers who lack experience with designing for circularity) (Ki et al., 2020; Moktadir et al., 2018). Explaining the answer to the third query about a second product-related problem, Franco (2017) pointed out that many textiles are intricate. When it comes to circular needs, it is often almost impossible to change all the inputs that need to be modified (zipper, dyes, glue, etc.). It is most often encountered with textile products with multiple parts rather than with seemingly more basic ones. Two examples in the current text are the fact that using blends of synthetic and natural fibres, for instance, makes recycling harder than when using a single material. Also, the application of only circularity-proof components reduces product functionality and, therefore, customer demand (Gardetti & Torres, 2013; Kim & Ko, 2010). According to Franco (2017), functional textiles should therefore not be developed at the expense of performance.

Jia et al. (2020) found that a third factor relates to the supply chain. In particular, they discovered that some organizations do not utilize recycled material because of such risks as contraction of quality. Related to it, there is also the problem of limited stock for recycled material availability. However, the enterprises experience some challenges and high cost and slow reverse logistics system (Jack et al., 2010; Ki et al., 2020).

For example, firms that collect used goods often receive merchandise from a variety of brands, thus making it difficult for them to know the content of materials – a piece of information that is crucial to the organization in charge of recycling the product (Jia et al., 2020). Similarly, it is difficult to predict when, how much and which quality products customers will return Franco (2017). Finally, one of the major challenges is the required financial investments (Ulgen & Forslund, 2015). The future sustainability of scaling circular firms and if that would make them financially viable remains highly unknown (Chesbrough, 2010).

Obstacles to CE Practices in the Textile Industry

Technical and Material Challenges

One of the major hurdles in the adoption of CE in textiles is the recycling of blended fabrics, which account for the majority of the market share because of their durability and versatility. Blended fibres, like polyester-cotton, have problems in separating and recycling individual components (Sandin & Peters, 2018). In addition, the absence of scalable technologies for chemical recycling limits the industry's ability to process textile waste effectively. For example, mechanical recycling is highly practiced, but it generally leads to downgraded fibre quality, which limits its applications (Zhao et al., 2020).

Economic Viability

CE transition involves significant capital costs by organizations in terms of infrastructure and technology as well as costs needed to retrain the workforce (Kirchherr et al., 2017). This situation shows that the cost of recycling and reuse is higher compared with the cost of preparing virgin materials. For example, the price of recycled polyester remains higher than that of virgin polyester due to labour-intensive sorting and washing requirements (Palm et al., 2015). Further, the mandates lack any form of financial incentives or subsidies to encourage organizations, particularly the small- and medium-sized enterprises (SMEs), to adopt CE models, because of its limited budgets (Ranta et al., 2018).

Regulatory and Policy Gaps

The textile industry lacks an appropriate establishment of comprehensible and general requirements and frameworks on applying CE. In fact, the policies of countries around the whole world vary considerably in terms of textile waste management, recycling goals, as well as extended producer responsibility (EPR) schemes (Bukhari et al., 2018). For instance, while the EU has put into force some policies, such as Waste Framework Directive, the force applied as well as compliance differ across its member countries.

Consumer Behaviour and Awareness

The major problems are the unwillingness of consumers to buy recycled or second-hand textiles. Most common reasons cited for not buying CE products are the low quality of products and hygiene issues (Henninger et al., 2016). Fast fashion culture is supporting the linear consumption based on cheap, short-time products. Lack of environmental knowledge on textile waste and its adverse impacts is yet another cause worsening this situation; education on sustainable consumption can be another requirement (Niinimäki et al., 2020).

Supply Chain Complexity

Circularity on the other hand is difficult to improve for textiles because of the complex structure of the globalized supply chain within a network with multi-stakeholders operating in different geographical locations. Lack of coordination, no full traceability of materials and minimal information flow provide challenges in the key area of completing the loop in textiles production and will be discussed in this work in relation to Franco's (2017) paper. In addition, the concentration and market fragmentation in the industry, as well as a powerful informal sector in the growing nations, are not encouraging of conventional CE practices (Singh & Ordoñez, 2016).

Champions of CE Solutions on the Textile Sector

Technological Innovations

Likely material challenges can be resolved through the advancement of technology in chemical recycling and fibre regeneration. For example, there are Renewcell, which uses blends made of cotton-type fabrics and produces fibres of equal quality, and Worn Again Technologies Other technologies can also improve communication and transparency in a supply chain, thus also benefiting the allocation and circulation of resources and their recycling: for example, blockchain (Saberi et al., 2019).

Increased Regulatory Support and Parameters

CE practice adoption enjoys high importance of the supportive policies with the appropriate regulatory frameworks. Local and global bodies are developing programmes that can enable sustainability of textiles. For instance, the circular economy action plan for the EU is also aimed at the reuse of textiles and minimizing waste together with encouraging sustainable production (European Commission, 2020). EPR strategies, where manufacturers are held accountable for managing products at their end of their useful life, have offered impetus to CE practices in many areas (Watson et al., 2018).

Business Model Innovation

Implementation of circular economy concepts for products like product-as-a-service, repair and resale or leasing decrease textile waste levels. Current examples of extended product life companies include Patagonia and Eileen Fisher take-back programmes and second-hand marketplaces (Hamid, 2019). Other models practiced are also environmentally friendly, and the increasing concern for environment by customers is also an added advantage.

Strategies in Planning (Collaboration and Stakeholder Engagement)

CE practice implementation is the process that must involve all members, from manufactures and retailers to policymakers and even consumers. Lately, there has been increased collaboration that has been spearheaded by industry alliances such as the Sustainable Apparel Coalition that has been at the forefront in the promotion of collective action towards achievement of the laid down sustainability objectives. Intersectoral cooperation also means cooperation with NGOs and research institutes for developing new solutions and for generating best practice examples (Fletcher & Grose, 2021).

Consumer Awareness and Education

While raising consumer awareness of the environmental impacts of textile waste and the benefits of CE practices is a key facilitator, educational campaigns, eco-labelling and certifications can help build trust with consumers and encourage sustainable purchasing behaviours (Testa et al., 2016). Also, the effectiveness of the messages can be boosted by proving it through social networks and partnering with influencers.

Financial Incentives and Market Opportunities

These are aspects of financial policy that can be used to facilitate increased use of renewable resources. While it is proposed that monetary rewards with subsidies or fiscal rebates and grants can be helpful to support various adopted circular business models. However, Neto et al (2019) have also identified the basic trend of sustainability and recycling as a raw material as another opportunity that the particular firms can capitalize on to develop the recognizable differentiation. For instance, consumer expectations for climate change, sustainable and ethical wear have given rise to sustainable brands and products that also promote more CE.

Of course, there are many challenges but migrating towards a more circular economy is timely in the textile sector. Since the interventions are associated with technical, economic, regulatory and/or behavioural challenges, then technologies, governments' policies and/or strategies, business models and last but not the least citizens' commitment can be the lasting solutions. Where these barriers are removed and facilitators optimally utilized, the textile industry will be able to record a novel level of enhanced environmental gained positive change. However, this conversion should be achieved with the blessings of the incumbent parties in the industrial sectors, the policymakers and the citizens for an environment that fosters circular economy.

More and more, businesses in outdoor sports present themselves as supporting the environment when they are not changing their practices dramatically. Firms like Patagonia and Arc'teryx really aim for environmental change through their circular fashion; however, several other companies use these stories just to celebrate their brand, sometimes without doing enough to help the environment. As a result of this, eco-illusion takes shape, making 'sustainability' seem like just a clever marketing strategy instead of something real. On the other hand, services like renting gear, selling goods and using 'product as a service' really show sustainability by making people use products less and keep using them longer. They guarantee adherence to ESG values (environmental, social, governance) by cutting their environmental footprint, supporting everyone's right to outdoor activities and acting with transparent business procedures. Besides, such transitions play a direct role in achieving the sustainable development goals (SDGs), mainly Goal 12 and Goal 13. But if brands do not put these practices into action properly and truthfully reveal the results, there is a chance the sharing economy will be used just for marketing. Hence, addressing eco-illusion needs us to use circular and shared-use systems, introduce laws and regulations and guide people to understand these claims for them to support global sustainability (European Outdoor Group, 2021; Kirchherr et al., 2017; Patagonia, 2020).

When businesses adopt genuine circles and sharing systems, it helps lower the risk of eco-illusion since it focuses more on actual changes to the whole economy. Companies resort to vague statements or solo projects, which may appear as sustainable, yet the results are not visible in their products, resources or how they do business with suppliers and employees. Alternatively, designs that are built for durability, collect products for recycling and repair or refurbish items add sustainability to the whole process of making and consuming. When rental, subscription and sharing schemes are used, companies reduce the amount they produce and help avoid wastes, proving that they fit ESG rules and SDG goals. Taken together, these actions support the environment and allow people can verify companies' claims. In addition, using shared-use means brands can record important data, for example, how many times an item is used and over its complete life, so people can see clear facts instead of vague green message. Embracing sustainability in how they operate and regularly checking the results with others helps them gain trust, as well as prove their commitment is real (Ellen MacArthur Foundation, 2020; European Outdoor Group, 2021; Geissdoerfer et al., 2017).

The CE establishes an appealing sustainability framework for environment and economy protection and social welfare but still meets difficulties during implementation in polluting industrial sectors such as textiles and outdoor sports products. Support from the EU and Chinese policy officials along with rising sustainable product demand has not produced consistent outcomes towards CE adoption within the outdoor sporting sector which displays superficial dedication at times. Companies waste their sustainability efforts by using single eco-initiatives to create misleading claims about complete eco-friendly policies which can result in greenwashing the market. Literature above illustrates how circular economy could reduce waste and other emissions while looking after the resources, although the real execution has multiple barriers particularly from return costs which is way higher than diverse products. The evaluation of true sustainability claims requires to be addressed immediately because it is necessary to support measurable and visible CE practices that produce real sustainability benefits that transcend beyond appearances.

Research Questions

This summary demonstrates the extensive study on obstacles to, and facilitators of, CE exercises pertaining to the industry based on textiles. We therefore seek resolutions to following research inquiries:

RQ1. To what extent do companies and sellers of outdoor sporting products actively adhere to the circular economy while simultaneously displaying instances of sustainability greenwashing in their claims?

RQ2. What significant obstacles and enablers affect the genuine application of the circular economy in the market for outdoor sporting products, and how does this affect sustainability transparency and credibility?

Methodology

The present research about circular economies depicts minimal industry-dedicated findings for specific challenges and facilitators, particularly regarding outdoor sporting goods. The current lack of information about this gap makes it unclear how obstacles and facilitators that emerged in other fields relate specifically to this outdoor sporting goods context. Qualitative exploratory research approaches proved appropriate for this situation according to academic guidance from Blaikie (2010) and Corbin and Strauss (2008) because it helps researchers reveal industry-specific insights and study unexplored fields. The study adopted a primary goal to present a new external viewpoint on CE by evaluating the validity of sustainability commitments during the rise of greenwashing concerns. Fundamental data came from independent industry experts as well as researchers who specialize in the field and leading brand owners who operate across the CE value chain (Wang, 2020). The research adopted three different methods, including snowball sampling alongside sustainability report analysis and thorough website evaluations of outdoor sporting organizations to establish relevant participants in the study (Heckathorn, 2011; Woodley & Lockard, 2016). Internal assessment focused on identifying the difference between sustainable promotional statements and actual performance despite investigating general sustainability issues affecting outdoor businesses. The increasing global discussion about CE within India's primary outdoor marketplaces guided our research to encompass both Indian companies and retailers for assessing local sustainability perspectives in comparison to worldwide sustainability shift. The research highlights the secrets of the market, while also investigates whether companies have actually adopted the sustainable circular practices or they are just depicting the manufactured appearances.

Findings and Discussions

The concept of CE is the new model of improving existing economic systems and reduce resource wastage. CE, unlike the conventional LE model of 'take-make-dispose', is focused on product durability, reuse and refurbishment and recycling (Kirchherr et al., 2017). It is, for this reason, that the promotion of this particular economic model is being urgently called for to help alleviate the rampant problem of environmental degradation and resource depletion. The Ellen MacArthur Foundation (2021) states that the CE presents itself as a realistic solution to develop sustainability between economic systems and ecological frameworks. The outdoor sporting industry faces difficulties implementing this promise because its products derive mainly from natural resources such as metals and thin plastics and synthetic fabrics. Industrial sustainability marketing efforts fail to stop the industry from following conventional high-waste patterns from other sectors because products often get thrown away early due to planned obsolescence and inadequate repairability and upgrade options (Rex et al., 2020). CEO mentions environmental responsibility through CE have become common in business communications, but these statements often hide ongoing linear business operations which still operate through the deception of green ideals. The need exists for immediate adoption of genuine CE while simultaneously requiring experts to evaluate corporate sustainability claims because greenwashing presents barriers to genuine sustainability achievements.

Barriers to Circular Economy Practices (RQ1)

Organizational and Financial Challenges

The main challenge that the outdoor sporting industry faces in adopting CE is the high cost of bringing in product changes for the purpose of being more durable, easy to repair and recyclable. One of the critical challenges is that SMEs admit that they have limited resources and financial capacities to invest in CE practices. Furthermore, the lack of awareness about and support for sustainability initiatives from top management deepen the problem, because sustainable development strategies perhaps may not fit well into available resources, and the firm needs to generate profits in the short term (Lüdeke-Freund et al., 2019).

Supply Chain Complexity

The outdoor sporting industry has intricate supply chains mainly being interconnected networks operated in different regions. Some of the challenges include difficulties in procuring secondary raw materials and – essentially, due to the reversibility of the CE supply chain – the problem of logistics when it comes to dealings in reused materials and products, which makes the implementation of CE practices challenging (Govindan & Hasanagic, 2018). Furthermore, lack of stakeholder integration in the supply network hampers the progress even more (Nußholz, 2017).

Technological Constraints

The technological factors also have a great influence, among them being the management of the material flow or tracking if and when a material can be recycled again can be hampered due to outdated systems or restricted access to new technologies in this field (Franco, 2017). This holds especially true when the sporting goods being considered are of high performance and incorporate composites which are extremely hard to recycle (Stahel, 2016).

Consumer Behaviour

Consumer behaviour is another challenge because people do not use or demand refurbished or second-hand outdoor sporting products frequently. Especially when it comes to higher-performance athletes, used goods are seen as less reliable than the new products and there emerges stigma around second-hand products (Michelini et al., 2017). Also, consumers lack adequate knowledge of the environmental benefits of CE practices and, therefore, are reluctant to engage in activities such as product returns (Ranta et al., 2018).

Regulatory and Policy Barriers

The second major challenge has to do with regulatory and policy barriers to the implementation of integrated reporting. Last but not the least; miniscule regulatory support and non-standard policies in different areas are very big challenges. Companies are lacking incentives or subsidies to introduce CE practices, and depending on some secondary materials has its limitations, which makes the implementation of CE challenging (Kirchherr et al., 2017; Korhonen et al., 2018).

Facilitators of Circular Economy Practices (RQ2)

Leadership Commitment and Organizational Vision

CE implementation has been more effective in companies that have a leadership commitment to sustainability. For example, Patagonia set up its mission as a circular economy business and introduced an extensive repair services facility and take-back initiatives in the sporting outfit market (Chaturvedi et al., 2021; Patagonia Sustainability Report, 2021).

Technological Innovations

This helps CE practices be adopted by enhancing technological advancements of the recycling technologies and tracking of product lifecycle of products. There are now technological solutions in the form of blockchain to document the origin and use of components and materials to conform to CE principles (Lacy & Rutqvist, 2015). Technological innovation can address material challenges by developing new methods for recycling composites and creating more sustainable fibres (Ellen MacArthur Foundation, 2019).

Collaboration Across the Value Chain

Action coordination by the various parties of the supply chain logistics stakeholders has also been found to boost the process. As cited by Adams et al., 2017, collaboration with recyclers, suppliers and even competitors may reduce logistical barriers and allow companies to get value for money on CE implementation. Intersectoral collaborations like the Circular Economy Initiative by the European Outdoor Group are some of the formats that have been proving that collective action could create change (European Outdoor Group, 2020).

Consumer Engagement and Education

Mainstreaming of the consumer through education and incentive programmes can be a powerful tool in enhancing consumer's take-up in CE practices. For example, encouraging greater consumption of used or refurbished products through incentive or reward programmes can foster circular consumption behaviour (Prendeville et al., 2017). For example, the use of humane-sensitive and relevant educational campaigns such as awareness creation for the purpose of discouraging carelessness in disposing of sporting equipment could also expand consumers' acceptance of the agenda (Bocken, de Pauw et al., 2016).

Policy-Based and Incentive-Based Mechanisms

The use of CE in organizations can only be enhanced by supportive organizational policies and regulations. EPR schemes, for example, hold companies responsible for the product lifecycle and motivate companies to plan products for recyclability and durability (Korhonen et al., 2018). Other fiscal incentives, such as tax deductions or subsidies for actions promoting CE, may motivate companies to invest in activities for sustainability (OECD, 2020).

Here, the barriers and facilitators suggest many of the challenges – such as financial and resource limitations, tangled supply chains, and consumer attitude and behaviour – remain but may be counterbalanced by collaborative efforts. This makes leadership commitment, technology development and partnership with other stakeholders along the value chain to become the enabling factors. Thus, efforts might be made to close the existing regulatory and policy gaps by providing coherent and supportive frameworks that could enhance the CE adoption in the outdoor sporting industry. The literature review presented in this paper discusses key implementation enablers and challenges in the industry producing outdoor sporting items. Still, the financial, technological and consumers' challenges are prohibiting the industry from moving forward; on the other hand, innovation, cooperation and supporting from regulation shall offer the way. More research works should be carried out for collecting observational data related to regional issues and solutions and the long term economic and eco-friendly consequences of CE implementation in this sector.

The move from a linear 'take-make-dispose' model to a circular economy system means working towards the optimum use of resources and minimum waste. When focusing on the challenges and enablers that one would come across when implementing a circular economy model is its fundamental elements which include: reduce, repair and reuse.

Reduce

Reduction at the root level of resource use is of prime importance. This includes, for instance, product design aimed at longevity and durability of the product as well as making sure that every aspect of product packaging is minimized as much as possible, which will help consequentially in advocating sustainable use of such products. If the initial percentages needed for the base materials to be used are less, then the impacts incurred such as extraction from the environment can be eliminated. Although those are sometimes interrelated, the primary goal of the categories that businesses target is to reduce energy, water, chemicals, waste and emissions. Since many products cannot function as effectively without fluorocarbons, or perfluorocarbons (PFCs), the main target of this compromise among functioning and element elimination is the major issue with chemicals. Although there appears to be disagreement among stakeholders over this issue, facilitators would also be prepared to exchange less sophisticated products. Further, overstock was mentioned by stakeholders as an environmental problem that also causes financial problems for companies. Both researchers hypothesized that, while it has many challenges, a more demand-oriented production strategy would be able to eliminate this problem. While in the case of energy, the emphasis was primarily placed on the use of renewables, with stakeholders mentioning that suppliers might be convinced to save energy because saving energy also saves them money. On the other hand, industry-wide multi-stakeholder cooperation, water treatment, natural materials, solution dyeing and shortage of water were the most frequently mentioned facilitators. Also, a vital barrier is the dissociating of growing and secretions because reducing secretions in turn will relate to reducing sales. This in large will go against the core performance indicators that the organizations use in culture will lead to the removal of many participants.

Repair

Replace and refurbishing services that elongate the life of a product are core ideas of circular economy. Among the opportunities highlighted, there is the potential to eliminate replacements by enhancing the importance of repair through easier access to services, spare parts and skills development. In a broad context, repair models and outdoor products have similarity with restoration and lasting attribute. Also, restore enhances durability. Unlike conventional construction processes, restoration implies the reinforcement and enhancement of the existing structures' endurance capacity. However, it appears that what really slows the effectiveness of repair is the price that results from manufacturing products in countries where wages remain low and then repairing them in places where wages are above average and have to be paid; this has the effect of putting the price up there with totally new production. Therefore, this makes it quite uncommon among users as those from business end are at least hard pressed to make the process make sense.

Reuse

Another important facet of the circular economy is the optimization of the assistance gained from the use of products via reuse and refurbishment. Some of these may be adapt and reuse initiatives, sharing and leasing initiatives and organization and management of markets for remanufactured as well as recycled items. Holding the products longer in use, one can minimize the demand for the new materials and in result, there will be less waste disposal. Although stakeholders have painted encouraging growth pictures, reuse models of outdoor gears appear more economically viable than rental-based models. Furthermore, the number of questions arising about the environmental aspects that are related to rentals appears to be somewhat limited. Since outdoor products themselves are very long-lasting, and people become fervently involved with them through their out-of-doors activities or even posted images, the primary issue is that outdoor products have an extremely low profit rate, which limits their supply. It takes a very long time for customers to return products, rather than return them immediately. The provider of EOL operations said that it is crucial to provide consumers with incentives to return products, and that the kind of incentive is not very significant. The choice of a seasoned service provider who can effectively assist (the initial stage of) re-commerce models is another crucial enabler.

Reduce, repair and reuse are the interventions that can help effectively tackle the barriers associated with the transition to a circular economy and build the future of our world – better and more resistant. Our findings are in line with the literature emphasizing some extent of unawareness and training required for internal threats Ki et al. (2020); Moktadir et al. (2018). The key concerns raised by the actors were a lack of expertise regarding circularity design and no clearness in companies on when to start with the circular economy journey. Although several of the interviewed executives reported occasional references to non-strategic methods, significantly more pointed out that so many organizations are in the process of raising strategic embedding. Recognized by the experts was that the outdoor sports products that were responsible had a high level of intrinsic motivation to advance sustainable procedures and therefore the requirement for management support did not limit them Bocken et al. (2017); Macchion et al. (2018). This was not considered as a barrier. Outdoor stakeholders pointed to pilots as a means to probe for possible economies of scale and, therefore, potentials contingently associated with scaling up, as suggested in the literature. This is significant given that realization of economic viability of circular economy transitions has been mooted as a major challenge for outdoor firms (Chesbrough, 2010).

Many of the features of this intricate product challenge for activities associated to the circular economy are particularly present in the outdoor industry (Franco, 2017). The use of many circular economy strategies, such as recycled, recyclable, bio-based and reduced amounts of specific chemicals, can be easier to find because some product categories, especially those used outdoors, have very high functional requirements (cold weather clothing, climbing equipment, etc.). This includes a vast array of vibrant items with distinct features in the footwear, apparel and equipment (outdoor sports) segments, where the circularity requirements vary greatly not just across and within the real segments but also within product types. Consequently, stakeholders recommend adopting circular processes based on product kinds. For less sophisticated items and products, it might also be possible to compromise functionality for circularity. This runs counter to Franco's (2017) argument that functional fabrics can never result in a situation where performance is compromised. Fewer studies have looked at this issue in the literature on textiles in general, even though durable and repairable design are mentioned as two of the six facilitators of circularity with reference to outdoor equipment. High complexity and high functionality needs are therefore trade-offs; nonetheless, combinations of highly and less technological products and services, as well as a low probability of product returns, make outdoor sports equipment appealing.

Additionally, there are outdoor-specific enablers like designing for durability, designing for reparability and linking product kinds to the predetermined degree of circularity. Uncertain and/or prolonged consumer needs, customer complexity issues, an unclear value chain, overproduction, decoupling issues and low-cost circularity are other general issues with outdoor sports items. According to the results, we think that the phrase 'reduce' should be used in circular practices as a foundation for other elements. This is why long-lasting, repairable technical outdoor equipment is favoured. However, this could change based on the situation or the product's features, such as less technical outdoor equipment.

Conclusion, Limitations and Future Scope

The main research objective was to develop a standardized explanation of circular economy implementation barriers and facilitators confronting outdoor sporting brands and vendors. The analysis questioned the appropriateness of CE solutions for athletic outdoor products while examining their usage as sustainability masks. The research makes an important scholarly contribution by exploring a critical gap in CE literature focused on outdoor sporting goods industry that provides useful knowledge for both scholars and practitioners. Organizations working in this sector should develop customized approaches to CE implementation which focus on real sustainability targets instead of artificial green practices. CE principles show promise but implementing them practically proves difficult mainly because of complex products alongside organization capacity limitations which sometimes lead to incomplete or surface-level implementation that amounts to greenwashing.

The analysis demonstrates that enhancing consumer awareness together with their engagement stands as an essential requirement. Consumer loyalty towards circular products depends on effective environmental and economic sustainability communication which strengthens their credibility and visibility. Brands should abandon non-specific sustainable statements by focusing new advertising messages on products which can be repaired together with durable components alongside explicit transparency communication. Industry-wide adoption of genuine CE became possible through the rise of important cooperative efforts between businesses to enable circular economy implementation. Companies should join collaborative platforms while actively advocating for policies which help solve common supply chain problems to establish responsibility while fighting the practice of greenwashing. True circular economy strategies beyond marketing purposes require transparent practices together with multi-sectoral alliances and consumer rights that establish actual sustainability measures in the outdoor sporting goods industry.

When we consider the essential principles of the circular economy as a base on which to stand, they would guide resource reduction activity, extend product life by way of reusability and ultimately help reduce the environmental impact, while achieving operational efficiencies as well. Firms that masterfully gaggle such practices will tend to carve a competitive edge that runs smoothly with the expectations of change on consumers and regulators. There are therefore some suggestions to practitioners: first, outdoor retailers and brands need to settle on a strategy for the circular economy idea. For them, representatives' thinking must seriously consider the implications of circular economy tricks and what this would inform about the broader company and sustainability programme. It is crucial that businesses communicate to why it is common sense to use circular economy thinking on process or products, as this has already been proven to present several challenges. Products come first when looking at either side of circularity, simply by adjusting for product specification (fewer or more complex items). Second, ensure saleability of circular products and services to customers by shedding more light on whatever lies ahead for them. Remediation, stalemate and repair are put in dire need of priority. Ideally, the coordination of collaboration within and between sectors should be directed by industrial associations.

This study faces several limitations, which arise due to presumed selective bias; the interviewed brands and retailers are exactly on the bright end of the circular economy-related practices, as opposed to circular economy-related limitations. While this indeed implies a selection-bias in the sampling process employed, we chose to adopt a stakeholder approach and embraced as wide a set of views as possible. Further, while we tried to remain objective on the issue, it is possible that the mentioned obstacles and facilitators may be in some way biased by questions asked during the interview. However, at least that serving brand preferential treatment, on the contrary, would be represented much more evidently than by suppliers or consumers, who work with product testers only.

Future academic work needs to research the real nature of CE initiatives in outdoor sporting goods industries and clarify methods to properly integrate circular practices. Researchers need to develop different communication techniques to demonstrate the actual benefits of circular products to disregard widespread biases against used or supposedly inferior goods. The elimination of this gap should lead to a societal revolution towards responsible purchasing along with decreasing dependence on fake sustainability messages. Eliminating this gap could result into societal revolution towards responsible purchasing alongside reducing the dependence on unauthorized sustainability claims. Future studies need to enhance qualitative findings by conducting quantitative analyses through representative research samples to properly measure how consumers perceive and what preferences they have regarding circular goods and services alongside their actual buying habits. Empirical evidence would both confirm previous research conclusions and help businesses target their sustainable product development towards genuine market consumer behaviours.

Another interesting area of inquiry involves the understanding of willingness by consumers to accept sacrifices in performance for environmental benefits, as that information can influence product design or marketing strategy formulation so that whatever is designed does not clash with welfare expectations and sustainability goals. Wider stakeholder participation will be required in future studies to achieve a more holistic appreciation of CE practices. Principles should entail input from suppliers, consumers and policymakers to account for the entire challenges and opportunities present throughout the supply chain. Comparative studies among different segments of the outdoor sporting goods industry and other high-impact sectors could serve as encouraging insights pertaining to the adoptability of CE practices and scalability of those practices within each sector. This would be very helpful in determining whether it is an industry-specific phenomenon or has wider significance.

For future studies, there is a need to investigate regulatory environment and policies more especially on issues like EPR and financial and non-financial incentives. Regional policies could be examined in terms of the CE with regard to best practice and in particular ongoing areas of relatively poor performance. Lastly, the sound environmental and economic performance indicators of circular products and practices in LCA will provide a quantitative expression of those numbers. This approach will help achieve a better balance between the long-term environmental benefits and the short-term costs of adopting circular economy practices in the outdoor sporting goods sector.

Implications

This study generates findings that present important consequences for three important business groups operating inside the outdoor sporting goods industry – businesses and policymakers as well as consumers. Businesses must now recognize that performing sustainability practices is no longer acceptable and should transition to genuine circular economy practices for sustainable long-term business development. The success of transitions demands a comprehensive method that connects organizational targets to CE methods and integrates them into product creation processes that target resilience and maintenance ability and material cycles. Organizations that properly align sustainability efforts gain competitive advantage in addition to delivering real sustainability, while customer groups focused on environmental concerns grow and specify beyond superficial branding claims.

The research shows that collaboration proves essential for challenges related to implementation while stopping overlapping symbolic efforts that stand alone. Industry alliances together with stakeholder partnerships act as drivers of true CE adoption since they unite groups to exchange knowledge and develop joint solutions which address shared supply chain obstacles. The research develops guidance for regulators to create transparency frameworks, whereas consumers need to investigate sustainability claims that do not reflect operational practices. The study directs all stakeholders towards meaningful participation in the measurable and credible circular transition by dropping illusions about sustainability.

For the policymakers, the study reiterates the call for strict regulatory frameworks, accompanied by incentive mechanisms that hasten the transition towards CE. Examples of such policies include EPR and value-added tax (VAT) refunds for sustainable practices, and regulations on waste and emissions which may encourage business to embrace its tenets. Government and industry should also strive to establish multi-stakeholder collaborations in knowledge-sharing forums and building funding ventures for technological interventions solving a very complex recycling conundrum.

Lastly, from the standpoint of consumers, it suggests huge implications for educational and awareness-raising initiatives as an aspect of attitudinal change for aligning with circular products. Some consumers often are shy to buy second-hand or refurbished products just because of their perceptions regarding quality and reliability. Approaches include having businesses and policymakers invest in initiatives allowing them to market CE practices' ideological and financial benefits to consumers: such as product take-back schemes and repair services. By building a sense of shared stewardship from consumers, businesses and regulators, the industry can unlock more sustainable consumption patterns and build an effective conservation strategy and minimize global environmental impact.

In other words, the transition to a CE framework in the context of outdoor sporting goods manufacturing and consumption cannot only create the prospects of an environmental salvation trail but is also a chance to redefine the value creation process, enhance customer bonds and leverage innovation in the industry. For CE practices to be implemented, it will require stakeholders' and government's support towards this direction right along the supply chain.

References

Adams, R., Jeanrenaud, S., Bessant, J., Denyer, D., & Overy, P. (2017). Sustainability-oriented innovation: A systematic review. *International Journal of Management Reviews*, *19*(4), 463–492. https://doi.org/10.1111/ijmr.12068

Arc'teryx. (2021). *ReBird program*. Arc'teryx. https://arcteryx.com

Blaikie, N. W. H. (2010). *Designing social research: The logic of anticipation*. Polity Press.

Bocken, N., Albareda, L., Ritala, P., Boons, F., Dembek, K., Gerardts, T., Kennedy, S., & Schaltegger, S. (2016). Sustainable business models: Towards meaningful organizations and organizing. *Journal of Industrial Production Engineering*, *33*, 308–320.

Bocken, N. M. P., de Pauw, I., Bakker, C., & van der Grinten, B. (2016). Product design and business model strategies for a circular economy. *Journal of Industrial and Production Engineering*, *33*(5), 308–320.

Bocken, N. M., Miller, K., Holgado, M., Weissbrod, I., & Evans, S. (2017). Business model experimentation for circularity: Driving sustainability in a large international clothing retailer. *Economics and Policy of Energy and the Environment*, *1*(2), 85–122.

Bogers, M., Chesbrough, H., & Moedas, C. (2018). Open innovation: Research, practices, and policies. *California Management Review*, *60*(2), 5–16.

Bressanelli, G., Adrodegari, F., Pigosso, D. C., & Saccani, N. (2019). Towards circular economy in the consumer goods sector. *Resources, Conservation and Recycling*, *141*, 21–31.

Bukhari, M. A., Carrasco-Gallego, R., & Ponce-Cueto, E. (2018). Developing a national programme for textiles and clothing recovery. *Waste Management & Research*, *36*(4), 321–331.

Chaturvedi, R., Brown, C., & Kilpatrick, K. (2021). *Patagonia: Sustainable innovation in the outdoor industry*. Harvard Business School Case Study.

Chesbrough, H. (2010). Business model innovation: Opportunities and barriers. *Long Range Planning*, *43*(2–3), 354–363.

Chistov, V., Aramburu, N., & Carrillo-Hermosilla, J. (2021). Open eco-innovation: A bibliometric review of emerging research. *Journal of Cleaner Production*, *311*, 127627.

Corbin, J., & Strauss, A. (2014). *Basics of qualitative research: Techniques and procedures for developing grounded theory* (4th ed.). Sage Publications.

de Jesus, A., Lammi, M., Domenech, T., Vanhuyse, F., & Mendonça, S. (2021). Eco-innovation diversity in a circular economy: Towards circular innovation studies. *Sustainability*, *13*(19), 10974.

Earley, R. (2017). Circular design futures. *The Design Journal*, *20*(4), 421–434.

Ellen MacArthur Foundation. (2013). *Towards the circular economy: Economic and business rationale for an accelerated transition*. Ellen MacArthur Foundation. https://ellenmacarthurfoundation.org

Ellen MacArthur Foundation. (2017). *A new textiles economy: Redesigning fashion's future*. Ellen MacArthur Foundation.

Ellen MacArthur Foundation. (2020). *The circular economy: A transformative approach to economic growth*. Ellen MacArthur Foundation. https://ellenmacarthurfoundation.org

European Commission. (2020). A new circular economy action plan for a cleaner and more competitive Europe. https://eur-lex.europa.eu/resource.html?uri=cellar:9903b325-6388-11ea-b735-01aa75ed71a1.0017.02/DOC_1&format=PDF

European Outdoor Group. (2020). *Sustainability insights for the outdoor industry*. EOG.

European Outdoor Group. (2021). Sustainability insights for the outdoor industry. https://europeanoutdoorgroup.com

European Parliamentary Research Service. (2018). Circular economy. https://www.europarl.europa.eu/thinktank/infographics/circulareconomy/public/index.html

Fletcher, K., & Grose, L. (2021). *Earth logic: Fashion action research plan*. The J.J. Charitable Trust.

Franco, M. A. (2017). Circular economy at the micro level: A dynamic view of incumbents' struggles and challenges in the textile industry. *Journal of Cleaner Production*, *168*, 833–845.

Fuchs, M., & Hovemann, G. (2022). Homogeneity or heterogeneity: An institutional theory view on circular economy practices in the outdoor sporting goods industry. *Sustainability*, *14*(10), 6279.

Gardetti, M. A., & Torres, A. L. (2013). Entrepreneurship, innovation, and luxury: The Aïny Savoirs Des Peuple case. *The Journal of Corporate Citizenship*, *52*, 55–75.

Geissdoerfer, M., Pieroni, M. P., Pigosso, D. C., & Soufani, K. (2020). Circular business models: A review. *Journal of Cleaner Production*, *277*, 123741.

Geissdoerfer, M., Savaget, P., Bocken, N. M. P., & Hultink, E. J. (2017). The circular economy: A new sustainability paradigm? *Journal of Cleaner Production*, *143*, 757–768.

Gleim, M. R., Smith, J. S., Andrews, D., & Cronin, J. J. (2013). Against the green: A multi-method examination of the barriers to green consumption. *Journal of Retailing*, *89*(1), 44–61.

Govindan, K., & Hasanagic, M. (2018). A systematic review on drivers, barriers, and practices towards a circular economy: A supply chain perspective. *International Journal of Production Research*, *56*(1–2), 278–311. https://doi.org/10.1080/00207543.2017.1402141

Grębosz-Krawczyk, M., & Siuda, D. (2019). Attitudes of young European consumers toward recycling campaigns of textile companies. *Autex Research Journal*, *19*(4), 394–399.

Hamid, S. (2019). Circularity in fashion: An analysis of take-back and resale models. *Journal of Fashion Technology & Textile Engineering*, *7*(1), 1–8.

Henninger, C. E., Alevizou, P., Goworek, H., & Ryding, D. (2016). Why do consumers buy second-hand apparel? *Journal of Fashion Marketing and Management*, *20*(4), 383–399.

Heckathorn, D. D. (2011). Comment: Snowball versus respondent-driven sampling. *Sociological Methodology*, *41*(1), 355–366.

Holtström, J., Bjellerup, C., & Eriksson, J. (2019). Business model development for sustainable apparel consumption: The case of Houdini Sportswear. *Journal of Strategic Marketing and Advertising*, *12*, 481–504.

Hvass, K. K. (2014). Post-retail responsibility of garments: A fashion industry perspective. *Journal of Fashion Marketing and Management*, *18*(4), 413–430.

Jack, E. P., Powers, T. L., & Skinner, L. (2010). Reverse logistics capabilities: Antecedents and cost savings. *International Journal of Physical Distribution & Logistics Management*, *40*(3), 228–246.

Jia, F., Yin, S., Chen, L., & Chen, X. (2020). The circular economy in the textile and apparel industry: A systematic literature review. *Journal of Cleaner Production*, *259*, 120728.

Ki, C. W., Chong, S. M., & Ha-Brookshire, J. E. (2020). How fashion can achieve sustainable development through a circular economy and stakeholder engagement: A systematic literature review. *Corporate Social Responsibility and Environmental Management*, *27*(6), 2401–2424.

Kim, A. J., & Ko, E. (2010). Impacts of luxury fashion brand's social media marketing on customer relationship and purchase intention. *Journal of Global Fashion Marketing*, *1*(3), 164–171.

Kirchherr, J., Reike, D., & Hekkert, M. (2017). Conceptualizing the circular economy: An analysis of 114 definitions. *Resources, Conservation and Recycling*, *127*, 221–232. https://doi.org/10.1016/j.resconrec.2017.09.005

Köhler, J., Sönnichsen, S. D., & Beske-Jansen, P. (2022). Towards a collaboration framework for circular economy: The role of dynamic capabilities and open innovation. *Business Strategy and the Environment*, *31*(6), 2700–2713.

Korhonen, J., Nuur, C., Feldmann, A., & Birkie, S. E. (2018). Circular economy as an essentially contested concept. *Journal of Cleaner Production*, *175*, 544–552. https://doi.org/10.1016/j.jclepro.2017.12.111

Lacy, P., & Rutqvist, J. (2015). *Waste to wealth: The circular economy advantage*. Palgrave Macmillan.

Lüdeke-Freund, F., Gold, S., & Bocken, N. M. P. (2019). A review and typology of circular economy business model patterns. *Journal of Industrial Ecology*, *23*(1), 36–61. https://doi.org/10.1111/jiec.12763

Macchion, L., Da Giau, A., Caniato, F., Caridi, M., Danese, P., Rinaldi, R., & Vinelli, A. (2018). Strategic approaches to sustainability in fashion supply chain management. *Production Planning & Control*, *29*(1), 9–28.

Masi, D., Day, S., & Godsell, J. (2017). Supply chain configurations in the circular economy: A systematic literature review. *Sustainability*, *9*(9), 1602.

Merli, R., Preziosi, M., & Acampora, A. (2018). How do scholars approach the circular economy? A systematic literature review. *Journal of Cleaner Production*, *178*, 703–722. https://doi.org/10.1016/j.jclepro.2017.11.246

Michelini, G., Moraes, R. N., Cunha, R. N., Costa, J. M. H., & Aldrighi, D. M. (2017). From linear to circular economy: PSS conducting the transition. *Procedia CIRP*, *64*, 2–6. https://doi.org/10.1016/j.procir.2017.03.012

Moktadir, M. A., Rahman, T., Rahman, M. H., Ali, S. M., & Paul, S. K. (2018). Drivers to sustainable manufacturing practices and circular economy: A perspective of leather industries in Bangladesh. *Journal of Cleaner Production*, *174*, 1366–1380. https://doi.org/10.1016/j.jclepro.2017.11.059

Neto, B., Oostra, M., & Vellenga, S. (2019). The textile circular economy: Opportunities for differentiation. *Sustainability*, *11*(23), 6778.

Niinimäki, K., Peters, G., Dahlbo, H., Perry, P., Rissanen, T., & Gwilt, A. (2020). The environmental price of fast fashion. *Nature Reviews Earth & Environment*, *1*, 189–200. https://doi.org/10.1038/s43017-020-0039-9

Nußholz, J. L. K. (2017). Circular business models: Defining a concept and framing an emerging research field. *Sustainability*, *9*(10), 1810. https://doi.org/10.3390/su9101810

OECD. (2020). *Business models for the circular economy: Opportunities and challenges from a policy perspective*. OECD Publishing. https://doi.org/10.1787/g2g9dd62-en

Palm, D., Elander, M., Watson, D., Kiørboe, N., & Salmenperä, H. (2015). *Towards a Nordic textile strategy: Collection, sorting, reuse and recycling of textiles*. Nordic Council of Ministers.

Parida, V., Burström, T., Visnjic, I., & Wincent, J. (2019). Orchestrating industrial ecosystem in circular economy: A two-stage transformation model for large manufacturing companies. *Journal of Business Research*, *101*, 715–725. https://doi.org/10.1016/j.jbusres.2019.04.028

Patagonia. (2020). Worn wear: Better than new. https://www.patagonia.com/worn-wear/

Prendeville, S., Sanders, C., Sherry, J., & Costa, F. (2017). Circular economy practices in the built environment: A systematic literature review. *Journal of Cleaner Production*, *142*, 3225–3235. https://doi.org/10.1016/j.jclepro.2016.10.084

Ranta, V., Aarikka-Stenroos, L., Ritala, P., & Mäkinen, S. J. (2018). Exploring institutional drivers and barriers of the circular economy: A cross-regional comparison of China, the US, and Europe. *Resources, Conservation and Recycling*, *135*, 70–82. https://doi.org/10.1016/j.resconrec.2017.08.017

Rex, E., Baumann, H., & Ryding, S. (2020). Beyond recycling: A framework for product life extension. *Journal of Industrial Ecology*, *24*(4), 841–854. https://doi.org/10.1111/jiec.13003

Sandin, G., & Peters, G. M. (2018). Environmental impact of textile reuse and recycling – A review. *Journal of Cleaner Production*, *184*, 353–365.

Sehnem, S., Campos, L. M., Julkovski, D. J., & Cazella, C. F. (2019). Circular business models: Level of maturity. *Management Decision*, *57*(4), 1043–1066. https://doi.org/10.1108/MD-10-2018-1110

Singh, J., & Ordoñez, I. (2016). Resource recovery from post-consumer waste: An assessment of end-of-life options for plastics. *Energy & Environmental Science*, *9*, 1744–1760.

Stahel, W. R. (2013). Policy for material efficiency—sustainable taxation as a departure from the throwaway society. *Philosophical Transactions of the Royal Society A: Mathematical, Physical and Engineering Sciences*, *371*(1986), 20110567. https://doi.org/10.1098/rsta.2011.0567

Stahel, W. R. (2016). Circular economy: A new relationship with our goods and materials would save resources and energy and create local jobs. *Nature*, *531* (7595), 435–438. https://doi.org/10.1038/531435a

Takacs, F., Frankenberger, K., & Stechow, R. (2020). Circular ecosystems: Business model innovation for the circular economy. *Journal of Business Research*, *101*, 642–651. https://doi.org/10.1016/j.jbusres.2019.11.052

Testa, F., Iraldo, F., Vaccari, A., & Ferrari, E. (2016). Why eco-labels can be effective: The role of environmental reputation. *Business Strategy and the Environment*, *24*(8), 1–15.

Turoń, K. (2022). From the classic business model to open innovation and data sharing—the concept of an open car-sharing business model. *Journal of Open Innovation: Technology, Market, and Complexity*, *8*(1), 36. https://doi.org/10.3390/joitmc8010036

Uhrenholt, J. N., Kristensen, J. H., Rincón, M. C., Jensen, S. F., & Waehrens, B. V. (2022). Circular economy: Factors affecting the financial performance of product take-back systems. *Journal of Cleaner Production*, *335*, 130319. https://doi.org/10.1016/j.jclepro.2021.130319

Ülgen, V. S., & Forslund, H. (2015). Logistics performance management in textiles supply chains: Best-practice and barriers. *International Journal of Productivity and Performance Management*, *64*(1), 52–75. https://doi.org/10.1108/IJPPM-03-2013-0046

Wang, B., Luo, W., Zhang, A., Tian, Z., & Li, Z. (2020). Blockchain-enabled circular supply chain management: A system architecture for fast fashion. *Computers in Industry*, *123*, 103324. https://doi.org/10.1016/j.compind.2020.103324

Watson, D., Aare, A., Trzepacz, S., Hansen, J., & Elander, M. (2018). *Designing circular systems for textiles*. Nordic Council of Ministers Report.

Winans, K., Kendall, A., & Deng, H. (2017). The history and current applications of the circular economy concept. *Renewable and Sustainable Energy Reviews*, *68*, 825–833. https://doi.org/10.1016/j.rser.2016.09.123

Woodley, X. M., & Lockard, M. (2016). Womanism and snowball sampling: Engaging marginalized populations in holistic research. *Qualitative Report*, *21*(2), 321–329. https://nsuworks.nova.edu/tqr/vol21/iss2/8

Chapter 11

Growth of Climate Finance Across the Nations and the Emergence of Greenwashing

Laiba Anwar and Rupesh Roshan Singh

Lovely Professional University, India

Abstract

Climate change has transformed from a distant concern to a visible reality that harms every individual in the world. The immediate need to tackle climate change has led to an increase in climate finance, over trillions of dollars committed to initiatives defined as 'green' or 'sustainable' as climate finance plays an important role in moving towards sustainable development. However, the increment in climate finance has increased the risk of 'greenwashing', which means the practice of deceiving investors by misrepresenting environmental advantages while in the absence of actual sustainability credentials. This chapter examines the landscape of international growth of climate funding across different nations, as well as climate finance commitments and contributions of developed and developing countries, and highlights insufficient funds as a major barrier for urgent climate action. Furthermore, this chapter explores the intricacies of greenwashing within climate finance. It assesses different forms of Greenwashing in Climate Finance, Motivations, Consequences of Greenwashing in Climate Finance, and lastly, best practices to prevent Greenwashing in Climate Finance. It also explains how greenwashing works against the climate initiative, reduces the trust of investors, and demands stricter regulatory measures. Considering the cases of worldwide companies involved in Greenwashing, this chapter highlights the need for public financial disclosures, standardized sustainability measures, and governance structures to ensure that climate financing effectively promotes environmental sustainability. The chapter concludes that understanding and combating greenwashing will be an effective tool to ensure that financial resources are put to actual use to

Eco Illusions, 229–252

doi:10.1108/978-1-83662-782-120261011

mitigate and adapt to climate, rather than lining the pockets of profits for greenwashers.

Keywords: Climate change; climate finance; green finance; greenwashing; zero carbon emissions

Introduction

Climate change can be described as long-term changes in weather patterns. Climate change can be the outcome of either natural or man-made processes. Variations in the sun's activity or massive volcanic eruptions can be natural causes, and major man-made causes are the burning of fossil fuels. By burning fossil fuels, greenhouse gases (GHGs) are released, which increases the temperature of the earth and warms the globe (United Nations, n.d.-a). Its ultimate consequences are very serious for all living beings on the earth, such as serious health issues, negative impact on agriculture, floods, and droughts. In order to address the climate change crisis, climate finance plays a significant role. According to UNFCCC, 'Climate finance refers to local, national or transnational financing drawn from public, private and alternative sources of financing that seeks to support mitigation and adaptation actions that will address climate change.' According to the Global Landscape of Climate Finance 2023, the average annual need of climate finance will be $8.1 to $9 trillion until 2030. Furthermore, from 2031 to 2050, the needs of climate finance are likely to increase by about $10 trillion annually. Although, in 2021–2022, climate funding flow was about $ 1.3 trillion. Thus, the need for climate finance is increasing rapidly in order to achieve net zero emissions by 2050. Climate change consequences are becoming more severe day by day which makes adequate Climate change funding very urgent. Therefore, the more we delay, the higher investment will be needed.

At a time when worldwide growth of climate funding is acknowledged as a significant tool to curb climate change, this chapter analyses whether this climate funding is actually addressing the environmental crisis or just creating an eco-illusion, a false perception of sustainability ignited by greenwashing. Nevertheless, environmental, social, and governance (ESG) metrics have also become popular and are attracting climate investments, but the risk of false claims has also increased. In this chapter, it is analyzed how greenwashing practices hinder the credibility of climate finance. Lastly, by exposing these relationships, it focuses on offering readers a way to distinguish between actual climate actions and misleading sustainability claims.

Literature Review

Forliano et al. (2024) studied the research on greenwashing in business and management using a systematic literature review approach, showing the analysis with the help of bibliometric and network analysis. With this regard, four cluster themes were generated – symbolic management and CSR communication, environmental regulations and institutional complexity, performance and sustainable practices, and marketing, perception, and trust – red, green, blue, and yellow, respectively. The prevalence of macro-level theories overall was emphasized. The results found that significant sustainability initiatives with environmental claims are necessary, since greenwashing presents considerable threats to business reputation and stakeholder confidence and sustained success. Dempere et al. (2024) examined the overall role of greenwashing in sustainable finance, including types, effects, and possible remedies. The study highlights that greenwashing can damage the reputation of a company, its financial performance and the trust of stakeholders which can distort the confidence of investors as well. The study suggested strict regulations and public education to fight greenwashing. Lastly, the application of the results will be to government agencies, corporates, and NGOs in order to increase responsibility and transparency in green finance. Lagoarde-Ségot (2024) investigated greenwashing and sustainable finance and questioned whether traditional financial frameworks are responsible for flawed ideas about reality, which further supports greenwashing problems. In addition, it was also argued that these misleading concepts misrepresent financial information and policies and affect ecology adversely. Lastly, the study suggested developing a new ecological finance paradigm from a critical realism point of view. Maria et al. (2024) analyzed the association between greenwashing and financial constraints of companies in the context of the capital market. With this regard, the researchers proposed an econometric model to measure how much a company is misleading with environmentally friendly claims, and further, the model was examined using multiple linear regression with panel data. Moreover, the results revealed a positive relationship between KZ index and Greenwash score. However, there is an adverse relationship between the Financial Risk and Debt Cost with the Greenwash score. This is how it provides insight into company behaviour with reference to ESG policies and how they impact market monitoring. Zhang (2023) explored the association between sustainable finance and the quality of ESG performance. The study found there is a strongly negative relationship between green finance and greenwashing, companies that are highly polluting reduce greenwashing initiatives in comparison to clean production companies, and green finance is received more by the companies that are highly environmentally regulated. Furthermore, Green finance reduces greenwashing by alleviating financial pressures, improving profitability, and strengthening ESG-related funding. Bernini & Rosa (2023) also evaluated what variables make a company more vulnerable or less vulnerable to greenwashing. In this regard, a conceptual framework was developed to highlight the multifaceted nature of greenwashing. Moreover, mandatory environmental disclosure and a comprehensive framework are necessary in order to reduce false practices. Liu et al. (2023) investigated the greenwashing phenomenon, that is, misrepresentation and environmental disclosure and performance. Moreover, an integrated framework was constructed to investigate the roots and implications of corporate greenwashing based on the corporate governance viewpoint. In addition, the paper discusses significant different theoretical aspects such as green marketing, green finance, signalling strategy, and corporate decoupling. Furthermore, factors such as internal and external governance mechanisms that affect greenwashing are also highlighted. Lastly, researchers suggested integrating ESG framework, internal governance mechanisms, and the influence of corporate greenwashing on different stakeholders. Mateo-Marquez et al. (2022) explored the association between corporate greenwashing conduct and control of climate change. The study depicts that the temperature control reduces the probability of corporations' greenwashing – that is, of presenting positive environmental performance in line with poor real performance. Using their carbon performance and CDP transparency scores, the study suggests a fresh method of identifying greenwashing businesses. It adds to the body of knowledge by underlining how important the regulatory environment is in determining business behaviour in supporting environmental claims. The result emphasized the need for efficient environmental law enforcement and monitoring. Ruiz-Blanco et al. (2021) studied the traits of companies that can make them less or more susceptible to greenwashing, which refers to the difference between company's claims and its real sustainable practices. In this regard, the researchers used content analysis and evaluated reporting levels using the information from the sustainability reports of the top 100 S&P companies. Moreover, the study found that companies that are following GRI standards and companies in vulnerable environmental areas are less vulnerable to greenwash. On the other hand, those companies that are high-profile are more susceptible to greenwashing because the limelight may mitigate the probability of adverse publicity related to misleading environmental claims. Lastly, the study highlights the necessity of a regulatory framework and public pressure in minimizing fraudulent advertising claims. Longa et al. (2022) analyzed climate finance studies using performance analysis and science mapping. The study found that the interest in climate finance has been higher since 2017 because of the Paris Agreement. Furthermore, it was also found that China, the United Kingdom, and the United States have been the highest contributors in climate finance studies. Moreover, the science mapping has generated six significant themes, including climate change, green finance, public policy, green bond valuation, green finance and banking, and green bonds and financial markets. Lastly, it is also highlighted that climate funding has evolved from green funding, with the scope of topics evolving more in recent times. Bhaskar & Srivastava (2021) investigated the climate finance in India, barriers to climate finance, and the commitments made by India under the Paris Agreement. Furthermore, the study highlights climate finance as a big challenge for developing countries like India. Although the UNFCCC provides financial support to emerging countries, India is highly vulnerable and exposed to climate change. Moreover, India has set its goal to invest $2.5 trillion to achieve its mitigation and adaptation targets by 2030, though it faces barriers to achieving them including high inflation and slowing growth. Finally, the study evaluates recent and existing mechanisms, activities, and challenges related to climate finance in India. Almazrouei & Nobanee (2021) explored the role of green finance in Sustainable Development Goals (SDGs). Furthermore, the study focused on addressing financing and ESG challenges, as well as how green

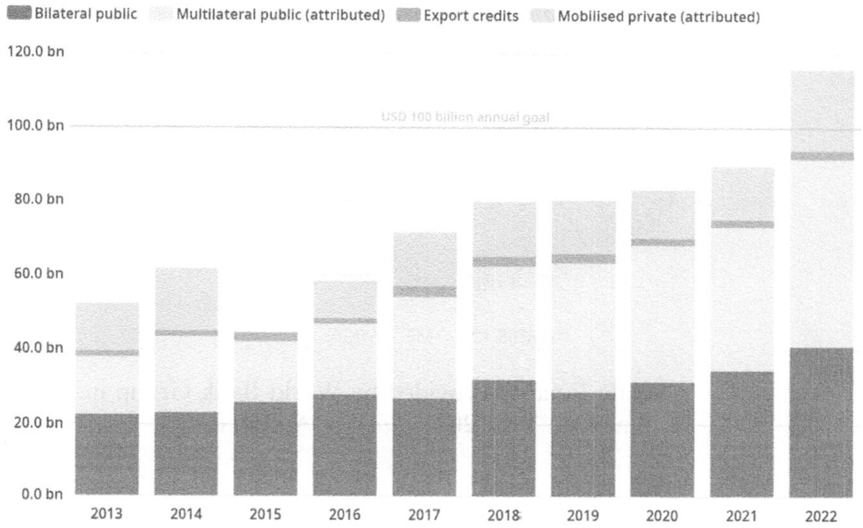

Fig. 11.1. Climate Finance Provided and Mobilized by Developed Countries in 2013–2022. *Source:* OECD, 2024 (OECD.ORG)

finance helps to achieve SDGs. It discusses about developments in green financing as well as the part both governmental and commercial sectors play. The study underlines the need for having one financial system equipped to support sustainable development. It recommends uniform green financial practices to generate similar markets all over. Yu et al. (2020) explored the relationship between ESG) and firm's greenwashing behaviour, particularly of large-cap firms. Moreover, researchers measured the level of greenwashing by firms, and the results found that the probability of greenwashing is reduced in companies that have stronger governance policies and evaluations. Furthermore, poor auditing and standardization were identified as barriers in ESG data disclosure. The study suggested that independent governance can discourage the practices of greenwashing.

Role of Developed Countries and Developing Countries in Climate Finance

Historically, developed countries have been the major cause for the current climate change crisis. Approximately 50% of the total GHGs emitted in the environment were from the wealthy nations in the previous 170 years (The New York Times, 2021). The development of wealthy nations cost the climate and harmed the climate to that extent. In the current scenario, the whole world is paying the cost and facing a climate crisis. Especially, developing nations are facing their

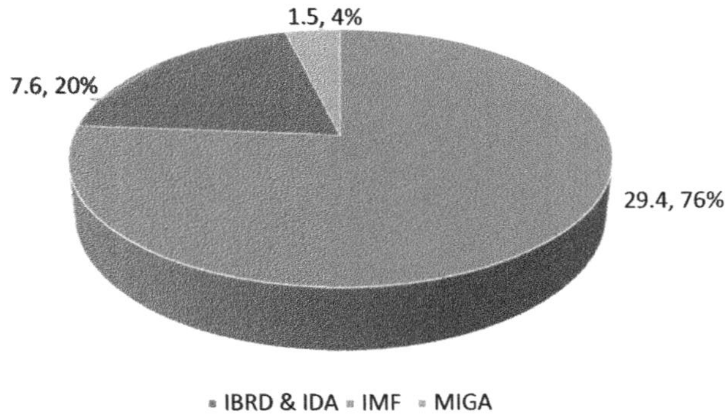

Fig. 11.2. Climate Finance Provided by World Bank Group in the Financial Year 2023. *Source:* Authors.

more severe consequences. Developing nations are on their way to development, hence struggling with both economic development and the climate change crisis simultaneously. Thus, if they move towards development as usual, the climate will be harmed even more. In order to overcome both these challenges simultaneously or move towards sustainable development, massive funding is required, and developing nations are incapable of gathering such massive funding for economic development, to mitigate and adapt to climate change impacts. In order to fight these challenges, developed nations should help developing nations.

As per the United Nations SDGs (2022), climate change is a worldwide crisis that demands cooperation at the international level to be addressed and emphasizes international cooperation with developing nations in transitioning to a low-carbon economy. In addition, according to UNFCCC, 'Developed country Parties (Annex II Parties) shall provide financial resources to assist developing country Parties in implementing the Convention.' In addition, at the 15th Conference of the Parties (COP15) of the UNFCCC, which was held in Copenhagen in 2009, developed nations pledged to raise $100 billion annually by 2020 for developing nations for climate change and promised 'Fast-start Finance' to commence the project immediately. This action was taken to help developing nations go ahead to low-carbon emissions (OECD, 2024; Romano, A. A. et al., 2018). Later at the 21st Conference of the Parties (COP21) of the UNFCCC in Paris in 2015, this commitment was extended to 2025. Furthermore, as per Article 9 of the Paris Agreement, developed nations must provide developing nations with financial resources for mitigation as well as adaptation to combat climate change and achieve the goal of 1.5°C. Furthermore, developing nations should keep taking the initiative to mobilize climate funding from diverse sources, including considering the requirements and priorities of developing nations. It also emphasized the balance of climate finance

Table 11.1. Major Companies Involved in Greenwashing and Their Penalties Globally (as of 2023).

S.R No.	Company	Penalty (in Million)	Purpose of Penalty	Data Sources
1.	Volkswagen	$34,690	Emissions tests circumvent	U.S. Department of Justice
2.	Toyota	$180	Report of emissions postponement	U.S. Department of Justice
3.	DWS	$25	Deception in marketing ESG funds	ESGInvestor.net, Markets Media Group
4.	Eni	$5.6	Faking 'Green' claim	S&P Global, The Wall Street journal
5.	Kohl's & Walmart	$5.5	False environment friendly manufacturing claim	U.S. Federal Trade Commission
6.	Goldman Sachs	$4	ESG fund claims	SEC.Gov, 2022, Financial Times, 2022
7.	Keurig	$2.2	False claim of single-use coffee pods can be recycled	Govt. of Canada, 2022,
8.	BNY Mellon	$1.5	Misstatements and Omissions concerning ESG Considerations	SEC.Gov, 2022
9.	Decathlon	$0.53	False sustainability claims	Business and Human Rights Resource Centre
10.	H&M	$0.43	False sustainability claims	Forbes.com, The Sustainable Fashion Forum

Source: Author creation.

between mitigation and adaptation as per the requirements of developing nations (Climate Finance Climate Change, n.d.). Later on, at the 27th Conference of the Parties (COP27), it was emphasized that developed countries have to fulfil their responsibilities on climate change. It was also emphasized that, in order to cut carbon emissions immediately, efforts need to be increased. Furthermore, losses and damages funds also need to be created (United Nations, Meetings Coverage and Press Releases, 2022; Climate United Nations Change, 2023).

As per OECD (2024), in the year 2022, climate finance provided by developed nations to developing nations finally reached $115.9 billion, surpassing the $100 billion goal unexpectedly. The total rise of $26.3 billion was a 30% increase in climate finance compared to the previous year. Thus, this is considered the biggest increment to date. This can be seen in Fig. 11.1.

Furthermore, public climate finance made up about 80% of the total climate finance in 2022. In addition, a threefold rise was seen in adaptation finance from 2016, as a total of $32.4 billion in adaptation finance was mobilized in 2022.

Furthermore, in the fiscal year 2023, $38.6 billion for climate finance was provided by the World Bank Group to assist initiatives to eradicate poverty on a liveable planet. There has been a rise of 22% in climate finance as compared to the prior year. The bank's new strategy to promote development is to assist developing nations by increasing financial resources to developing nations. Out of the total funding provided by the World Bank Group in climate finance in the fiscal year 2023, about $29.4 billion was provided by IBRD and IDA. From which about $12 billion in investment assisted adaptation and resilience. In addition, $7.6 billion was provided by IFC and MIGA in 1.5 billion in climate finance (The World Bank, 2023). It can be seen in Fig. 11.2.

Barriers and Opportunities of Climate Finance

Climate change is a global challenge to fight, and it needs vast funding to combat. Although climate finance is increasing, it is still not sufficient to move towards zero carbon emissions by 2050. Thus, the funding gap is the most significant barrier to moving towards zero carbon emissions by 2050. In addition, the growth of climate finance is not consistent across sectors and geographical areas. Most of the increment seen in global climate change was due to a rise in clean energy investment in a few geographical regions, such as China, the United States, Europe, Brazil, Japan, and India. However, funding gaps exist even in these regions. Furthermore, mitigation and adaptation funds are also not in a balanced proportion. Finance for adaptation is still lacking, even though it has reached its high record of $63 billion. In addition, private finance can help bridge the vast climate funding gaps, but it is not increasing at the desired rate and quantity. Thus, the obstacles that are hindering the way to climate finance are the high cost of capital, real and perceived investment risks, and competing political priorities. Overcoming these barriers can help foster climate finance at the required rate and scale (Climate Policy Initiative, 2023).

Furthermore, in order to gather desired capital for climate change, CPI recommended a few priorities to expand the unfolding opportunities such as to transform the financial system by changing international financial institutions and by providing concessional funding to attract private finance, to combine the needs of development with the climate through cooperation and cutting the use of fossil fuel with a fair transition, to obtain local funding, and to ensure proper discloser of data related to climate finance (Climate Policy Initiative, 2023).

Climate Finance Need in India

India is the third highest GHGs emitter after China and the United States in the world (Emissions Database for Global Atmospheric Research, 2023). Also, emerging market and developing economies (EMDEs) are more vulnerable to climate change than developed nations. Thus, India, as an emerging nation and third-highest GHG emitter, has been facing the severe consequences of climate change. India's GDP will also be affected by climate change. As per the Indian Institute for Human Settlement report 2023, India GDP will lose 2.6%, 6.7%, and 16.9% by 2030, 2050, and 2100, respectively, due to climate change. Therefore, it becomes very urgent to tackle climate change by moving towards zero carbon emissions and aligning with the global target of 1.5°C. Thus, the only way to stay on the safe side is to highly invest in climate change mitigation as well as climate change adaptation. Furthermore, in order to achieve these targets, India needs to spend 7–18% of its GDP, or an expected annual funding of $167 billion, till 2030. However, annual climate finance achieved $44 billion in 2020 by increasing 150% between 2017 and 2019; climate funding still lacks in India. India needs massive investments to mitigate and adapt to climate change. However, this is a very challenging situation for India, as it still relies on fossil fuel sources and generates 57% of its electricity through fossil fuel sources. Furthermore, shifting from fossil fuel to renewable energy sources is another challenge for India because more than 7 million civilians' employment relies on fossil-fuel-based sectors.

Greenwashing

The term 'greenwashing' originates from the fusion of 'green' and 'brainwashing,' with the latter being contextualized within environmental discourse (Bernini & Rosa, 2023). Greenwashing is a technique of fabricating false and misleading claims about environmentally beneficial practices or commodities (NRDC, 2023). Greenwashing describes deceptive misrepresentation that tricks stakeholders about the environmental advantages of products and services and investments (United Nations, n.d.-b). Companies perform deceptive practices to show environmental responsibility even though they avoid real operational changes. During green bond promotion, within climate financing entities manage to market these financial products as environmentally sustainable yet maintain no visible proof of their genuine sustainability influence (Dempere et al., 2024b).

Examples of greenwashing in climate finance:

- A fund is being invested heavily in promoting fossil fuel activities while claiming to be invested in renewable energy.
- A company is misrepresenting its products as emissions-free but has no credible offsetting measures.
- Green bonds for sustainable projects are being offered by a financial institution, but with minimal environmental benefits.

Greenwashing in Climate Finance

Greenwashing represents environmental deception through which financial institutions, together with corporations and investment funds, produce artificial sustainability messages to draw funds from environmentally conscious investors (Chaube, n.d.). The practice of greenwashing plays a vital role in climate finance because crucial environmental attributes within financial products experience integrity issues. The popularity of sustainable investment products among customers creates new risks of misleading advertisements that hinder the advancement of sustainable environments (Delmas & Burbano, 2011b). Companies fabricate sustainability statements about their financial products because environmental investing trends have increased their prevalence of greenwashing. The ongoing fight against climate change continues because deliberate falsification in marketing makes stakeholders and investors fall for deceitful promises. Default marketing practices demonstrate their distinct type of greenwashing beyond the green bond misrepresentations and tampering of ESG metrics, which target financial sectors together with unverifiable net-zero commitments. Many world-famous companies are also involved in greenwashing, as can be seen in Table 11.1. The following table presents some notable corporate green claim abuses, emissions test frauds, and false claims on sustainability across different industries. The Volkswagen comes at the top of the list, headed by a fine of $34,690 for circumventing emissions tests. It is an example against the integrity of regulations on emissions. The image of corporations as honest players in business has been soiled. Nevertheless, Toyota was charged by the United States of America Department of Justice for the offence of withholding emissions tests, an offence that is even more pervasively symptomatic of disrespect for environmental legislation. The law was cited by the department, though the corporation only had to pay $1,180 in fines. Other stakeholders, such as DWS, were charged a fine of $25 for greenwashing ESG loans following a wider probe of firms that self-certify to be compliant with ESG requirements through the use of deceptive measures. Eni paid a $5.6 million fine for issuing a deceptive 'green' statement, and this is the context of the broader situation of firms profiting from people's desire for sustainable products without really adhering to sustainability. Kohl's and Walmart, two of America's upper-end department store chains, were penalized $5.5 million for dishonesty when they say they have green production processes. This is a case of the 'greenwashing' one is normally used to seeing in the fashion world, as well as throughout the wider retail business. Moreover, Goldman Sachs was also reported to the authorities, and the Securities and Exchange Commission (SEC) imposed a four-million-dollar penalty on the company for giving misleading information about its ESG management fund. Similar to the above case, Decathlon, BNY Mellon, and Keurig were all fined between $1.5 million and $2.2 million for giving either unsubstantiated or false information about sustainability. Another example of the prevalent practice of exaggerating the role that companies play in the environment is given by this specific case. This can be found in a very wide variety of sectors, ranging from banks to coffee makers. The reason that other fashion clothing companies like

H&M and Decathlon were also found to have been guilty of misleading claims about sustainability and were fined a paltry sum of $0.43 million and $0.53 million, respectively, is enough proof for anyone to know how much effort the fashion world is taking to present itself as being eco-friendly, but what it is really doing is causing a great deal of harm to the planet. This is reflective of there being an emerging trend whereby corporate titans are encountering an increasing rate of legal activity and proceedings as a result of their failure to meet standards of morality in the environment and greenery-friendly operations. While it is correct that the severity of punishments differs, they offer further proof of growing expectation that companies declare their environmental impact to customers and other stakeholders honestly and openly.

Forms of Greenwashing in Climate Finance

- ***Deceptive ESG Investment Assertions:*** Some investment funds market themselves as sustainable with large investments in fossil fuels, and deforestation and other harmful environmental industries. The absence of consistent ESG reporting standards makes this situation worse.
- ***False Carbon Offsetting Claims:*** Corporations may use claims of eco-friendly or green terms without providing concrete evidence or make unsupported carbon offsetting claims through procedures which fail to achieve proper verification measures or deliver insignificant actual impacts. Carbon offset projects that involve replanting trees in protected areas or projects that do not guarantee sustained carbon storage have been demonstrated by The University of BritishColumbia, 2023.
- ***Green Bonds with Confined Impact:*** The surge of 'green bonds' in recent years does not indicate that all these bonds support authentic sustainable projects. Corporate organizations issue green bonds to back projects which deliver small environmental advantages or were planned for implementation irrespective of obtaining the bonds (Flammer, 2021).
- ***Selective Disclosure and Data Manipulation or Cherry-picking data:*** Some financial institutions or organizations display their sustainable investments through selective advertising, yet they simultaneously hide their less sustainable business operations. The restricted disclosure practice produces misleading assessments of how companies affect the environment.
- ***Insufficient or Unsubstantiated Net-Zero Commitments:*** Many businesses, together with financial institutions, claim a net-zero commitment through 2050 with no defined interim targets (Lütkehermöller et al., 2023). Business commitments usually omit clear information about the emissions produced during supply chain activities and product use cycles (Scope 3).
- ***Misallocation of funds:*** when the fund is raised for sustainable projects but using those funds for projects that don't genuinely contribute to climate solutions. A lack of effective fund distribution happens when organizations send money towards activities that produce no genuine benefits for climate solutions (Stein, 2023).

- ***False or Misleading Labels:*** Greenwashing misleads the public into believing that a corporation or entity is more environmentally responsible than it actually is. Misleading labels can create an illusion of sustainability that does not reflect actual practices (United Nations, n.d.-a).
- ***Lack of Transparency:*** Insufficient disclosure about how funds from green bonds are utilized can obscure the true environmental impact of projects.

Motivations for Greenwashing in Climate Finance

The motivations for greenwashing in climate finance are complex and often intertwined:

- ***Attracting investment:*** Most of the companies use greenwashing tactics to attract the maximum number of investors. The demand of investors has grown for sustainable funds that create an attractive market for green financial instruments. In order to attract funds from environmentally conscious investors, companies may indulge in greenwashing (Flammer, 2021).
- ***Enhancing reputation:*** Sustainability has become a new trend to attract the public as well as investors. Thus, to position the sustainable image in people's minds or to improve a company's public image and reputation, greenwashing has started to be used, portraying it as environmentally responsible even if its core business practices are unsustainable.
- ***Avoiding regulation:*** In some cases, companies try to bypass the robust or stricter environmental regulations. In such cases, greenwashing can be used to avoid or delay the implementation of stricter environmental regulations.
- ***Gaining competitive advantage:*** Companies may also use greenwashing tactics in order to be seen as more sustainable among all the competitors and to differentiate themselves from all competitors and gain a competitive advantage in the market.

Consequences of Greenwashing in Climate Finance

Greenwashing in climate finance has significant implications for the global transition to a sustainable economy:

- ***Erosion of Investor Trust:*** Greenwashing can destroy the trust of investors in all the other companies even when they are genuinely investing in green activities. Due to greenwashing, scepticism is developed by investors towards ESG claims that can lower their propensity to invest in sustainable activities (Kim & Lyon, 2014, United Nations, n.d.-a, Lyon & Montgomery, 2015b).
- ***Misallocation of capital:*** When the fund is raised for sustainable projects but using those funds for projects that don't genuinely contribute to climate solutions. It develops mistrust in investors and shifts financial resources from authentically environmentally friendly projects to projects that may worsen environmental issues (ClientEarth in Asia, 2025).

- ***Regulatory and Legal Risks:*** When regulations become stricter, as imposed by the regulators, companies engaging in greenwashing suffer legal consequences, financial penalties and reputational harm to their brand (Van der Lugt et al., 2020).
- ***Undermining Market Credibility:*** If greenwashing becomes the norm, then the credibility of the sustainable finance market will suffer, and efforts to reach a low-carbon economy will be deterred (Forest Stewardship CouncilInternational, 2024).

Regulatory and Market-Based Responses

Several regulatory frameworks have been introduced to combat greenwashing and enhance transparency in climate finance:

- ***EU Sustainable Finance Disclosure Regulation (SFDR):*** SFDR came into existence in March 2021 and mandates obligatory ESG disclosure requirements for asset managers and other participants in financial markets, encompassing significant aspects of the legislation (Gannon et al., 2021). The European Commission has made the disclosure of data compulsory and authorizes the Commission to enact delegated and implementing acts to delineate the compliance requirements for competent authorities and market participants as stipulated in the directive. It mandates financial market participants to disclose sustainability risks and classify investments based on sustainability criteria (European Commission, n.d.).
- ***Green Taxonomies:*** As per Institute for Energy Economics and financial analysis, 2022, 'A green taxonomy is a classification system that defines which economic activities and assets are "green" or environmentally sustainable.' The European Union and other jurisdictions have developed classification systems to define what constitutes a truly sustainable investment (Organisation for Economic Co-operation and Development, 2021). Green taxonomies are developed to enhance transparency to improve risk evaluation, integrate financial markets to net-zero objectives and foster an ecologically sustainable economy (Institute for Energy Economics and financial analysis, 2022).
- ***US SEC Climate Disclosure Rules:*** The US Securities and Exchange Commission (SEC) implemented regulations to improve and standardize climate-related disclosures by publicly traded corporations and in public offerings from March 2024 (SEC.Gov, 2024).
- ***Third-Party Verification and Certification:*** Third-party certification states that an autonomous entity has evaluated the production process of a product and has independently ascertained that the final product adheres to designated standards for safety, quality, or performance (NSF.Org, 2020). Organizations such as the Climate Bonds Initiative (CBI) and the Science-Based Targets Initiative (SBTi) provide independent verification of sustainability claims, reducing the risk of greenwashing.

Best Practices to Prevent Greenwashing

To mitigate greenwashing risks and ensure credible climate finance, financial institutions and investors should adopt the following best practices:

- ***Standardized ESG Metrics:*** By implementing internationally acknowledged ESG reporting frameworks, such as the Task Force on Climate-related Financial Disclosures (TCFDs) and the Global Reporting Initiative (GRI), the potential risk of greenwashing can be reduced.
- ***Enhanced Transparency and Disclosure Requirements:*** By guaranteeing transparent, quantifiable, and thoroughly validated sustainability assertions (Ioannou et al., 2021). Companies should be obligated to present comprehensive reports on the application of cash from green bonds and their actual environmental effects. The requirement for comprehensive reporting on spending and environmental consequences might offer stakeholders enhanced understanding of investment effects.
- ***Stricter Regulation:*** The development of more rigorous norms and criteria for defining a 'green' investment is important to promoting openness and accountability in financial markets and can help mitigate greenwashing.
- ***Accountability Mechanisms:*** By enforcing strict legal penalties for deceptive environmental declarations and enhancing impartial procedures for auditing, we can also help avoid greenwashing.
- ***Investment in Impact-Driven Projects:*** By encouraging initiatives that showcase visible environmental benefits, like energy from renewable sources, circular economy efforts, and climate resilience infrastructure, can also help mitigate greenwashing in the market.
- ***Investor Education:*** By teaching and training investors on recognizing authentic, environmentally friendly investments, we can enable them to make sound decisions and dodge greenwashed offerings.

Environmental, Social, and Governance

ESG is a collection of guidelines used by companies to evaluate their social and environmental influence (International Business MachinesCorporation, 2024). The organizations utilize the ESG framework to disclose how the opportunities and risks in the domain of environmental aspects, social accountability, and corporate governance are being managed. ESG metrics are also used by investors, the general public, and stakeholders such as customers, suppliers, and employees to measure the ethical and long-term effects of investments of the companies (International Business MachinesCorporation, 2024; CharteredGovernance Institute UK & Ireland, n.d.).

The ESG has three dimensions: Environmental, Social, and Governance, where the environmental aspect measures the impact of the company and its activities on the environment, also considering the impact of the environment on the company, which includes issues such as climate change, carbon emission, loss of biodiversity, energy consumption, waste management and land and water management. Furthermore, the social aspect considers the responsibility of the company towards society and its impact on stakeholders and other people. The social issues include health and safety, fair pay, health, safety and well-being of the workforce, organizational culture, charity, fair pricing, social equity and inclusion. Lastly, the term governance considers a collection of guidelines, procedures and policies that are directed and controlled by the company. The issues concerned with governance include data privacy, cybersecurity, internal controls, succession planning, shareholder rights, bribery and corruption risk (International Business Machines Corporation, 2024; The Harvard Law School Forum on Corporate Governance, 2020; Chartered Governance Institute UK & Ireland, n.d.).

Although the term ESG was originally used in 2004, it had its roots since the 20th century. In the 1970s, socially conscious investing became a path for people who felt their portfolios should represent their values. Further, during apartheid, this progressed even more under the South African divestment movement. Later, in the 1990s, ESG became mainstream in investment ideas when the US Social Investment Forum tracked record sustainable investments in North America in 1995. Furthermore, institutional investors came to see that companies addressing ESG issues, including greenhouse gases, improve financial performance and risk control. In this regard, the Global Reporting Initiative (GRI) started to grow in 1997 to handle environmental concerns and political and social issues as well. After a year, John Elkington first made the triple bottom line concept in 1998, that is, people, planet, and profit, widely known. In 2000, in the Millennium Summit, basic concepts evolved in human rights, working conditions, the environment, and corruption. In this regard, the Millennium Development Goals were formed, and in the same year, the Carbon Disclosure Project (CDP) was also formed. It aimed to begin institutional investor tracking and reporting of their carbon footprint. Then in 2004, the term ESG officially came into use (IBM, 2024).

Significance of ESG

The term ESG indicates a standard of non-financial factors utilized by stakeholders, investors, and policymakers for assessing the ethical and sustainability influence of a company or investment. The awareness of ESG is increasing day by day, and people are becoming more concerned with sustainable investment. This altered behaviour is making a global shift towards more ethical and disclosed business practices that aim for SDGs. The significance of ESG is given below:

Enhanced Investor Confidence and Better Management Of Risk: The ESG elements help to determine and address significant long-term risks, including climate change issues, legislative changes, and governance failures (Macek & Vitásek, 2024; Yébenes, 2024b). Additionally, companies with better ESG performance can gather capital from investors more easily than other companies because investors evaluate businesses depending on their ESG performance.

Lastly, it is also revealed by the studies that companies with higher ESG ratings have smoother operational performance, lower capital costs, and have stable returns.

Regulatory Compliance and Global Standards: ESG has created an opportunity to set global integrated standards for ESG reporting. In this regard, governments and financial regulators globally have incorporated mandatory ESG disclosure reporting, including SEBI BRSR in India and the EU Taxonomy. Nevertheless, the companies that make ESG practices a top priority are more likely to be prepared to adjust to potential social and environmental regulations and are less prone to being fined or to suffering reputation damage.

Competitive Advantage and Brand Reputation: Companies that embrace ESG principles often attract more consumers and talented employees. This is because consumers have become more conscious of social responsibility and environmental care; thus, they prefer to support those brands that support ESG. Furthermore, these companies are more likely to draw and retain bright employees, particularly among younger generations that respect social responsibility. Nevertheless, ESG also drives innovation such as mindful resource usage, sustainable business models using renewable energy, and sustainable product design.

Contribution to SDGs: ESG directly contributes to SDGs, particularly to Goal 13, Goal 8, Goal 5 and Goal 12, that is, climate action, decent work, gender equality, and responsible consumption and production, respectively (Semet, 2020; Gerber, 2023). Companies that actively implement ESG strategies demonstrate proactive support to participants in creating a fairer, more sustainable global economy.

Enhanced Corporate Governance and Accountability: Companies that follow ESG guidelines strictly have ethical and strong governance practices that lead to a reduction in mismanagement, fraud, and corruption, and enhance transparency, which fosters long-term trust among investors, stakeholders, and communities (Akinsola et al., n.d.).

Financial Performance and Valuation: The integration of ESG into business practices not only serves ethics but it has a positive correlation with financial performance and provides value for shareholders, also as the market usually perceives higher value and lower risks for the companies that are ESG-compliant (Zubeltzu-Jaka et al., 2018). Thus, better ESG performance of a company is not limited to ethics but is also a tool for value creation. It serves as a gap filler between the profitability of a company and sustainability and aligns with societal and environmental goals.

Relationship Between ESG and Greenwashing

The terms Greenwashing and ESG are interrelated despite being opposite in nature. Although ESG aims to encourage open and ethical business operations towards achieving sustainability, greenwashing aims to mislead with false sustainability claims and data to demonstrate a company as environmentally and socially concerned (Zervoudi et al., 2025). Nevertheless, better ESG performance enhances a company's chance to gain more ESG investments (Cherkasova & Nenuzhenko, 2022). Thus, when some companies fail to achieve global ESG metrics, they try to portray their companies as a good ESG performer by using false data, thereby engaging in greenwashing. This practice by a few companies distorts the trust and confidence of investors and also affects capital allocation and the global growth of sustainable development (Poiriazi et al., 2025). Thus, it becomes significant to reduce greenwashing to enhance the global growth of sustainable development. With this regard, there is an enhanced demand for stricter standards for ESG disclosure, stricter regulatory frameworks, and third-party verification certification (Ye, 2024). This is how greenwashing can be reduced, while a strong and transparent ESG system can be promoted — thereby restoring investor trust, confidence, and long-term value creation.

Interconnection Between ESG and Climate Finance

ESG and climate finance have an interconnection with each other; both of these terms promote sustainable development and aim to achieve a carbon-neutral economy (D'Orazio, 2023). ESG is significant in gathering climate finance for sustainable infrastructure, particularly in carbon-neutral technologies, green bonds, and renewable energy infrastructure. Nevertheless, the projects that have high ESG performance have more potential to receive climate finance. Furthermore, ESG metrics promote climate finance by helping investors and companies to measure the environmental and social performance and risks of a company, which is used to promote climate action projects (D'Orazio, 2023). Additionally, ESG metrics also guide companies to utilize climate finance in more mindful projects, including renewable energy, sustainable infrastructure and green technology and buildings, that enhance transparency, responsibility and effective use of climate finance and reduce greenwashing. In conclusion, climate funding serves as a backbone or assessment tool for ESG to evaluate and achieve sustainability as well as financial returns (Institute of Company Secretaries ofIndia, 2022).

Interconnection Between ESG and SDG

The concepts of ESG and SDGs are positively related to each other. ESG investment decisions are made based on alignment with the goals of sustainable development (SDGs) that can build long-term value for a company as well as for society (Hussain, M. A., 2024). The goals of sustainable development help achieve inclusive and sustainable economic growth and social welfare. The companies recognize ESG as easier to connect with SDGs based on a governance perspective, but if SDGs are seen from other perspectives, then only the social and environmental issues of ESG can be connected to SDGs. The interconnection of ESG with SDGs encourages organizations to facilitate returns earlier and also helps investors to make sustainable investments to support worldwide goals (Institute of Company Secretaries ofIndia, 2022).

Integrated Role of ESG, Climate Finance and Greenwashing

The integration of ESG indicates a multifaceted mechanism that impacts SDGs (Zervoudi et al., 2025). As ESG is a regulatory framework that helps businesses make sustainable investments and measure the environmental and social behaviour of companies, and climate finance helps companies gather the funding needed to invest to address climate change, including mitigation, adaptation, and renewable energy. With this regard, ESG metrics make sure that the funds for climate are actually invested in sustainable and significant projects (Kotsantonis et al., 2016). This helps investors determine and invest in actual sustainable projects and contribute to sustainable development. Nevertheless, increased climate finance has also led to greenwashing, where companies make false claims or misrepresent their ESG performance to deceive investors into investing in their company while they use those investments for other purposes (Bo & Battisti, 2024). This act of greenwashing distorts the trust of investors and the credibility of climate finance and hinders the growth of climate goals. This challenge must be addressed for market transparency and credibility and to ensure transparent and effective use of climate finance by implementing a stricter regulatory framework, standard disclosure reporting and strong ESG governance (Yébenes, 2024). Thus, in order to build a credible and outcome-driven sustainable financial environment, including promoting green technologies, renewable energy and green buildings, ESG and climate finance need to be aligned while avoiding greenwashing.

Confronting the Eco-Illusion

Eco-illusion is a misleading belief of any company, consumer, media, or other public that a company, product, or policy is environmentally friendly, which in reality it is not (Davis, 2024). This happens due to a lack of information, improper knowledge, false claims, and cognitive bias. Eco-illusion is a significant challenge encouraged by greenwashing for climate finance. The action of false claims of 'environmentally sustainable' projects has increased due to the higher need for climate funding and the willingness of investors to invest in sustainable projects and products (Adamo et al., 2025). Furthermore, insufficient disclosure rules, an inconsistent ESG framework and a lack of a worldwide responsibility system have made companies exaggerate their data and indulge in greenwashing to get more climate funding. Thus, these increased claims of greenwashing have encouraged eco-illusion as both of these concepts are interrelated. This chapter shows the significant dependence of the integrity of climate finance on transparent and strong ESG governance, and also ways that ultimately reduce greenwashing, and so is eco-illusion. It is essential to establish accountability at the centre of climate finance to be sure that investments produce practical outcomes. Therefore, eco-illusion is not just an academic learning opportunity, but it is essential to restore confidence in green finance and achieve a carbon-neutral and just transition globally (Parguel, B., & Johnson, G. (2021).

Conclusion

The issue of climate finance greenwashing is a major hurdle towards the attainment of global sustainability targets. In this regard, the global mobilization of climate funds has primarily resulted in a global transition towards a green and low-carbon economy. Nevertheless, green projects are funded by governments, banks and private financiers in a growing trend with a perspective towards climate change mitigation and environmental sustainability, renewable energy and climate-resilient infrastructure growth. But with this fast growth, greenwashing cases have also grown to become a major problem spoiling the reputation of environmental projects and climate money, and creating eco-illusion as well. Thus, many companies and banks have been proven to be culpable of misleading stakeholders, overstating or understating their green projects, thereby diluting the effect of green financial programmes. The current climate finance greenwashing challenges demand robust standards, stable ESG ratings and transparency in investment practices and sustainability reports. With rectification of these issues, they can go on to regain the trust of stakeholders and ensure that funds intended for climate change are being utilized to their desired end. This can help in addressing the same for financial flows to be able to contribute towards environmental sustainability and the targets set out both through environment audits and initiatives like the United Nations SDGs. Furthermore, growing popular consciousness and government, business, and civil society pressure will work to see that industry gets put in its place and a real commitment towards environmental sustainability is guaranteed.

Future Directions of Work

The rapid spread of climate financing in countries presents both policy-wise and academically interesting possibilities as well as difficulties. Since climate finance is crucial in funding the low-carbon transition, the associated rise of greenwashing threatens to destroy the credibility of sustainable investment. Future field research will aim to rationalize laws and enforcement techniques in order to counteract the dissemination of greenwashing. In addition, a comparative study of the control of claims on sustainability and climate financing reporting can help supply information concerning ideal policies as well as initiatives harmonizing. Furthermore, research by financial institutions towards boosting the transparency of green investment is rather necessary in countries within the developing world where regulation could be more lenient.

Moreover, using ESG grading systems as effective markers of sustainable investment is another vital area of research. Generally, a non-syndicated wide ESG rating treats rated companies equally with respect to their environmental performance. In the coming years, research should prioritise the development of globally defined ESG standards that reduce the risks of greenwashing and misinformation. Nevertheless, policymakers and academics have to investigate how the climate money affects real-time emissions and sustainability targets. Although green businesses receive a lot of funding, not much specific information exists about whether such an investment benefits the earth or not. Long-term follow-up monitoring of climate finance initiatives guides follow-up investment as well as helps define success. Future research should look at how technologies such as artificial intelligence and blockchain may be applied to create hacker-proof, sustainable systems of reporting so that reliable data supports green claims. Second, studies grounded in behavioural economics, finance and environmental science can provide a deeper understanding of investor, corporate business and legislative reactions to incidents of greenwashing and policy recommendations. Later on, one has to consider public opinion and customer understanding of green financing and business sustainability statements.

Understanding why and how people view and respond to greenwashing will help one build better laws for regulation and communication strategies correspondingly. Future studies can also look at how media, NGOs, and activist investors hold companies responsible for supporting unfounded sustainability claims. By use of salient feature analysis, scholars and professionals can assist in building a larger, more transparent system of climate financing, therefore enabling the world to proceed towards sustainability.

References

Adamo, R., Federico, D., & Notte, A. (2025). Green finance for sustainable financing. In *World sustainability series* (pp. 39–59). https://doi.org/10.1007/978-3-031-80969-9_4

Akinsola, O. K., & Kingsley Onu, D. Y. O. (n.d.). *Regulatory and legal challenges in the energy sector: How corporate governance affects compliance and risk management*. Unpublished manuscript. ResearchGate.

Almazrouei, H., & Nobanee, H. (2021). *Green finance and sustainable growth*. https://www.researchgate.net/publication/354371920_Green_Finance_and_Sustainable_Growth

Bernini, F., & La Rosa, F. (2023). Research in the greenwashing field: Concepts, theories, and potential impacts on economic and social value. *Journal of Management & Governance*, *28*(2024), 405–444. https://doi.org/10.1007/s10997-023-09686-5

Bhaskar, R., & Srivastava, B. (2021). An overview of climate finance in India. *Nimitmai Review Journal*, *4*(1), 25–33.

Bo, S., & Battisti, E. (2024). Green finance and greenwashing: Charting a sustainable path forward. *Qualitative Research in Financial Markets*. https://doi.org/10.1108/qrfm-05-2024-0125

Chaube, N. (n.d.). *Greenwashing for financial institutions in India: Challenges and the way ahead*. Legal Service India. https://www.legalserviceindia.com/legal/article-18261-greenwashing-for-financial-institutions-in-india-challenges-and-the-way-ahead.html. Accessed on January 15.

Cherkasova, V., & Nenuzhenko, I. (2022). Investment in ESG projects and corporate performance of multinational companies. *Journal of Economic Integration*, *37*(1), 54–92.

ClientEarth in Asia. (2025, January 24). *ClientEarth*. https://www.clientearth.asia/

Climate Policy Initiative. (2023). *Global landscape of climate finance 2023 - CPI*. CPI. https://www.climatepolicyinitiative.org/publication/global-landscape-of-climate-finance-2023/

Climate Policy Initiative. (2024, June 7). *Global landscape of climate finance 2023 - CPI*. CPI. https://www.climatepolicyinitiative.org/publication/global-landscape-of-climate-finance-2023/

Davis, M. B. (2024). *Eco-Illusions: Unveiling greenwashing techniques on corporate social media*. Digital Commons @ Salve Regina. https://digitalcommons.salve.edu/pell_theses/147/

Delmas, M. A., & Burbano, V. C. (2011). The drivers of greenwashing. *California Management Review*, *54*(1), 64–87. https://doi.org/10.1525/cmr.2011.54.1.64

Dempere, J., Alamash, E., & Mattos, P. (2024). Unveiling the truth: Greenwashing in sustainable finance. *Frontiers in Sustainability*, *5*. https://doi.org/10.3389/frsus.2024.1362051

D'Orazio, P. (2023). The politics of climate finance and policy initiatives to promote sustainable finance and address ESG issues. In *Sustainable finance and ESG: Risk, management, regulations, and implications for financial institutions* (pp. 145–171). Springer International Publishing.

EDGAR - the emissions database for global atmospheric Research. (n.d.). https://edgar.jrc.ec.europa.eu/report_2023#:~:text=all%20world%20countries-,Main%20findings,61.6%25%20of%20global%20GHG%20emissions

European Commission. (n.d.). *Sustainable Finance Disclosures Regulation (SFDR) – Implementing and delegated acts*. European Commission. https://finance.ec.europa.eu/regulation-and-supervision/financial-services-legislation/implementing-and-delegated-acts/sustainable-finance-disclosures-regulation_en

Flammer, C. (2021). Corporate green bonds. *Journal of Financial Economics*, *142*(2), 499–516. https://doi.org/10.1016/j.jfineco.2021.01.010

Forliano, C., Battisti, E., De Bernardi, P., & Kliestik, T. (2025). Mapping the greenwashing research landscape: A theoretical and field analysis. *Review of Managerial Science*. https://doi.org/10.1007/s11846-025-00856-3

Gannon, F., Holland, C., & Nelson, I. (2021, March 9). *What is the SFDR? KPMG*. https://kpmg.com/ie/en/home/insights/2021/03/what-is-the-sfdr-sustainable-futures.html

Gerber, A. (2023). *Analysis of manufacturing businesses in addressing the 17 UN sustainable development goals*. Theseus. https://www.theseus.fi/handle/10024/810164

IBM. (2024). *The history of ESG: A journey towards sustainable investing*. IBM. https://www.ibm.com/think/topics/environmental-social-and-governance-history

Hussain, M. A. (2024). Sustainable finance and investment strategies for SDG alignment. *Sustainable Development Goals & Business Sustainability*, *473*.

Ioannou, I., & Serafeim, G., & London Business School, & Harvard Business School. (2021). *Corporate sustainability: A strategy?* (Working Paper 19-065). https://www.hbs.edu/ris/Publication%20Files/WP19-065rev4-23-21_aefe2c98-5fa6-44c4-bbae-f68e6f283642.pdf

Kim, E., & Lyon, T. P. (2014). Greenwash vs. Brownwash: Exaggeration and undue modesty in corporate sustainability disclosure. *Organization Science*, *26*(3), 705–723. https://doi.org/10.1287/orsc.2014.0949

Kotsantonis, S., Pinney, C., & Serafeim, G. (2016). ESG integration in investment management: Myths and realities. *Journal of Applied Corporate Finance*, *28*(2), 10–16. https://doi.org/10.1111/jacf.12169

Lagoarde-Ségot, T. (2024). Greenwashing and sustainable finance: An approach anchored in the philosophy of science. *Current Opinion in Environmental Sustainability*, *66*, 101397. https://doi.org/10.1016/j.cosust.2023.101397

Liu, Y., Li, W., Wang, L., & Meng, Q. (2023). Why greenwashing occurs and what happens afterwards? A systematic literature review and future research agenda. *Environmental Science and Pollution Research*, *30*(56), 118102–118116. https://doi.org/10.1007/s11356-023-30571-z

Long, S., Lucey, B., Kumar, S., Zhang, D., & Zhang, Z. (2022). Climate finance: What we know and what we should know? *Journal of Climate Finance*, *1*, 100005. https://doi.org/10.1016/j.jclimf.2023.100005

Lütkehermöller, K., Marquardt, M., Kachi, A., NewClimate Institute, Lütkehermöller, K., Marquardt, M., & Kachi, A. (2023). *Investigating financial institutions' net zero portfolio commitments* NewClimate Institute, Ed.. https://newclimate.org/sites/default/files/2024-01/from_rhetoric_to_reality_investigating_financial_institutions_net_zero_portfolio_commitments.pdf

Lyon, T. P., & Montgomery, A. W. (2015b). The means and end of greenwash. *Organization & Environment*, *28*(2), 223–249. https://doi.org/10.1177/1086026615575332

Macek, D., & Vitásek, S. (2024). ESG risk analysis and preparedness of companies in the Czech Republic. *International Journal of Economic Sciences*, *13*(2), 38–54.

Maria, M. M. L., Da Silva Zonatto, V. C., Júnior, E. M., Louzada, L. C., & Nascimento, S. P. (2024). The practice of green washing Motivated by Financial constraints: An analysis in Global Economies. *Revista de Gestão Social e Ambiental*, *18*(7), e06084. https://doi.org/10.24857/rgsa.v18n7-060

Mateo-Márquez, A. J., González-González, J. M., & Zamora-Ramírez, C. (2022). An international empirical study of greenwashing and voluntary carbon disclosure. *Journal of Cleaner Production*, *363*, 132567. https://doi.org/10.1016/j.jclepro.2022.132567

Natural Resources Defense Council. (n.d.). *What is greenwashing? NRDC*. https://www.nrdc.org/stories/what-greenwashing

Organisation for Economic Co-operation and Development (OECD). (2024). *Climate finance provided and mobilised by developed countries in 2013-2022*. [Climate Change]. https://www.oecd.org/climate-change/finance-usd-100-billion-goal/

Organisation for Economic Co-operation and Development [OECD]. (2024, May 29). *Developed countries materially surpassed their USD 100 billion climate finance commitment in 2022*. [Press release]. https://www.oecd.org/environment/growth-accelerated-in-the-climate-finance-provided-and-mobilised-in-2021-but-developed-countries-remain-short.htm

Parguel, B., & Johnson, G. (2021). Beyond greenwashing: Addressing 'the great illusion'of green advertising. *Responsible Organization Review*, *16*(2), 59–66.

Poiriazi, E., Zournatzidou, G., Konteos, G., & Sariannidis, N. (2025). Analyzing the interconnection between environmental, social, and governance (ESG) criteria and corporate corruption: Revealing the significant impact of greenwashing. *Administrative Sciences*, *15*(3), 100. https://doi.org/10.3390/admsci15030100

Romano, A. A., Scandurra, G., Carfora, A., & Ronghi, M. (2018). *Climate finance as an instrument to promote the green growth in developing countries.* Springer International Publishing.

Ruiz-Blanco, S., Romero, S., & Fernandez-Feijoo, B. (2021). Green, blue or black, but washing–what company characteristics determine greenwashing? *Environment, Development and Sustainability*, *24*(3), 4024–4045. https://doi.org/10.1007/s10668-021-01602-x

Semet, R. (2020). *The social issue of ESG analysis. Available at SSRN 3838372.*

Stein, Z. (2023). *Green fund.* Carbon Collective. https://www.carboncollective.co/sustainable-investing/green-fund. Accessed January 18, 2025.

U.S. Securities and Exchange Commission. (n.d.). *SEC adopts rules to enhance and standardize climate-related disclosures for investors.* U.S. Securities and Exchange Commission. https://www.sec.gov.

United Nations. (2022). *Developed countries must deliver on climate change, finance commitments, delegates stress, as Second Committee continues its general debate.* [Press release] United Nations. https://press.un.org/en/2022/gaef3566.doc.htm

United Nations. (2023). *COP27: Delivering for people and the planet.* United Nations. https://www.un.org/en/climatechange/cop27. Accessed on January 15.

United Nations. (n.d.-a). *Greenwashing – the deceptive tactics behind environmental claims.* United Nations. https://www.un.org/en/climatechange/science/climate-issues/greenwashing

United Nations. (n.d.-b). *Greenwashing – the deceptive tactics behind environmental claims.* United Nations. https://www.un.org/en/climatechange/science/climate-issues/greenwashing#:~:text=Through%20deceptive%20marketing%20and%20false,hampering%20the%20trust%2C%20ambition%2C%20and

United Nations Framework Convention on Climate Change (UNFCCC). (2018, November 29). *Introduction to climate finance.* https://unfccc.int/topics/introduction-to-climate-finance

United Nations Framework Convention on Climate Change (UNFCCC). (n.d.). *Climate finance in the negotiations.* https://unfccc.int/topics/climate-finance/the-big-picture/climate-finance-in-the-negotiations

van der Lugt, C., van de Wijs, P. P., & Petrovics, D. (2020). *Carrots & sticks: Sustainability reporting policy: Global trends in disclosure as the ESG agenda goes mainstream.* Global Reporting Initiative (GRI) and the University of Stellenbosch Business School (USB).

World Bank Group. (2023). *Climate Finance update.* World Bank Publications. https://www.worldbank.org/en/news/factsheet/2023/10/10/climate-finance-update

Ye, Z. (2024, September). Comparative analysis of global ESG information disclosure regulatory frameworks and challenges. In *2024 10th International Conference on Humanities and Social Science Research (ICHSSR 2024)* (pp. 942–950). Atlantis Press.

Yébenes, M. O. (2024). Climate change, ESG criteria and recent regulation: Challenges and opportunities. *Eurasian Economic Review*, *14*(1), 87–120. https://doi.org/10.1007/s40822-023-00251-x

Yu, E. P., Van Luu, B., & Chen, C. H. (2020). Greenwashing in environmental, social and governance disclosures. *Research in International Business and Finance*, *52*, 101192. https://doi.org/10.1016/j.ribaf.2020.101192

Zervoudi, E. K., Moschos, N., & Christopoulos, A. G. (2025). From the corporate social responsibility (CSR) and the environmental, social and governance (ESG) criteria to the greenwashing phenomenon: A comprehensive literature review about the causes, consequences and solutions of the phenomenon with specific case studies. *Sustainability*, *17*(5), 2222. https://doi.org/10.3390/su17052222

Zhang, D. (2023). Does green finance really inhibit extreme hypocritical ESG risk? A greenwashing perspective exploration. *Energy Economics*, *121*, 106688. https://doi.org/10.1016/j.eneco.2023.106688

Zubeltzu Jaka, E., Andicoechea-Arondo, L., & Etxeberria, I. A. (2018). Corporate social responsibility and corporate governance and corporate financial performance: Bridging concepts for a more ethical business model. *Business Strategy & Development*, *1*(3), 214–222. https://doi.org/10.1002/bsd2.29

Chapter 12

Eco-Fashion Facades: How Rebranding and Influencer Culture Fuel Greenwashing in Fast Fashion

Shamily Jaggi[a], *Shabnam Gulati*[c] *and Arvind Kumar*[b]

[a]Indus International University, India
[b]University of Strathclyde, UK
[c]Lovely Professional University, India

Abstract

The fast fashion industry has embraced sustainability as a marketing strategy, often resorting to greenwashing to align with evolving consumer preferences for eco-friendly products. This chapter aims to explain how influencer marketing and rebranding strategies by fast fashion brands contribute to greenwashing by creating a façade of environmental responsibility. It critically explores the intersection of social media endorsements, strategic rebranding and consumer psychology to unveil how these tactics by the fast fashion brands are misleading consumers and perpetuating unsustainable practices. Eco-illusions deepen the issue more by fostering a false sense of environmental responsibility among customers. Key themes include the role of micro/macro influencers, social media hashtags in legitimizing green claims and an increase in eco-labels that make consumers susceptible to deceptive marketing. This chapter also highlights the difference between claimed and actual sustainability efforts by fast fashion brands that demonstrate how superficial changes in branding products obscure deeper environmental and ethical violations. It emphasizes the importance of robust consumer awareness, consumer education and strict enforcement of sustainability claims to counteract the influence of greenwashing. This study serves as a critical resource for academics, industry stakeholders and policymakers who aim to understand and mitigate the adverse impact of greenwashing in the fast fashion industry.

Eco Illusions, 253–271

doi:10.1108/978-1-83662-782-120261012

Keywords: Greenwashing; fast fashion; influencer culture; rebranding; consumer behaviour; sustainability; ethical fashion; eco-labels; social media marketing; eco-illusions

Introduction: The Rise of 'Eco-Fashion' in Fast Fashion Brands

The fashion industry is in a growing trend due to the inclination of today's consumer towards the environment and high preference for eco-friendly products (Lochab et al., 2024; Singh et al., 2024). It acts as a junction point of two prime marketing factors, that is, growing environmental accountability and consumer's consciousness (Gulati et al., 2023). The fast fashion brands are adopting the practice of rebranding themselves by launching eco-friendly clothes collections in semblance with 'Eco-fashion' (Gulati et al., 2024). By strategic thinking and collaborations with high-profile social media influencers, these brands are positioning themselves as the big ambassadors in the fight for environmental change. Through glossy campaigns highlighting the eco-friendliness of their products, they are turning researcher's attention towards a harsh reality, that is 'GREEN WASHING' where the companies exaggerate the sustainability claims and often mislead the consumer. Fast fashion brands, which are mostly criticized for exploitative labour practices and majorly for unsustainable operations, have increasingly turned to sustainability measures to reinvent the public image (Becker-Leifhold & Iran, 2018). The brands are using buzzwords like 'organic', 'sustainable', 'conscious' and 'eco-friendly' in their marketing campaigns that showcase their sustainable practices like recycled materials, circular economy initiatives and eco-friendly products. Influencers have played a pivotal role in validating and promoting these advertising campaigns on their social media platforms. By adopting 'eco-fashion' branding, different brands launch their collections and marketed them as eco-friendly, sustainable or ethically produced and often promoted them by social media influencers. These influencers, with their high fan followings, amplify the company's sustainability claims and persuade consumers (eco-conscious) to engage with these rebranded fast fashion brands (Jung et al., 2020). By leveraging the influencer power, fast fashion brands are able to reach high audience and many of them treat these endorsements as a more authentic representation of the company's values. The influencers are often unaware of the nuances of sustainability and endorse these brands, inadvertently legitimizing their claims (Carfora et al., 2021). Despite the allure of these glossy campaigns, there is growing scepticism about their authenticity. Delmas and Burbano (2011) stated in their study that 'many fast fashion brands make minimal changes to their operations while heavily investing in marketing campaigns to create a perception of sustainability'. Words like 'carbon-neutral collections' and 'recycled fabrics' are mostly used with inappropriate transparency that leaves consumers in big doubt about claims. Grappi et al. (2013) stated that 'terms such as 'recycled materials' or 'sustainable collections' are frequently employed without adequate transparency about their environmental impacts or production processes'. Therefore, this study is investigating the intersection of rebranding strategies and influencer culture in perpetuating greenwashing in the fast fashion industry by highlighting the strategies to construct eco-fashion facades, exploring the role of influencers in exaggerating these claims and highlighting the implications for customer trust. This will unmask the brand's greenwashing practices for more transparency and accountability in the fast fashion industry.

Eco-fashion in the fast fashion industry has become the buzzword among national as well as international companies to position their brands as eco-friendly and, moreover, more sustainable brands. Many of these efforts have been scrutinized for greenwashing. Some notable examples of fast fashion brands embracing Eco-fashion are as follows:

International Brands

Shaw (2025) wrote in his article titled 'Top 50 fast fashion brands' about the top international brands in the fast fashion industry. Some are listed below:

- H&M (Sweden): Introduced the 'Conscious Collection' and claimed that it uses sustainable materials in the entire production process, but the critics argued that the company's overall production volume negates its eco-friendly initiatives.
- Nike (USA): Promoted sustainability through its Move to 'Zero' campaign by using recycled materials in shoes/apparel while still maintaining mass production.
- Zara (Spain): Launched its 'Join Life' collection, which claims to use organic and recycled materials, but the concerns remain over transparency in its supply chain.
- Uniqlo (Japan): Introduced its 'Re.Uniqlo' recycling initiative and sustainable fabrics, but reports highlighted the ethical concerns in their labour practices.
- Adidas (Germany): Collaborated with 'Parley' for the Oceans to create sneakers from ocean plastic but continues to face challenges in reducing its overall impact on the environment.
- Shein (China): Recently launched a sustainability-focused 'EvoluSHEIN' line, but the company's actions raise doubts about its true commitment to sustainability.

National Brands

In today's times, wearing branded clothes is not only just fashion; it shows one's status and lifestyle. Luthfi (2024) has listed 35 top clothing brands in India for 2024 in his article on BLINKSTORE. Some national brands are listed below:

- FabIndia: The brand markets itself as a 'sustainable and ethical' brand using traditional craftsmanship and organic fabrics, but has faced criticism over greenwashing claims.

- Lifestyle (Pantaloons, Max Fashion): Introduced eco-conscious lines such as 'Pantaloons Earth' and 'Max Eco', focusing on recycled and organic fabrics but still operating within the fast fashion model.
- W for Woman: The brand has begun incorporating sustainable textiles in select collections but lacks a comprehensive sustainability framework.
- Biba: Introduced sustainable cotton collections, but sustainability efforts remain limited compared to the scale of production.
- Raymond: Launched 'Ecovera', a sustainable fabric initiative using recycled polyester, yet continues large-scale production with synthetic materials.

The increasing demand for eco-conscious fashion among consumers has made fast fashion brands think more about effective sustainable marketing strategies. Feeling the need for the same, some brands have made genuine efforts to incorporate sustainable changes such as optimal water usage, more use of recycled materials and promotion of ethical sourcing, while others are still engaged in superficial greenwashing activities to enhance the value of their brand without making any significant systemic changes. International brand's eco-friendly product lines, like Zara's *'Join Life' or* H&M's *'Conscious Collection'*, often work on mass production models that result in exploitation of labour and depletion of natural resources. Similarly, national brands such as Raymond and FabIndia claim sustainable initiatives, but they still rely on conventional production processes that raise authenticity concerns. These major concerns within the fast fashion industry have mandated the critical scrutiny of company's sustainability claims so that an informed consumer can be able to differentiate between genuine eco-fashion efforts by brands and their mere marketing facades.

Eco-illusions: The Hidden Façade of Sustainability in Fast Fashion

In this growing era of the fashion world, eco-illusions are emerging as a powerful tool for fast brands that capitalizes on growing customer demand for sustainability without implementing substantive environmental reforms. These illusions are greatly crafted by strategic rebranding strategies and using the social media influencer's magic and power that create a façade of eco-consciousness that masks the underlying unsustainable practices. By promoting 'green' fashion collections, limited edition recycled lines, or emphasizing resale/rental platforms within the sharing economy, fast fashion brands enhance a perception of environmental responsibility that often fails to address the systemic issues of labour exploitation, overproduction, excessive resource use etc. Eco-illusions perpetuate greenwashing, misleading customers into believing they are supporting sustainable fashion. This phenomenon underscores the critical need for transparency and authentic accountability within the fashion industry, especially as sharing economy models gain prominence as purported solutions to fast fashion's environmental impact.

Rebranding Strategies: Fast Fashion's Shift to 'Green'

The fast fashion world has rebranded itself as more environmentally conscious due to an increase in eco-conscious consumerism. Many are launching and promoting their 'Sustainable' fashion collections with buzzwords like 'green', 'organic' or 'eco-conscious' and use of recycled materials and ethical practices in their various marketing stunts. Building strong brands has become an imperative part of every firm (Nim et al., 2022), and it is very important to study the factors that influence the customer switching behaviour for sustaining market share and fostering brand loyalty (Jaggi et al., 2024). The companies keep on designing effective marketing strategies to meet the latest trends among consumers. For example, 'Conscious Collection' of H&M, 'Join Life" of Zara and 'Primark Cares' of Primark, initiatives by the brands that exemplify this fast-growing trend to present themselves as the 'Big Ambassadors' of 'Sustainability' while still doing practices that lead to environmental degradation. Henninger et al., 2016 stated that 'These initiatives are crafted to resonate with modern consumers who value brands aligned with their ethical and environmental concerns'. By using creative advertising, emotional appeals and aesthetically pleasing themes, these brands have painted a picture of 'Sustainability' that needs to be scrutinized. When looking deep into these rebranding strategies, one can uncover the reliance on symbolic actions more than any systemic change. For example, many brands promote recycling programmes in their production houses without highlighting the other energy-intensive processes which are involved in their production which are harmful to the environment. In the 'garment recycling program' initiative by H&M, only a fraction of the materials collected are truly recycled into new textiles, with the majority incinerated or downcycled (Jorgensen et al., 2021). 'Join Life' campaign by Zara promoted the use of sustainable fabrics, but these products make up a very small portion of its overall product offerings, leaving its core fast fashion business model largely unchanged. McKinsey & Company (2020) report stated that 'Primark has pledged to make all its clothes from recycled or sustainably sourced materials by 2030, but critics argue that the timeline and lack of transparency make the claims questionable.' Moreover, these campaigns side-step the broader issues of the fast fashion brands, like unethical labour practices, excessive overproduction, emphasis on low-cost production and disposable clothing.

Another crucial element of rebranding is the manipulation of certifications and partnerships with sustainability organizations. Brands mostly highlight certifications like Worldwide Responsible Accredited Production (WRAP) or Global Organic Textile Standard (GOTS) to authenticate their sustainability commitment. These certifications may apply to their few product lines only, but brands use these certifications to fool customers about their entire product offerings. Perry et al. (2019) stated in their study that 'H&M highlights its association with the Better Cotton Initiative (BCI), a program aimed at improving global cotton production. However, reports have raised concerns about the effectiveness of such programs in ensuring real sustainability improvements, particularly in addressing labour issues and environmental degradation'. Fast fashion brands are having partnerships with various sustainable organizations to provide a stamp of approval to bolster their sustainability image further.

Brand's rebranding strategies have also aimed to harness the digital and social media influencer's power, where popular people on social media platforms are highly paid by the brands to validate their claims about sustainability to the audiences. By using influencer's fan followings and high networks, fast fashion brands are authenticating their sustainability narratives by embedding them into daily lives of consumers who rely on these social media influencers for fashion advice and guidance. Brands like Levis, H&M, Zara and Nike collaborate with green-conscious social media influencers to authenticate their sustainability claims. These campaigns may attract eco-conscious consumers, but they frequently gloss over the deeper environmental and ethical issues tied to fast fashion (Carfora et al., 2021). These rebranding tactics are effective in the short term only and raise critical questions about the authenticity and ethicality of such marketing initiatives. The fast fashion brands positioned themselves as a solution to the environmental problems, but they distract from their major role as the key contributors to the problem.

Influencer's Influence: The Role in Crafting Green Narratives

Influencers play a very crucial role in strengthening the fast fashion brands' sustainability claims by acting as mediators between brands and eco-conscious consumers. These personalities, with their strong fan following and high networks, promote and authenticate the brands' sustainability claims among the consumers. For example, H&M collaborated with Brittany Xavier and Leonie Hanne (green-conscious influencers) for its 'Conscious Collection' promotion by posts on YouTube and Instagram highlighting the use of ecofriendly designs and recycled fabrics. Similarly, ASOS leveraged the power of influencers to launch its curated selection of products titled 'Responsible Edit,' using hashtags like #ASOSResponsible to boost its visibility and engagement rate (Jung et al., 2020). Zara promoted its 'Join Life' collection through social media influencers, highlighting the use of organic and sustainable fabrics with hashtags like #JoinLife to engage and align the brand with eco-conscious values (Jung et al., 2020). Shein (a fast fashion giant) has collaborated with social media influencers to promote its Shein Cares Program, which emphasized their green efforts. Danielle Bernstein has shared the content about the programme and showcased Shein's products effectively to blend social responsibility messaging with aspirational fashion (Carfora et al., 2021). Similarly, Boohoo partnered with prominent social figures like Kourtney Kardashian Barker to promote its 'Sustainable Fashion' line, a significant step towards greener practices, but the critics accused the initiative of greenwashing tactics (Mintel, 2023). Micro-influencers also play an important role in targeting niche and eco-conscious demographics. For example, Primark's 'Primark Cares' marketing programme has leveraged the power of micro influencers to showcase their recycling and sustainable initiatives through social media platforms like Instagram and TikTok to reach the young audience. These efforts help the fast fashion brands to align with sustainability trends (Henninger et al., 2016). As per many researchers, sometimes influencers may unintentionally be involved in greenwashing tactics by endorsing the brands without even verifying the authenticity of their sustainability claims. No one can doubt the power of influencers in increasing the visibility of the company's green initiatives, but their participation in advertising campaigns can raise concerns about the transparency and accountability of these claims. Influencers from celebrities to micro-influencers have become pivotal in brand marketing. Fast fashion brands collaborate with social media influencers who advocate sustainability, gifting them 'eco-friendly' collections or sponsoring content that promotes companies' green initiatives. Some influencers genuinely support the sustainable practices; many unintentionally (or intentionally) become participants in greenwashing by endorsing brands without conducting due diligence. For example, Zara's *Join Life* and H&M's *Conscious Collection* were widely promoted by social media influencers who emphasized the use of organic and recycled fabrics but failed to highlight the broader issue of mass production and textile waste. Due to high turnover of clothing and reliance on cheap labour, fast fashion brands remain inherently unsustainable, but influencer-driven marketing is successful in shifting the focus of customers to select 'green' product lines, obscuring the industry's ethical and environmental issues. The credibility that social media influencers lend to these fast fashion brands makes greenwashing more effective, as followers trust their recommendations, often without questioning their authenticity of the sustainability claims. Another key factor in social media-driven greenwashing is *hashtag activism and curated branding*. Fast fashion invests in viral hashtags related to sustainability, aligning themselves with movements such as #GoGreen and #WhoMadeMyClothes to craft a sustainable and ethical brand image. The visual feature of social media platforms like Instagram allows brands to create aesthetically pleasing content like images of models, clothing labelled with eco-friendly symbols and minimalist, green-themed packaging etc. to reinforce the illusion of sustainability. Trending hashtags like #Gogreen, #EcoChic, #SustainableFashion and #ConsciousLiving rule the platforms of Facebook, Instagram, YouTube and Pinterest to create an ecosystem where 'sustainability' is more about 'perception' than 'action'. For example, H&M used the hashtag #ConsciousFashion to promote its Conscious Collection (Jung et al., 2020). Similarly, Zara used the hashtag #JoinLife to promote its collection on Instagram to draw the attention of the audience to the companies' eco-friendly practices while avoiding discussions about its larger environmental footprint (Henninger et al., 2016). McKinsey & Company (2020) report stated that 'Fast fashion giant Shein has faced backlash for employing green hashtags and sustainability-themed content on TikTok under initiatives like #SheinCares. While these campaigns generate millions of views, critics highlight the inconsistency between Shein's social media messaging and its mass-production model, which remains highly unsustainable.' ASOS has also capitalized on social media trends and promoted its Responsible Edit line with the use of the hashtag #ASOSResponsible, though only a fraction of its collections met the true criteria of sustainability. Influencers mostly unintentionally endorse the greenwashing by reposting brand's content or participating in sponsored collaborations with brands without fully understanding the environmental impact of the promoted products (Carfora et al., 2021). For example, when influencers highlight the clothing recycling programmes without even discussing the various challenges of textile recycling, which contribute to the green hype that masks systemic issues in the fashion industry. By creating a façade of engagement and transparency, social media platforms allow fast fashion brands to craft green hype that resonates with eco-conscious consumers while avoiding scrutiny. The strategic use of sustainability-related hashtags and carefully curated digital storytelling allows brands to engage in performative activism, and their commitment to the environment should exist in their actual operations rather than in marketing. Social media further reinforces greenwashing by *prioritizing engagement over authenticity*. Algorithm-driven content distribution means that posts that generate high interaction, such as likes, shares and comments, are promoted more aggressively, benefiting the brands that produce eye-catching, creative, feel-good sustainability content, even if it lacks substance. A fast fashion brand announcing a new sustainable initiative by a professionally shot video with social media influencers highlighting the use of recycled materials and corporate social responsibility efforts is more likely to go viral regardless of whether the initiative represents a meaningful commitment to sustainability or not. Meanwhile, the critical analyses or various investigation reports that expose greenwashing often struggle to reach as broad an audience because they do not generate the same level of immediate engagement. This creates an imbalance where misleading sustainability claims receive widespread attention while genuine critiques remain confined to niche circles. Furthermore, the *rise of corporate social media accounts engaging in direct consumer dialogue* has contributed to the perception of transparency, even when brands provide little actual accountability. Many fast fashion brands have sustainability pages on and Twitter, Facebook, Instagram etc., where they respond to their customer enquiries about their eco-friendly initiatives and sustainability claims. This gives the appearance of openness and often serves as a carefully controlled PR strategy of the company rather than a platform for genuine accountability. Responses are often vague, and testimonials are often misleading, deflecting critical questions with the most generic statements about company's commitment to sustainability without providing specific data on labour practices, carbon emissions, material used or supply chain transparency. By managing the perception of the public through controlled digital engagement, fast fashion brands are effectively sidestepping deeper scrutiny.

Despite various limitations, social media platforms also present numerous opportunities for the fast fashion brands to counteract greenwashing and promote genuine sustainability practices. The platforms that facilitate misleading marketing can be leveraged to hold the brands accountable for their sustainability claims. The fashion activists, investigative journalists and watchdog organizations have increasingly used the power of social media to expose the fast fashion brand's greenwashing tactics. Hashtags such as #FastFashionExposed or #Greenwashing have gained the audience's attention and encouraged them to question the brands about their sustainability claims and ask for more transparency. These campaigns educate them on how they can identify misleading marketing tactics by making them aware of the tools, such as guides and brand rating apps for ethical fashion choices. Social media-driven audience awareness has led to greater demand for certifications like Fair Trade Certified and the GOTS to distinguish between genuine sustainability efforts and greenwashing. Hence, social media has acted as a double-edged sword in shaping the sustainability narrative in the fast fashion world. On one hand, it helps in spreading awareness about ethical fashion, providing a platform for advocacy and giving customers access to information on sustainability. On the other hand, it has enabled and amplified greenwashing, allowing fast fashion brands to manipulate the perception of the people through social media influencer partnerships, viral trends, hashtag marketing and carefully curated branding.

Consumer Perception: The Truth Dilemma in Eco-Fashion Marketing

As sustainability becomes a key selling point in the apparel sector, customers are faced with an increasingly challenging decision. How can one distinguish genuinely environmentally conscientious companies from those engaging in greenwashing? According to studies, customers are often suspicious of sustainable fashion despite its growing demand due to misleading advertising, a lack of transparency and conflicting statistics. Contemporary studies on the psychological effects of greenwashing, how consumers understand eco-fashion promises and the challenges of making informed purchasing decisions are reviewed in this section. The eco-fashion industry has emerged as a significant driver of sustainable development, mirroring the values of modern consumers on environmental stewardship and ethical production. However, considering the disparity between consumer perception and reality, questions are raised about the integrity of eco-fashion marketing techniques. Nowadays, consumers are highly motivated by sustainability. According to studies, consumers are willing to spend more for eco-friendly apparel because they expect companies to respect social and environmental responsibility. Eco-fashion benefits from this increased attention, yet it also draws criticism. Products are frequently portrayed as sustainable through certifications, labels and narratives in eco-fashion marketing. However, what is commonly referred to as 'greenwashing' results from imprecise statements and a lack of openness. This leads to a predicament where customers find it difficult to distinguish truly sustainable items from deceptive advertising. Customers lose faith in eco-fashion firms when they learn about greenwashing tactics. In addition to harming brand reputations, this violation impedes the general shift towards sustainable consumption. In the marketplace, genuine brands are sometimes overwhelmed by mistrust. The increasing trend of eco-fashion marketing has left the consumers in a true dilemma state, to understand the brand's claims, where sustainability claims often blur the line between genuine efforts and greenwashing. Fast fashion brands strategically and intentionally use buzzwords like 'sustainable', 'conscious', 'Go green' and 'eco-friendly' in their various marketing campaigns, leaving consumers unsure about the actual impact of their purchases on the environment. Various researchers have studied about these types of marketing campaigns by the fast fashion brands. Henninger et al. (2016) found that 'H&M's "Conscious Collection" is marketed as a sustainable alternative, yet studies reveal that the brand provides limited transparency on how these products significantly differ from its standard offerings'. Jorgensen et al. (2021) found that 'Zara's "Join Life" initiative emphasizes the use of organic or recycled materials but fails to address the larger environmental toll of its high-volume production model.' The dilemma is further strengthened by the use of various certifications, ecolabels and partnerships with eco-friendly organizations. According to Perry et al. (2019), 'Certifications like BCI (Better Cotton Initiative) or OEKO-TEX are often highlighted in advertising campaigns but might only pertain to a small percentage of a brand's products'. A failure to have open discussion on the extent of these certifications could lead consumers to overvalue their importance and believe a more general dedication to sustainability than truly exists. Additionally, social media influencers have a significant impact on how consumers perceive products. As revealed by Shein's 'Shein Cares' program, which promotes sustainability initiatives while upholding a fast-paced, unsustainable production cycle, 'influencers who encourage eco-collections without questioning their authenticity can inadvertently reinforce greenwashing narratives,' according to Carfora et al. (2021). The truth dilemma not only damages the trust of the consumer but also undercuts the sincere efforts by fast fashion brands dedicated to sustainability. Both customers and brands need to actively engage in order to close the gap between perception and reality. Consumers must expect more accountability from brands, and brands must act on their claims. Creating a culture in which sustainability is the rule rather than the exception is the ultimate objective. The way that consumers view sustainable fashion is a vicious cycle of optimism and disappointment. Despite rising awareness, consumers face a 'truth dilemma' when trying to choose truly ethical businesses due to greenwashing and varying standards. Moving beyond catchphrases to verifiable responsibility, more openness, independent verification and regulatory enforcement are essential for the future of eco-fashion marketing.

The Real Environmental Costs of 'Eco' Fast Fashion

'Eco' fast fashion has gained popularity as a remedy for the industry's well-known ethical and environmental issues. But beyond the recycled textiles, carbon-neutral promises and biodegradable tags comes a disturbing truth: a lot of these efforts are either inadequate or purposefully deceptive. Many fast fashion brands have adopted 'eco-friendly' lines while continuing harmful practices. Greenwashing or deceiving customers about the advantages for the environment, is very common. Examples are imprecise statements such as 'green' or 'conscious' that lack certification. Many supposedly sustainable techniques may result in more complicated ecological effects than their eco-friendly names suggest. Hidden environmental costs may be discovered by looking at the activities of the entire lifecycle-manufacturing, use and disposal. Materials like bamboo, recycled polyester and organic cotton are promoted by brands as green substitutes, yet they have significant drawbacks like Toxic chemicals are frequently used in the processing of bamboo fabric (e.g. viscose manufacturing). Large tracts of arable land and a lot of water are needed for organic cotton. It can nevertheless contribute to land erosion and water scarcity when grown on a large scale for quick fashion (Fiorilli, 2023; Zhang et al., 2023). Fast fashion, including 'sustainable' lines, depends on short trend cycles and low pricing. Brands are now developing 'eco' lines while still pushing disposable apparel, which has been made worse by the advent of ultra-fast fashion (Shein, Boohoo, Temu). Although recycled polyester lessens the need for virgin plastics, its production still requires a lot of energy. Furthermore, while washing, it releases microplastics that damage marine habitats by getting into waterways (Dey, Santra, et al., 2024). Numerous items in fast fashion collections are modestly constructed to keep costs down, even though they are marketed as eco-friendly. This promotes disposal since it causes rapid wear and tear (Rahaman et al., 2024; Wang et al., 2024). Furthermore, overproduction wastes resources and releases carbon emissions because unsold goods are frequently landfilled or burnt. Although some companies advertise their garment recycling initiatives, less than 1% of textiles are turned into new apparel (Dey, Veerendra et al., 2024; Sharma & Sharma, 2024). Because many 'sustainable' clothing items combine different materials (such as organic cotton and recycled polyester), they are challenging to recycle when their useful lives are over (Robert et al., 2023). However, the process of making paper frequently uses a lot of energy, water and wood. Even forests that are managed sustainably might not be able to stop the loss of biodiversity. Exploitative labour methods are still used by many 'eco' brands, especially in the Global South, like land grabs for materials like organic cotton or bamboo that displace local communities, low salaries in factories making 'ethical' apparel and unsafe working conditions even in certified companies. Although paper recycling uses less energy than original manufacture, each cycle degrades the quality of the paper, requiring additional material inputs. In many areas, the demand for popular plant-based foods like avocados and almonds has resulted in deforestation and water-intensive production. Due to energy consumption and packaging waste, highly processed plant-based substitutes, such as imitation meats, have a considerable carbon footprint. Furthermore, Lithium, cobalt and nickel are necessary for EV batteries; their mining is energy-intensive and frequently raises ethical concerns about hazardous labour approaches and environmental damage. The electricity grid determines the environmental benefits of EVs. Emissions are reduced less dramatically if fossil fuels are the main source of electricity. Battery recycling and disposal are still major problems, because of inadequate infrastructure; many batteries wind up in landfills (Rouhana et al., 2024). From the energy-intensive recycling of polyester to the difficulties in handling EV batteries and the water and land requirements of organic cotton, these practices can exacerbate environmental harm rather than lessen it. Furthermore, the low-quality 'eco' items of quick fashion and the carbon footprint of plant-based alternatives show that sustainability claims can be flimsy. 'Eco' fast fashion frequently acts as a Band-Aid solution, enabling companies to capitalize on environmental trends without tackling issues of overproduction, waste and exploitation. Going beyond corporate greenwashing and reconsidering our entire relationship with clothing – valuing durability over fads and ethics above ease of use – necessary for real change.

Consumer Awareness and Accountability

Brands have responded to consumers' growing concerns about the environment by emphasizing sustainability in their marketing and product offerings. Greenwashing, the practice of businesses misleading customers about their environmental initiatives, has increased as a result of the rise in eco-friendly branding. In addition to misleading consumers, greenwashing erodes sincere environmental efforts. Greenwashing is the unethical practice of companies marketing themselves as sustainable or eco-friendly without actually reducing their environmental impact. Because customers are knowledgeable and critical, they can help hold brands accountable for the widespread greenwashing in the fashion sector (Kohli and Corpus, 2023; Sammons, 2024). The fashion business has changed as a result of growing customer awareness of environmental issues and their desire for sustainable options. But this growing demand has also made it easier for businesses to engage in 'greenwashing,' a dishonest marketing tactic in which they make their goods or operations appear to be more ecologically friendly than they actually are. In order to tackle this issue and ensure that true sustainability prevails over false claims, consumer awareness and accountability are crucial. In the eco-fashion sector, greenwashing can acquire many different shapes. It encompasses everything from ambiguous, unsupported statements like 'natural' or 'eco-friendly' to fake certifications and comprised stories. Businesses may highlight the one sustainable feature of their product while ignoring the adverse consequences of their whole supply chain. As an example, a company may advertise a t-shirt designed with organic cotton while neglecting the difficult working environment in the factory or the labour-intensive colouring process. Customers who genuinely want to make ethical decisions are misled by this selective disclosure, which affects the perception of sustainability.

The use of misleading words and images is another popular approach. Businesses may employ images of the outdoors, green colours or terms like 'sustainable collection' to convey an eco-friendly image even when their operations don't have any environmental value. By appealing to consumers' emotional desire to contribute to a greener future, this deception exploits their good intentions.

The problem became complicated due to a lack of uniform rules and precise meanings for words like 'sustainable' and 'eco-friendly'. Because of a lack of clarity, businesses are able to interpret these terms in a broad range, which leads to contradictory and frequently inaccurate claims. It is challenging for consumers to distinguish genuine sustainability from weak branding because they must navigate a perplexing network of unsupported claims. This discussion revealed consumer awareness, business responsibility and the broader ramifications of greenwashing in the eco-fashion industry. Raising consumer awareness and encouraging accountability are important to addressing greenwashing. Customers should carefully examine product labelling, brand transparency and components.

Product Labels and Materials:

- *Ambiguous and Vague Terms:* Words like 'natural,' 'eco-friendly' or 'sustainable' that don't provide specifics should be avoided. These may be deceptive.
- **Prioritize Just One Aspect:** Labels that simply emphasize one feature, like organic cotton, may be downplaying other environmental effects (Boström & Klintman, 2008; Medvecka, 2024).
- **Fictitious Certifications:** Some companies generate their own certifications without having them verified by a third party. Seek out reputable certifications such as Oeko-Tex, Fairtrade, or GOTS (Global Organic Textile Standard) (Baker & McNeill, 2024; Sahoo & Dash, 2024).
- *Unexplored Chemicals:* Hazardous chemicals can be used to treat even 'natural' materials. Find out about the procedures used for processing and finishing (Pranta, A. D., & Rahaman, 2024; Sfameni et al., 2023)
- **Recycling vs Downcycling:** Downcycling is not the same as recycling because it involves turning garbage into inferior items. Seek assertions of real recycling procedures.

Brand Transparency:

- **Lack of Information: A brand should be avoided if it is evasive regarding its production or supply chain procedures.**
- **Emphasis on promoting Over Action: A brand is probably engaging in greenwashing if it invests more in promoting sustainability than in putting practices into place.**
- **Social and Environmental Impact Reports: Trustworthy companies will provide open and honest reports outlining their sustainability initiatives.**
- **Traceability: Seek out companies that guarantee ethical sourcing by being able to track the origin of their materials** (Chen, 2022).

Regulatory Frameworks and Future Directions for Sustainable Fashion

The fashion business is one of the biggest causes of waste generation, social inequality and environmental deterioration. Global regulatory frameworks are being developed in response to these issues in order to promote sustainability in fashion (Thorisdottir & Johannsdottir, 2020). Strong regulatory frameworks are required to ensure true environmental and social responsibility in light of the growing demand for sustainable fashion. Greenwashing is common, and confusion is caused by the fragmented nature of the current environment, which has different standards and enforcement. Harmonization, accountability and openness must be the main priorities of future developments. Current laws frequently concentrate on particular facets of the supply chain, such as labour standards or chemical limitations (such as REACH in the EU). But there isn't a thorough, lifecycle-focused method. This creates opportunities for businesses to focus on the positive features while disregarding the negative ones. Although certifications like GOTS, Fair Trade and Bluesign provide useful guidelines, their voluntary nature prevents them from being widely used. Furthermore, effective regulation is hampered by inconsistent enforcement across borders. It explores current regulatory regulations and future directions to create a more sustainable fashion ecosystem.

Current Regulatory Frameworks

European Union Initiatives

- **EU Green Deal**: By 2050, the EU wants to have a circular economy. The Sustainable Products Initiative, which encourages eco-design standards for textiles, is part of the agreement (Horner Bussolo et al., 2024).
- **EU Textile Strategy**: Waste reduction, extended producer responsibility (EPR) and obligatory recycling goals for textile waste by 2030 are the main focuses of this plan (Hofgärtner et al., 2024).

The United States Policies

- **Fabric Act:** The purpose of this proposed law is to promote sustainable production methods and enhance working conditions in the fashion sector (Pastran et al., 2021).
- **State-Level Regulations**: States like California have taken action against wage theft and poor working conditions by enacting laws like the Garment Worker Protection Act (Fritz-Mauer, 2016).

Asian Market Regulations

- **China's EPR**: Encourages manufacturers to take responsibility for the entire lifecycle of their products.
- **India's Draft Textile Policy**: Focuses on reducing pollution through stricter effluent treatment norms and promoting organic cotton production.

Global Standards and Voluntary Initiatives

- **Global Organic Textile Standard**: From raw material gathering to socially and environmentally conscious manufacture, it guarantees organic status (Jiang & Zhang, 2023; Tong et al., 2024).
- **Higg Index**: a set of instruments for quantifying social and environmental effects throughout the supply chain.

Future Directions

Adopting circular economy models, cutting-edge materials and environmentally friendly production techniques, as well as utilizing digital transformation and encouraging conscientious consumer behaviour are key components of the future of sustainable fashion (Abdelmeguid et al., 2024). Companies will use bio-based or lab-grown textiles, recycle, upcycle and rent and use technologies like waterless dyeing and renewable energy (Yun, 2016). Government regulations and educational initiatives will raise consumer awareness and industry accountability, while blockchain and artificial intelligence will improve efficiency and transparency (Chauhan & Sahoo, 2024; Manda et al., 2024). Fashion will become more ethical and ecologically conscious with cross-sector collaboration, fair labour practices and local, artisan-based production, opening the door to a more inclusive and sustainable business (Beida, 2023). Deceptive methods pose a serious threat to the viability of eco-fashion. 'Eco-facades' will become more prevalent as fast fashion companies use influencer relationships and strategic rebranding to cover up their unsustainable business methods. Anticipate exaggerated yet shallow 'green' fashion collections and deceptive social media marketing. Influencers will propagate these façades, obscuring authenticity, since they frequently lack in-depth environmental understanding.

Conclusion

The combination of influencer culture, social media and rebranding strategies has led to a rise in greenwashing in the fast fashion sector. Fast fashion industries portray an eco-friendly image by using influencers to promote their claims and adopting the language of sustainability, yet this image frequently falls far short of actual environmental policies. Although manufacturers have been under pressure to adopt sustainability narratives due to the rise of eco-conscious consumption, these initiatives usually don't address the deeper environmental and social issues associated with fast fashion's fundamental economic model. The labels 'organic,' 'recycled' and 'sustainable' are commonly used in an unclear manner and are reinforced by partnerships and selective certifications that don't really make meaningful change. Social media influencers endorse campaigns and brands without carefully evaluating their claims, which either purposefully or unknowingly contributes to this dynamic. A multifaceted approach is needed to fight against greenwashing. Customers must be vigilant, thoroughly reviewing certifications, product labels and marketing claims critically while holding companies responsible and open. Governments and international organizations should enact stricter legislation to prevent dishonest practices and advance true sustainability. Cross-sector collaborations and technical advancements, like blockchain for supply chain transparency; can further increase efficiency and accountability. Systemic change is ultimately required to create a truly sustainable fashion industry. This includes enforcing the ideas of the circular economy, making investments in cutting-edge materials, implementing moral labour standards and encouraging thoughtful consumerism. The growing number of consumers who care about the environment has forced fast fashion businesses to rebrand themselves as sustainability advocates. However, under the facade of recycled collections, carbon-neutral pledges and influencer-backed marketing campaigns, the industry's fundamental problems – overproduction, abusive labour and environmental harm – remain unsolved. The industry may advance towards a more open, equitable and environmentally conscientious future by uncovering greenwashing and promoting true sustainability.

References

Abdelmeguid, A., Afy-Shararah, M., & Salonitis, K. (2024). Towards circular fashion: Management strategies promoting circular behaviour along the value chain. *Sustainable Production and Consumption*, *48*, 143–156.

Baker, K., & McNeill, L. S. (2024). A five-stage framework for sustainability certification for fashion brands: Can a standardised approach work in the fashion industry? *International Journal of Fashion Design, Technology and Education*, 1–15.

Becker-Leifhold, C., & Iran, S. (2018). Collaborative fashion consumption – drivers, barriers and future pathways. *Journal of Fashion Marketing and Management*, *22*(2), 189–208.

Beida, L. (2023). *Women's artisan livelihoods, networks of care and multi-sitedness among the Shipibo-Konibo in the Ucayali, Peruvian Amazon* (Master's thesis). University of Toronto.

Blinkstore. (2024, April 24). 35 Top clothing brands in India for 2024. https://blinkstore.in/blog/top-clothing-brands-in-india/

Boström, M., & Klintman, M. (2008). *Eco-standards, product labelling and green consumerism* (pp. 17–26). Palgrave Macmillan.

Business of Fashion. (2024). The year ahead: Deconstructing fast fashion's future. https://www.businessoffashion.com/articles/professional/the-state-of-fashion-2024-report-fast-fashion-retail-customer-experience-regulation-shein-temu/

Carfora, V., Caso, D., Sparks, P., & Conner, M. (2021). Moderating effects of social influence on intention-behavior consistency: A meta-analysis. *Journal of Environmental Psychology*, *75*, 101577.

Chauhan, M., & Sahoo, D. R. (2024). Towards a greener tomorrow: Exploring the potential of AI, blockchain, and IoT in sustainable development. *Nature Environment and Pollution Technology*, *23*(2), 1105–1113.

Chen, J. Y. (2022). Responsible sourcing and supply chain traceability. *International Journal of Production Economics*, *248*, 108462.

Delmas, M. A., & Burbano, V. C. (2011). The drivers of greenwashing. *California Management Review*, *54*(1), 64–87.

Dey, S., Santra, M., Choudhury, M., Ghosh, A. R., & Samanta, P. (2024). Food waste generation and its industrial utilization: An overview. *Environmental Science and Pollution Research*, 1–20.

Dey, S., Veerendra, G. T. N., Babu, P. A., Manoj, A. P., & Nagarjuna, K. (2024). Degradation of plastics waste and its effects on biological ecosystems: A scientific analysis and comprehensive review. *Biomedical Materials & Devices*, *2*(1), 70–112.

Fiorilli, E. (2023). *Sustainable textile processing: An in-depth analysis of environmental and workers well-being in the fashion industry*. (Master's thesis). Politecnico di Milano.

Fritz-Mauer, M. (2016). Lofty laws, broken promises: Wage theft and the degradation of low-wage workers. *Employment Rights and Employment Policy Journal*, *20*, 71.

Grappi, S., Romani, S., & Bagozzi, R. P. (2013). Consumer response to corporate social responsibility initiatives: The role of consumer–company identification. *International Journal of Research in Marketing*, *30*(1), 26–38.

Gulati, S., Singh, G., & Kumar, A. (2023). Interceding of repurchase intention between e-loyalty and word of mouth advocacy: A study of behavioural consequences and antecedents of e-loyalty. *International Journal of Electronic Business*, *18*(3), 299–319.

Gulati, S., Singh, G., & Kumar, A. (2024). Ascendancy of SNS information and age difference on intention to buy eco-friendly offerings: Meaningful insights for e-tailers. *International Journal of Electronic Business*, *19*(4), 435–450. https://doi.org/10.1504/IJEB.2024.10061502

Henninger, C. E., Alevizou, P. J., & Oates, C. J. (2016). What is sustainable fashion? *Journal of Fashion Marketing and Management*. *20*(4), 400–416.

Hofgärtner, R., Bachus, K., & Multani, M. (2024). *Weaving a circular workforce: Competences in a circular textile industry in Flanders* (CE Center Report). HIVA–KU Leuven.

Hörner Bussolo, G., Bressanelli, G., Visintin, F., & Saccani, N. (2024, September). Toward the European Union 2030 strategy for textiles: A review. In *IFIP International Conference on Advances in Production Management Systems* (pp. 382–397). Springer Nature Switzerland.

Jaggi, S., Nasir, M., & Chopra, P. (2024). Switching barriers and E-loyalty: Deciphering the mediating role of E-satisfaction for baby care products. *Asia Pacific Journal of Information Systems*, *34*(4), 1048–1073.

Jiang, C., & Zhang, Y. (2023). Does extended producer responsibility system promote green technological innovation in China's power battery enterprises? *Sustainability*, *15*(16), 12318.

Jørgensen, K. M., Knudsen, M. H., & Dreyer, H. C. (2021). Sustainability paradoxes in fast fashion recycling: A review. *Sustainability*, *13*(5), 2915.

Jung, S., Kim, H., & Choi, H. (2020). Influencer marketing on Instagram: The impact of number of followers and product divergence on brand attitude. *Journal of Fashion Marketing and Management*, *24*(3), 337–353.

Kohli, V. (2023). Greenwashing in the fashion industry: A manipulative facade in the name of corporate environment responsibility. *Jus Corpus LJ*, *4*, 28.

Lochab, A., Salman, M., Mor, K., & Kumar, A. (2024). The relationship between fashion consciousness and personality traits of generation Y with moderating effect of social influence: An empirical investigation from India. *International Journal of Business Excellence*, *32*(3), 394–412.

Luthfi (2024). https://blinkstore.in/blog/top-clothing-brands-in-india/

Manda, V. K., Sagi, S., & Yadav, A. (2024). Blockchain in advertising and marketing: Revolutionizing the industry through transparency and trust. In T. K. Tarnanidis & N. Sklavounos (Eds.), *New trends in marketing and consumer science* (pp. 89–112). IGI Global.

McKinsey & Company. (2020). *The State of Fashion 2020: Navigating uncertainty* (in partnership with The Business of Fashion). McKinsey & Company. https://www.mckinsey.com/~/media/mckinsey/industries/retail/our%20insights/the%20state%20of%20fashion%202020%20navigating%20uncertainty/the-state-of-fashion-2020-final.pdf

Medvecka, J. (2024). (Un) believably green: Understanding what influences perceived green label. *European Journal of Marketing*, *56*(2), 351–374.

Mintel. (2023). *Boohoo accused of greenwashing over Kourtney Kardashian collaboration* [Mintel Reports].

Nim, D., Jaggi, S., & Singh, G. (2022). Role of brand experience, brand trust and brand love in assessing brand loyalty: A study of fashion jewellery brands among women. *International Journal of Internet Marketing and Advertising*, *17*(1–2), 200–216.

Pastran, A., Colli, E., & Nor, H. M. (2021). Public policy and legislation in sustainable fashion. In M. Á. Gardetti & R. P. Larios-Francia (Eds.), *Sustainable fashion and textiles in Latin America* (pp. 171–189). Springer Singapore.

Perry, P., Wood, S., & Fernie, J. (2019). The impact of ethical consumption on fashion retailing. *International Journal of Retail & Distribution Management*, *47*(2), 123–140.

Pranta, A. D., & Rahaman, M. T. (2024). Extraction of eco-friendly natural dyes and biomordants for textile coloration: A critical review. *Nano-Structures & Nano-Objects*, *39*, 101243.

Rahaman, M. T., Pranta, A. D., Repon, M. R., Ahmed, M. S., & Islam, T. (2024). Green production and consumption of textiles and apparel: Importance, fabrication, challenges and future prospects. *Journal of Open Innovation: Technology, Market, and Complexity*, 100280.

Roberts, H., Milios, L., Mont, O., & Dalhammar, C. (2023). Product destruction: Exploring unsustainable production-consumption systems and appropriate policy responses. *Sustainable Production and Consumption*, *35*, 300–312.

Rouhana, F., Zhu, J., Chacon-Hurtado, D., Hertel, S., & Bagtzoglou, A. C. (2024). Ensuring a just transition: The electric vehicle revolution from a human rights perspective. *Journal of Cleaner Production*, 142667.

Sahoo, M. S. K., & Dash, B. P. (2024). Sustainable fabric production methods. *Green Fashion and Sustainability*, *199*.

Sammons, E. (2024). Green" is the new black: Enforcing consumer protection laws against greenwashing in the fashion industry. *Emory International Law Review*, *38*, 191.

Sfameni, S., Rando, G., & Plutino, M. R. (2023). Sustainable secondary-raw materials, natural substances and eco-friendly nanomaterial-based approaches for improved surface performances: An overview of what they are and how they work. *International Journal of Molecular Sciences*, *24*(6), 5472.

Sharma, G. K., & Sharma, S. D. (2024). Optimizing the fashion supply chain: A game-changing strategy for reducing inventory waste. In *Illustrating digital innovations towards intelligent fashion: Leveraging information system engineering and digital twins for efficient design of next-generation fashion* (pp. 203–229). Springer Nature Switzerland.

Shaw, S. (2025, March 8). *Top 50 fast fashion brands: Best 4 ways to avoid risks.* Leeline Sourcing. https://leelinesourcing.com/fast-fashion-brands/

Singh, G., Kaur, J., & Kumar, A. (2024). Do brand coolness and brand romance synchronize with sustainability? Insights from mixed method approach. *Marketing Intelligence and Planning*. Advance online publication. https://doi.org/10.1108/MIP-11-2023-0604

Thorisdottir, T. S., & Johannsdottir, L. (2020). Corporate social responsibility influencing sustainability within the fashion industry. A systematic review. *Sustainability*, *12*(21), 9167.

Tong, X., Wang, T., Li, J., & Wang, X. (2024). Extended producer responsibility to reconstruct the circular value chain. *Circular Economy*, *3*(1), 100076.

Wang, S. (2024). *Communicating the environmental impact and sustainability of fashion: Developing new labels for consumer awareness* (Doctoral dissertation). Politecnico di Torino. http://webthesis.biblio.polito.it/id/eprint/30243

Yun, J. J. (2016). Open innovation: Technology, market and complexity in South Korea. *Science, Technology and Society*, *21*(3), 319–323.

Zhang, Z., Huang, J., Yao, Y., Peters, G., Macdonald, B., La Rosa, A. D., . . ., & Scherer, L. (2023). Environmental impacts of cotton and opportunities for improvement. *Nature Reviews Earth & Environment*, *4*(10), 703–715.

Chapter 13

Green Promises and Platform Realities: Regulatory Responses to Greenwashing in the Sharing Economy

Sonal Jain

QA Higher Education, UK

Abstract

The sharing economy, powered by digital platforms like Airbnb and Uber, has reshaped how goods and services are accessed, exchanged, and monetized. While these models are often marketed as environmentally sustainable, empirical research increasingly questions the validity of such claims. This chapter critically explores the concepts of greenwashing and eco-illusion within the sharing economy, emphasizing the gap between platform narratives and actual environmental outcomes. Greenwashing—originally rooted in false advertising—has evolved into a sophisticated strategy embedded in corporate governance and sustainability disclosures, often supported by selective data and misleading ESG metrics. Eco-illusion, in contrast, extends this critique by highlighting the systemic reinforcement of false sustainability perceptions by firms, regulators, and consumers alike.

Drawing on case studies and empirical data, the chapter evaluates how platform businesses strategically use sustainability frameworks, such as the Circular Economy (CE), Environmental, Social, and Governance (ESG) standards, and the United Nations Sustainable Development Goals (SDGs), to construct appealing but often misleading narratives. It also examines the rebound effects and systemic trade-offs obscured by these claims, such as increased emissions from tourism or overuse of shared vehicles. Further, it analyzes emerging regulatory responses, focusing on the European Union's proposed Green Claims Directive (GCD) and similar initiatives in the United States and national jurisdictions. These frameworks aim to counter unsubstantiated environmental claims through third-party verification and scientific substantiation.

Eco Illusions, 273–298

doi:10.1108/978-1-83662-782-120261013

Ultimately, the chapter underscores the need for robust regulation and critical policy discourse to ensure accountability in the sharing economy. Without meaningful oversight, greenwashing and eco-illusion risk misleading consumers and distorting sustainable market competition.

Keywords: Sharing economy; greenwashing; eco-illusion; sustainability narratives; Green Claims Directive (GCD)

Introduction

One of the most significant disruptive transformations of the 21st century is the rise of the sharing economy. Driven by the advancements in digital technologies, the sharing economy—through platforms like Airbnb, Uber, BlaBlaCar, and Turo (Sharma, 2022)—has transformed the way people access, exchange, and monetize goods and services. The sharing economy is founded on the principle of the underutilization of resources, enabling peer-to-peer transactions (Aloni, 2016) and, in theory, enhances efficiency and reduce consumption. Within this evolving landscape, environmental sustainability has become a central theme for platform-based businesses. Sharing economy firms often frame themselves in both the marketing and justification of platform-based business models the environmentally responsible alternative to traditional industries (Martin, 2016).

Despite the promising portrayals and remarkable growth of the sharing economy, it is not without criticism (Schor, 2020), a large majority of empirical studies argue that the environmental benefit of the sharing depends heavily on institutional structures, users' practices, and market dynamics, rather than solely on inherent features of peer-to-peer exchange. As a result, a growing number of empirical studies and policy makes have raised concern about the validity of environmental claims. Further, the issue of platforms holding operational data and limiting access to independent academic researchers is a well-know and significant critique in research circles (Frenken & Schor, 2019). This has led to a rising interest in the sharing economy and its green credentials, not only among researchers but policymakers as well.

Although there is growing interest among researchers in this field, greenwashing and eco-illusion within sharing economy presents a complex domain for study. This complexity stems, first and foremost, from the inherent nature of the greenwashing and eco-illusion, which is a dynamic, interdisciplinary, and multifaceted phenomenon. In addition to these challenges, the structural uniqueness of the sharing economy (Langley & Leyshon, 2017) further complicates the issue, which operates though decentralized platforms and are highly flexible models, distinguishing from the traditional business structure.

This chapter investigates how regulatory frameworks are responding to greenwashing and eco-illusion within the sharing economy by comparing the European Union (EU), the United States, and selected national contexts. Furthermore, it explores the existing limitations of the current approaches and evaluate emerging enforceable regulations to unsure a robust accountability.

This discussion comes at an important moment, as sharing economy is growing, and the way they present environmental credentials is going to shape the consumers decision and sustainability. Without a strong regulation, greenwashing and eco-illusion may not only mislead consumers but also distort fair competition. By critically examining existing regulatory frameworks and identifying gaps in enforcement and accountability, this chapter aims to help a more informed policy debate around greenwashing and eco-illusion.

Greenwashing, Eco-Illusion the Sharing Economy

Greenwashing is an established concept and is a significant concern in the business practices, as firms are facing rising pressure across stakeholders—customers, employees, policymakers—to demonstrate environmental responsibility. The term was first introduced by Jay Westerveld in 1986 (Pearson, 2010).

Greenwashing, originally grounded in simple advertising misrepresentations (Pearson, 2010; TerraChoice Environmental Marketing, 2010), has evolved into a sophisticated, multidimensional phenomenon embedded within corporate governance, financial reporting, and sustainability disclosures (ESMA, 2023). No longer confined to overt false claims, modern greenwashing encompasses nuanced corporate strategies that selectively emphasize positive environmental narratives while concealing negative externalities, systemic rebound effects, and incomplete sustainability trade-offs (De Freitas Netto et al., 2020; Lyon & Maxwell, 2011). Parallel to this evolution is the emergence of *eco-illusion*—a structural phenomenon in which false perceptions of sustainability are maintained not solely by corporations but by consumers, regulators and markets themselves (Delmas & Burbano, 2011).

This increasingly complex landscape has unfolded alongside the institutionalization of key global sustainability frameworks, including the Circular Economy (CE), Environmental, Social, and Governance (ESG) standards, and the United Nations Sustainable Development Goals (SDGs). While each of these frameworks aims to steer firms toward sustainable business models, they have also provided fertile ground for increasingly sophisticated forms of narrative manipulation. Corporations now routinely appropriate CE, ESG, and SDG language to signal sustainability alignment, often without corresponding changes in underlying operational realities. For example, Coco-Cola offers a textbook examples of strategic sustainability signals using CE, ESG, and SDG narratives to align with stakeholders' expectations (Arijeniwa et al., 2024). However, it retains its business model on single-use plastics and linear growth. Similarly, companies like H&M and Zara promotes "conscious collection" and circular initiatives while continuing mass production cycle.

The CE—widely positioned as an antidote to the resource depletion and waste generation inherent in linear "take-make-dispose" models—advocates for resource circulation through reuse, repair, remanufacturing, and recycling (Ghisellini et al., 2016; Kirchherr et al., 2017). However, when loosely applied, it allows platforms such as Airbnb and Uber to rhetorically frame their models as sustainable simply because they maximize asset utilization (Frenken & Schor, 2019; Martin, 2016). This narrative appeals directly to SDG 12 (Responsible Consumption and Production) and SDG 13 (Climate Action), as platforms argue that shared access reduces resource extraction, waste generation, and emissions (Airbnb, 2018). Yet empirical studies demonstrate that these gains are often offset by rebound effects: increased tourism, higher vehicle miles traveled (VMT), and displacement of public transportation usage (Erhardt et al., 2019; Guttentag, 2015; Henao & Marshall, 2019). This creates a form of "narrative greenwashing," where platforms selectively emphasize the CE-aligned benefits while ignoring systemic trade-offs.

The ESG framework further complicates this terrain. As ESG disclosures increasingly influence investment decisions and corporate valuation, firms face growing financial incentives to project favorable sustainability credentials. Yet, ESG metrics often rely on narrow or self-reported data, offering firms opportunities to strategically amplify positive indicators while excluding or downplaying rebound effects, upstream emissions, and embedded socio-economic trade-offs (Lyon & Maxwell, 2011). This convergence between ESG disclosures and selective sustainability narratives intensifies the scope for both greenwashing and eco-illusion.

Similarly, the SDGs, designed as global development benchmarks, are routinely invoked by sharing economy firms without binding obligations or enforceable standards. Platforms may reference SDG goals in marketing (e.g., poverty alleviation via flexible work, environmental gains via asset sharing) without demonstrating verifiable, material contributions to these targets (Frenken & Schor, 2019). In this sense, SDGs serve as "discursive resources" that provide reputational benefits without substantive operational transformation.

Modern greenwashing increasingly incorporates executional greenwashing (Parguel et al., 2011), wherein firms deploy symbolic and aesthetic devices—such as green color schemes, nature imagery, and emotionally charged language—to construct subconscious associations with ecological virtue. In digital platform markets, where user interfaces heavily shape consumer perceptions, these symbolic strategies operate largely free from regulatory oversight, thereby facilitating eco-illusion at scale (Seele & Gatti, 2017).

The sharing economy represents one of the most pronounced arenas where these dynamics converge. Platforms such as Airbnb, Uber, and BlaBlaCar extensively leverage circular economy rhetoric to position their business models as environmentally beneficial through increased asset utilization and access-based consumption (Frenken & Schor, 2019; Martin, 2016). These platforms claim alignment with CE principles and multiple SDG targets by purportedly reducing resource consumption, emissions, and infrastructure demands (Airbnb, 2018).

However, empirical studies reveal that these environmental claims are highly contingent and frequently offset by systemic rebound effects. For example, while Airbnb asserts that short-term rentals displace hotel construction, studies show that platform-enabled tourism expands total travel demand, exacerbates urban

Table 13.1. FTC Cases.

Case Name	FTC Filing Date	Industry/Sector	Nature of Greenwashing
Kohl's Inc.	May 4, 2022	Retail/Textiles	False marketing of rayon as eco-friendly bamboo
Walmart	April 8, 2022	Retail/Textiles	False marketing of rayon as eco-friendly bamboo
Volkswagen Group of America, Inc.	July 27, 2020	Automotive	Misleading "clean diesel" vehicle emissions claims
Truly Organic Inc.	September 19, 2019	Personal care products	False organic product claims
Lights of America, Inc.	July 19, 2019	Energy products (LED lighting)	Exaggerated lifespan and efficiency of LED bulbs
YOLO Colorhouse	April 27, 2018	Paint/Building materials	Misleading "zero-VOC" paint claims
ICP Construction, Inc.	April 27, 2018	Paint/Building materials	Misleading "zero-VOC" paint claims
Imperial Paints	April 27, 2018	Paint/Building materials	Misleading "zero-VOC" paint claims
Benjamin Moore & Co., Inc.	April 27, 2018	Paint/Building materials	Misleading "zero-VOC" paint claims
Moonlight Slumber	December 12, 2017	Baby products (Mattresses)	Misleading organic and eco-friendly claims
ECM BioFilms, Inc.	March 16, 2017	Plastic additives	False biodegradability claims
California Naturel	December 12, 2016	Personal care (Sunscreen)	Misrepresented organic content of sunscreen
Trans-India Products, Inc.	July 13, 2016	Personal care (Sunscreen)	Misleading natural sunscreen claims
Beyond Coastal	July 13, 2016	Personal care (Sunscreen)	Misleading natural sunscreen claims
The Erickson Marketing Group Inc.	July 13, 2016	Personal care (Sunscreen)	Misleading natural sunscreen claims
ABS Consumer Products	July 13, 2016	Personal care (Sunscreen)	Misleading natural sunscreen claims

(Continued)

Table 13.1. *(Continued)*

Case Name	FTC Filing Date	Industry/Sector	Nature of Greenwashing
Nordstrom, Inc.	December 10, 2015	Retail/Textiles	False bamboo textile marketing
Backcountry.com, LLC	December 9, 2015	Retail/Textiles	False bamboo textile marketing
Bed Bath & Beyond Inc.	December 9, 2015	Retail/Textiles	False bamboo textile marketing
J.C. Penney Company, Inc.	December 9, 2015	Retail/Textiles	False bamboo textile marketing

Source: Authors own, based on FTC data.

congestion, and contributes to housing shortages (Garcia-Ayllon, 2018; Guttentag, 2015). Similarly, Uber's claims of reducing car ownership are contradicted by evidence showing that ride-hailing services substitute for public transit, walking, and cycling, thereby increasing VMT and urban emissions (Erhardt et al., 2019; Henao & Marshall, 2019). In these cases, platform business models sustain eco-illusion by externalizing environmental responsibility while enjoying reputational benefits from circular economy narratives.

Regulatory Asymmetry: The Case of FTC Enforcement

While both greenwashing and eco-illusion are conceptually well-established (De Freitas Netto et al., 2020; Delmas & Burbano, 2011; Lyon & Maxwell, 2011), empirical regulatory enforcement remains heavily skewed toward traditional sectors. An analysis of Federal Trade Commission (FTC) enforcement actions from 2015 to 2022 (Table 13.1) reveals that the vast majority of formal greenwashing cases target conventional manufacturing and retail industries—textiles, personal care products, consumer goods, energy products, and automotive firms. These cases primarily involve direct product misstatements, such as false claims about biodegradability, organic content, emissions, and energy efficiency.

These cases reflect on three significant trends. First, all these cases pertain to traditional firms engaged in a wide range of sectors such as retails, textiles, personal care, energy, and consumer goods. None of the regulatory actions features sharing economy platform such as Airbnb, Uber, or Zipcar despite their frequent reliance on environmental narratives. For example, according to Frenken (2017), in 2014 Airbnb commissioned its own environmental study, claiming that Airbnb guest consumes less energy (by 63–78%), water (by 12–48%), fewer GHG emission (by 61–89%), and achieved more waste avoidance (by 0–32%) when compared to hotel guests. Similar claim was made by

BlaBlaCar of saving 1,000,000 tons CO_2 over the past two years (Frenken, 2017). This absence raises an academic and regulatory gap as on one hand where traditional firms' environmental claims are increasingly scrutinized while digital platforms due to their inherent nature remain under regulated in this regard.

Second, the structural detachment of sharing economy creates a grey zone of environmental accountability, where platforms takes the benefits from users eco-conscious behaviors but distance themselves from the negative externalities (Cohen & Kietzmann, 2014; Martin, 2016). For example, UberPool marketed itself as environmentally friendly alternatives to traditional transportation by suggesting that users are contributing to reduce emissions and traffic conjunction. However, this narrative has the potential to decrease individual car usage but is being criticized for creating a shift away from public transportation, walking, or cycling. Further, as the Uber business model relies on individuals using their personal vehicles, it allows the company to distance itself from the direct environmental impact of its operations. These dynamics reflect a broader neoliberal governance model in which environmental responsibility is individualized and marketized while systemic accountability is fragmented or absent. This is consistent with the work of scholars in environmental sociology and political economy who critique the commodification of sustainability and the depoliticization of ecological responsibility.

Lastly, the rising focus of regulatory bodies and a need to adopt more proactive enforcement strategies. What is interesting to notice is besides the FTC, no other regulatory bodies have published a complete centralized list of greenwashing cases. The absence of these centralized transparency at international level hamper comparative analysis and regulatory benchmarking. More international efforts and a case-by-case investigation with public reporting would help in strengthening comparability and comprehensive academic analysis. In addition, as sharing and gig economy continue to dominate the global economy, the platform business model will continue to expand their influence and concurrently the case of greenwashing. It would demand a critical assessment of existing regulatory frameworks, and the following sections turns to this task by examining the current significant regulatory frameworks that address greenwashing.

Existing Regulatory Frameworks

Historically, the greenwashing and eco-illusion were guided by soft law instruments rather than legal binding standards, such as US FTC Green Guides. However, with rise in cases and globalization, the need for more robust enforceable mechanism became pertinent, leading to merging initiatives from European Union, France, and Germany.

The European Union: Toward a Legal Definition of Greenwashing

The EU has taken an increasingly proactive stance against greenwashing, recognizing its potential to mislead consumers and undermine genuine environmental progress (Machado, 2025). The centerpiece of this effort is the proposed Green Claims Directive (GCD), introduced in March 2023, which builds upon prior initiatives such as the Unfair Commercial Practices Directive (Directive 2005/29/EC) and the EU Taxonomy for Sustainable Activities. The GCD specifically targets unsubstantiated or misleading environmental claims by requiring companies to substantiate such statements with scientific evidence and to undergo independent third-party verification (European Commission, 2023b). This marks a partial regulatory response not only to overt greenwashing but also to subtler forms of eco-illusion, where firms create the appearance of sustainability through curated narratives and selective data disclosure without material environmental change.

A 2020 screening by the Commission found that more than 50% of green claims in the EU were vague, misleading, or unsubstantiated (European Commission, 2023b), prompting the move toward legally binding measures. Under the GCD, terms such as "climate neutral," "eco," or "green" must be anchored in quantifiable environmental performance, with full lifecycle considerations. In doing so, the EU aims to reduce consumer confusion while aligning market behavior with the objectives of the European Green Deal.

However, the Directive also raises normative questions about the standardization of environmental truth claims. As scholars have argued, environmental standards are often embedded in culturally contingent assumptions about nature, risk, and responsibility. By codifying specific metrics of sustainability, the EU risks privileging a technocratic and potentially exclusionary model of environmental governance (Behr, 2021). Moreover, the focus on product-level claims may overlook systemic sustainability concerns—such as the platform economy's broader contribution to resource-intensive consumption patterns—even when individual services appear green.

Critics have also noted enforcement challenges. The burden of proof remains with firms, but resource-strapped enforcement agencies across the EU may struggle to systematically verify compliance. This creates opportunities for strategic compliance, where firms invest more in the appearance of verification than in actual sustainability (Lyon & Maxwell, 2011). In sum, the GCD is a step toward legal accountability, but it requires careful implementation and monitoring to avoid becoming another box-ticking exercise.

The United States: A Framework Built on Soft Law

In contrast to the EU's movement toward binding regulation, the United States has favored a soft law approach to environmental marketing through the FTC's Green Guides. First introduced in 1992 and last updated in 2012, the Green Guides offer interpretive guidance for companies to avoid making deceptive environmental claims under Section 5 of the FTC Act (FTC, 2012). They emphasize the importance of clear language, qualification of claims, and substantiation based on reliable evidence.

While the Guides have shaped marketing norms and been cited in enforcement actions—such as the FTC's 2013 case against ECM BioFilms for falsely advertising plastic additives as biodegradable—their non-binding nature limits their reach. Moreover, the Guides have not kept pace with recent developments in sustainability discourse, particularly regarding carbon offsets, ESG metrics, and platform-based environmental claims. Recognizing these gaps, the FTC opened a public comment period in 2022 to inform a long-awaited revision (FTC, 2025).

A key limitation of the US framework is its reactive orientation: enforcement is complaint-driven, and the FTC typically intervenes after misleading practices have already occurred. As Schor and Attwood-Charles (2017) note, this approach may suffice in traditional consumer markets, but it falters in digital environments where platforms constantly recalibrate their claims and operate across multiple jurisdictions. Moreover, the Green Guides focus on direct claims, leaving platforms free to benefit from associative greenwashing and eco-illusion—the strategic use of green aesthetics or sustainability narratives without making explicit claims (Delmas & Burbano, 2011).

Furthermore, platform-based firms often situate their environmental messaging within larger ESG narratives, which fall outside the FTC's narrow consumer protection remit. This fragmentation invites regulatory arbitrage, allowing firms to tailor disclosures and green narratives based on the weakest applicable standards. Without a unified national or federal sustainability reporting framework, as seen in the EU, US regulators lack leverage to impose consistent environmental accountability across digital service providers.

France: Codifying Greenwashing as Deception

France has moved more aggressively than most EU member states in addressing greenwashing through legally binding domestic legislation. Its Climate and Resilience Law (Loi Climat et Résilience), passed in 2021, specifically recognizes greenwashing as a form of misleading commercial practice, codified in the French Consumer Code (Article L121-2). The law prohibits companies from claiming that a product or service is carbon-neutral or climate-neutral unless they can demonstrate precise and verified offsetting measures and emissions data (Assemblée nationale, 2025).

France's approach is noteworthy for several reasons. First, it anchors greenwashing within consumer rights law rather than environmental or commercial regulation alone. This framing treats deceptive green claims not merely as reputational issues but as infringements on consumer autonomy and market fairness (De Freitas Netto et al., 2020). Second, the law mandates lifecycle transparency: firms must demonstrate environmental performance across production, distribution, and post-use phases, thereby challenging platform firms' habitual focus on downstream user behavior while neglecting upstream emissions.

Third, the law includes advertising restrictions. Any sustainability-related claim in public communication (e.g., digital ads, social media, influencer marketing) must meet the same standards of verifiability, with steep fines for non-compliance. This provision directly addresses the aesthetics of greenwashing and eco-illusion—its reliance on imagery, metaphors, and symbols—rather than solely its textual content.

Nonetheless, enforcement has been uneven. Critics argue that while France has pioneered the codification of greenwashing as deception, enforcement agencies like the DGCCRF (Directorate-General for Competition, Consumer Affairs and Fraud Control) have limited capacity to systematically audit claims, especially in dynamic digital sectors (Gbadegesin et al., 2025) like the sharing economy. Furthermore, large platforms may simply adapt their narratives in ways that remain suggestive but legally ambiguous, avoiding outright falsehoods while maintaining green appeal.

Germany: The Supply Chain Due Diligence Act

Germany's Lieferkettensorgfaltspflichtengesetz (Supply Chain Due Diligence Act), effective from January 2023, introduces a more structural response to greenwashing by targeting environmental risks embedded within global supply chains. Applicable to companies with 3,000+ employees (and from 2024, those with 1,000+), the law mandates companies to identify, prevent, and remedy environmental and human rights risks within their operations and those of their suppliers (Federal Ministry for Economic Cooperation and Development, 2023).

Although not explicitly framed as an anti-greenwashing measure, the Act is significant in shifting the focus from marketing to material practices. Rather than policing advertising claims, it requires firms to develop due diligence policies, conduct risk analyses, establish complaint mechanisms, and report annually on their mitigation strategies. Violations can lead to fines and exclusion from public procurement.

For platform firms, the implications are substantial. While many sharing economy companies claim minimal environmental footprints due to their non-ownership model, the Supply Chain Act challenges this assumption by considering network effects and externalized risks. For example, if a ride-hailing platform exerts algorithmic control over fleet usage or indirectly incentivizes fossil fuel-intensive behavior, it may be held accountable for these outcomes under due diligence principles (Tang, 2022).

Yet, the Act has limitations. It currently applies only to direct and tier-one suppliers, excluding many of the subcontracted or gig-based arrangements typical of the platform economy. Moreover, enforcement remains concentrated in Germany, with no automatic spillover to the EU level unless incorporated into the broader Corporate Sustainability Due Diligence Directive (CSDDD). The Act thus represents a critical innovation but must evolve to address the complexities of digital and transnational business models.

Taken together, these frameworks reveal a shifting but uneven landscape in the regulation of greenwashing. The EU's GCD and Germany's supply chain act emphasize structural accountability and lifecycle metrics while the FTC's Green Guides rely more on interpretive flexibility and post-hoc enforcement. France bridges the two by combining legally binding restrictions with normative standards on corporate communication. Yet major gaps remain:

(1) *Platform Exceptionalism:* Most regulatory schemes struggle to account for the unique structure of platforms, which act as orchestrators rather than producers or owners. This blurs legal responsibility and allows greenwashing to flourish in a regulatory blind spot (Van Doorn & Badger, 2020).
(2) *Lack of Enforcement Infrastructure:* Even when laws exist, their enforcement depends on institutional capacity, political will, and technological resources. Regulatory authorities often lack the tools to audit algorithmically optimized marketing or to interpret dynamic sustainability metrics (Schor, 2020).
(3) *No Common Taxonomy:* A major impediment to cross-border enforcement is the absence of a global taxonomy of sustainability claims. Without standardized definitions, what qualifies as "sustainable" in one jurisdiction may be deemed misleading in another, enabling regulatory arbitrage (Lambin et al., 2014).
(4) *Voluntary Standards as Substitutes:* The rise of voluntary certifications (e.g., B Corps, LEED, ISO 14001) has created a false sense of accountability. While such systems can promote best practices, they are often co-opted for legitimacy purposes and lack enforcement teeth (Pope & Wæraas, 2016).

Addressing these gaps requires a shift from fragmented enforcement to integrated, adaptive governance. First, regulators must adopt a multi-scalar approach, combining national laws with transnational frameworks like the OECD Due Diligence Guidelines or the UN's Business and Human Rights Principles. Second, greenwashing should be treated not merely as false advertising but as a form of market manipulation, with implications for securities law, trade agreements, and ESG disclosures.

Third, regulators must leverage digital tools—such as natural language processing and AI audits—to track, verify, and flag deceptive sustainability claims in real time (Pasquale, 2015). Finally, governance structures should include civil society and affected communities in the verification process, ensuring that the lived consequences of false environmental narratives inform legal interpretations and penalties.

Gaps and Challenges in Regulating Greenwashing and Eco-illusion in the Sharing Economy

Despite notable progress in developing legal and policy mechanisms to regulate greenwashing, existing regulatory frameworks remain incomplete, unevenly enforced, and often ill-suited to the structural idiosyncrasies of the sharing economy. This section critically examines the persistent gaps in greenwashing by focusing on five core challenges: (1) definitional ambiguity, (2) jurisdictional fragmentation, (3) platform-mediated accountability gaps, (4) enforcement limitations, and (5) systemic underestimation of rebound effects.

Definitional Ambiguity and Semantic Flexibility

One of the significant challenges is the lack of clear, universally accepted definitions for key environmental terms. Claims such as "carbon neutral," "eco-friendly," or "sustainable" are often used without a shared conceptual or scientific basis, creating space for strategic manipulation.

Airbnb, for instance. The company often promote Eco-Conscious Travel by encouraging guests to "travel like a local" and reduce their carbon footprint by using underutilized space rather than supporting new hotel construction (Airbnb, 2018; Hati et al., 2021). However, such claims often ignore the indirect environmental impacts of increased tourism, short-term rentals, and infrastructure overuse (Guttentag, 2015). Without clear criteria for what constitutes "eco-conscious" behavior, these slogans remain rhetorically potent but substantively hollow.

Similarly, Uber's commitment to becoming a "zero-emissions mobility platform" by 2040 appears ambitious (Uber, 2023), but it hinges on conditions outside its immediate control, such as drivers' adoption of electric vehicles. Uber's app interface now allows users to select "Uber Green," yet no lifecycle data or emissions offset calculations are disclosed, and the metrics behind "greenness" remain opaque. The company thus benefits reputationally from green narratives without facing binding standards of evidence or performance.

Jurisdictional Fragmentation and Regulatory Arbitrage

Greenwashing in the sharing economy is also complicated by fragmented jurisdictional authority, especially for transnational platforms (Buttigieg & Pulis, 2024). Firms like Airbnb, Uber, or Turo operate across hundreds of legal environments, each with its own standards for consumer protection, environmental regulation, and commercial advertising.

This fragmentation enables regulatory arbitrage, whereby firms selectively comply with the least stringent regulations available. For example, Uber's marketing practices differ across jurisdictions. While its UK website prominently features commitments to electric vehicles and net-zero ambitions, its operations in regions with looser oversight often contain little or no environmental reporting. This discrepancy exemplifies the uneven and market-driven diffusion of standards that allows firms to optimize compliance for economic efficiency over not ethical consistency.

Moreover, digital platforms are often headquartered in jurisdictions with favorable regulatory climates (e.g., Delaware for US-based corporations or

Ireland for EU firms), which can shield them from more aggressive enforcement efforts in other territories. As Van Doorn and Badger (2020) argue, platform firms thrive on legal ambiguity, presenting themselves as "tech intermediaries" rather than service providers. This allows firms to elude sector-specific regulation that would apply to traditional hospitality or transport firms.

Accountability Gaps in Platform Intermediation

The sharing economy operates through a platform-mediated logic in which asset ownership, labour provision, and service delivery are externalized to users (Codagnone et al., 2016). This allows platforms to claim environmental credit for activities over which they exert control only indirectly—via nudges, algorithms, or incentive structures—while disclaiming responsibility for adverse environmental effects (Benlian et al., 2022).

Consider the case of Lyft, which claims that its services help reduce car ownership and support sustainable urban mobility. Yet studies have shown that ride-hailing apps contribute significantly to increased VMT, often substituting for walking, cycling, or public transit (Erhardt et al., 2019; Henao & Marshall, 2019). Because Lyft does not own the vehicles or employ the drivers, it is not legally liable for emissions under most regulatory regimes. This represents a broader problem in attributional accountability: platform firms create environmental externalities but are not required to internalize them.

This accountability gap also manifests in data asymmetry. Platforms tightly control access to operational data—such as fleet emissions, trip distances, energy use—which hampers third-party verification and public oversight. Even when regulators seek information, it may be delivered in aggregate or obfuscated formats, limiting transparency.

Enforcement Deficiencies and Institutional Capacity

Even where regulations exist—such as the EU's GCD or France's greenwashing provisions under the Climate and Resilience Law—enforcement remains uneven and under-resourced. Most environmental authorities and consumer protection agencies operate with limited budgets, staffing, and technological expertise, especially when compared to the legal and lobbying capacities of global tech firms.

For example, in 2022, France's consumer watchdog, DGCCRF, launched an investigation into environmental claims made by online travel agencies and accommodation platforms. While the probe identified numerous violations—such as unverified use of eco-labels and vague sustainability assertions—only a few resulted in fines or public corrective actions, largely due to evidentiary and jurisdictional constraints.

In the United States, the FTC's reliance on post-hoc enforcement and voluntary compliance means that only the most egregious cases are prosecuted. The FTC's case against Truly Organic (2019), which falsely marketed synthetic products as certified organic, was a notable success, but it remains an exception. The sharing economy's more subtle, suggestive forms of greenwashing typically fall below the FTC's enforcement threshold, creating a permissive environment for incremental deception.

Moreover, enforcement tends to focus on product-based claims, leaving systemic issues—such as digital labor exploitation, energy-intensive server infrastructure, or platform-driven consumption patterns—outside the regulatory spotlight. As Lyon and Maxwell (2011) contend, greenwashing often resides not in outright falsehoods but in strategic omissions and calculated ambiguity, which existing laws are poorly equipped to handle.

Rebound Effects and the Illusion of Efficiency

A final and often overlooked challenge is the rebound effect: the phenomenon whereby efficiency gains lead to increased consumption, ultimately offsetting or even reversing environmental benefits. This is particularly pronounced in the sharing economy, where platforms encourage access over ownership, but may also stimulate latent demand and overuse thereby producing eco-illusion: the false impression that operational efficiency equates to genuine sustainability.

Airbnb exemplifies this dilemma. While the platform may reduce per-capita resource use in specific instances (e.g., shared heating or lighting), it also lowers the cost of travel and expands market access, leading to increased tourism, higher carbon footprints, and the displacement of long-term residents (Zervas et al., 2017). The platform's green claims thus rest on partial environmental accounting, ignoring second-order effects that erode aggregate sustainability.

Similarly, peer-to-peer car-sharing services like Getaround or Turo claim to reduce car ownership, but studies suggest that such platforms may encourage users to purchase vehicles for rental purposes, thereby increasing the total vehicle stock and emissions in urban centers (Shaheen & Cohen, 2013). Without lifecycle analysis and macro-level modeling, regulators may be misled by the appearance of efficiency and fail to anticipate longer-term ecological costs.

These five challenges reveal that greenwashing in the sharing economy is not merely a problem of miscommunication or marketing abuse—it is symptomatic of deeper structural and epistemic asymmetries. The platform model decentralizes responsibility, diffuses regulation, and obscures environmental impacts through rhetorical and data-driven means. To address these challenges, future regulatory designs must move beyond linear command-and-control models and embrace networked, anticipatory, and multi-scalar approaches to sustainability governance.

Robust greenwashing regulation will require:

- Clear legal definitions of environmental claims.
- Mandated data disclosure and third-party environmental audits.
- Jurisdictional coordination across national and supranational levels.
- Enforcement bodies empowered with digital tools for real-time verification.

- Lifecycle- and rebound-aware metrics for evaluating platform impact.

Only through such multi-pronged reforms can regulators begin to close the credibility gap between what platforms claim and what they do in environmental terms.

Case Studies: Greenwashing in Practice

Case studies serve as valuable empirical touchpoints for interrogating how greenwashing plays out within the operational dynamics and rhetorical strategies of sharing economy platforms. This section provides a deeper analysis of two emblematic cases: Airbnb and Uber. These firms exemplify the contradictory logics of sustainability promotion and environmental impact obfuscation. While both companies have publicly committed to environmental responsibility, their actions often fall short of their claims. By situating their green narratives within the broader context of platform capitalism and environmental governance, we can more clearly trace the disjunction between marketing discourse and material practices.

Airbnb and the Myth of Sustainable Tourism

Airbnb's environmental branding hinges on its characterization as a low-impact alternative to traditional hospitality. The company frequently frames its core model—home-sharing—as a form of ecological efficiency, suggesting that repurposing existing residential spaces avoids the carbon-intensive development of hotels and resorts (Airbnb, 2023). However, empirical evidence increasingly challenges this assumption.

Rebound Effects and Increased Tourism Flows

One of the most significant critiques concerns the rebound effect. Rather than reducing total travel, Airbnb has contributed to an expansion of tourism demand, especially in urban centres and previously untapped residential neighborhoods. Research by Guttentag (Guttentag, 2015) demonstrates that the platform's growth correlates with increased air travel, over-tourism, and higher localized emissions—particularly in cities already grappling with environmental stress and gentrification pressures.

In Barcelona, for example, the proliferation of Airbnb listings has coincided with unsustainable spikes in tourist density and a rise in anti-tourism sentiment, leading the municipal government to impose strict regulations on short-term rentals (Garcia-Ayllon, 2018). Despite this, Airbnb has continued to promote its services as supporting "local, sustainable tourism," often using selective success stories to reinforce this narrative. This is a clear instance of narrative greenwashing and eco-illusion, wherein anecdotal or symbolic examples are substituted for systemic accountability (Delmas & Burbano, 2011).

Opaque Data and Selective Reporting

Another concern is Airbnb's selective data transparency. While the company periodically releases reports on its environmental footprint—such as energy savings compared to hotels—these are often based on proprietary models and lack third-party verification. Critics, including Slee (2017), have noted that Airbnb's sustainability claims typically omit indirect emissions from travel (e.g., flights, car rentals), and the environmental costs associated with increased housing turnover, waste production, and resource use in tourist-saturated areas.

Moreover, Airbnb does not provide city-specific data on carbon emissions or consumption patterns (Airbnb, n.d.), making it difficult for researchers or regulators to validate its claims. The platform's reliance on user self-reporting (e.g., hosts tagging properties as "eco-friendly") further reduces the reliability of its green narrative. The absence of clear metrics, audit procedures, or independent assessments indicates a lack of operational integration of environmental responsibility despite robust public communication around sustainability.

Green Aesthetics vs. Systemic Change

Airbnb's marketing frequently features imagery of solar panels, natural materials, and eco-retreats—what Schor and Attwood-Charles (2017) call "eco-chic aesthetics"—but these visuals rarely correspond to measurable sustainability outcomes. The company has piloted initiatives such as sustainable tourism funds or partnerships with local governments (e.g., the Healthy Tourism Commitment), but these remain marginal to its core business model and often lack binding sustainability metrics or performance evaluations (Airbnb, 2022).

In short, Airbnb exemplifies a high-visibility, low-substance form of greenwashing, where strategic storytelling and user-led responsibility substitute for platform-level ecological governance.

Uber and the Problem of Conditional Emissions Reduction

Uber has positioned itself as a transformative force in urban mobility, repeatedly asserting its role in reducing car ownership, promoting multimodal transport, and accelerating the transition to electric vehicles (Khosrowshahi, 2020). In 2020, Uber pledged to become a zero-emissions platform in North America and Europe by 2030 (Khosrowshahi, 2020) and globally by 2040. It introduced features such as "Uber Green," allowing riders to select hybrid or electric vehicles, and committed to investing in driver EV incentives, charging infrastructure, and carbon offsets. Yet critical scrutiny reveals that these pledges are structurally contingent and often more aspirational than operational.

Carbon Emissions and VMT Increases

A foundational issue is the documented increase in VMT and associated emissions since the introduction of ride-hailing services. Erhardt et al. (2019), using data from major US cities, found that Uber and Lyft have increased VMT by between 160% and 180% relative to their share of urban trips. Rather than replacing private car trips, ride-hailing services often displace public transit, walking, and biking, leading to net environmental harms.

This contradicts the company's frequent claims about greener urban mobility and exposes the problem of assumed substitution—where firms imply that their services replace more harmful alternatives without providing the empirical basis for this displacement. Despite these findings, Uber continues to assert environmental progress by emphasizing potential rather than current performance—i.e., promoting what could be, not what is.

Structural Dependence on Fossil-Fueled Vehicles

Uber's emissions profile remains heavily tied to gasoline-powered vehicles operated by independent contractors. Although "Uber Green" is marketed as a sustainable option, it constitutes a small minority of total rides, especially outside major metropolitan areas with policy incentives. Moreover, Uber lacks ownership over its fleet and cannot mandate vehicle choice among drivers, reducing the feasibility of achieving emissions targets (Cramer & Krueger, 2016).

Uber's reliance on driver incentives and rebates (e.g., for electric vehicle purchases) shifts environmental responsibility to workers—many of whom lack the financial capacity to invest in EVs (Humphrey et al., 2019). This reflects a broader trend of externalizing environmental compliance onto gig workers, enabling the platform to maintain a green brand while minimizing operational accountability.

Offsetting and Climate Claims

Uber also employs carbon offsetting as a pillar of its environmental strategy. While offsets are a legitimate tool under some conditions, they are widely criticized for enabling "carbon laundering"—paying for emissions reductions elsewhere while continuing polluting practices locally (Bumpus & Liverman, 2008). Uber provides little detail on the quality, permanence, or additionality of its offsets, raising concerns about their credibility.

The platform's framing of "net zero" thus masks the persistence of carbon-intensive operations behind a veneer of market-based mitigation, a classic manifestation of eco-illusion. This fits Lyon and Montgomery's (2015) model of symbolic corporate environmentalism, where green initiatives are designed more for reputational benefit than for substantive transformation.

These case studies highlight distinct but complementary forms of greenwashing. Airbnb engages primarily in narrative greenwashing, using emotionally resonant stories and selective data to frame its operations as environmentally beneficial. Uber, by contrast, employs a more metric-driven strategy, relying on ambitious targets, pilot programs, and offsetting schemes to project environmental leadership—despite empirical contradictions.

Both firms benefit from the platform structure that enables them to externalize environmental impacts while retaining branding control. They also exploit regulatory ambiguity, operating in legal grey zones that allow them to issue broad, unverifiable claims with limited consequences.

Policy Recommendations: Building a Regulatory Infrastructure for Environmental Integrity in the Sharing Economy

The evidence presented throughout this article illustrates that greenwashing in the sharing economy is not merely a matter of individual marketing infractions, but a systemic issue deeply embedded in platform business models. To mitigate these risks and ensure that sustainability narratives reflect measurable environmental outcomes, regulatory frameworks must evolve in ways that are both context-sensitive and globally harmonised. What follows is a set of interrelated policy strategies, grounded in comparative governance analysis and environmental law, designed to address the regulatory, epistemic, and structural conditions that enable greenwashing to persist.

A critical starting point is the development of platform-specific environmental reporting standards. Current sustainability disclosure frameworks, such as the Global Reporting Initiative (GRI) or the Sustainability Accounting Standards Board (SASB), are often modeled on vertically integrated corporations with centralized operations. These models poorly reflect the operational dynamics of digital platforms, which influence consumption and emissions indirectly through algorithms, user incentives, and service design. For example, Uber and Lyft do not own the vehicles in their networks, yet exert considerable control over ride frequency and route optimization through their algorithms. To capture such diffuse environmental impacts, regulators must establish customized reporting obligations that account for platform-specific variables—such as gig worker emissions, rebound effects, and cross-sectoral data on user behaviors (Cohen & Kietzmann, 2014; Martin, 2016). These reporting frameworks should mandate disaggregated disclosures by region and service type, paired with annual public reporting subject to independent verification, much like emerging EU requirements under the Corporate Sustainability Reporting (European Commission, n. d.).

Concomitantly, the legal meaning of environmental claims must be clarified and codified. As studies by Lyon and Montgomery (2015) and Delmas and Burbano (2011) have shown, vague and emotionally resonant terms such as "eco," "green," or "climate-neutral" are routinely employed in ways that escape regulatory scrutiny due to their semantic ambiguity. The EU's GCD (2023a) and France's Climate and Resilience Law (Ministères Aménagement du territoire Transition écologique, 2023) provide early models of what more stringent legal definitions might look like. These instruments mandate that environmental claims be substantiated by full life-cycle analysis and third-party verification, while prohibiting unsubstantiated or misleading labels in consumer-facing advertising. Regulators outside the EU should draw on these examples to implement legally binding definitions of sustainability terms, alongside a public registry of certified environmental claims and labeling schemes. This would help reduce consumer confusion and elevate the evidentiary burden for firms making environmental assertions.

A third avenue for reform involves the institutionalization of independent auditing procedures. Many platform firms—including Airbnb and Uber—self-report their environmental progress using internal metrics, selectively disclosing favorable data while withholding information on rebound effects, life-cycle impacts, or algorithmic nudges (Slee, 2017). In response, regulators should mandate annual sustainability audits for platforms above a defined threshold (e.g., in revenue or user base), modeled on the third-party assurance processes used in financial accounting or emissions trading schemes (Fung et al., 2007). These audits should cover not only firm-reported data but also the platforms' use of carbon offsets, the effectiveness of EV adoption programs, and compliance with regional emissions standards. Transparency mechanisms such as those used in the EU Emissions Trading System (EU ETS) could serve as templates for public disclosure and review.

Central to the challenge of enforcing environmental claims in the platform economy is the issue of liability allocation. Sharing economy firms often exert significant operational influence without legal accountability for downstream consequences. Uber's reliance on driver-owned vehicles, for example, allows it to market sustainability pledges while distancing itself from emissions outcomes (Cramer & Krueger, 2016). Airbnb similarly benefits from "eco-" listings without guaranteeing their environmental performance. To address this structural misalignment, legal frameworks must explicitly assign environmental liability to platforms when they influence consumption patterns through algorithms, pricing, or interface design (Van Doorn & Badger, 2020). This approach would extend principles of producer responsibility into the digital sphere, ensuring that platforms cannot externalize sustainability obligations to users while internalizing reputational gains.

Jurisdictional fragmentation poses another critical obstacle to effective regulation. Given that most major platforms operate transnationally, they often exploit regulatory differentials between jurisdictions—a practice commonly referred to as regulatory arbitrage (Levi-Faur, 2006). For instance, a platform may comply with stringent EU regulations in one region while continuing to make unverified environmental claims in regions lacking similar protections. To combat this, countries and regulatory bodies must pursue multilateral cooperation on sustainability governance in the digital economy. The OECD, WTO, or UNCTAD could play convening roles in developing model guidelines for environmental claims, akin to the OECD Guidelines for Multinational Enterprises. Regional coalitions such as the EU–Canada Comprehensive Economic and Trade Agreement (CETA) or the USMCA could incorporate binding commitments to transparency in green marketing. Harmonized definitions, mutual recognition of auditing standards, and cross-border data sharing agreements would help to close gaps and establish a minimum global threshold for claim substantiation.

Finally, any regulatory reform must involve a robust transparency and accountability infrastructure that engages civil society and consumers directly. While legal enforcement is essential, regulatory capacity is often limited, and oversight cannot rest solely with state agencies. Digital tools—such as open-access dashboards showing platform emissions data, user-flagging mechanisms for misleading claims, or browser plugins that assess sustainability ratings—can democratize oversight and empower informed consumption (Pasquale, 2015). Transparency can also be enhanced by integrating traceability features directly into platforms, for instance by tagging rides with emissions estimates or requiring third-party verification for "eco-friendly" accommodation labels. Analogous to the EU's "nutrition label" approach in food regulation, platforms should be required to present standardized sustainability information at the point of service. Such reforms would both enhance consumer autonomy and generate bottom-up pressure for platform compliance.

Together, these policy recommendations reflect a shift in focus from post-hoc enforcement to anticipatory and systemic governance. Greenwashing in the sharing economy is facilitated by opaque business models, decentralized responsibility, and weak regulatory coordination. Effective policy must therefore operate on multiple levels: clarifying legal definitions, requiring verified data, assigning platform liability, coordinating across jurisdictions, and empowering consumers. These measures are not only feasible but necessary to ensure that sustainability transitions in the platform economy are based on material environmental integrity rather than symbolic compliance.

Recommendations

Incentivizing Transparency: Building a Culture of Voluntary Disclosure

Incentivizing transparency is often promoted as a non-coercive, market-compatible regulatory strategy. It encourages platforms to proactively disclose their environmental performance by rewarding good behavior with reputational benefits, access to green finance, or preferential regulatory treatment (Fung et al., 2007). For instance, Uber's rollout of emissions tracking features and its public pledges to electrify its fleet can be seen as attempts to gain trust from investors and consumers through self-reported sustainability efforts.

Transparency-based approaches are particularly effective in early-stage regulation, where the goals are to raise awareness, encourage innovation, and create benchmarking norms. They also work well in complex, data-rich environments—like platform ecosystems—where regulators may lack full information and where soft law mechanisms, such as environmental ratings, voluntary codes, or ESG frameworks, can trigger peer pressure and investor scrutiny (Gunningham & Sinclair, 2019).

However, the sharing economy has demonstrated that voluntary disclosure is often incomplete, strategically curated, and susceptible to selective transparency. Airbnb's sustainability reports, for instance, omit critical data on the platform's contribution to overtourism and energy consumption in tourist-saturated neighborhoods. Moreover, firms may "greenwash by association" by emphasizing partnerships with NGOs or certification bodies without undergoing meaningful transformation (Delmas & Burbano, 2011). Transparency without enforceability often results in reputational laundering rather than true accountability.

Enforcing Penalties: Deterrence Through Legal Accountability

Where transparency falters or is strategically exploited, legal penalties and deterrence-based strategies become necessary. These approaches draw from command-and-control regulatory models, imposing fines, legal sanctions, or even operational restrictions on firms that mislead the public or violate environmental advertising laws.

Recent regulatory developments in the European Union—such as the GCD—signal a shift toward enforcement. Under the directive, environmental claims must be verified by independent assessors, and violations can result in fines up to 4% of annual turnover (European Commission, 2023a). France has already prosecuted firms for climate-related misrepresentation under its Climate and Resilience Law, recognizing greenwashing as a deceptive commercial practice (Ministères Aménagement du territoire Transition écologique, 2023).

In the context of the sharing economy, enforcement mechanisms are crucial to correct structural asymmetries. Platform firms often hold significant power over data, narrative, and operational design, allowing them to profit from sustainability rhetoric while displacing environmental responsibility onto users (Van Doorn & Badger, 2020). Enforceable penalties compel firms to align marketing with operations and create a legal floor beneath voluntary disclosures.

However, enforcement-heavy approaches face two challenges. First, regulatory capacity is often lacking, especially in emerging markets or jurisdictions without robust consumer protection frameworks. Second, overly punitive regimes may discourage experimentation and innovation, especially for smaller or newer platforms trying to implement novel sustainability models.

An Integrated Approach: Regulatory Hybridity and Escalating Intervention

The most effective policy regime is not a binary choice between incentives and penalties but a graduated or "escalating" model of intervention. As Gunningham and Sinclair (2019) argue in their theory of smart regulation, governance should begin with voluntary and market-based tools but progressively incorporate coercive instruments for persistent non-compliance.

This means designing regulation that:

- Starts with transparency incentives (e.g., tax benefits, preferential listing, or ESG investor access for verified disclosures).
- Moves to auditing requirements and mandatory reporting thresholds as firms scale.
- Escalates to penalties and prohibitions when firms persistently greenwash or obstruct verification efforts.

Such a hybrid model can also be adaptive and sector-specific. For example, car-sharing platforms with quantifiable emissions data may be held to more stringent standards earlier while decentralized accommodation platforms might first undergo collaborative benchmarking exercises before enforcement kicks in.

Conclusion: Prioritizing Policy Fit Over Preference

In sum, the question is not whether to incentivize or penalize but when, where, and how to combine both approaches. Incentivizing transparency can cultivate a culture of disclosure and reduce regulatory friction, particularly in dynamic digital sectors. However, without enforceable penalties, it risks becoming a fig leaf for continued environmental obfuscation.

In the sharing economy—characterized by data asymmetry, decentralized impact, and high reputational sensitivity—a hybrid model with escalating enforcement linked to platform size, impact, and claim frequency is the most pragmatic and effective route forward.

Further research is needed to explore how AI and machine learning could assist regulators in real-time detection of deceptive environmental narratives. Similarly, the potential for blockchain technologies to improve supply chain traceability and platform emissions transparency remains underexplored. Expanding the geographic scope of greenwashing analysis to include the Global South and incorporating indigenous and non-Western environmental governance models could significantly enrich both regulatory theory and practice. By expanding both analytical tools and normative frameworks, future scholarship can more fully interrogate the promises and perils of sustainability in the platform economy.

References

Airbnb. (2018). How the Airbnb community supports environmentally-friendly travel worldwide. *Airbnb Newsroom*. https://news.airbnb.com/how-the-airbnb-community-supports-environmentally-friendly-travel-worldwide/

Airbnb. (2022). Healthy tourism commitment: Supporting the UK's sustainable tourism recovery. *Airbnb Newsroom*. https://news.airbnb.com/en-uk/healthy-tourism-commitment-supporting-the-uks-sustainable-tourism-recovery/

Airbnb. (2023). An update on environmental sustainability at Airbnb. *Airbnb Newsroom*. https://news.airbnb.com/an-update-on-environmental-sustainability-at-airbnb/

Airbnb. (n.d.). *Support selected climate protection projects with your stay*. Airbnb. https://www.airbnb.co.uk/help/article/3439. Accessed on April 21, 2025.

Aloni, E. (2016). Pluralizing the sharing economy. *Washington Law Review*, *91*, 1397.

Arijeniwa, V. F., Akinsemolu, A. A., Chukwugozie, D. C., Onawo, U. G., Ochulor, C. E., Nwauzoma, U. M., Kawino, D. A., & Onyeaka, H. (2024). Closing the loop: A framework for tackling single-use plastic waste in the food and beverage industry through circular economy-a review. *Journal of Environmental Management*, *359*, 120816.

Assemblée nationale. (2025). *Proposition de loi visant à abroger l'article L. 435-1 du code de la sécurité intérieure, n° 1212. 17e législature.* https://www.assemblee-nationale.fr/dyn/17/textes/l17b1212_proposition-loi

Behr, H. (2021). Technocracy and the tragedy of EU governance. *Journal of Contemporary European Research, 17*(2). https://jcer.net/index.php/jcer/article/view/1178

Benlian, A., Wiener, M., Cram, W. A., Krasnova, H., Maedche, A., Möhlmann, M., Recker, J., & Remus, U. (2022). Algorithmic management: Bright and dark sides, practical implications, and research opportunities. *Business & Information Systems Engineering, 64*(6), 825–839. https://doi.org/10.1007/s12599-022-00764-w

Bumpus, A. G., & Liverman, D. M. (2008). Accumulation by decarbonization and the governance of carbon offsets. *Economic Geography, 84*(2), 127–155. https://doi.org/10.1111/j.1944-8287.2008.tb00401.x

Buttigieg, C. P., & Pulis, S. (2024). Strategic initiatives to address greenwashing. *ERA Forum, 25*(3), 327–337. https://doi.org/10.1007/s12027-024-00815-7

Codagnone, C., Biagi, F., & Abadie, F. (2016). *The passions and the interests: Unpacking the 'sharing economy'.* Institute for Prospective Technological Studies, JRC Science for Policy Report. https://papers.ssrn.com/sol3/papers.cfm?abstract_id=2793901

Cohen, B., & Kietzmann, J. (2014). Ride on! Mobility business models for the sharing economy. *Organization & Environment, 27*(3), 279–296. https://doi.org/10.1177/1086026614546199

Cramer, J., & Krueger, A. B. (2016). Disruptive change in the taxi business: The case of Uber. *The American Economic Review, 106*(5), 177–182.

De Freitas Netto, S. V., Sobral, M. F. F., Ribeiro, A. R. B., & Soares, G. R. D. L. (2020). Concepts and forms of greenwashing: A systematic review. *Environmental Sciences Europe, 32*(1), 19. https://doi.org/10.1186/s12302-020-0300-3

Delmas, M. A., & Burbano, V. C. (2011). The drivers of greenwashing. *California Management Review, 54*(1), 64–87. https://doi.org/10.1525/cmr.2011.54.1.64

Erhardt, G. D., Roy, S., Cooper, D., Sana, B., Chen, M., & Castiglione, J. (2019). Do transportation network companies decrease or increase congestion? *Science Advances, 5*(5), eaau2670. https://doi.org/10.1126/sciadv.aau2670

ESMA. (2023). *ESAs put forward common understanding of greenwashing and warn on risks.* https://www.esma.europa.eu/press-news/esma-news/esas-put-forward-common-understanding-greenwashing-and-warn-risks

European Commission. (2023a). *Green claims.* https://environment.ec.europa.eu/topics/circular-economy/green-claims_en

European Commission. (2023b). *Green claims—European commission.* https://environment.ec.europa.eu/topics/circular-economy/green-claims_en

European Commission. (n.d.). *Corporate sustainability reporting.* https://finance.ec.europa.eu/capital-markets-union-and-financial-markets/company-reporting-and-auditing/company-reporting/corporate-sustainability-reporting_en. Accessed on April 21, 2025.

Federal Ministry for Economic Cooperation and Development. (2023). *The German Act on corporate due diligence obligations in supply chains: Implications for businesses in partner countries and support from the German Government.* Federal Ministry for Economic Cooperation and Development. https://www.bmz.de/resource/blob/154774/lieferkettengesetz-faktenpapier-partnerlaender-eng-bf.pdf

Frenken, K. (2017). Political economies and environmental futures for the sharing economy. *Philosophical Transactions of the Royal Society A: Mathematical, Physical and Engineering Sciences, 375*(2095), 20160367. https://doi.org/10.1098/rsta.2016.0367

Frenken, K., & Schor, J. (2019). Putting the sharing economy into perspective. In *A research agenda for sustainable consumption governance* (pp. 121–135). Edward Elgar Publishing. https://www.elgaronline.com/edcollchap-oa/book/9781788117814/book-part-9781788117814-17.xml

FTC. (2012). *FTC issues revised "green guides"*. https://www.ftc.gov/news-events/news/press-releases/2012/10/ftc-issues-revised-green-guides

FTC. (2019). *Truly Organic Inc*. Federal Trade Commission. https://www.ftc.gov/legal-library/browse/cases-proceedings/192-3077-truly-organic-inc

FTC. (2025). *FTC launches public inquiry into anti-competitive regulations*. https://www.ftc.gov/news-events/news/press-releases/2025/04/ftc-launches-public-inquiry-anti-competitive-regulations

Fung, A., Graham, M., & Weil, D. (2007). *Full disclosure: The perils and promise of transparency*. Cambridge University Press. https://books.google.com/books?hl=en&lr=&id=DvnAEAAAQBAJ&oi=fnd&pg=PR11&dq=Full+disclosure:+The+perils+and+promise+of+transparency&ots=UXE35eerqd&sig=13a13lZvnqfDZ4Xs2O0xQzqnzHM

Garcia-Ayllon, S. (2018). Urban transformations as an indicator of unsustainability in the P2P mass tourism phenomenon: The Airbnb case in Spain through three case studies. *Sustainability, 10*(8), 2933.

Gbadegesin, O. A., Komolafe, O. S., Ayodele-Olajire, D., Omotoye, O., & Gbadegesin, A. (2025). Unmasking greenwashing: strengthening Nigeria's legal framework for a sustainable green economy. *Green and Low-Carbon Economy*. https://ojs.bonviewpress.com/index.php/GLCE/article/view/4335

Ghisellini, P., Cialani, C., & Ulgiati, S. (2016). A review on circular economy: The expected transition to a balanced interplay of environmental and economic systems. *Journal of Cleaner Production, 114*, 11–32.

Gunningham, N., & Sinclair, D. (2019). Regulatory pluralism: Designing policy mixes for environmental protection. In *Environmental law* (pp. 463–490). Routledge. https://www.taylorfrancis.com/chapters/edit/10.4324/9781315194288-9/regulatory-pluralism-designing-policy-mixes-environmental-protection-neil-gunningham-darren-sinclair

Guttentag, D. (2015). Airbnb: Disruptive innovation and the rise of an informal tourism accommodation sector. *Current Issues in Tourism, 18*(12), 1192–1217. https://doi.org/10.1080/13683500.2013.827159

Hati, S. R. H., Balqiah, T. E., Hananto, A., & Yuliati, E. (2021). A decade of systematic literature review on Airbnb: The sharing economy from a multiple stakeholder perspective. *Heliyon, 7*(10). https://www.cell.com/heliyon/fulltext/S2405-8440(21)02325-2

Henao, A., & Marshall, W. E. (2019). The impact of ride-hailing on vehicle miles traveled. *Transportation, 46*(6), 2173–2194. https://doi.org/10.1007/s11116-018-9923-2

Humphrey, J., Provencher, D., Gasior, N., Baugher, M., & Watroba, J. (2019). *Electric vehicle adoption among Uber and Lyft drivers*. https://kb.osu.edu/items/ccceb32f-f1b1-43aa-a009-d2647e503e53

Khosrowshahi, D. (2020). Driving a green recovery. *Uber Newsroom.* https://www.uber.com/en-IE/newsroom/driving-a-green-recovery/

Kirchherr, J., Reike, D., & Hekkert, M. (2017). Conceptualizing the circular economy: An analysis of 114 definitions. *Resources, Conservation and Recycling, 127*, 221–232.

Lambin, E. F., Meyfroidt, P., Rueda, X., Blackman, A., Börner, J., Cerutti, P. O., Dietsch, T., Jungmann, L., Lamarque, P., & Lister, J. (2014). Effectiveness and synergies of policy instruments for land use governance in tropical regions. *Global Environmental Change, 28*, 129–140.

Langley, P., & Leyshon, A. (2017). Platform capitalism: The intermediation and capitalisation of digital economic circulation. *Finance and Society, 3*(1), 11–31.

Levi-Faur, D. (2006). Regulatory capitalism: The dynamics of change beyond telecoms and electricity. *Governance, 19*(3). https://www.researchgate.net/profile/David-Levi-Faur/publication/228026925_Regulatory_Capitalism_The_Dynamics_of_Change_Beyond_Telecoms_and_Electricity/links/59e06cc4a6fdcca9842f3607/Regulatory-Capitalism-The-Dynamics-of-Change-Beyond-Telecoms-and-Electricity.pdf

Lyon, T. P., & Maxwell, J. W. (2011). Greenwash: Corporate environmental disclosure under threat of audit. *Journal of Economics and Management Strategy, 20* (1), 3–41. https://doi.org/10.1111/j.1530-9134.2010.00282.x

Lyon, T. P., & Montgomery, A. W. (2015). The means and end of greenwash. *Organization & Environment, 28*(2), 223–249 https://doi.org/10.1177/1086026615575332

Machado, S. M. D. C. (2025). The fight against greenwashing in the European Union: Directive (EU) 2024/825 of the European parliament and the council, of February 28, 2024, and the Portuguese case. *Cuadernos de Derecho Transnacional, 17*(1), 353–365.

Martin, C. J. (2016). The sharing economy: A pathway to sustainability or a nightmarish form of neoliberal capitalism? *Ecological Economics, 121*, 149–159.

Ministères Aménagement du territoire Transition écologique. (2023). *Loi climat et résilience: Bilan à 2 ans.* https://www.ecologie.gouv.fr/actualites/loi-climat-resilience-bilan-2-ans

Parguel, B., Benoît-Moreau, F., & Larceneux, F. (2011). How sustainability ratings might deter 'greenwashing': A closer look at ethical corporate communication. *Journal of Business Ethics, 102*(1), 15–28. https://doi.org/10.1007/s10551-011-0901-2

Pasquale, F. (2015). *The black box society: The secret algorithms that control money and information.* Harvard University Press. https://doi.org/10.4159/harvard.9780674736061

Pearson, J. (2010). Are we doing the right thing? Leadership and prioritisation for public benefit. *The Journal of Corporate Citizenship, 37*, 37–40.

Pope, S., & Wæraas, A. (2016). CSR-washing is rare: A conceptual framework, literature review, and critique. *Journal of Business Ethics, 137*(1), 173–193. https://doi.org/10.1007/s10551-015-2546-z

Schor, J. (2020). *After the gig: How the sharing economy got hijacked and how to win it back.* Univ of California Press. https://books.google.com/books?hl=en&lr=&id=5WDiDwAAQBAJ&oi=fnd&pg=PR9&dq=After+the+gig:+How+the+

sharing+economy+got+hijacked+and+how+to+win+it+back&ots=J6pR-G33Ez&sig=RlwIDTMo46FDq-R3ZZkrFLriO9E

Schor, J. B., & Attwood-Charles, W. (2017). The "sharing" economy: Labor, inequality, and social connection on for-profit platforms. *Sociology Compass, 11* (8), e12493. https://doi.org/10.1111/soc4.12493

Seele, P., & Gatti, L. (2017). Greenwashing revisited: In search of a typology and accusation-based definition incorporating legitimacy strategies. *Business Strategy and the Environment*, *26*(2), 239–252. https://doi.org/10.1002/bse.1912

Shaheen, S. A., & Cohen, A. P. (2013). Carsharing and personal vehicle services: Worldwide market developments and emerging trends. *International Journal of Sustainable Transportation*, *7*(1), 5–34. https://doi.org/10.1080/15568318.2012.660103

Sharma, P. (2022). Sharing economy: The concepts and cases. In J. Bhattacharyya (Ed.), *Dealing with socially responsible consumers* (pp. 51–68). Springer Nature. https://doi.org/10.1007/978-981-19-4457-4_4

Slee, T. (2017). *What's yours is mine: Against the sharing economy*. Scribe Publications.

Tang, Z. (2022). *The dark side of artificial intelligence: Understanding the role of perceived algorithm unfairness on ride-hailing driver discontinuance*. Mississippi State University. https://search.proquest.com/openview/f7befbf47534b6bd0646933ff7ca8049/1?pq-origsite=gscholar&cbl=18750&diss=y

TerraChoice Environmental Marketing. (2010). *The sins of greenwashing: Home and family edition*. Industry Research Report. https://www.twosides.info/wp-content/uploads/2018/05/Terrachoice_The_Sins_of_Greenwashing_-_Home_and_Family_Edition_2010.pdf

Uber. (2023). *Measuring corporate sustainability*. Uber for Business. https://www.uber.com/gb/en/business/articles/measuring-corporate-sustainability/

Van Doorn, N., & Badger, A. (2020). Platform capitalism's hidden abode: Producing data assets in the gig economy. *Antipode*, *52*(5), 1475–1495. https://doi.org/10.1111/anti.12641

Zervas, G., Proserpio, D., & Byers, J. W. (2017). The rise of the sharing economy: Estimating the impact of Airbnb on the hotel industry. *Journal of Marketing Research*, *54*(5), 687–705. https://doi.org/10.1509/jmr.15.0204

Chapter 14

The Evolution of Greenwashing Research in the Context of the Shared Economy: Insights from a Bibliometric Study

Animesh Kumar Sharma[a], *Rahul Sharma*[a] *and Rohit Duggal*[b]

[a]Lovely Professional University, India
[b]CIC Higher Education, Australia

Abstract

Greenwashing has been a prominent topic in sustainability discourse, especially in reference to the shared economy. The bibliometric study employed VOSviewer to analyze publications from 2006 to 2024, focusing on citation networks, and co-authorship analysis. The analysis showed that studies around greenwashing are in the starting phase; however, it would have a significant influence on hereafter work. Authors frequently referred to early publications highlighting the disparity between environmental claims and real behavior. Furthermore, co-authorship patterns revealed substantial coordination among scholars in the United States and Europe, reflecting regional apprehension for corporate liability in ecological claims. This concern was expanded by the absence of regulatory frameworks controlling eco-friendly promises around this time. Therefore, the foundations for more powerful analytical tools and ethical directions for addressing greenwashing were laid. The findings of the study elucidate the early academic interest in greenwashing within the shared economy and give a base for future research to investigate its better implications. The study spotlights the active character of research in greenwashing and the shared economy, pushed by global sustainability issues and the growing need for transparent and ethical business behavior.

Keywords: Greenwashing; shared economy; sustainability; corporate social responsibility; ethical business practices; sustainable business practices

Eco Illusions, 299–323

doi:10.1108/978-1-83662-782-120261014

Introduction

In the modern-day world scenario, sustainability has appeared as a base of both administrative law and corporate strategy (Ashrafi et al., 2020; Park, 2018). Amid mounting concerns over environmental change, resource reduction, and atmospheric declination, businesses are under growing compulsion to embrace sustainable practices and communicate their commitment to eco-consciousness (Sun et al., 2024). Simultaneously, the shared economy has gotten a grip as a transformative model that promotes collaborative utilization and resource efficiency (Muñoz & Cohen, 2017; Eckhardt et al., 2019). However, as these patterns converge, a critical challenge emerges; in distinguishing sincere attempts to sustain from dishonest behavior like greenwashing (Wang et al., 2023). Greenwashing is the usage of presenting misleading or exaggerated claims about the environmental benefits of a product, service, or company (Spaniol et al., 2024). The term greenwashing had first came in 1980s and it shows how businesses may exploit customer demand for sustainability by marketing themselves as ecologically conscious while failing to make substantive modifications to their business practices (de Freitas Netto et al., 2020). Greenwashing can be in a variety of forms, such as vague environmental statements, irrelevant eco-labels, or outright false advertising (Atkinson & Kim, 2015; Şenyapar, 2024). For example, an organization can tout its packaging as '100% recyclable' without addressing the carbon footprint of its production process or the actual recyclability rates in various areas. At its core, greenwashing damages credibility and delays the development of real sustainability (Bricker & Justice, 2022). It misleads environmentally conscious consumers, creates unfair competition for truly sustainable organization, and weakens the effect of legitimate environmental initiatives. More importantly, greenwashing can eternalize adverse practices by giving the illusion of sustainability, thereby delaying systemic change (Yoganandham et al., 2024). In some cases, these deceptive claims have even led to lawful outcomes, as regulatory agencies across the globe begin to crack down on false advertising related to environmental claims (Szabo & Webster, 2021).

Growth of Shared Economy

The shared economy, also named as the collaborative economy, shows a change from ownership-based consumption to access-based consumption (Saravade et al., 2021). Airbnb, Uber, and Zipcar platforms demonstrate this model by making it possible for people to share underutilized resources—be it accommodation, transportation, or skills—in exchange for monetary or nonmonetary benefits (Khalek & Chakraborty, 2023). This method ensures relevant environmental and social benefits, including degraded resource consumption, minimized waste, and increased community engagement (Lee et al., 2024). Proponents of the shared economy argue that it conforms to the sustainability principles by fostering efficient resource use and lessening the impact on the environment (Carrigan et al., 2020; Wang et al., 2022). For instance, car-sharing services can reduce the necessity of personal automobile ownership, leading to fewer automobiles on the road and reduced emissions of carbon gases. Identically, the reuse of existing assets, such as homes or tools, can curtail the demand for new production and the associated resource extraction. Despite the advantages to the environment, the shared economy can also promote social equity by providing an affordable approach to services for individuals who might otherwise be unable to afford them (Schor, 2017).

The Intersection of Greenwashing and the Shared Economy

While the shared economy offers substantial possibilities for advancing sustainability, it is not immune to the pitfalls of greenwashing (Hao et al., 2024; Jones, 2019). As businesses within the shared economy seek to position themselves as ecologically conscious, they may resort to superficial claims (Badhwar et al., 2024). For example, a ride-sharing company might stress the ecological advantages of carpooling while neglecting to address the emissions generated by its fleet or the impact of heightened traffic jams (Guyader et al., 2021). Likely, a vacation rental app might promote itself as a sustainable substitute for conventional hotels without considering the environmental consequences of the energy consumption of its listed properties (Fudurich & Mackay; 2020). This intersection brings up significant issues regarding transparency, accountability, and the function of legislation in promoting true sustainability in the shared economy (Light & Miskelly, 2019). How can customers discern authentic environmental claims from greenwashed narratives? What criteria and measurements ought companies to follow when showcasing their dedication to sustainability? And what role do policymakers, nongovernmental organizations, and the media play in ensuring that the shared economy contributes significantly to environmental goals? The shared economy's potential to run sustainably depends on the integrity of its actors and the strength of its governance (Grinevich et al., 2019). It provides creative answers to some of the most urgent environmental problems facing the planet, on the one hand. However, the ubiquity of greenwashing and the lack of strict control pose a threat to its contributions. For example, even though shared mobility platforms may lower emissions per person, if they are not properly managed, their activities may worsen traffic and pollution in cities. Furthermore, greenwashing in the shared economy might damage public confidence and make people doubt the industry's sustainability claims (Mu & Lee, 2023). This, in turn, can hinder consumer participation in shared economy initiatives, ultimately stalling progress toward environmental aims. Therefore, addressing greenwashing is not merely a matter of ethical marketing but a critical step in unlocking the full potential of the shared economy (Vangeli et al., 2023; Qayyum et al., 2023).

Greenwashing and Technology

The growth of technology may play an important role in combating greenwashing within the shared economy (Zhang, 2024). Blockchain gives a clear and tamper-proof method for tracking the environmental effect of products (Ling & Wang, 2024; Nygaard & Silkoset, 2023). By using blockchain, companies can offer verifiable data on their carbon discharge, resource usage, and waste management practices. Similarly, big data analytics and artificial intelligence (AI) can help monitor and evaluate sustainability claims, ensuring that companies are held responsible for their environmental promises (Boedijanto & Delina, 2024; Singh et al., 2024). Additionally, platforms in the shared economy can incorporate sustainability monitoring tools to help customers make wise choices (Huang & Leau, 2024; Lashitew, 2021). For example, a ride-sharing platform could show the carbon footprint of each travel, allowing users to choose greener options. Such inventions not only increase transparency but also encourage companies to implement more environmentally friendly procedures to stay competitive.

Research Gap

The field of greenwashing and the shared economy remains an underexplored domain, despite the growing prominence of both notions in sustainability discourse. While existing studies have examined greenwashing as a deceptive practice in corporate sustainability initiatives and the shared economy as a model for resource efficiency, limited research addresses the interplay between these phenomena. Specifically, there is a lack of comprehensive analyses on how greenwashing impacts consumer confidence and involvement in the shared economy, or how shared economy platforms offer environmental benefits versus superficial claims. Additionally, methodological gaps exist in assessing the pervasiveness and outcomes of greenwashing within the shared economy. Quantitative tools such as bibliometric analyzes can offer a complete outline of research trends, collaboration networks, and thematic development in this area, but such studies are scarce. Perspectives on geographic patterns, interdisciplinary ways, and the addition of technological solutions to combat greenwashing within shared economy platforms are also underrepresented. Filling up these disparities could advance the understanding of sustainability problems and opportunities in the shared economy.

Research Questions

Research questions for the bibliometric study on the research study are listed below.

RQ1: What are the publication trends in studies addressing greenwashing within shared economy models?

RQ2: Who are the top authors, journals, and affiliations contributing to the greenwashing and the shared economy?
RQ3: How has the volume of publications on greenwashing and the shared economy evolved across the world and disciplines?
RQ4: Which fields and sectors are leading in studies addressing greenwashing within the shared economy?
RQ5: What are the most frequently cited works and methodologies in studies addressing greenwashing within shared economy models?
RQ6: How does the literature address the role of technology in reducing greenwashing within the shared economy?

Research Methodology

This study employs a bibliometric approach to analyze the research landscape on greenwashing and the shared economy. Bibliometric analysis is a quantitative approach to scrutinize the structure, development, and patterns within a particular body of academic literature (Donthu et al., 2021; Passas, 2024). It provides insights into research output, influential authors, institutional collaborations, thematic clusters, and citation patterns, thereby fostering a thorough comprehension of the field.

Data Collection

The bibliometric dataset was extracted from Scopus using specific search strings customized based on the research focus. Keywords such as 'greenwashing,' 'shared economy,' 'collaborative consumption,' and 'sustainability' were combined with Boolean operators to polish the search. The search was restricted to articles published between 2006 and 2024 to capture contemporary developments while ensuring a manageable dataset. There was a total of 936 publications extracted from the database. The PRISMA framework was applied for further identification of data for the study. Language restrictions were applied to include only articles published in English. Irrelevant publications were excluded through manual screening, focusing on studies directly handling the intersection of greenwashing and the shared economy. Finally, a total of 640 publications was selected for the analysis (Fig. 14.1).

Data Analysis

The bibliometric analysis was conducted by using the VOSviewer software.

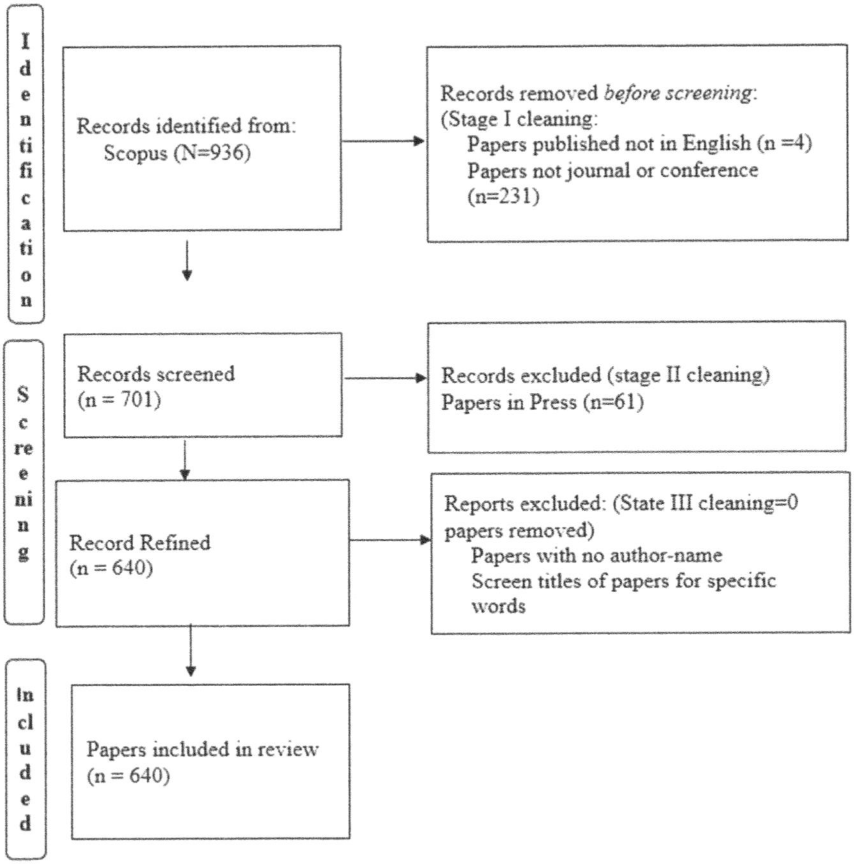

Fig. 14.1. PRISMA Framework. *Source:* Authors' Own Elaboration.

Results and Analysis

Publications Trends

Fig. 14.2 provides a breakdown of Open Access publications related to their models. A total of 389 publications are categorized under Open Access. Among these, 155 are classified as Gold Open Access, where the entire content is freely available immediately upon publication, generally sponsored through APCs (Article Processing Charges). Another 133 fall under the Hybrid Gold category, authorizing authors to make specific articles Open Access in journals that normally work on a subscription model. Additionally, 16 publications are marked as Bronze Open Access, which provides temporary free access without a clear license for reuse. Lastly, 111 publications are identified as Green Open Access, where authors self-archive their work, such as preprints or postprints, in

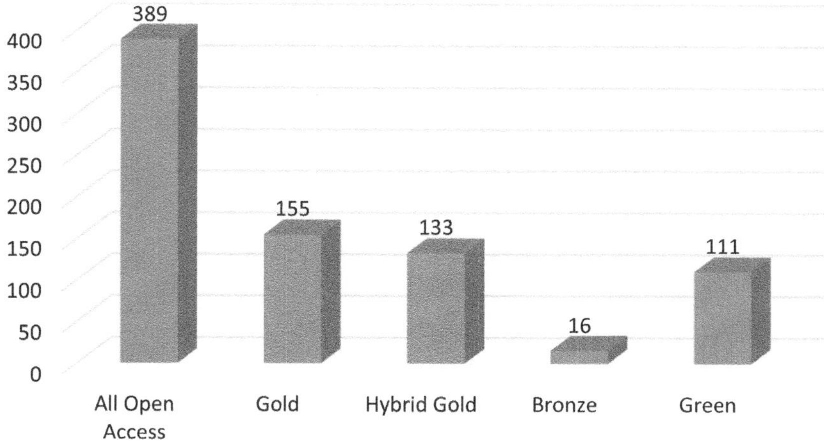

Fig. 14.2. Open Access Publication. *Source:* Authors' Own Elaboration.

repositories, often alongside the published version. This distribution highlights the different ways within Open Access publishing and offers to numerous accessibility and licensing preferences.

Fig. 14.3 depicts the distribution of publications across many setups. A majority, totaling 705, are journal articles, reflecting a prominence on publishing in peer-reviewed academic journals. In addition, 189 publications are in the form of books, showcasing significant contributions to comprehensive, standalone academic or professional works. Furthermore, 29 publications are part of a book series, showing thematic collections. Lastly, 13 publications are classified as conference proceedings, representing research presented at academic or professional conferences. This table gives a diverse range of publication formats, with journals being the predominant way of spreading research.

Fig. 14.4 shows an overview of publications categorized by document type. The majority, 635 publications, are articles, underscoring their dominance as the main channel for sharing research results. This is followed by 128 publications in the form of books, indicating a substantial contribution to detailed and comprehensive scholarly works. Additionally, 83 book chapters highlight participation in collaborative research volumes. Sixty-three reviews demonstrate efforts in synthesizing existing understanding in different fields, while 19 conference papers reflect active engagement in scholarly works. Further, five editorials and two notes represent more focused or opinion-based contributions, and a single short survey showcases targeted work on a special field. This distribution illustrates a wide range of scholarly outputs, with articles being the most prominent.

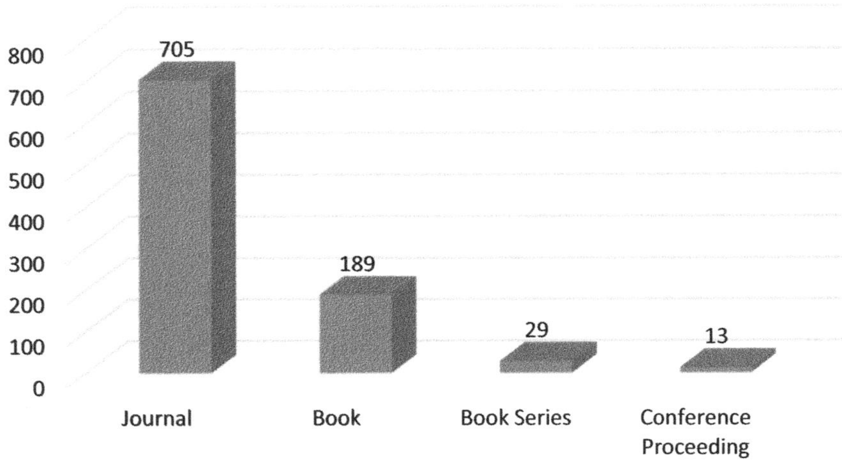

Fig. 14.3. Publication Distribution. *Source:* Authors' Own Elaboration.

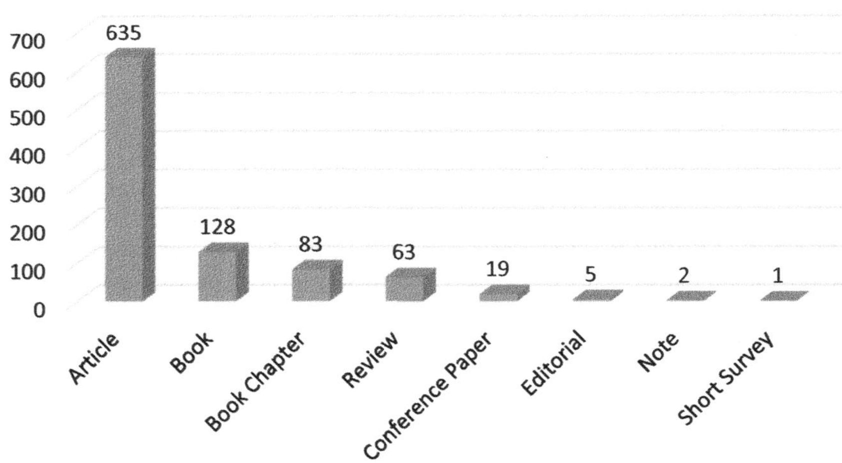

Fig. 14.4. Publication Type. *Source:* Authors' Own Elaboration.

Year-wise Publications

Fig. 14.5 presents a year-wise distribution of publications, underlining the growth and trends over time. The highest number of publications is observed in 2024, with a total of 276, reflecting a peak in research works. This is followed by 180 publications in 2023 and 135 in 2022, showcasing a steady rise in recent

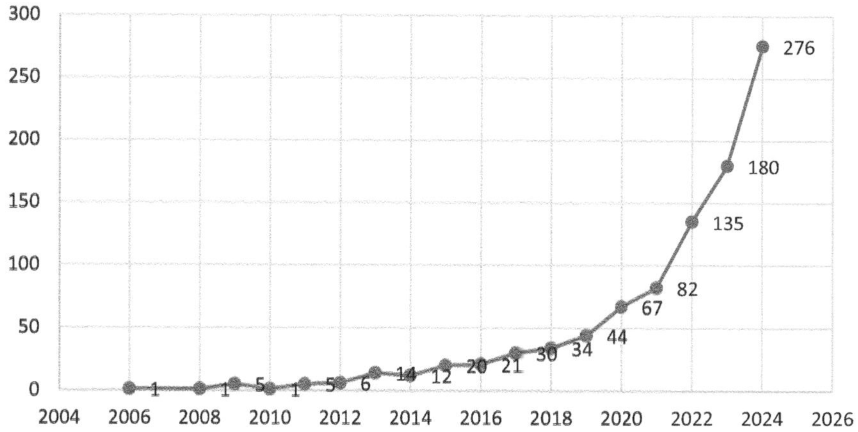

Fig. 14.5. Year-wise Publications. *Source:* Authors' Own Elaboration.

years. Earlier years exhibit a gradual decrease, with 82 publications in 2021, 67 in 2020, and 44 in 2019. Contributions from the late 2000s and early 2010s are sparse, with single-digit outputs such as 6 in 2012 and 5 in 2009 and 2011, indicating a modest beginning. Notable early contributions include 1 publication in 2006, 2008, and 2010, reflecting the initial stages of scholarly dissemination. Overall, the table shows a significant acceleration in research output in the last decade, particularly post-2020.

Top Publications Venue

Fig. 14.6 provides an overview of the sources where publications are disseminated, highlighting key academic journals in the field of sustainability and business ethics. The journal Sustainability Switzerland stands out as the leading source with 66 publications, pointing to its main role in publishing research related to sustainability. *Journal of Cleaner Production* follows with 28 publications, reflecting its focus on environmental management and sustainable production practices. The *Corporate Social Responsibility and Environmental Management* journal, with 27 publications, showcases research on corporate responsibility and environmental management practices. Other prominent sources include the *Journal of Business Ethics*, with 25 publications, which explores ethical business practices, and *Business Strategy and the Environment*, with 18 publications, emphasizing the intersection of business strategy and environmental sustainability. Journals such as *Environment, Development, and Sustainability and Environmental Science and Pollution Research*, each with 11 publications, further highlight scholarly work in environmental science and sustainable development. Other noteworthy sources like *Business and Society*,

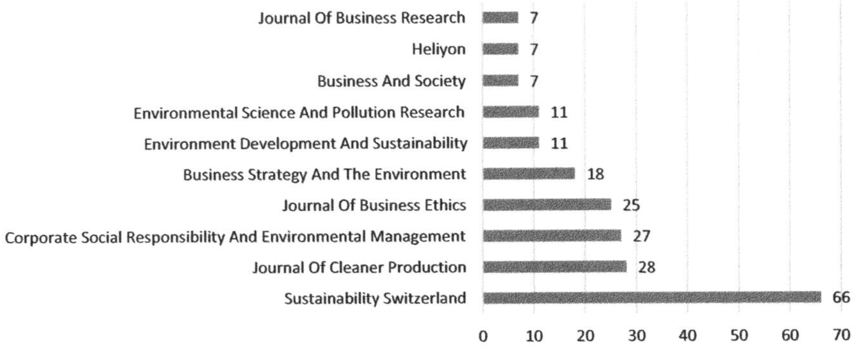

Fig. 14.6. Top Publications Venues. *Source:* Authors' Own Elaboration.

Heliyon, and the *Journal of Business Research*, each with 7 publications, contribute to a broader discussion on the relationship between organization, society, and sustainability.

Keywords Occurrences

Fig. 14.7 lists various keywords and the number of publications associated with each, providing insight into the prominent work within sustainability and business ethics. Sustainability is the most significant keyword, appearing in 155 publications, underlining its central role in academic discussions around environmental responsibility and enduring methods. Sustainable Development comes next with 119 publications, showing key attention on achieving economic, social, and environmental equilibrium for long-term growth. Corporate Social Responsibility (CSR), mentioned in 103 publications, demonstrates the increasing attention on how businesses contribute to societal happiness, while CSR itself, with 33 mentions, further reinforces its significance in business practices. The environmental problems like Climate Change (42) and Greenwashing (40) are also key themes, reflecting concerns about the environmental impact of corporate actions and the genuineness of their sustainability claims. Other notable keywords include Innovation (33), emphasizing the role of modern technologies and creative solutions in increasing sustainability, and China (32), indicating the country's increasing relevance in global sustainability discussions. Stakeholder (30) and Environmental Economics (24) underscore the involvement of different stakeholders in shaping sustainable policies, in addition to the financial effects of environmental measures. Ultimately, 3 Fig. 14.8 shows the keywords cloud, and it reflects a varied research focus on sustainability, its integration into business practices, and its influence on universal and local environmental issues.

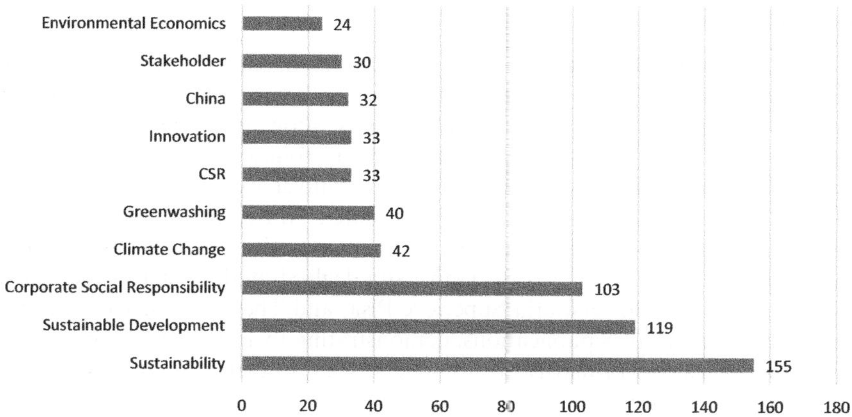

Fig. 14.7. Keywords Occurrences. *Source:* Authors' Own Elaboration.

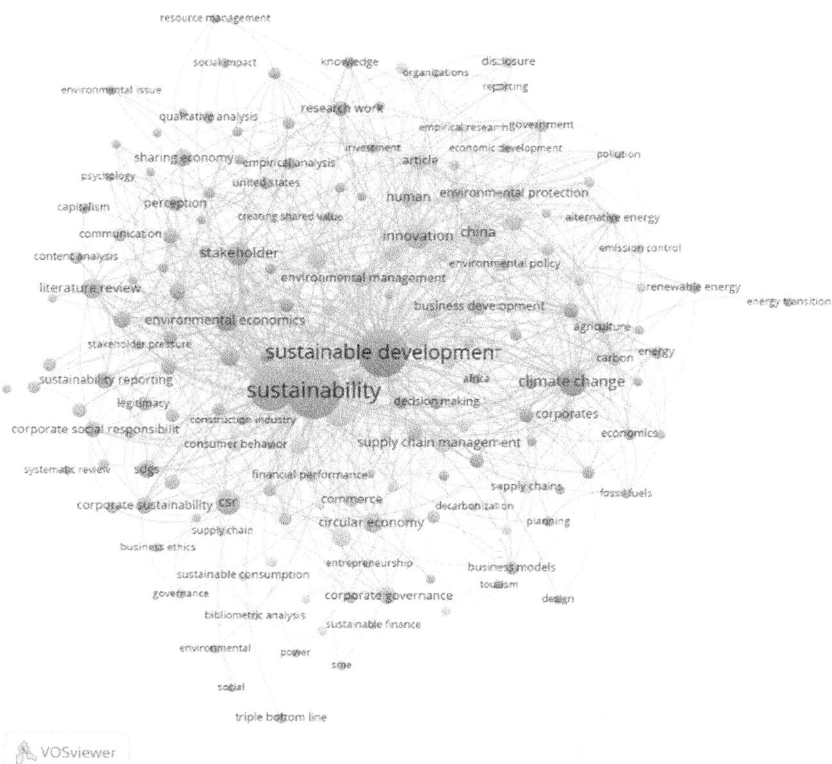

Fig. 14.8. Keywords Cloud. *Source:* VOSviewer

Top Affiliations

Fig. 14.9 describes the distribution of publications based on institutional affiliations, showcasing contributions from notable academic institutions. Copenhagen Business School leads with 19 publications, showing its important role in research output. Leuphana Universität Lüneburg follows with 14 publications, indicating active scholarly engagement. The University of Sydney has contributed 10 publications, while Vrije Universiteit Amsterdam has produced 9 publications, showcasing their strong research initiatives. Several institutions, including the University of Sussex, Università degli Studi di Roma Tor Vergata, Sant'Anna Scuola Universitaria Superiore Pisa, and The University of Queensland, each account for 8 publications, demonstrating their cooperative initiatives to further research. Primarily, the University of Manchester and Newcastle University have each contributed 7 publications, highlighting their active participation in academic research. This distribution, which includes noteworthy contributions from institutions in Europe, Australia, and the United Kingdom, highlights the international and cooperative nature of research.

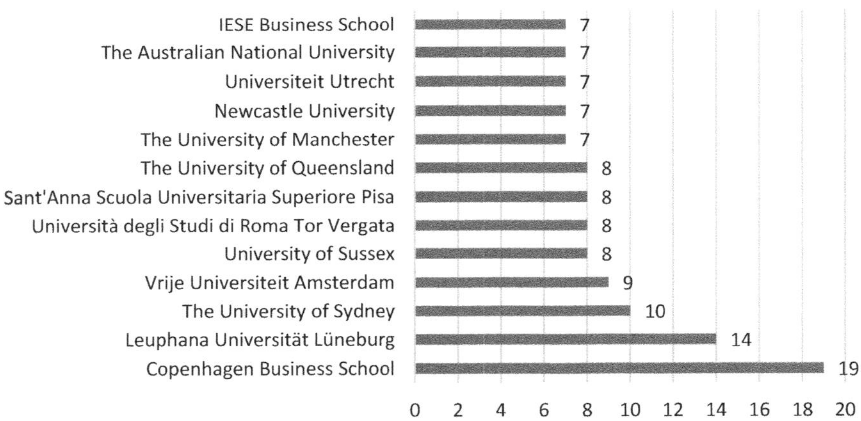

Fig. 14.9. Top Affiliations. *Source:* Authors' Own Elaboration.

Top Countries

Fig. 14.10 provides a breakdown of publications by country, demonstrating the worldwide reach of research in the field of sustainability and business ethics. The United States leads with 177 publications, followed closely by the United Kingdom with 155 publications, indicating these two countries as major contributors to the academic discourse in this area. China ranks third with 112 publications, showcasing its increasing effect on sustainability-related research, specifically in the field of rapid industrialization and environmental challenges. European countries also play an important role, with Italy contributing 79

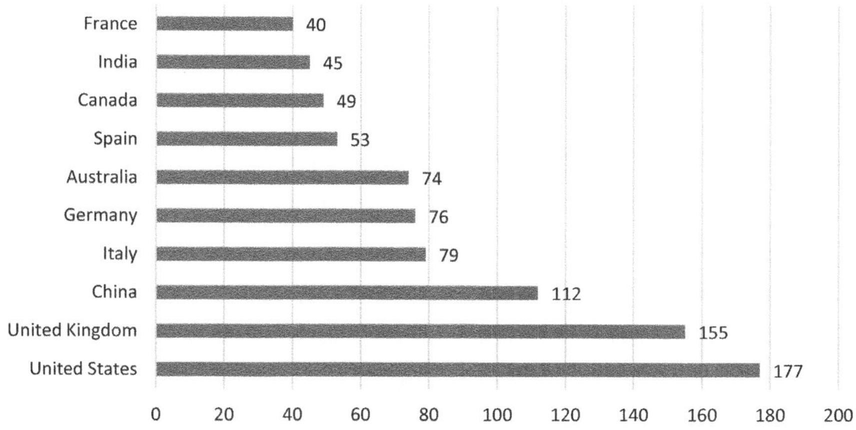

Fig. 14.10. Country Wise Publications. *Source:* Authors' Own Elaboration.

publications and Germany publishing 76, highlighting their engagement in environmental and sustainability research. Australia, with 74 publications, emphasizes its commitment to environmental problems, while Spain (53) and Canada (49) also show significant advancements in the field. India (45) and France (40) complete the list of top contributors, each with a notable field of work focused on sustainability practices and their effect on business and society. This distribution reflects the global nature of sustainability research, with countries across North America, Europe, Asia, and Oceania actively participating in the conversation. The United States and the United Kingdom stand out as key leaders, while other nations, particularly in Europe and Asia, keep up the important contributions to the ongoing dialogue on sustainable development and environmental responsibility.

Top Authors

Fig. 14.11 presents a list of authors and the number of publications they have contributed to in the field of sustainability, business ethics, and corporate social responsibility. Morsing, M. stands out as the leading author with 6 publications, indicating a significant influence on research in this domain. Authors such as Chang, T.W., and Light, A., each with 5 publications, also demonstrate substantial participation in the academic literature. Other notable authors include Lee Park, C., Miskelly, C., Panait, M., Schaltegger, S., Siano, A., Testa, F., and Vollero, A., each contributing 4 publications. These authors are participating in different features of sustainability, including environmental management, corporate social responsibility, and sustainable business. The distribution of publications across these authors demonstrates the collaborative character of

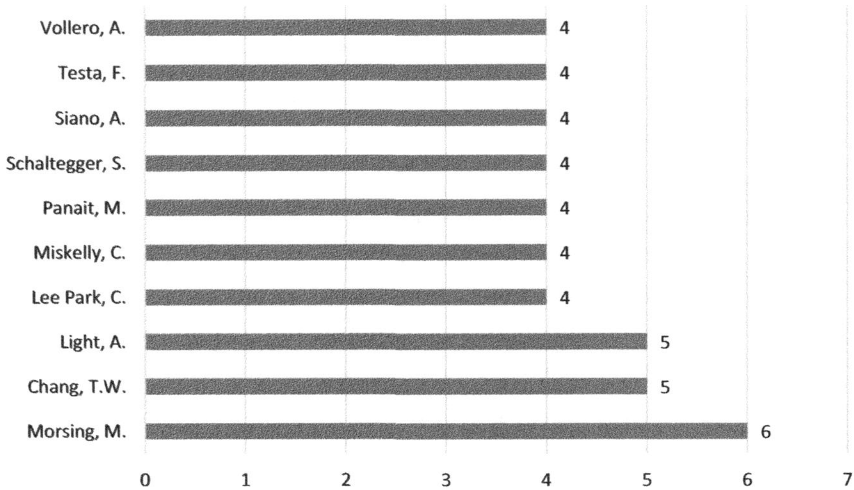

Fig. 14.11. Author-wise Publications. *Source:* Authors' Own Elaboration.

research in this sector, with several academics participating in the development of knowledge around sustainability and corporate ethics. These authors, through their collaborative work, have profoundly influenced the academic conversation on sustainability, reflecting the growing importance of these problems in modern research.

Co-Citation Analysis

Fig. 14.12 shows the co-citation network in the study. The network visualization shows clusters, each of which represents a field's research domain or theme. The larger nodes, like 'Freeman E.E.—Strategic Management' and 'Delmas M.A.—Burbano V.C.' denote significant writers or works that are regularly referenced in the literature. These main findings emphasize seminal works on sustainability, corporate social responsibility, and greenwashing tactics. According to authors like 'Ostrom E.' and 'Hamari J.', the links between clusters point to important overlaps and interdisciplinary conversations, especially on subjects like governance, resource sharing, and sustainability in the shared economy. Distant nodes, which address topics like energy sustainability and socioeconomic inequality, include 'Arruda G.M.—Sustainable Energy' and 'Piketty T.—Capital in the Twenty-First Century,' which give various viewpoints or less often co-cited publications. These nodes depict more general relationships between global issues and shared economy and greenwashing studies. All things considered, our co-citation analysis recognizes significant contributions, draws

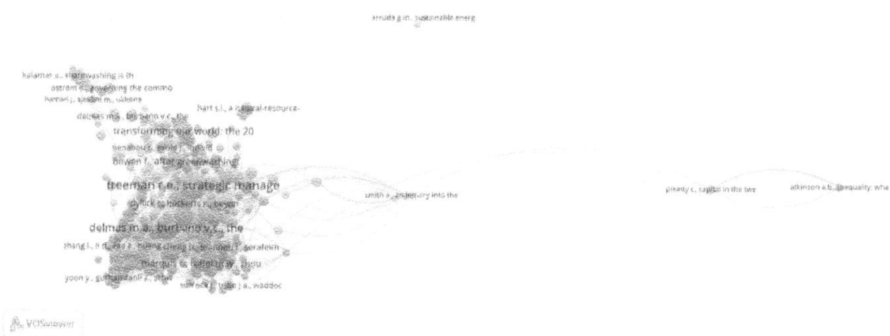

Fig. 14.12. Co-Citation Network. *Source:* VOSviewer.

attention to related topics, and recommends fields that could use more interdisciplinary research.

Discussion

This research study has provided insightful information about the current situation of research on greenwashing and the shared economy. By inspecting publication trends, influential authors, journals, institutions, and regional contributions, it clarifies how these subjects are developing and how they relate to the larger conversation about sustainability and business ethics. The findings answer the research questions posed and give a greater comprehension of how these concepts are addressed in the academic literature.

Evolution of Greenwashing

Greenwashing is an industry practice where businesses mislead consumers by misrepresenting their product, service, or policy as green. The phrase gained popularity in the 1980s when environmentalist Jay Westerveld found that hotels were promoting towel reuse 'for the environment' but had unsustainable operations going on behind the scenes. Greenwashing has evolved over the decades from mere symbolic actions like green packaging and vague labels to more sophisticated strategies that include sustainability reports, unverifiable certifications, and ESG metric-based branding. In the 1990s and 2000s, firms started issuing corporate social responsibility reports to highlight their green initiatives; however, most of these reports were not verified by an independent auditor. With the 2010s' frenzy of investor demand for ESG performance, firms started incorporating sustainability into their business model and branding, though not always honestly. Today, such a practice has moved into a digital era, with green claims amplified through social media, influencer marketing, and even AI-generated sustainability narratives, making it difficult for stakeholders to separate fact from fiction.

The rise of the sharing economy, characterized by peer-to-peer platforms for collaborative consumption of goods and services like cars, homes, and apparel, has been widely viewed as a move away from unsustainable consumption. In line with the principles of the circular economy, where reuse, repurposing, or redistribution of goods is preferred over disposal, the sharing economy has the promise of reduced consumption of resources and a reduced environmental footprint. From car-sharing schemes to furniture hire businesses, such models seem to promote a progression of Environmental, Social, and Governance (ESG) goals by reducing carbon footprints, facilitating inclusive consumption, and improving transparency. In addition, they align with the United Nations Sustainable Development Goals (UNSDGs). But this promise is not always matched by reality. While the sharing economy has potential for sustainability, it is not free of greenwashing. Some companies market marginal environmental benefits while ignoring hidden costs such as increased travel generated by ride-sharing, disposable goods used in short-term rentals, or abusive labor. In doing so, they can produce an 'eco illusion,' where consumers perceive that they are making a sustainable choice, while the net effect can be negligible or even negative. For example, selling sustainability through making reuse possible without calculating emissions, waste, or social impact can be misleading. This undermines both the credibility of ESG and the progress of SDGs.

To avoid the eco-illusion and actually unlock the potential of the sharing economy, platforms must adopt greater transparency, standardized environmental measurements, and independent audits. ESG assertions must be fact-based, and circular practices must be embedded in operations, not just in marketing. Public awareness about greenwashing must be increased so end-users and investors make smart decisions. With real circular models and in accordance with ESG and SDG frameworks, the sharing economy can reduce environmental impact and encourage sustainable consumption. Otherwise, it could become another facade of sustainability, contributing to the very eco-illusion it seeks to address.

Publication Trends in Greenwashing within Shared Economy Models

The publication trends reveal a notable increase in research output over the last decade, with a notable increase in publications in 2024 (276 articles). This acceleration indicates growing academic interest in greenwashing and the shared economy, particularly in the wake of increased global environmental consciousness and corporate transparency concerns. The relatively sparse contributions before 2019 suggest that greenwashing in the context of the shared economy is a relatively recent area of focus, highlighting a developing field of academic work. The change towards more substantial publication activity post-2020 indicates the heightened importance of addressing greenwashing practices within shared economy models, spurred by growing customer demand for sustainability and corporate responsibility (Park, 2021; Treepongkaruna, 2024).

Influential Authors, Journals, and Institutions

The analysis identifies key authors, journals, and institutions that have contributed importantly to the research area. Notably, Morsing, M. is the most influential author, contributing significantly to the body of work on sustainability and organizational ethics. The journal *Sustainability Switzerland* appears as a main outlet for research on greenwashing and the shared economy, underscoring the journal's importance in the sustainability field. Similarly, prestigious establishments such as Copenhagen Business School and Leuphana Universität Lüneburg have played a crucial part in influencing scholarly discourse, reflecting the worldwide collaboration on these issues. The identification of these influential authors, journals, and institutions highlights the collaborative and multidisciplinary character of this field's study, including a range of stakeholders from academic, governmental, and corporate spheres (Enginkaya Erkent & Sağlam, 2024; Leseure & Bennett, 2024).

Evolution of Publications Across Regions and Disciplines

The geographical distribution of publications reveals a strong presence from countries such as the United States, the United Kingdom, and China, with noteworthy contributions from European countries like Italy, Germany, and Spain. This distribution highlights the worldwide reach of research on greenwashing and the shared economy, with North America, Europe, and Asia leading the way in terms of scholarly contributions. The increasing number of publications from China suggests the country's rising importance in conversations around sustainability and environmental practices, driven by swift industrialization and the need for corporate accountability. The regional trends also reflect different degrees of involvement with sustainability topics, with some regions emphasizing greenwashing in relation to corporate practices, while others concentrate on the shared economy as a model for sustainable consumption (Aref, 2024; Qiang, 2024).

Leading Disciplines and Industries

The disciplines leading the charge in addressing greenwashing within the shared economy are primarily business ethics, sustainability studies, and environmental management. The frequency of keywords like *Corporate Social Responsibility (CSR)*, *Climate Change*, and *Environmental Economics* points to a strong junction between environmental sciences and business practices. This confluence of disciplines indicates a multidisciplinary approach to studying greenwashing, with scholars utilizing a range of fields to analyze how businesses in the shared economy can cultivate sustainable practices while avoiding misleading environmental claims (von Flüe et al., 2024; Naumova & Naumova, 2024). Industries such as transportation, energy, and tourism are particularly prominent in these discussions, with the shared economy model offering opportunities to promote minimizing environmental effects and increasing resource efficiency, albeit with the risk of greenwashing.

Frequently Cited Works and Methodologies

The most often referenced works emphasize the value of empirical research as well as theoretical frameworks in expanding our knowledge of greenwashing in the shared economy. Case studies, content analysis, and surveys are important approaches used in this research; these are especially useful for analyzing business practices and customer perceptions of greenwashing. These approaches enable academics to examine the subtleties of shared economy enterprises' sustainability claims and evaluate their veracity. It also seems that a common strategy for figuring out how consumers feel about greenwashing and its effects on sustainable purchasing is the use of qualitative techniques like focus groups and interviews (Boermans et al., 2024).

The Role of Technology in Mitigating Greenwashing

In the shared economy, technology is essential for combating greenwashing; developments in data analytics, blockchain, and AI are being mentioned more and more as instruments to improve accountability and transparency. AI-powered tools, for example, are being employed to track and verify sustainability claims, offering consumers a more reliable way to evaluate whether businesses are truly sticking to sustainable practices or merely engaging in greenwashing (Pata et al., 2024). Similarly, blockchain technology has been emphasized for its potential to ensure that sustainability-related claims are precisely documented and publicly accessible (Udeh et al., 2024). These technical solutions are seen as key enablers in the fight against greenwashing, as they can help bridge the trust gap between customers and businesses in the shared economy.

This research offers a thorough examination of the shared economy and greenwashing, including a summary of the major players, trends, and significant approaches in the industry. The results show that although scholarly interest in these subjects is growing, there are still a lot of unanswered questions, especially when it comes to interdisciplinary collaboration and technical advancements to counteract greenwashing. Future study on technology's role is fascinating since it has the potential to improve transparency and encourage more sustainable practices in the shared economy. For the shared economy to reach its full potential for sustainable growth, further research into practical tactics and solutions will be necessary as greenwashing continues to present difficulties for both consumers and businesses.

The findings of this study on greenwashing and the shared economy are profoundly aligned with several of the UNSDGs, especially those related to sustainability, responsible consumption, and climate action. The main idea of greenwashing, where businesses make misleading assertions about their environmental practices, directly aligns with the objective of responsible consumption and production (SDG 12). The prevalence of greenwashing in the shared economy models, as identified in this study, undermines efforts to cultivate sustainable practices by misleading customers into trusting they are holding up environmentally responsible businesses. The research highlights the need for more transparent and accountable business models to ensure that assertions about sustainability are substantiated and align with true ecological impact. It emphasizes the consequence of precise communication and accountability in advancing SDG 12, which focuses on developing sustainable consumption patterns, reducing waste, and promoting ecologically friendly manufacturing methods. Greenwashing is closely tied to SDG 13, which calls for drastic action to battle climate change and its impacts. False sustainability claims hinder initiatives to lower greenhouse gas emissions and alleviate climate-related risks. The literature reviewed in this study indicates that firms employing the shared economy model must be investigated for their environmental claims to avoid perpetuating ineffective practices. As the shared economy grows, especially in areas like mobility and resource sharing, the role of genuine sustainable initiatives becomes more critical in mitigating the climate crisis. This bibliometric analysis reveals the urgent need for the acceptance of ethical behavior and openness in both the shared economy and broader industries, ensuring that the environmental profits of these models are not overshadowed by deceptive marketing strategies. The research also connects to SDG 17, which emphasizes the importance of partnerships for achieving the SDGs. Many of the top contributing institutions, authors, and countries involved in sustainability research are working collaboratively to make the global discourse on sustainable business work.

Conclusion

This study reveals significant insights into the growing research on greenwashing within the shared economy. The findings draw attention to the growing volume of publications over recent years, particularly post-2020, reflecting heightened academic bring attention to the expansion of sustainability, business ethics, and environmental responsibility. The important journals, authors, and institutions have come out as central contributors, with a noticeable focus on sustainability, corporate social responsibility, and environmental management. The study also reinforces the worldwide nature of this research, with contributions spanning different areas, specifically North America, Europe, and Asia. However, despite the promising upgrade in this field, the prevalence of greenwashing presents a considerable problem to achieving genuine sustainable practices. As commercial organizations within the shared economy model continue to rise, the need for transparency, ethical communication, and accountability becomes more crucial to ensuring that sustainability claims are not misleading. This study adds to the current conversation about sustainability and advocates for a more thorough, sincere strategy to incorporate green concepts into business models worldwide.

The finding of the study imply that addressing greenwashing in shared economy models will require multisector collaboration, including policymakers, businesses, and researchers. These stakeholders can create frameworks using transdisciplinary cooperation that incentivize genuine sustainability efforts and discourage greenwashing, ultimately contributing to the achievement of SDG 17 by encouraging international collaborations towards sustainable growth. This study emphasizes the relationship between corporate ethics, environmental responsibility, and social accountability by relating greenwashing and the shared economy to the larger SDG framework. The implications of these findings emphasize how crucial it is to align corporate practices with the global sustainability agenda, ensuring that the shared economy can fulfill its commitment to lessening the impact on the environment without being tarnished by false promises.

Implications

Theoretical Implications

The findings of the study contribute to the understanding of the theoretical frameworks related to greenwashing and environmental ethics, where, in new business models , the distinction between sustainability promises and real actions is blurred. This study highlights the significance of incorporating technology solutions into sustainability frameworks to fight greenwashing, suggesting a potential route for further theoretical exploration. It requires more sophisticated theoretical models that can handle the complex dynamics of consumer trust, business transparency, and sustainable consumption in the fast-developing shared economy sector.

Practical Implications

The practical implications of this study offer valuable guidance for enterprises, policymakers, and researchers seeking to combat greenwashing within the shared economy. For businesses, the findings stress the value of transparency and authenticity in sustainability claims, urging companies to adopt clear, verifiable practices that are in line with worldwide sustainability standards. This is especially significant in the shared economy; trust and credibility are vital for long-term success. Policymakers can utilize these findings to tighten rules and build frameworks that encourage more corporate accountability in environmental claims, ensuring that enterprises in the shared economy adhere to ethical standards. This research also signifies that integrating new technologies could help mitigate greenwashing by furnishing verifiable evidence of a company's environmental impact.

Managerial Implications

This research emphasizes the responsibility of managers in maintaining the authenticity and openness of sustainability activities within the shared economy. Managers must hierarchize the development and execution of clear, measurable sustainability practices that exceed outermost claims, thereby avoiding the hazards involved with greenwashing. Managers should increase customer trust and protect the brand's image by using ethical marketing tactics and using technology like blockchain or AI to verify sustainability promises. This research also recommends that managers focus on continual monitoring and reporting of environmental consequences, aligning their company operations with global sustainability norms and legislation. This study suggests that managers build a culture of accountability inside their firms, ensuring that sustainability is ingrained throughout all business operations, from supply chain management to customer interactions.

Limitations and Scope of Future Work

This study is limited to the data in the Scopus database. Future research can be done on the other database sources, such as Web of Science and Google Scholar. This study does not investigate the specific mechanisms of greenwashing practices, which could give a more in-depth understanding of how these practices unfold in problems. Future work can expand on these limitations by conducting qualitative case studies or interviews with industry experts to explore the implications and challenges of greenwashing in the shared economy. Additionally, further investigations could explore the role of specific technologies in mitigating greenwashing and assess their efficacy in different industry contexts.

References

Aref, M. (2024). Sharing economy from the sustainable development goals perspective: A path to global prosperity. *Journal of Internet and Digital Economics*, *4*(2), 116–138. https://doi.org/10.1108/JIDE-02-2024-0007

Ashrafi, M., Magnan, G. M., Adams, M., & Walker, T. R. (2020). Understanding the conceptual evolutionary path and theoretical underpinnings of corporate social responsibility and corporate sustainability. *Sustainability*, *12*(3), 760. https://doi.org/10.3390/su12030760

Atkinson, L., & Kim, Y. (2015). "I drink it anyway and I know I shouldn't": Understanding green consumers' positive evaluations of norm-violating non-green products and misleading green advertising. *Environmental Communication*, *9*(1), 37–57. https://doi.org/10.1080/17524032.2014.932817

Badhwar, A., Islam, S., Tan, C. S. L., Panwar, T., Wigley, S., & Nayak, R. (2024). Unraveling green marketing and greenwashing: A systematic review in the context of the fashion and textiles industry. *Sustainability*, *16*(7), 2738. https://doi.org/10.3390/su16072738

Boedijanto, F. J. O., & Delina, L. L. (2024). Potentials and challenges of artificial intelligence-supported greenwashing detection in the energy sector. *Energy Research and Social Science*, *115*, 103638. https://doi.org/10.1016/j.erss.2024.103638

Boermans, D., Jagoda, A., Lemiski, D., Wegener, J., & Krzywonos, M. Environmental awareness and sustainable behavior management in Poland, Germany, and The Netherlands: A qualitative focus group study. *Germany, and The Netherlands: A Qualitative Focus Group Study*. https://doi.org/10.1016/j.jenvman.2024.122515

Bricker, B., & Justice, J. (2022). Identifying and challenging greenwashing through conciliatio. *Western Journal of Communication*, *86*(4), 521–540. https://doi.org/10.1080/10570314.2022.2087893

Carrigan, M., Magrizos, S., Lazell, J., & Kostopoulos, I. (2020). Fostering sustainability through technology-mediated interactions: Conviviality and reciprocity in the sharing economy. *Information Technology and People*, *33*(3), 919–943. https://doi.org/10.1108/ITP-10-2018-0474

de Freitas Netto, S. V., Sobral, M. F. F., Ribeiro, A. R. B., & Soares, G. R. D. L. (2020). Concepts and forms of greenwashing: A systematic review. *Environmental Sciences Europe*, *32*, 1–12. https://doi.org/10.1186/s12302-020-0300-3

Donthu, N., Kumar, S., Mukherjee, D., Pandey, N., & Lim, W. M. (2021). How to conduct a bibliometric analysis: An overview and guidelines. *Journal of Business Research*, *133*, 285–296. https://doi.org/10.1016/j.jbusres.2021.04.070

Eckhardt, G. M., Houston, M. B., Jiang, B., Lamberton, C., Rindfleisch, A., & Zervas, G. (2019). Marketing in the sharing economy. *Journal of Marketing*, *83*(5), 5–27. https://doi.org/10.1177/0022242919861929

Enginkaya Erkent, E., & Sağlam, M. (2024). Recycling reinforced: The synergistic dynamics of sustainable behavior. *Sustainability*, *16*(9). https://doi.org/10.3390/su16093827

Fudurich, G., & Mackay, K. (2020). Greening the guest bedroom: Exploring hosts' perspectives on environmental certification for Airbnb. *Tourism and Hospitality Research*, *20*(4), 423–434. https://doi.org/10.1177/1467358420911987

Grinevich, V., Huber, F., Karataş-Özkan, M., & Yavuz, Ç. (2019). Green entrepreneurship in the sharing economy: Utilising multiplicity of institutional logics. *Small Business Economics*, *52*, 859–876. https://doi.org/10.1007/s11187-017-9935-x

Guyader, H., Friman, M., & Olsson, L. E. (2021). Shared mobility: Evolving practices for sustainability. *Sustainability*, *13*(21), 12148. https://doi.org/10.3390/su132112148

Hao, X., Miao, E., Wen, S., Wu, H., & Xue, Y. (2024). Executive green cognition on corporate greenwashing behavior: Evidence from A-share listed companies in China. *Business Strategy and the Environment*. https://doi.org/10.1002/bse.4095

Huang, S. L., & Leau, Y. R. (2024). Understanding how consumers' perceived sustainability influences their continuance intention to use sharing economy services. *Sustainability*, *16*(17), 7753. https://doi.org/10.3390/su16177753

Jones, E. (2019). Rethinking greenwashing: Corporate discourse, unethical practice, and the unmet potential of ethical consumerism. *Sociological Perspectives*, *62*(5), 728–754. https://journals.sagepub.com/doi/abs/10.1177/0731121419849095#tab-contributors

Khalek, S. A., & Chakraborty, A. (2023). Access or collaboration? A typology of sharing economy. *Technological Forecasting and Social Change*, *186*, 122121. https://doi.org/10.1016/j.techfore.2022.122121

Lashitew, A. A. (2021). Corporate uptake of the Sustainable Development Goals: Mere greenwashing or an advent of institutional change? *Journal of International Business Policy*, *4*(1), 184–200. https://doi.org/10.1057/s42214-020-00092-4

Lee, E. J. H., Rindfleisch, A., & Kopalle, P. K. (2024). Innovation in the sharing economy: Examining Uber's transformation. *Journal of Product Innovation Management.* https://doi.org/10.1111/jpim.12768

Leseure, M. J., & Bennett, D. (2024). Adopting the materiality principle in sustainable operations management. *Sustainability*, *16*(15), 6572. https://doi.org/10.3390/su16156572

Light, A., & Miskelly, C. (2019). Platforms, scales and networks: Meshing a local sustainable sharing economy. *Computer Supported Cooperative Work*, *28*(3), 591–626. https://doi.org/10.1007/s10606-019-09352-1

Ling, X., & Wang, H. (2024). Green behavior strategies in the green credit market: Analysis of the impacts of enterprises' greenwashing and blockchain technology. *Sustainability*, *16*(11), 4858. https://doi.org/10.3390/su16114858

Mu, H., & Lee, Y. (2023). Greenwashing in corporate social responsibility: A dual-faceted analysis of its impact on employee trust and identification. *Sustainability*, *15*(22), 15693. https://doi.org/10.3390/su152215693

Muñoz, P., & Cohen, B. (2017). Mapping out the sharing economy: A configurational approach to sharing business modeling. *Technological Forecasting and Social Change*, *125*, 21–37. https://doi.org/10.1016/j.techfore.2017.03.035

Naumova, O., & Naumova, M. (2024). Sustainable development and greenwashing: AN analysis of sufficient consumption in the fashion industry. *Economics, Finance and Management Review*, *1*(17), 16–24. https://doi.org/10.36690/2674-5208-2024-1-16

Nygaard, A., & Silkoset, R. (2023). Sustainable development and greenwashing: How blockchain technology information can empower green consumers. *Business Strategy and the Environment*, *32*(6), 3801–3813. https://doi.org/10.1002/bse.3338

Park, S. B. (2018). Multinationals and sustainable development: Does internationalization develop corporate sustainability of emerging market multinationals? *Business Strategy and the Environment*, *27*(8), 1514–1524. https://doi.org/10.1002/bse.2209

Park, S. K. (2021). Legal strategy disrupted: Managing climate change and regulatory transformation. *American Business Law Journal*, *58*(4), 711–749. https://doi.org/10.1111/ablj.12194

Passas, I. (2024). Bibliometric analysis: The main steps. *Encyclopedia*, *4*(2). https://doi.org/10.3390/encyclopedia4020065

Pata, U. K., Si Mohammed, K., Nassani, A. A., & Ghosh, S. (2024). Discovering the sustainable development role of fintech credit and the pilot low carbon project on greenwashing in China. *Environment, Development and Sustainability*, 1–20. https://doi.org/10.1016/j.ribaf.2024.102481

Qayyum, A., Jamil, R. A., & Sehar, A. (2023). Impact of green marketing, greenwashing and green confusion on green brand equity. *Spanish Journal of Marketing-ESIC*, *27*(3), 286–305. https://doi.org/10.1108/SJME-03-2022-0032

Qiang, J. (2024). Reflections on the progress of green consumption within the sharing economy. *The Frontiers of Society, Science and Technology*, *6*(4). https://doi.org/10.25236/FSST.2024.060410

Saravade, S., Felix, R., & Fırat, A. F. (2021). From solidity to liquidity: Macro-level consumption patterns in the sharing economy. *Journal of Macromarketing*, *41*(2), 284–296. https://doi.org/10.1177/0276146720958184

Schor, J. B. (2017). Does the sharing economy increase inequality within the eighty percent? Findings from a qualitative study of platform providers. *Cambridge Journal of Regions, Economy and Society*, *10*(2), 263–279. https://doi.org/10.1093/cjres/rsw047

Şenyapar, H. N. D. (2024). Unveiling greenwashing strategies: A comprehensive analysis of impacts on consumer trust and environmental sustainability. *Journal of Energy Systems*, *8*(3), 164–181. https://doi.org/10.30521/jes.1436875

Singh, S., Yadav, S., Singh, A., Krishna, Y. J., & Singh, A. (2024). Harnessing technology for a sustainable future in finance: The role of artificial intelligence in promoting environmental responsibility. *Anticipating Future Business Trends: Navigating Artificial Intelligence Innovations* (Vol. 2, pp. 367–378). Springer Nature Switzerland. https://doi.org/10.1007/978-3-031-63402-4_30

Spaniol, M. J., Danilova-Jensen, E., Nielsen, M., Rosdahl, C. G., & Schmidt, C. J. (2024). Defining greenwashing: A concept analysis. *Sustainability*, *16*(20), 9055. https://doi.org/10.3390/su16209055

Sun, J., Sarfraz, M., & Ozturk, I. (2024). Eco-consciousness to eco-consumption: Unraveling the drivers of sustainable consumption behavior under the mediated-moderated model. *Environmental Science and Pollution Research*, 1–20. https://doi.org/10.1007/s11356-024-33560-y

Szabo, S., & Webster, J. (2021). Perceived greenwashing: The effects of green marketing on environmental and product perceptions. *Journal of Business Ethics*, *171*, 719–739. https://doi.org/10.1007/s10551-020-04461-0

Treepongkaruna, S. (2024). Corporate sustainability and biodiversity reporting: A proactive business strategy to mitigate litigation and reputational risks. *Business Strategy and the Environment*. https://doi.org/10.1002/bse.3840

Udeh, E. O., Amajuoyi, P., Adeusi, K. B., & Scott, A. O. (2024). The role of Blockchain technology in enhancing transparency and trust in green finance markets. *Finance & Accounting Research Journal*, *6*(6), 825–850. https://doi.org/10.51594/farj.v6i6.1181

Vangeli, A., Małecka, A., Mitręga, M., & Pfajfar, G. (2023). From greenwashing to green B2B marketing: A systematic literature review. *Industrial Marketing Management*, *115*, 281–299. https://doi.org/10.1016/j.indmarman.2023.10.002

von Flüe, L., Efferson, C., & Vogt, S. (2024). Green preferences sustain greenwashing: Challenges in the cultural transition to a sustainable future. *Philosophical Transactions of the Royal Society B*, *379*(1893), 20220268. https://doi.org/10.1098/rstb.2022.0268

Wang, W., Ma, D., Wu, F., Sun, M., Xu, S., Hua, Q., & Sun, Z. (2023). Exploring the knowledge structure and hotspot evolution of greenwashing: A visual analysis based on bibliometrics. *Sustainability*, *15*(3), 2290. https://doi.org/10.3390/su15032290

Wang, D., Yan, L., Ruan, F., & Zeng, X. (2022). An abductive analysis of debates on the impact of the sharing economy: A systematic review in a sustainable framework. *Sustainability*, *14*(7), 3996. https://doi.org/10.3390/su14073996

Yoganandham, G., Kareem, A. A., & Khan, E. M. I. (2024). Unveiling the shadows-corporate greenwashing and its multifaceted impacts on environment, society, and governance-A macro economic theoretical assessment. *Humanities*, *11* (S3), 20–29. https://doi.org/10.34293/sijash.v11is3-feb.7237

Zhang, D. (2024). The pathway to curb greenwashing in sustainable growth: The role of artificial intelligence. *Energy Economics*, *133*, 107562. https://doi.org/10.1016/j.eneco.2024.107562

Chapter 15

Age and Gender Differences in Consumer Attitudes Towards Cruelty-free Cosmetics: Integrating Social Identity Theory Within the Stimulus-Organism-Response Framework

Jyoti Malik[a], *Jyoti Grover*[a], *Deepak Bisht*[b] *and Pawan Kumar*[b]

[a]Maharishi Markandeshwar (Deemed to be university), India
[b]Lovely Professional University, India

Abstract

In recent years, a growing social consciousness and post-pandemic lifestyle shifts have prompted consumers to scrutinise the ethical implications of their choices, particularly in the beauty industry. The growing preference for cruelty-free cosmetics reflects this shift towards values-driven consumption. This study examines the psychological processes that diverse consumer demographics undergo when purchasing cruelty-free cosmetic products, a trend gaining momentum in socially aware markets. By integrating Social Identity Theory (SIT) into the Stimulus-Organism-Response (S-O-R) framework, it examines how gender moderates the relationship between key stimuli, such as cruelty-free labels, awareness, social media influence (SMI) and regulatory standards, and consumer responses, as measured by perceived value (PV). Using covariance-based structural equation modelling (CB-SEM) on data from 468 validated participants, the study reveals significant gender-based disparities in consumer behaviour. Findings indicate that Social Identity (SI) substantially moderates the relationship between stimuli and PV, suggesting that gender influences how consumers process information and make purchasing decisions about cruelty-free products. These insights provide practical implications for stakeholders in ethical consumerism, enabling them to align marketing and

Eco Illusions, 325–350

doi:10.1108/978-1-83662-782-120261015

communication strategies with evolving consumer values. The study's originality lies in its integration of SIT into the S-O-R framework, providing a fresh perspective on ethical consumption and highlighting the pivotal role of gender in shaping attitudes and behaviours towards cruelty-free cosmetics. Ultimately, it advances theoretical understanding and provides actionable insights to engage different consumer segments more effectively.

Keywords: Consumer attitudes; purchase intentions; social identity theory; Stimulus-Organism-Response (S-O-R) framework; cruelty-free cosmetics

Introduction

Consumer behaviour is being increasingly influenced by social consciousness, particularly in the cosmetics industry, where there is a growing demand for sustainable and ethical practices (Drobac et al., 2020). The transition to natural and organic products is being driven by consumers, who are encouraging companies to incorporate renewable, biodegradable and ethically sourced ingredients (Hussain & Dar, n.d.). Such products are identified through certification schemes and sustainability indices; however, consumers often become perplexed by the ambiguous terminology, underscoring the need for more precise guidelines and verification (Ainsworth, 1990; Hennigs et al., 2015). A broader concern for animal welfare and ethical issues is reflected in the increasing interest in cruelty-free cosmetics (Cavender, 2019). Research indicates that consumers' purchasing decisions are substantially influenced by their awareness of corporate social responsibility (CSR) and their values. Informed consumers exhibit a strong preference for cruelty-free products (Hansen et al., 2012; Kim & Bae, n.d.; Mishra, 2018). Despite this trend, there is a scarcity of research on the psychological processes underlying consumer attitudes towards cruelty-free cosmetics, particularly among different age and gender groups (Hansen et al., 2012). Systematic data collection is necessary to investigate the impact of regulatory norms, social media and cruelty-free labels on consumer behaviour, as these psychological aspects are often overlooked in existing research (Hansen et al., 2012; Hennigs et al., 2015; Kim & Bae, n.d.; Mishra, 2018).

This study examines the psychological mechanisms that influence the purchase of cruelty-free cosmetics by young consumers and whether these findings can be applied to older males as well. The research is based on the Social Identity Theory (SIT) , which is employed as an organism in the Stimulus-Organism-Response (SOR) model. The SOR framework provides a comprehensive framework for understanding the potential impact of external factors on the internal cognitions and behavioural psychology of consumers. This research aims to provide a comprehensive map of factors and customer behaviours that academicians and stakeholders can understand by integrating and validating theoretical work.

Theoretical Framework

The S-O-R Framework

The S-O-R framework, developed by Mehrabian and Russell in 1974, is a foundational model for studying human behaviour, particularly in consumer contexts. It consists of three key components:

Stimulus: An external event or situation that triggers a response.
Organism: The individual's internal processes, such as emotions, motivations and characteristics, which influence how they respond to the stimulus.
Response: The observable behaviour or reaction exhibited by the individual in response to the stimulus.

The S-O-R model is used to understand how various factors, such as the shopping environment or product qualities, influence consumer behaviour. It examines how external stimuli influence internal states and behaviours, emphasising that individuals' reactions are shaped by both the external environment and their internal characteristics. Researchers across various fields utilise this model to examine how environmental factors influence individual performance and behaviour, highlighting the dynamic interplay between stimuli, internal processes and responses.

S-O-R Framework in Social Consciousness Solution

The S-O-R framework provides a comprehensive approach to understanding human behaviour in response to environmental stimuli and consumer types. It suggests that cognitive and emotional responses to stimuli, including negative ones, are crucial for human adaptability. The S-O-R model helps explain consumer behaviour, including preferences for cruelty-free products, by linking human reactions to concerns about animal welfare. The framework has been applied to various non-verbal reaction theories that involve aesthetics and sensory experiences, such as colour, smell and music. These stimuli can influence emotional responses and subsequent decision-making. Research on the impact of age and gender within the S-O-R framework is mixed, with some studies showing significant effects while others do not. For example, findings by Islam and Rahman (n.d.) contrast with those by Wu and Li (2017) regarding the impact of gender on customer loyalty in online social commerce. This study aims to explore these dynamics further using the S-O-R framework.

Social Identity Theory

From this, SIT suggests that people draw on their memberships in these groups as explicit sources of self-definition and actively strive to maintain a positive image (Brown, 2000; Hogg & Williams, 2000). This highlights the relevance of in-group and out-group dynamics (Figueiredo et al., 2014), where individuals often favour their intragroup members over other intergroup counterparts to enhance self-esteem and social identity (SI) (Hogg & Williams, 2000). As a generalisation, this bias is illustrated in consumer behaviour – people tend to choose products that align with their in-group identity, for example, not buying cosmetics tested on animals. In making this selection, both brands have demonstrated their commitment to ethical consumption and social responsibility (Moghaddam, 2017). Such alignment not only reinforces the individual's self-perception but also serves to unite and create a shared identity among customers with similar beliefs and preferences (Brewer, 2001). The desire to belong has a psychological impact on consumer preferences.

Another example is the purchase of cruelty-free makeup, in which a buyer invests in a particular process that demonstrates their commitment and belief in caring for animals. The association and interaction of personal predicates, collective norms, provenance or place branding ideals and specific consumer predilections are particularly salient within the cosmetics industry (e.g. Hennigs et al., 2015; Reed, 2002), as well as in the work of Starr. Growth in demand for cruelty-free products – Growth sectors Cruelty-free growth driven by therapy (Lamont & Molnár, n.d.). Awareness of consumer social and environmental issues, especially a sense that these areas can be addressed to some extent.

Introduction of the Moderating Effects: Age and Gender

Research suggests that age and gender can influence memory and information processing, potentially impacting decision-making (Belham et al., 2017; Parola et al., 2018). Younger adults employ different cognitive strategies in situations of high emotional content, which may explain the motives behind consumers' purchasing of cruelty-free products. Gender differences also exist in working memory and information processing, with females performing better in socially relevant tasks (Belham et al., 2017). Younger consumers are more likely to consider product information in their purchasing decisions, as they are more attuned to brand stories that emphasise responsible practices (Elst et al., 2007). They are more likely to use alternative-based processing when emotion and cognition conflict, leading to different purchase intentions (PIs) (Kim & Bae, n.d.). SIT in the animal-friendly cosmetics field has found direct associations between environmental concern, awareness of sustainable production practices and ethical buying intention, which can be moderated by age and gender.

Building the Research Model and Hypotheses

Cruelty-free labels on food products indicate that they have not been tested on animals and have not been harmed during preparation (Hennigs et al., 2015). While cosmetic companies like CoverGirl and Maybelline have been associated with misleading advertising practices, cruelty-free food products have not been linked to false advertising (Duran et al., 2014; Mishra, 2018). However, these labels do not necessarily influence consumer behaviour to be healthy for animals (Wuisan & Februadi, 2018). Existing studies provide limited insights into how these labels affect consumer behaviour in the food industry (Sharma, 2020). Labels are generally accepted as important indicators of food quality, providing consumers with peace of mind and added benefits, which are considered part of the perceived value (PV) (Grewal, Roggeveen, & Nordfält, Year; Sirieix, Remaud, & Issanchou, 2012).

Hypothesis 1 (H1): Cruelty-free labelling (CFL) as a stimulus has a positive influence on the organism's Social Identity (SI) regarding cosmetic shopping during the transition to social consciousness.

Consumer Behaviour Awareness

Consumer choice behaviour is a key focus in marketing research, with a growing emphasis on consumer awareness (Hennigs et al., 2015). Understanding consumer behaviour is crucial for marketers and researchers to comprehend the factors that influence consumer purchasing decisions. Chang and Chen's (2022) study highlighted consciousness phenomena, with concerns about animal rights and safety influencing consumer decisions. Awareness of product qualities, such as those labelled as cruelty-free, influences consumer choices.

Hypothesis 2 (H2): Awareness (AW) as a stimulus positively influences the organism's SI regarding cosmetic shopping during the transitional age of social consciousness.

Impact of Social Media on Customers' Perception

Social media is a powerful tool for sharing marketing content and influencing customer engagement, attitude and intention (Schreiner, Körner, & Gössling, 2019). It involves information exposure, information seeking and social interaction (Ali et al., 2023). Perception is crucial in decision-making, and a brand's approach should focus on improving consumer awareness of cruelty-free labels and promoting animal welfare. People's attitudes towards cruelty-free labels can be influenced by their perceptions of the brand's social media marketing efforts. Express: Buyers as Info Seekers July 27, New Express: Info Seeking – When customers seek your marketing content that they like enough to interact with social platforms alone, it could be highly effective at changing customer opinions and behaviours. Positive perceptions are associated with favourable thoughts about a company, strong purchasing intentions for excellent products and a willingness to pay indirectly (Macgoldrick & Freestone, n.d.). Additionally, people form deeper emotional ties to their social media, spreading facts and reminding them of the importance of compassion towards animals (Ali et al., 2023). Adequate visibility aims to help individuals recognise and recall the brand more effectively.

Hypothesis 3 (H3): Social Media Influence (SMI) as a stimulus has a positive effect on the organism's Social Identity (SI) regarding cosmetic shopping during the transition period of social consciousness.

Legal and Regulatory Standards for the Beauty Industry

The beauty and personal care industry has shifted towards cruelty-free cosmetics due to campaigns and increased concerns for animal welfare (Rita da Silva Pereira, 2018). Consumer demand for cruelty-free cosmetics is driven by awareness and brand acceptance. Regulations worldwide have adopted animal welfare and legal standards for the cosmetic use of animals, but prosecution may impact the irrational practice of animal testing (Magano et al., 2022). This paper highlights regulatory and legal barriers as impediments to consumers' awareness and acceptance of cruelty-free cosmetics.

Hypothesis 4 (H4): Regulatory and Legal standards (RLS) as a stimulus positively determine the organism's Social Identity (SI) concerning cosmetic shopping during the transition age of social consciousness.

Environmental orientation and social compliance concepts influence consumer perceptions of cruelty-free labels and products. Environmental orientation refers to the relationship humans have with nature, while social compliance focuses on a brand's efforts to promote CFL. Research shows that consumers' understanding of cruelty-free labels is influenced by social indication characteristics. SIT, which relates to self-categorisation and social comparison, is crucial for understanding consumer behaviour. Pro-sustainable and environmentally friendly food is considered in terms of organic, green or ecological food.

Hypothesis 5 (H5): Social Identity (SI) as an organismic factor positively determines the perceived value (PV) of cosmetic shopping during the transition age of social consciousness.

Hypothesis 6 (H6): Social Identity (SI) as an organism positively determines the purchase intention (PI) concerning cosmetic shopping during the transition age of social consciousness.

Response Components: PV and PI

In this research, PV is defined as the sum of all perceptions a customer holds towards a particular service or technology. It has been more accurately considered in work such as Zeithaml et al. (1988). This research explores the impact of acquiring and investing in PV, which encompasses all customer perceptions of a service or technology. It also considers other acceptable value references, such as production price, bargaining tactics, emotional response quality and reputation. PV also encompasses instrumental, hedonic and social value perceptions.

Hypothesis 7 (H7): Customers' perceived value (PV) positively determines purchase intention (PI) concerning cosmetic shopping during the transition age of social consciousness.

Moderation Hypothesis

Numerous studies have empirically demonstrated the impact of gender and age on various adoption models, with their findings suggesting that both are moderators in certain instances (Alwahaishi & Snasel, 2013). As shown in Fig. 15.1, the moderating variables of gender and age are considered as multi-group controls, which are intended to enhance the model's ability to account for any inconsistent results. Nonetheless, the moderation hypotheses in this study were developed through an exploratory method, as was the case in previous studies, due to the initial development of the proposed model. Following the overall

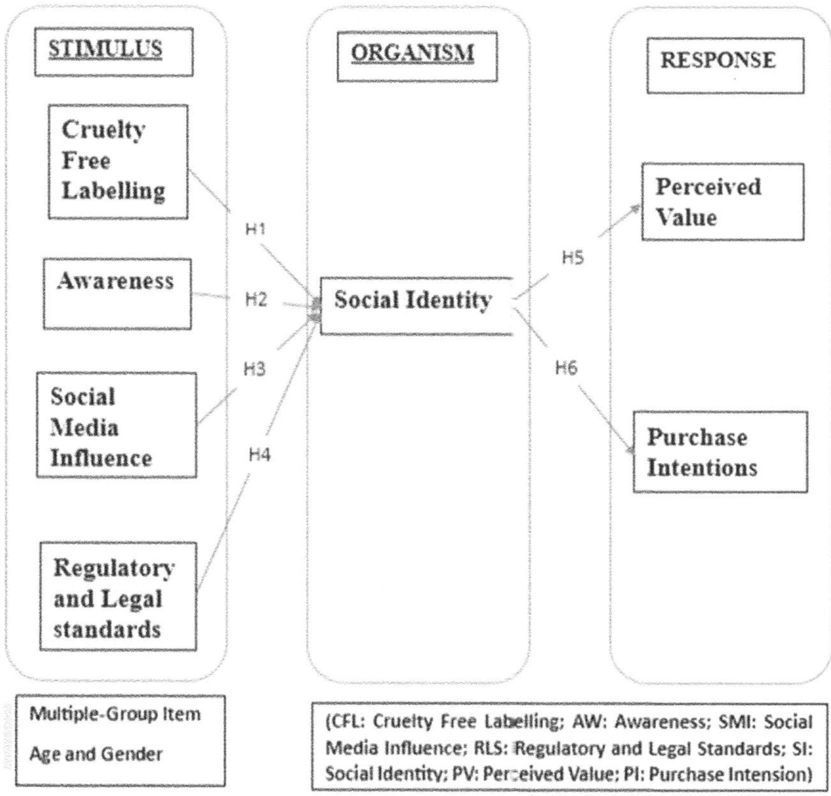

Fig. 15.1. Proposed Research Model. *Source:* Compiled for this study.

model evaluation, subgroup analysis will assess the moderating effect. Therefore, the following hypotheses are proposed to explore the age and gender differences in moderating cosmetic buying psychological processes throughout the social consciousness transition period.

Hypothesis 8 (H8): Gender moderates the relationship among all the constructs of the proposed model.

Hypothesis 9 (H9): Age moderates the relationship among all the constructs of the proposed model.

Conceptual Framework

This study employs a conceptual framework based on the Stimulus-Response Model and SIT, examining seven constructs: Cruelty-Free Labels, Awareness, SMI, RLS and SI, which affect PV and PI.

The research is divided into three groups: stimuli (cruelty-free labels, awareness, SMI, regulatory standards and SI), unconditional and dependent variables (PV and PI) and SI as a mediator. Table 15.1 provides definitions and measurement items for each construct.

Methodology and Data Demographic Distribution

The study employed a web-based questionnaire survey in Haryana, India, to evaluate the proposed model of CFL and its impact on PI. The survey collected demographic information and assessed various aspects of CFL, awareness, SMI, regulatory and legal SI, PV and PI. The questionnaire was designed in English to minimise linguistic and cultural biases and was created using Google Forms. The survey collected 507 empirical data points, with a response rate of 93.5%. The Kolmogorov-Smirnov test and Shapiro-Wilk test were used to analyse the data, revealing no statistically significant differences between early responders and late respondents. The results indicated that the data were not normally distributed.

Demographic Characteristics of the Data

The survey involved 55.8% of participants from Yamuna Nagar, 22.1% from Hissar and 21.5% from Rohtak, Haryana. The demographic consisted of female and male cosmetic consumers, with 27.01% aged 21–35 years and 51.07% under 36 years old. 24.06% of participants engaged in weekly cosmetic purchasing, with over 39% purchasing cosmetics on a weekly basis. Demographic data is presented in Table 15.2.

Data Analysis

Wang and Hwan analysed the demographic data of cosmetic consumers in Haryana, India, using online and random sampling techniques. The majority of participants were from Yamuna Nagar, Hissar and Rohtak, the most populous

Table 15.1. Constructs Used in the Study.

Constructs	***Items***	***Related Documents***
Cruelty-Free Label	CFL1: Buying cruelty-free products gives me pleasure. CFL2: Buying cruelty-free products would make me feel like a better person. CFL3: Consuming cruelty-free products would improve my quality of life. CFL4: The act of purchasing cruelty-free products is a source of personal satisfaction and empowerment. CFL5: Choosing cruelty-free products would reflect my commitment to ethical values.	Kim and Chung (n.d.); Kesari and Atulkar (n.d.); Ghazali et al. (2017)
Awareness	AW1: I understand cruelty-free products well. AW2: I have good experience in using cruelty-free products. AW3: I understand the advantages of cruelty-free products. AW4: I understand the impact of cruelty-free products. AW5: I can tell which products are cruelty-free and which are not.	Ghazali et al. (2017); Zollo et al. (2020)
Social Media Influence	SMI1: My engagement on social media influences my cruelty-free cosmetic purchases. SMI2: I use social media to search for information about cruelty-free cosmetics. SMI3: Contents about cruelty-free cosmetics on social media are trustworthy. SMI4: Content about cruelty-free cosmetics on social media is clear and concrete.	Gunawan & Huarng (2015) Goldsmith et al. (2000)

(Continued)

Table 15.1. *(Continued)*

Constructs	***Items***	***Related Documents***
	SMI5: I feel more confident in my cosmetic purchases when I see positive reviews from social media influencers.	
Regulatory and Legal Standards	RLS1: Regulations ensure the purchase of cruelty-free cosmetics. RLS2: Clear and consistent regulatory standards are crucial for cruelty-free cosmetics. RLS3: Due to insufficient regulation, most cosmetic products must be more accurate about their cruelty-free status. RLS4: Stricter regulatory standards would increase the number of cruelty-free products available. RLS5: Regulatory bodies or third-party certifications authenticate cruelty-free claims.	Gough and Thompson (2021)
Social Identity	SI1: Buying cruelty-free products would make me feel more accepted in society. SI2: Buying cruelty-free products would enhance my self-image. SI3: Buying Cruelty-Free products would improve my self-image. SI4: Buying cruelty-free products would make me feel more valued by myself. SI5: Buying cruelty-free products would make me feel more valued by myself.	Kumar and Ghodeswar (n.d.). Ghazali et al. (2017); Zollo et al. (2020)
Perceived Value	PV1: Cruelty-free products are eco-friendly. PV2: Cruelty-free products are in line with environmental preservation. PV3: I believe cruelty-free products are manufactured with full responsibility for the environment. PV4: Cruelty-free products are better	Bauer et al. (2013); Ghazali et al. (2017)

Table 15.1. *(Continued)*

Constructs	***Items***	***Related Documents***
	for the environment than regular products. PV5: Cruelty-free products contribute positively to sustainability efforts.	
Purchase Intention	PI1: I intend to purchase cruelty-free products in the future.	Ghazali et al. (2017); Zollo et al. (2020)
	PI2: I intend to learn more about cruelty-free products.	
	PI3: In the future, I intend to pay more attention to whether products are non- or cruelty-free.	
	PI4: I will purchase cruelty-free personal care products when needed.	

Source: Compiled for this study.

districts. The primary demographic consisted of individuals aged 21–35 years, with 27.01% of participants under 36 years. The study employed covariance-based structural equation modelling (CB-SEM) to measure the predicted underlying concepts and their corresponding indicators (Hair et al., 2014). The CB-SEM approach demonstrated excellent accuracy, surpassing both PLS-SEM and regression in small sample sizes (Bagozzi & Yi, 2012; Hair et al., 2010). The study used a two-step approach, including measurement model assessment and structural model review, to ensure the model's reliability and validity. The dataset appropriateness was evaluated using the Exploratory Factor Analysis (EFA) (SPSS) (Goodhue et al., 2012). The Kaiser criterion and scree plot were used to determine the number of underlying factors (Cattell, 1966). The findings suggest that eight components can be derived, consistent with the proposed model (Gefen et al., 2000).

Measurement Model

The measurement model's reliability and validity were assessed using Cronbach's alpha, with composite reliability, convergent validity and average variance extracted (AVE) exceeding recommended thresholds. The model's adequacy was confirmed by goodness-of-fit results, which met the criteria set by each index.

Table 15.2. Demographic Distribution of Participants.

Measure	Item	N	%
Gender	Male	194	41.13
	Female	274	57.87
Age	Below 20 Years	47	10
	21–35 Years	127	26.3
	36–50 Years	227	48.5
	Above 51 years	71	15.2
Frequency of Cosmetics Purchase	At least 1 time per day	28	6.0
	At least 1 time per week	114	24.4
	Every week	184	39.7
	At least 1 time per month	74	14.3
	At least 1 time in every 3 months	41	8.8
	At least 1 time per 6 months	26	5.6
	Never bought any cosmetics	06	1.3

Source: Compiled for this study.

The study also assessed the possibility of standard method bias using Harman's one-factor test and the adequacy of a single-factor model. The results showed that the model fits the data well and that a single factor does not account for the majority of the variance. The model is suitable for additional evaluation of its structural model, as it meets the requirements set forth by Podsakoff et al. (2003).

Table 15.3 presents the results for *construct reliability, convergent validity and discriminant validity* measures for all latent constructs in the study. Internal consistency reliability was assessed using Cronbach's alpha (CA) and composite reliability (CR). All CA values ranged from 0.934 (Cruelty-Free Label and PI) to 0.964 (RLS), exceeding the recommended minimum of 0.70 (Nunnally & Bernstein, 1994). Similarly, CR values ranged from 0.931 (SMI) to 0.964 (RLS), surpassing the 0.70 threshold (Hair et al., 2014), thus confirming strong reliability. Convergent validity was examined through the AVE, with all constructs exceeding the minimum criterion of 0.50 (Fornell & Larcker, 1981).

Discriminant validity was assessed using the Fornell–Larcker criterion (Fornell & Larcker, 1981) as shown in Table 15.4, wherein the square root of the AVE for each latent construct should be greater than its correlations with other constructs. As shown in Table 15.4, the square root of AVE values (presented on the diagonal in bold) ranged from 0.883 (SI) to 0.920 (PI), all exceeding the recommended threshold of 0.70 (Hair et al., 2014). These values were

Table 15.3. Latent Constructs' CA, CR, AVE, MSV and Items' Factor Loading.

Factors	**CA**	**CR**	**AVE**	**MSV**	**Items**	**Loadings**
Cruelty-free label	0.934	0.934	0.810	0.509	CFL1	0.873
					CFL2	0.910
					CFL3	0.907
					CFL4	0.899
					CFL5	0.900
Awareness	0.937	0.934	0.824	0.325	AW1	0.894
					AW2	0.878
					AW3	0.915
					AW4	0.834
					AW5	0.879
Social media influence	0.950	0.931	0.800	0.270	SMI1	0.898
					SMI2	0.910
					SMI3	0.930
					SMI4	0.904
					SMI5	0.899
Regulatory and legal standards	0.964	0.964	0.828	0.412	RLS1	0.864
					RLS2	0.891
					RLS3	0.902
					RLS4	0.869
					RLS5	0.865
Social identity	0.945	0.946	0.779	0.414	SI1	0.903
					SI2	0.887
					SI3	0.837
					SI4	0.898
					SI5	0.873
Perceived value	0.956	0.941	0.785	0.445	PV1	0.909
					PV2	0.925
					PV3	0.927
					PV4	0.907
					PV5	0.928
Purchase intention	0.934	0.956	0.874	0.505	PI1	0.881
					PI2	0.902
					PI3	0.910
					PI4	0.904

Source: Compiled for this study.

CA, Cronbach's alpha; *CR*, Composite reliability; *AVE*, average variance extracted; *MSV*, maximum shared squared variance.

Table 15.4. Latent Constructs' Square Root of AVE and Correlation.

	CFL	AW	SMI	RLSS	SI	PV	PI
CFL	**0.895**						
AW	0.569	**0.904**					
SMI	0.515	0.412	**0.884**				
RLS	0.654	0.410	0.421	**0.905**			
SI	0.626	0.421	0.461	0.561	**0.883**		
PV	0.664	0.510	0.464	0.568	0.532	**0.887**	
PI	0712	0.521	0.469	0.594	0.591	0.634	**0.920**

Source: Compiled for this study.

Number in Bold: Latent constructs' square root of AVE.

consistently greater than the corresponding inter-construct correlations, which ranged from 0.410 to 0.712. For instance, the square root of AVE for Cruelty-Free Label (0.895) was higher than its highest correlation with PI (r = 0.712). This pattern held across all constructs, indicating that each construct measured a conceptually distinct phenomenon and confirming discriminant validity for the measurement model. The highest observed correlation (0.712 between Cruelty-Free Label and PI) remained below the square root of AVE for both constructs (0.895 and 0.920, respectively), further supporting the adequacy of the measurement model. Consequently, the constructs – Cruelty-Free Labels, Awareness, SMI, RLS, SI, PV and PI – are empirically distinct within the context of the SOR framework integrated with SIT.

Here, Table 15.5 presents the fit indices for the single-factor, measurement and structural models, along with subgroup models for age and gender. The single-factor model demonstrated poor fit (χ^2/df = 12.741, CFI = 0.524, RMSEA = 0.178), indicating that common method bias was not a significant concern. In contrast, the measurement model showed excellent fit (χ^2/df = 1.197, CFI = 0.998, RMSEA = 0.021), meeting all recommended criteria (Hair et al., 2010). The original structural model (χ^2/df = 1.413, CFI = 0.981, RMSEA = 0.031) and subgroup models by age and gender also met acceptable thresholds, confirming the model's robustness across demographic groups.

Structural Model

The research developed a structural equation model using AMOS, which was then divided into two variants for age and gender subgroups, as shown in Table 15.6. All models met goodness-of-fit criteria, indicating satisfactory fit. The R_2 values of endogenous variables were analysed, with gender-subgroup models showing the highest explanatory power for CFL, SI and PI, and age-subgroup models showing the most robustness for PV.

Table 15.5. The Model Fit of Each Model.

	X^2/df	CFI	GFI	AGFI	NFI	TLI	RMSEA
Recommend value	<3	>0.9	>0.8	>0.8	>0.9	>0.9	<0.08
Single-factor model	12.741	0.524	0.394	0.395	0.502	0.527	0.178
Measurement model	1.197	0.998	0.917	0.908	0.901	0.949	0.021
Original structural model	1.413	0.981	0.923	0.900	0.882	0.941	0.031
Model with age subgroups	1.401	0.967	0.965	0.824	0.786	0.901	0.034
Model with gender subgroups	1.392	0.971	0.960	0.830	0.810	0.902	0.032

Source: Compiled for this study.

Table 15.6. R_2 Values of Endogenous Variables in Different Models.

	R^2		
Endogenous Variables	**Original Structural Model**	**Model with Age Subgroups**	**Model with Gender Subgroups**
CFL	0.32	0.31	0.34
SI	0.55	0.58	0.77
PV	0.59	0.56	0.48
PI	0.46	0.41	0.49

Source: Compiled for this study.

Furthermore, the hypotheses were meticulously tested using the coefficient of each path. The comprehensive results are depicted in Table 15.7. Specifically, except for H4 (RLS→SI) being rejected (β = 0.061, p = 0.048), all the other hypotheses were supported in the original structural model and sorted by the significance from high to low, shown as follows: H1 (CFL→SI, β = 0.281, $p <$ 0.001), H2 (AW→SI, β = 0.206, $p <$ 0.001), H3 (SMI→SI, β = 0.202, $p <$ 0.001), H5 (SI→PV, β = 0.841, $p <$ 0.001), H6 (SI→PI, β = 0.542, $p <$ 0.001), H7 (PV→PI, β = 0.311, $p <$ 0.001).

Table 15.7. Hypothesis Testing of the Original Structural Model.

		Original Model→				
H	**Relations**	**Estimates**	**S.E.**	**T**	***P***	**Decision**
H1	CFL→SI	0.2810	0.0517	3.4581	***	Supported
H2	AW→SI	0.2062	0.0429	3.2234	***	Supported
H3	SMI→SI	0.2021	0.0436	4.3191	***	Supported
H4	RLS→SI	0.0610	0.0324	1.5244	0.048	Rejected
H5	SI→PV	0.8410	0.0345	5.1961	***	Supported
H6	SI→PI	0.5420	0.0465	7.3321	***	Supported
H7	PV→PI	0.3113	0.0691	6.3840	***	Supported

Source: Compiled for this study.

Est., estimate; *S.E.*, standard error; *T*, t-value; *P*, *p*-value; ***, *p*-value <0.01.

Hypothesis Testing and Multi-Group Analysis

Tables 15.8, 15.9 and 15.10 summarise the results of hypothesis testing for the original model and multi-group analyses by gender and age. In the original structural model (Table 15.8), all hypotheses were supported ($p < 0.001$) except H4 (RLS → SI), which was rejected ($p = 0.048$). The strongest relationship was found for H5 (SI → PV; $\beta = 0.841$, $p < 0.001$).

Gender-based analysis (Table 15.9) revealed differences in path significance. H1 (Cruelty-Free Label → SI) was supported for both males and females, with a Z-score of 0.436 indicating no significant gender difference. H2 (Awareness → SI)

Table 15.8. Hypothesis Testing of the Original Structural Model.

		Original Model				
H	**Relations**	**Est.**	**S.E.**	**T**	***P***	**Dec.**
H1	CFL→SI	0.281	0.051	3.458	***	Supported
H2	AW →SI	0.206	0.042	3.22	***	Supported
H3	SMI→SI	0.202	0.043	4.319	***	Supported
H4	RLS→SI	0.061	0.032	1.524	0.048	Rejected
H5	SI→PV	0.841	0.034	5.196	***	Supported
H6	SI→PV	0.542	0.046	7.332	***	Supported
H7	PV→PI	0.311	0.069	6.384	***	Supported

Est., estimate; *S.E.*, Standard error; *T*, tValue; *P*, *p*-Value; Dec, Decision; Sup, Supported; Rej, Rejected; ***, *p*-value<0.01.

Table 15.9. Hypothesis Testing of the Subgroup.

Model with Gender Subgroups												
		Male					Female					
H	**Relations**	**Est**	**S.E.**	**T**	***P***	**Dec.**	**Est.**	**S.E.**	**T**	***P***	**Dec.**	**Z-score**
H1	CFL→ SI	0.158	0.067	2.401	0.017	Sup.	0.176	0.069	2.735	0.007	Sup.	0.436
H2	AW→ SI	0.162	0.044	3.014	0.004	Sup.	0.048	0.065	0.498	0.556	Rej.	−1.495
H3	SMI→ SI	0.365	0.056	4.009	***	Sup.	0.141	0.071	20251	0.033	Sup.	−1.273
H4	RLS→ SI	0.293	0.066	5.075	***	Sup.	0.134	0.069	1.766	0.052	Rej.	−1.783
H5	SI→ PV	0.307	0.062	5.154	***	Sup.	0.455	0.089	5.397	***	Sup.	3.99
H6	SI→ PV	0.317	0.065	5.697	***	Sup.	0.422	0.089	4.321	***	Sup.	2.531
H7	PV→ PI	0.395	0.073	5.447	***	Sup.	0.339	0.078	5.245	***	Sup.	0.045
Model with Gender Subgroups												
		< 35					>35					
H	**Relations**	**Est**	**S.E.**	**T**	***P***	**Dec.**	**Est.**	**S.E.**	**T**	***P***	**Dec.**	**Z-score**
H1	CFL→ SI	0.197	0.062	3.101	0.001	Sup.	0.172	0.081	2.58	0.01	Sup.	1.421
H2	AW→ SI	0.074	0.057	1.342	0.19	Rej.	0.074	0.087	1.253	0.556	Rej.	−0.253
H3	SMI→ SI	0.143	0.066	2.141	0.032	Sup.	0.275	0.071	4.087	0.033	Sup.	−0.311
H4	RLS→ SI	0.21	0.065	3.329	***	Sup.	0.285	0.052	3.285	0.052	Sup.	0.098
H5	SI→ PV	0.282	0.067	4.373	***	Sup.	0.165	0.072	1.872	***	Rej..	−0.056
H6	SI→ PV	0.201	0.077	2.656	0.007	Sup.	0.332	0.085	4.518	***	Sup.	−1.249
H7	PV→ PI	0.478	0.075	6.572	***	Sup.	0.267	0.083	3.673	***	Sup.	1.283

Est., estimate; *S.E.*, Standard error; *T*, tValue; *P*, *p*-Value; Dec, Decision; Sup, Supported; Rej, Rejected; ***, *p*-value$<$0.01; **: *p*-value$<$0.05; *, *p* value $<$ 0.01.

Table 15.10. Comparison Between the Models of Gender and Age Subgroups.

	Model with Gender Subgroups			Model with Age Subgroups		
	Chi-square	**df**	**p-Value**	**Chi-square**	**df**	**p-Value**
Unconstrained	1501.519	1204		1564.315	1204	
Fully constrained	1551.458	1148		1596.514	1148	
Number of groups		2			2	
Difference	49.939	36	0.056	32.199	36	0.650
Model in variant		No			Yes	

Source: Compiled for this study.

Table 15.11. The Significant Determinants of Each Subgroup.

Mediator	**Sub-Group**	**Stimulus**	**Organism**	**Response**
Gender	Male	Cruelty Free label; awareness; social media influence; regulatory and legal standards	Social identity	Perceived value; Purchase intention
	Female	Cruelty Free label; social media influence	Social identity	Perceived value; Purchase intention
Age	Below 35 years	Cruelty Free label; social media influence; regulatory and legal standards	Social identity	Perceived value; Purchase intention
	Above 35 years	Cruelty Free label; social media influence; regulatory and legal standards	Social identity	Perceived value; Purchase intention

Source: Compiled for this study.

was significant for males ($p = 0.004$) but not for females ($p = 0.556$). H3 (SMI → SI) was significant for both genders, with a more substantial effect for males. H4 (RLS → SI) was significant for males ($p < 0.001$) but marginal for females ($p = 0.052$). H5 (SI → PV) showed a notable gender effect, being rejected for males but strongly supported for females. H6 (SI → PI) also revealed gender disparity, though both genders supported H7 (PV → PI). Age-based analysis showed fewer differences. Most relationships held across groups, except H5 (SI → PV), which was significant only for participants under 35 years.

Table 15.10's chi-square difference tests indicated no significant difference for age groups ($p = 0.650$), but near-significant model non-invariance for gender ($p = 0.056$). This suggests that gender moderates several structural paths, whereas age has minimal moderating influence.

Discussion

This research examines the psychological shopping processes of customers seeking cruelty-free cosmetic products during the transition to an ethical consciousness, focusing on the S-O-R components and their determinants, as summarised in Table 15.11.

This study examines the convergence of SIT and S-O-R models, explaining three alternative processes regarding consumer attitudes towards cruelty-free cosmetics, depending on age/gender. This interpretation essentially argues that group membership and personality traits related to social identification influence consumer behaviour – in this case, attitudes towards animal conservation (Hogg & Williams, n.d.; Hogg et al.). The results indicated that younger and female individuals with high social group membership hold positive beliefs about cruelty-free products. There are issues regarding prioritising cruelty-free cosmetics among women more than men that warrant reflection – research by Graça et al. Levendosky et al. (2018) also discovered that women tended to be more empathetic towards animals. In line with this effect, Magano et al. reported higher empathy, resulting in a greater dislike for products containing substances associated with animal cruelty (2022). This humane response reflects a broader moral concern for the well-being of those non-human animals, leading many women to opt for cruelty-free products.

For a long time, women have been considered the primary target audience for beauty and cosmetic products due to their pervasive association with ideas about beauty and attractiveness (Pervin & Ranchhod, n.d.). As a result, the public is becoming increasingly receptive to marketing and advocacy efforts that address concerns over the ethics of animal testing. This cultural affiliation makes women more likely to integrate cruelty-free products into their beauty routine. In addition, the beauty industry has garnered a significant shift towards ethical and sustainable practices driven mainly by female consumer demand (Wuisan & Februadi, 2018). Women tend to have a greater preference for products – and the companies that produce them – across industries whose values align more closely with their own. If a product is cruelty-free or environmentally responsible, then you know she will back it. Such a tendency is exacerbated by promoter social media and influencers, where female voices campaigning for cruelty-free products are preponderant (Magano et al., 2022).

Additionally, the psychological components are essential because women often feel a more profound internal connection to the ethical implications of their purchasing decisions. In my experience, beauty is the creation of a beautiful human being who nurtures themselves and their gifts. By using cruelty-free beauty products, individuals can align their ethical stance with their cosmetic behaviour, creating consonance in values and outward actions (Hennigs et al., 2015).

Ultimately, the cosmetics industry is designed with women in mind, as they are the primary purchasers. Consequently, cruelty-free products are often marketed more aggressively to women, thus reinforcing the idea that esteemed beauty choices derive mostly from femininity (Jones, 2006). This targeted advertising helps establish a connection between women and cruelty-free makeup. In general, women have increased their use of poor-cell cosmetics by a complex mix of ethical considerations, cultural practices in raising children, consumer behaviour, psychological aspects, marketing strategies, business interests and incentives to view these goods as more important than those for males. Epoch. When marketers segment the market by age, it reveals consumer perceptions prominently, and gender has a more substantial impact on these beliefs. Inserting SIT in the S-O-R model suggests that social identities provide a fuller explanation of psychological responses beyond what can be predicted only by S-O-R. In conclusion, the study suggests that further research could be conducted to investigate the influence of age and gender on customer perceptions of cruelty-free cosmetics.

Conclusion

This study examined how incorporating SIT into the S-O-R framework could be pivotal in understanding consumer attitudes towards cruelty-free cosmetics, particularly in the context of CSR marketing. The research model was empirically tested on a sample of 474 subjects from Haryana, encompassing both males and females across all age groups. This article examines the impact of being part of communities focused on environmental issues versus other attitudes towards cruelty-free cosmetics. These results confirm the successful inclusion of SIT within the explanatory scope of customer behaviour through a theoretical lens such as S-O-R. Young consumers show a greater preference for living beings compared to older generations, and the liberal view of female consumer rights for life has led to an increased interpretation of animal experiments as a form of free productivism.

Contributions Finding

This study contributes to the existing literature on the academic underpinnings and real-world applications of consumer behaviour, marketing and SI. One of their main findings was the importance of social identities (the authors focused on age and gender) as determinants for how customers perceive cruelty-free cosmetics, which, to my knowledge, have not been examined before. The findings suggest that cosmetic manufacturers must integrate their marketing strategies to appeal to Millennial and Gen Z buyers while also targeting customers of older age groups. The significance of consumer awareness of cosmetic components reinforces the role of attitude.

Limitations and Future Works

The study has limitations, including hypothetical scenarios, the risk of social desirability bias and the sampling of individuals from limited demographics. Future research may investigate whether in-person interviews, orientation assessments of animal welfare measures, and financial incentives influence cruelty-free shopping decisions or examine individual differences in the drivers of conspicuous consumption. Future research can also investigate how authoritarian attitudes and gender gaps affect ethical consumption behaviours. However, the role of SI in shaping brand engagement and identification should also be taken into consideration.

References

Ainsworth, R. (1990). Buying organic: An exploration of consumer perceptions. British Food Journal, 92, 24–28.

Ali, L., Islam, T., & Jahan, S. (2023). Social media marketing effect on consumer behaviour: A study on the fast fashion industry of Bangladesh. *South Asian Journal of Business Studies.*

Alwahaishi, S., & Snasel, V. (2013). Factors affecting the adoption of mobile banking in Saudi Arabia: An exploratory study. *International Journal of Marketing Studies, 5*, 151.

Anderson, J. C., & Gerbing, D. W. (1988). Structural equation modeling in practice: A review and recommended two-step approach. *Psychological Bulletin, 103*(3), 411–423. https://doi.org/10.1037/0033-2909.103.3.411

Bagozzi, R., & Yi, Y. (2012). Specification, evaluation, and interpretation of structural equation models. *Journal of the Academy of Marketing Science, 40*(1), 8–34. https://doi.org/10.1007/s11747-011-0278-x

Bauer, H. H., Heinrich, D., & Schäfer, D. B. (2013). The effects of organic labels on global, local, and private brands: More hype than substance? *Journal of Business Research, 66*, 1035–1043. https://doi.org/10.1016/j.jbusres.2011.12.028

Belham, F. S., Henson, R. N., & Dritschel, B. H. (2017). Age-related changes in the neural response to emotional distraction. *Journal of Cognitive Neuroscience, 29*, 1286–1300.

Bollen, K. A. (1989). *Structural equations with latent variables.* Wiley.

Brewer, M. B. (2001). The many faces of social identity: Implications for political psychology. *Political Psychology, 22*, 115–127.

Brown, S. L. (2000). Group processes and team decision making. *Reviews of Industrial and Organizational Psychology, 19*, 143–172.

Cattell, R. B. (1966). The screen test for the number of factors. *Multivariate Behavioral Research*, *1*(2), 245–276. https://doi.org/10.1207/s15327906mbr0102_10

Cavender, B. (2019). *The Sustainable fashion handbook*. Thames & Hudson.

Chang, C. H., & Chen, Y. S. (2022). Predicting young consumers' intention to purchase vegan food: The role of food attributes, consumer attitude, and social influence. *Foods, 11*, 1604.

de Luna, I. R., Liébana-Cabanillas, F., Sánchez-Fernández, J., & Muñoz-Leiva, F. (2018). Mobile payment is not all the same: The adoption of mobile payment systems depends on the technology applied. *Technological Forecasting and Social Change*, *146*, 931–944. https://doi.org/10.1016/j.techfore.2018.01.015

Doll, W., Xia, W., & Torkzadeh, G. (1994). A confirmatory factor analysis of the end-user computing satisfaction instrument. *MIS Quarterly*, *18*(4), 453–461. https://doi.org/10.2307/249524

Drobac, D., Gržinić, J., & Dulčić, Ž. (2020). Sustainable consumption in the beauty and personal care market: A cross-cultural study. *Sustainability*, *12*, 7504. https://doi.org/10.3390/su12187504

Duran, I., Bikfalvi, A., & Llach, J. (2014, November 1). New facets of quality: A multiple case study of green cosmetic manufacturers. *Journal of Business Ethics*, *44*, 44–61. https://doi.org/10.26595/eamr.2014.1.1.3

Duran, S., Vidal, T., & Ares, G. (Year). When cause-related marketing enhances consumers' willingness to pay: The role of ethical judgment and price consciousness. *Journal of Business Ethics, 124*, 47–57.

Elst, J. V. D., Van Boxtel, M. P., Van Breukelen, G. J., & Jolles, J. (2007). The influence of age and education on cognitive function: An overview of cross-sectional and longitudinal studies. *Neuropsychology Review, 17*, 289–309.

Ewi, W. W. A., & Avicenna, F. (2020, July 14). Social media marketing: Consumer behavior on the cruelty-free concern of beauty brands. *Universitas Pembangunan Nasional Veteran Yogyakarta*, *17*(1), 95. https://doi.org/10.31315/jik.v17i1.2379

Figueiredo, P. S., Grau, L., & Folgado, M. J. (2014). The influence of consumer innovativeness on fashion involvement, impulse buying, and brand switching. *Journal of Fashion Marketing and Management: International Journal*, *18*, 538–554.

Fornell, C. G., & Larcker, D. F. (1981). Evaluating structural equation models with unobservable variables and measurement error. *Journal of Marketing Research*, *18*(1), 39–50. https://doi.org/10.1177/002224378101800104

Gefen, D., Straub, D., & Boudreau, M. C. (2000). Structural equation modeling and regression: Guidelines for research practice. *Communications of the Association for Information Systems*, *4*(1), 7. https://doi.org/10.17705/1CAIS.00407

Ghazali, E. M., Mutum, D. S., & Ariswibowo, N. (2017). Impact of religious values and habits on an extended green purchase behaviour model. *International Journal of Consumer Studies*, *42*, 657–669. https://doi.org/10.1111/ijcs.12472

Goldsmith, R. E., Lafferty, B. A., & Newell, S. J. (2000). The impact of corporate credibility and celebrity credibility on consumer reaction to advertisements and brands. *Journal of Advertising, 29*, 43–54.

Goodhue, D. L., Lewis, W., & Thompson, R. (2012). Does PLS have advantages for small sample sizes or non-normal data? *MIS Quarterly*, *36*(3), 981–1001. https://doi.org/10.2307/41703491

Gough, L. R., & Thompson, K. H. (2021). Regulating animal testing in the cosmetics industry: The impact of legal standards on consumer behavior and industry practices. *Journal of Business Ethics*, *174*(3), 455–470. https://doi.org/10.1007/s10551-020-04500-1

Graça, J., Calheiros, M. M., Oliveira, A., & Milfont, T. L. (2018, July 1). Why are women less likely to support animal exploitation than men? The mediating roles of social dominance orientation and empathy. *Personality and Individual Differences*, *129*, 66–69. https://doi.org/10.1016/j.paid.2018.03.007

Grewal, W. B. D. K. B. M. D. (2023, November 10). Effects of price, brand, and store information on buyers' product evaluations. *Journal of Marketing*, *28*, 305. https://doi.org/10.1177/002224379102800305

Grewal, D., Roggeveen, A. L., & Nordfält, J. (Year). Value-based pricing in a digital world. *Journal of the Academy of Marketing Science*, *51*, 3–23.

Gunawan, D. D., & Huarng, K. H. (2015). Viral effects of social networks and media on consumers' purchase intention. *Journal of Business Research*, *68*, 2237–2241. https://doi.org/10.1016/j.jbusres.2015.02.004

Hair, J. F., Black, W. C., Babin, B. J., & Anderson, R. E. (2010). *Multivariate data analysis* (7th ed.). Prentice-Hall.

Hair, J. F., Gabriel, M. L. D. S., & Patel, V. K. (2014). AMOS covariance-based structural equation modeling (CB-SEM): Guidelines on its application as a marketing research tool. *Brazilian Journal of Marketing*, *13*(2), 44–55.

Hansen, H., Busch, J., & Jacobsen, E. (2012). Consumers, stakeholders, and dolphin-friendly tuna: What influences consumers to buy, and keep buying, dolphin-friendly tuna? *Journal of Consumer Behaviour*, *11*, 71–81.

Hennigs, N., Karampournioti, E., & Wiedmann, K. P. (2015, December 31). *Do as you would be done by: The importance of animal welfare in the global beauty care industry* (pp. 109–125). Springer Nature. https://doi.org/10.1007/978-981-10-0111-6_5

Hennigs, N., Karampournioti, E., & Wiedmann, K. P. (n.d.). Do as you would be done by: The importance of animal welfare in the global beauty care industry. *Journal of Business Ethics*, *128*, 549–568.

Henseler, J., Ringle, C. M., & Sarstedt, M. (2014). A new criterion for assessing discriminant validity in variance-based structural equation modeling. *Journal of the Academy of Marketing Science*, *43*(1), 115–135. https://doi.org/10.1007/s11747-014-0403-8

Hess, T. M., Germain, A., & Hodges, E. A. (n.d.). Aging and emotional memory: Cognitive mechanisms and neuroimaging findings. *Current Opinion in Behavioral Sciences*, *17*, 85–93.

Hogg, M. A., & Williams, K. D. (n.d.). From I to we: Social identity and the collective self. *Group Dynamics: Theory, Research, and Practice*, *4*, 80–99.

Hussain, A., & Dar, S. H. (n.d.). Impact of social media marketing on consumer purchase intention: The mediating role of brand image and brand awareness. *Journal of Global Marketing Insights*, *6*, 60–77.

India, K. S. U. O. D. D. (2023, November 10). *Label perceptions and consumer decision-making: An empirical investigation* (Vol. 283). Springer. https://link.springer.com/chapter/10.1007/978-3-319-47331-4_283

Islam, J. U., & Rahman, Z. (n.d.). Linking e-satisfaction to customer loyalty: Moderating roles of perceived value, habit, and switching cost in online retail banking. *International Journal of Bank Marketing*, *35*, 232–252.

Jannoo, Z., Yap, B. W., Auchoybur, N., & Lazim, M. A. (2014). The effect of nonnormality on CB-SEM and PLS-SEM path estimates. *International Scholarly and Scientific Research & Innovation*, *8*(2), 285–291.

Jones, M. (2006). *Stimulus-organism-response framework: Definition & examples* [Website Name].

Kesari, B., & Atulkar, S. (n.d.). Satisfaction of mall shoppers: A study on perceived utilitarian and hedonic shopping values. *Journal of Retailing and Consumer Services*, *31*, 242–249. https://doi.org/10.1016/j.jretconser.2016.03.005

Kim, M. H., & Bae, S. (n.d.). Impact of consumer environmental concern in the post-COVID-19 era on purchase intention of environmentally friendly cosmetics with awareness of sustainability management activities from cosmetics companies as a medium. *Sustainability*, *13*, 10424.

Kim, Y., & Bae, S. (n.d.). The effect of consumer ethnocentrism on willingness to buy cruelty-free cosmetics: Focusing on the mediating effect of animosity and consumer awareness of animal experiments. *Asian Journal of Sustainability and Social Responsibility*, *6*, 1–14.

Kim, H. Y., & Chung, J.-E. (n.d.). Consumer purchase intention for organic personal care products. *Journal of Consumer Marketing*, *28*, 58–67. https://doi.org/0736-3761

Kumar, P., & Ghodeswar, B. M. (n.d.). Factors affecting consumers' green product purchase decisions. *Marketing Intelligence & Planning*, *33*, 386–399. https://doi.org/10.1108/MIP-09-2013-0185

Lamont, M., & Molnár, V. (n.d.). National identity and national pride in a changing world: The case of Britain and Hungary. *European Sociological Review*, *17*, 293–317.

Lynn, P. (2008). The problem of non-response. In E. D. De Leeuw, J. Hox, & D. Dillman (Eds.), *International handbook of survey methodology* (pp. 35–55). Erlbaum.

Ma, Y., & Chen, G. (n.d.). Ethical consumption and social identity: A cross-cultural comparison of Chinese and American consumers. *Journal of Business Ethics*, *129*, 121–134.

Macgoldrick, W., & Freestone, O. (n.d.). Saying one thing, selling another: An investigation into the prevalence and impact of misleading cruelty-free claims in the cosmetics industry. *Journal of Business Ethics*, *1*, 1–22.

Magano, J., Au-Yong-Oliveira, M., Ferreira, B., et al. (2022). A cross-sectional study on ethical buyer behavior towards cruelty-free cosmetics: What consequences for female leadership practices? *Sustainability*, *14*, 7786.

Mehrabian, A., & Russell, J. A. (n.d.). *An approach to environmental psychology*. MIT Press.

Mishra, S. (2018, January 1). Understanding consumer behaviour towards toxic chemical-free cosmetics using Schwartz values - a study from India. *International Journal of Indian Culture and Business Management*, *17*(2), 185. https://doi.org/10.1504/ijicbm.2018.094253

Mishra, A. (n.d.). Cruelty-free cosmetics: Understanding consumer perception. *Journal of Business Ethics*, *153*, 971–988.

Mishra, A. (n.d.). Exploring consumer acceptance of eco-friendly packaging: An empirical investigation. *Journal of Retailing and Consumer Services*, *40*, 224–231.

Moghaddam, F. M. (n.d.). Mutual radicalization: How groups and countries are driven into extremes. *American Psychologist*, *72*, 585–593.

Nunnally, J. C., & Bernstein, I. H. (1994). The assessment of reliability. In *Psychometric theory* (3rd ed.). McGraw-Hill.

Park, J., Ahn, J., Thavisaya, T., & Ren, T. (2018). Examining the role of anxiety and social influence in the multi-benefits of mobile payment service. *Journal of Retailing and Consumer Services*, *47*, 140–149. https://doi.org/10.1016/j.jretconser.2018.11.004

Parola, A., Bellelli, G., & Bizzini, L. (n.d.). Age differences in emotional memory: A meta-analysis. *Developmental Review*, *48*, 1–23.

Pervin, M., & Ranchhod, A. (n.d.). Social media marketing adoption and its impact on the profitability of small and medium enterprises in South Africa. *Mediterranean Journal of Social Sciences*, *5*, 1296–1302.

Podsakoff, P. M., MacKenzie, S. B., Lee, J. Y., & Podsakoff, N. P. (2003). Common method biases in behavioral research: A critical review of the literature and recommended remedies. *Journal of Applied Psychology*, *88*(5), 879–903. https://doi.org/10.1037/0021-9010.88.5.879

QuestMobile. (2020). 2020 Double 11 E-commerce insight. Retrieved December 20, 2020, from https://www.questmobile.com.cn/research/reportnew/132

Reed, D. (n.d.). Critical marketing perspectives on corporate social responsibility. *Academy of Marketing Science Review*, *1*, 1–20.

Rita da Silva Pereira, A. (n.d.). Cruelty-free beauty: An overview of the legislation in the European Union and the challenges for the future. *European Journal of Law and Technology*, *9*, 1–23.

Ryans, A. B. (1974). Estimating consumer preferences for a new durable brand in an established product class. *Journal of Marketing Research*, *11*(4), 434–443.

Schreiner, M., Fischer, T., & Riedl, R. (2019, May 10). Impact of content characteristics and emotion on behavioral engagement in social media: Literature review and research agenda. *Electronic Markets*, *21*(2), 329–345. https://doi.org/10.1007/s10660-019-09353-8

Schreiner, M., Körner, A., & Gössling, S. (2019). Exploring the relationship between social media use and environmental concern: Does exposure to pro-environmental content matter? *Journal of Sustainable Tourism*, *27*, 1016–1031.

Sharma, K. (2020). Impact of eco-friendly packaging on consumer buying behavior: A literature review. *International Journal of Management, Technology and Social Sciences*, *4*, 115–122.

Sirieix, L., Delanchy, M., Remaud, H., Zepeda, L., & Gurviez, P. (2012, May 30). Consumers' perceptions of individual and combined sustainable food labels: A UK pilot investigation. *International Journal of Consumer Studies*, *37*(2), 143–151. https://doi.org/10.1111/j.1470-6431.2012.01109.x

Sirieix, L., Remaud, H., & Issanchou, S. (2012). Consumers and healthy eating: How far do attitudes, norms, and control determine the food decision process? *Food Quality and Preference*, *24*, 133–144.

Starr, A. (2009). The social economics of ethical consumption: Theoretical and empirical advances. *The Journal of Socio-Economics*, *38*, 914–925.

Sustainability: How the cosmetics industry is greening up. (n.d.). *Organic monitor*.

UK, P. J. M., & L, L. (2023, November 10). Ethical product premiums: Antecedents and extent of consumers' willingness to pay. *The Journal of Product and Brand Management*. https://www.tandfonline.com/doi/abs/10.1080/09593960701868431

Westland, J. C. (2010). Lower bounds on sample size in structural equation modeling. *Electronic Commerce Research and Applications*, *9*(6), 476–487. https://doi.org/10.1016/j.elerap.2010.07.003

Wu, Y. L., & Li, E. Y. (2017). Marketing mix, CRM, and loyalty in social commerce: A stimulus-organism-response perspective. *Electronic Commerce Research and Applications*, *28*, 39–52.

Wuisan, E. C., & Februadi, A. (2018). Consumers' attitude towards the cruelty-free label on cosmetic and skincare products and its influence on purchase intention. *Jurnal Manajemen dan Bisnis*, *2*, 279–290.

Zheng, X., Akhter, S., & Dabija, D. C. (2023). Going green to be seen: A study on the influence of social identity on green food purchase intention. *Foods*, *12*, 842.

Zollo, L., Carranza, R., Faraoni, M., Díaz, E., & Martín-Consuegra, D. (2020). What influences consumers' intention to purchase organic personal care products? The role of social reassurance. *Journal of Retailing and Consumer Services*, *58*, 102432. https://doi.org/10.1016/j.jretconser.2020.102432

Printed and bound by CPI Group (UK) Ltd, Croydon, CR0 4YY

13/09/2026

14961028-0006